M000198781

Abolition's Public Sphere

Abolition's Public Sphere

Robert Fanuzzi

University of Minnesota Press
Minneapolis • London

MINNESOTA

An earlier version of chapter 2 appeared as "'The Organ of an Individual': William Lloyd Garrison and *The Liberator*," *Prospects* 23 (1998): 107–27; reprinted with the permission of Cambridge University Press. An earlier version of chapter 3 appeared as "The Trouble with Douglass's Body," *American Transcendental Quarterly* 13, no. 1 (March 1999): 27–49; reprinted by permission of the University of Rhode Island. An earlier version of chapter 4 appeared as "Everybody's Faneuil Hall: The Imaginary Institution of Democracy," *Arizona Quarterly* 54 (1998): 1–23; reprinted by permission of the Regents of the University of Arizona. An earlier version of chapter 5 appeared as "Thoreau's Urban Imagination," *American Literature* 68 (1996): 321–46; copyright Duke University Press; reprinted by permission of Duke University Press.

Published by the University of Minnesota Press
111 Third Avenue South, Suite 290
Minneapolis, MN 55401-2520
http://www.upress.umn.edu

Printed in the United States of America on acid-free paper

Library of Congress Cataloging-in-Publication Data

Fanuzzi, Robert.
  Abolition's public sphere / Robert Fanuzzi.
     p. cm.
Includes bibliographical references and index.
  ISBN 0-8166-4089-0 (alk. paper) — ISBN 0-8166-4090-4 (pbk. : alk. paper)
  1. Antislavery movements—United States—History—19th century.
2. Antislavery movements—United States—Public Relations. 3. Antislavery
movements—United States—Public opinion. 4. Publicity—History—19th century.
5. Public opinion—United States—History—19th century. 6. Abolitionists—
United States—History—19th century. 7. Protest literature, American—
History and criticism. 8. Material culture—United States—History—
19th century. 9. Political culture—United States—History—19th century. I. Title.
E449 .F16 2003
326).8)0973—dc21

                                                  2003004031

The University of Minnesota is an equal-opportunity educator and employer.

12 11 10 09 08 07 06 05 04 03   10 9 8 7 6 5 4 3 2 1

Contents

Acknowledgments

It seems a long time since Americanists, myself included, first encountered Jürgen Habermas's *Structural Transformation of the Public Sphere*, and for that discovery I owe a lasting debt of gratitude to Michael Warner and John Brenkman, both of whom helped to inspire a graduate student community at Northwestern University uniquely oriented toward critical and social theory. Included in that community were Bruce Burgett, Glenn Hendler, Douglas Payne, and Carla Kaplan, fellow travelers and dear friends who have done so much over the years to bring intellectual ferment to my life. The generous, unflagging attention they have given my ideas has never failed to help me crystallize them.

As I began my research into abolitionist publicity and the liberal public sphere, Kenneth Warren and James Oakes, also then at Northwestern, were particularly helpful in helping me address historical issues of race and slavery, while Julia Sterne and Carl Smith gave indispensable advice and moral support for preparing my manuscript for publication. My book research took a striking conceptual turn, however, when I wrote an essay on Thoreau for *American Literature* in which I left behind my familiarity with political history and theory and presented the ideal of civic space as explicitly utopian, the product and evidence of the imagination. For prompting me to think hard about the aesthetic value of the public sphere and then emphatically seconding my findings, I will always be thankful to the then editors, Michael Moon and Cathy

Davidson. Their belief in that essay did so much to influence the course of this book. I owe similar thanks to the editorial board of *Arizona Quarterly* for enthusiastically publishing a sort of follow-up essay on the imaginary public space of Faneuil Hall.

The 1999 NEH Summer Institute, "Futures of American Studies," proved to be the perfect setting for presenting this new research before a superbly attentive audience of scholars. I particularly benefited from Don Pease's interest in my work, and from a wonderfully incisive reading from Robyn Weigman. The critical language of citizenship, racial otherness, and marginalization that emerges at the end of this book is owed directly to their contributions and to those of my fellow institute participants. I received similarly careful commentary on my work on Douglass and black oratory from Dana Nelson, Robert Levine, Philip Gould, Philip Barnard, and Sandra Gustafson. Todd Vogel gave me the perfect forum for my essay on Douglass's and Garrison's racial politics in his pathbreaking collection of essays on the black press, while Jack Salzman did the same for an essay on Garrison in *Prospects*. I reserve special praise for Russ Castronovo, whose sympathetic, sagacious reading of my work helped me to keep my eye on the ball.

While at St. John's, I have enjoyed the support of two chairs, Gloria Seminara and Stephen Sicari, in obtaining research leaves and teaching reductions, and the intellectual cameraderie of my colleagues Kevin McLaughlin, Stephen Paul Miller, and the late Michael Hart. The librarians at the New York Public Library and the Boston Public Library collectively demonstrated unrivaled expertise in archival research, a great boon to me. And I just cannot say enough about the conviction of Will Murphy, the acquisitions editor who first brought this project to Minnesota, or the integrity of Doug Armato, director of the humanities division at the press, who staked his own claim to the project during a hiatus between editors. Richard Morrison extended me such grace, guidance, and civility during the long process of readers' reports and revisions that it became a special incentive to produce the best manuscript possible.

I save my last words and lasting devotion for the final reader and arbiter of my work, my wife Joann. In addition to uttering the immortal words, "Finish the damn thing," that ensured the completion of this manuscript, she served as the most patient and perceptive of listeners, helping me to articulate verbally ideas that would not have otherwise come to life on the page. And my darling daughter Mia, all of two years old, actually did find a typo, as if I needed a reason to be grateful for her presence.

The Lessons of Repeated Experience

William Lloyd Garrison operated literally in the forefront of the American abolition movement, soliciting subscribers and readers for his newspaper before there were organized, nonsectarian abolition societies. Inspired by the mass pamphleteering campaign of the English emancipation movement, he published the first issue of *The Liberator* in 1831 and thereafter linked the progress of the cause to the circulation of the newspaper and other printed articles. When the first national gathering of abolitionists did occur in 1833, he wrote a *Declaration of Sentiments* for the American Anti-Slavery Society that committed the abolitionist agenda to the publicity campaign he was already pursuing. "We shall circulate, unsparingly and extensively, antislavery tracts and periodicals," Garrison's manifesto promised, and the national society and the regional but no less aggressive Massachusetts Anti-Slavery Society followed suit, sending annually almost a million newspapers, pamphlets, and tracts into national circulation by the year 1837.[1] The effect of this initiative was to instigate the discussion of the slavery question among an often hostile populace and to bring the issue of abolition to the forefront of reform, developments that left Garrison declaring victory for the cause. A "multitude of journals," he crowed to the abolitionist lecturer Wendell Philips in 1837, together with a number of pamphlets "that is impossible to calculate ... [are] scattered over the land, thicker than rain-drops, and as nourishing to the soil of freedom."[2]

Garrison's faith in the agency of these publications was under-written by the Massachusetts Anti-Slavery Society, which dedicated a large proportion of its meager resources to printing and distribution while systematically excluding other forms of political action—partisan organizing, slave insurrection, and even voting—from its political plat-form.[3] This ideological and material investment in the utility of literate discussion made the creation of a reading public the principle goal of antislavery agitation, the practical equivalent of abolition itself. "Those who can be induced to *Read*, will most assuredly be abolitionized, and THOROUGHLY converted," read the frontispiece to Maria Weston Chap-man's *Right and Wrong in Massachusetts*; as defined by this source, to "abo-litionize" meant to turn the residents of "almost any town or village" into readers.[4] Of course, Garrison and his fellow members did not intend to stop circulating their publications until all Americans had been "aboli-tionized," for what they imagined was not just a nation free of slavery but a public sphere of literate discussion superimposed on the nation.

With this ambition, New England abolitionists betrayed the frankly utopian scale of their publicity campaign, and, at first glance, it is a scale that would seem to expand on the ideological dimension that Jürgen Habermas inscribed in his representation of the liberal public sphere. In *The Structural Transformation of the Public Sphere*, Habermas described eighteenth-century Anglo-European civic culture as a mate-rial and discursive space of free discussion, conducive to the critical inspection of the state, the political participation of an emergent bour-geoisie, and ultimately the liberal democratic resistance to monarchical government.[5] The circulation of abolitionist publications might well have been intended to reproduce the effect of "rational-critical debate" on the American polity and to reinstate the antagonism between a public and the state—and yet we can differentiate straightaway the abolition-ists' institution of a public sphere from the idealized portrait sketched by Habermas on two important grounds.

For one, the New England abolitionists expressly sought to define their reading public so that it did not coincide with the legal and polit-ical definition of a citizenry. To "abolitionize," according to Garrison's

"Prospectus" for *The Liberator*, was to engage "the people, the whole people . . . in the work; every man, and every woman, and every child"; in pursuit of this goal, abolitionists addressed their articles of publicity to the literate and illiterate noncitizens of antebellum society. Garrison took special care to dedicate *The Liberator*, the flagship abolitionist newspaper he founded and edited, to "the people of color" so that the free African Americans of the North might consider it "their organ."[6] For the benefit of illiterate "readers," the enslaved of the South, he included on the masthead the graphic depiction of a kneeling slave, adapted from Wedgwood's famous engraving for the English antislavery movement, and, even more famously, repeated the efforts of David Walker by reprinting his *Appeal to the Colored Citizens of the World*.[7] The million abolitionist tracts and newspapers blanketing the nation thus signified the prospect of an indiscriminately composed public sphere and the threat of full civic participation by disenfranchised Americans.

The women members of the New England abolition movement demonstrated the truth of this proposition by wearing kerchiefs imprinted with abolitionist slogans and catechisms. In this fashion, they circulated literally as emblems of publicity that betokened not only their political visibility but a strikingly new incarnation of the public sphere. As feminist scholars have shown, abolitionists such as Chapman, Lucretia Mott, Angelina and Sarah Grimké, and Lydia Maria Child sponsored the discussion of abolition in a way that created new spaces and forms of literate discussion as well as socially particular, embodied alternatives to the self-transcending ideals of citizenship.[8] The abolitionists' printed articles might even be considered women's medium of embodiment, reversing the symbolic value of literate discussion in the antislavery struggle and rendering the slavery question a subject worthy of "mere" women. Child's preface to her seminal abolitionist treatise *An Appeal in Favor of that Class of Americans Called Africans* implicitly drew an analogy between antislavery literature and the new cultural phenomenon of politically involved women in addressing the inevitability of a hostile reception. "Reader, I beseech you," she wrote, employing the conventional self-deprecating inflection of a woman's authorial voice, "not to throw down this volume as soon as you have glanced at the title. . . . If I have the most trifling claims upon your good will, for an hour's amusement for yourself, or benefit to your children, read it for *my* sake."[9] In her apologia for abolitionist publicity, Angelina Grimké deployed still more solicitous tropes of femininity to defuse the claims of its "incendiary" value, its purported tendency to foment insurrection among the enslaved: "Scattered over our land as abundantly as the leaves of Autumn, . . . [abolitionist publications] will be as leaves for the healing of the nation."[10]

An important effect of this institution of the public sphere was to take from even white male abolitionists what Lauren Berlant has called the "privilege of abstraction."[11] One unlucky traveling agent was captured by a hostile mob and tarred and feathered with the pages of his own publications, a sure indication that abolitionist publicity had done nothing to abstract the abolition movement into the image of a rational citizenry and instead could lend it the corporeal aspect of the most victimized slave.[12] The circulation of abolitionist newspapers and pamphlets indeed would give the entire movement the signal qualities that distinguished it from the rank of citizens: the status and social standing of the disenfranchised, as well as a cultural representation shared with women and African Americans. This was consistent with Garrison's hope, as expressed in his *Declaration of Sentiments*, that the literate discussion of abolition would link the fate of the largely white male movement not only with the cause of women but with the suffering of the "oppressed one-sixth of our countrymen" (4).

However, the abolitionists' publicity campaign also had a far different object that seemed to run contrary to the spirit of social egalitarianism and to sever any connection between an "abolitionized" reading public and an inclusive, pluralist community. This second, potentially contradictory feature of the abolitionists' public sphere is evident in one of the more obscure journals in the antislavery corpus, a short-lived penny press called the *Cradle of Liberty*.[13] This newspaper was not successful enough and did not last long enough to serve as a mode of socialization. It served instead as an instrument of civic pedagogy that would institute the memory of a public sphere among its readers and represent the small but noisome abolition movement as nothing less than the people of revolutionary legend. The key, Garrison seemed to realize, was to appropriate for his newspaper the local symbolism of the public sphere—in this case, the figurative appellation for Faneuil Hall, Boston's most renowned public space and its monument to the democratic assemblies of the Revolutionary era—so that the abolitionists' *Cradle of Liberty* could circulate as a trace or reminder of a past struggle for liberty and bear the promise of similarly public agitation.

The slogan for this penny press, "Abolition's Public Forum," indicates that Garrison and his fellow abolitionists did not conceive their public sphere independently of these historical associations. On the contrary, they meant the circulation of newspapers, journals, and pamphlets to sustain an analogy between the literate discussion of the slavery question and the democratic politics of another era. In other words, even as they sought to "abolitionize" a socially diverse reading public in their own time, the New England abolitionists hoped to create a deliberately anachronistic public sphere that would be home to unlimited exercise of free speech, the disinterested consideration of the public good, and above all, the resistance of a liberty-loving people. Of course, they knew all these objectives would make their movement irrelevant, out-of-step, and incongruous with the freewheeling, fractious public sphere of Jacksonian political culture. They stared at the outbreak of violent mobs against their public assemblies, at the nearly unanimous opposition of elected officials, and at a federally coordinated policy of censorship directed against the discussion of abolition and concluded that a publicity campaign that appealed to an eighteenth-century theory of libertarian politics and a republican standard of citizenship was fundamentally untimely.[14] However, the abolitionists' mode of political resistance had as much to do with counterpoising an obsolete ideal of the public sphere with its contemporary manifestations as it did with counterpoising a socially heterogeneous reading public with an ideologically exclusive definition of a citizenry. They based their opposition to slavery as well as their challenge to American citizenship on the prospect of dating their public sphere as a recognizably historical institution.

The abolitionists' determination to provide a historically incongruous context for their movement can be seen in the striking incidence of obsolete political idioms in their discourse of publicity. A republican ethic of self-denial, Anglo-American libertarian theory of free speech, Enlightenment rationalism, the classical ideal of the polis, and an auspiciously dated concept of democratic revolution were all invoked with an imaginative awareness that would transform the New England abolition movement, a struggling newcomer to the antebellum reform scene, into a liberty-loving, insurgent people. Garrison was quite flagrant in his borrowings, or "conjurations," as Derrida would call them (a transliteration meaning both to pledge resistance and to incant).[15] He dedicated *The Liberator* "to those who believe with JEFFERSON, that the 'error of opinion may be safely tolerated where reason is left to combat it'"[16]; with equal historical consciousness, he borrowed the slogan for the newspaper, "Our Country is the World, Our Countrymen Mankind," from the radical lexicon of Tom Paine. The success of *The Liberator* thus would herald the arrival of a new era of rational progress and universal emancipation that only the most optimistic philosophes of the Enlightenment had dared to imagine. The future of abolition, Garrison was arguing, lay in the past, or in resurrecting an obsolete ideal of historical progress in the era of Manifest Destiny and the equally expansive "great transformation."[17]

The function of the abolitionists' printed articles in this politics of anachronism was to mediate between distinct historical eras so that successive visions of the American republic could be brought to bear on each other. Newspapers like *The Liberator* and the *Cradle of Liberty* could be even considered the medium for summoning what Derrida would call the "specters" of a democratic revolution from a venerated but, at the same time, repudiated past. The "spirit of revolution," he argues in a rejoinder to Marx's "The Eighteenth Brumaire," "*is fantastic and anachronistic through and through*"; its appearance in the outmoded guises of lapsed revolutions, the "'battle-slogans and costumes'" of the past, is said to be indicative of not only a political crisis but of a "period in crisis," a present "'out of joint.'"[18] To be sure, the Jacksonian era did coincide with the birth of a national historiography that enshrined the words and deeds of founding fathers in cultural narratives and rituals of remembrance. However, Garrison's intention in conjuring the ghosts of Jefferson and Paine was to disrupt this reproduction of citizenship, to introduce what Eric Sundquist has called "the first serious fractures in the sense of 'continuing Revolutionary time,'" and to precipitate the awareness of a historical crisis among his contemporaries.[19] He thus inaugurated the abolitionists' publicity campaign in his *Declaration of Sentiments* with a conventional homage to the "band of patriots" who convened in Philadelphia as well as for the "three millions of people" who "deem[ed] it more glorious to die instantly as freemen, than desireable to live one hour as slaves" before reminding his listeners that the hour of revolution really had not passed and that the task of the forebears was, in his words, "incomplete" (3, 4). The untimeliness of this appeal in the 1830s, the era of organized slave insurrections and equally violent counterrevolutionary popular demonstrations, only furthered Garrison's strategy, which was to present the abolition movement itself as discordant with its own time.

Garrison's hope for the New England abolition movement was that it would be "fantastic and anachronistic," but the movement could only be as fantastic and anachronistic as its printed articles allowed it to be. The abolitionists' publicity campaign, in other words, supplied the historical medium for resurrecting a public identity from another era; the obsolete idioms of republicanism, of Enlightenment, and of progressive democratic revolution with which Garrison symbolized the progress of the abolition cause were all native to the print culture in which the movement situated itself. Garrison, a former printer's apprentice and self-declared "mechanic," was especially attuned to the historical resonances within this culture that could cast the abolition movement as an eighteenth-century movement. He could sound like an Enlightenment philosophe in calling for "Revolutions wrought by reason, not force," but he was more closely and professionally connected to the radical artisan politics of the antebellum printing trade, which contested the emergence of liberal capitalism and its contribution to growing social inequality with eighteenth-century ideals of republican equality, public virtue, and active, insurgent citizenship. The currency of these ostensibly anachronistic ideals in nineteenth-century America can be seen in the creation of important third-party political movements as well as in the number of artisan newspapers.[20] From the evidence of this political activity and many other reform movements, many scholars of the antebellum era have rightly concluded that the conventional Americanist linear model of ideological succession—first republicanism, then liberalism—needs to be replaced with a model of synchronism and dialectical interdependence.[21]

Garrison, however, developed his politics of the printing trade so that it was deliberately commemorative and backward-looking, an homage to a lapsed revolution and scathing denunciation of the present moment. He did so by forging a logistical alliance with an intensely controversial movement called Freethought, nominally an extension of eighteenth-century deism but which had its origins in printers' radical democratic societies.[22] Without an invitation from Boston's Protestant establishment and with no place for the nascent movement to gather, Garrison accepted an offer from Abner Kneeland, the city's leading Freethinker, to assemble at his society's Julien Hall. For the rest of his abolitionist career, Garrison would face accusations that he was in league with Kneeland, with the more fiery, New York–based spokesperson of the Freethought movement Frances Wright, and ultimately with Thomas Paine himself, the "Patron Saint," so to speak, of free thinking mechanics since the publication of *Age of Reason* and *Rights of Man*. As I show in the first two chapters, Paine, or a refracted image of Paine, seemed to shadow Garrison and to have lent his historical reputation as jacobin, insurrectionist, infidel, and traitor to the reception of both the abolitionist editor and of the abolition movement itself.

Garrison did not help matters when he seemed to summon effortlessly the iconoclasm of both the *Rights of Man* and *Age of Reason* to explain his insistence on the discussion of abolition:

All things are interrogated as to their origin, intent, tendency, and law-
fulness, without regard to their antiquity, or the authority with which
they are clothed. The cry is everywhere heard for free speech and free
inquity, that Right may prevail, and Imposture put to flight.[23]

Critics of abolition, especially those who belonged to the Protestant-led
colonization movement, made sure that no one would miss the resemblance. "This was the plea," one said of Garrison's call for universal
emancipation, "of Thomas Paine . . . of Fanny Wright Daresmont—this
is the plea of all the infidels on the face of the earth!"[24] Although Garrison sought to portray the New England abolitionists as righteous,
nondenominational followers of Christ, his investment in the politics of
the printing trade and an institutional alliance with the Freethinkers
seemed to make such comparisons inevitable. "Should Washington and
his followers have surrendered at discretion to British despotism, because
Paine was an infidel?" Garrison demanded of his clerical critics, antagonizing a Protestant "benevolent empire" that, until his own ascendance,
had been the principle sponsor of the antislavery movement and had
made Christian evangelism synonymous with reform.[25]

While Garrison publicly claimed to be inspired by the stirring
example of English emancipation (also based in Protestant evangelism)
and to have patterned the abolitionists' publicity campaign after Wilber-
force's successful pamphleteering strategy, a historical analogy with
Paine seemed to trump these contemporary associations and to make the
New England abolition movement into a threat that was all the more
scandalous for seeming to have emerged from the past and disturbed a
sense of orderly succession.[26] One of the many antiabolitionist tracts
that criticized abolitionists as fellow travelers of Wright and Paine saw
this threat in the well-orchestrated and seemingly well-financed publicity campaign that Garrison had conceived in his *Declaration of Sentiments*.
According to one Calvin Colton, author of *Abolition a Sedition*, the otherwise small and fragile movement had been emboldened by the "amazing
power of its vast political machinery" to become "like the Jacobins of revolutionary France . . . enough to revolutionize any State, any nation."[27]

Thomas Paine, jacobinism, revolutionary terror—in what decade were Garrison and the Massachusetts Anti-Slavery Society waging the antislavery struggle? Although the effort to "abolitionize" the nation with the distribution of abolitionist publications might have been intended to interpellate the disenfranchised of their own era as a reading public, the more immediate effect of this initiative was to pitch their struggle into past and particularly into the 1790s, when Paine gained his lasting infamy as an infidel and insurrectionist, so-called self-created societies of artisans and laborers agitated for a continuing democratic revolution, and an even more radical revolution in France set off a "jacobin phrenzy" that had Americans looking in their midst for agents of foreign insurrection.[28] For critics of the abolition movement and, more significantly, for legislators of southern states, the agitation of the slavery question promised the immanent success of the French Revolution, or even worse, of the French-inspired revolution in Saint-Domingue, and in response they proposed a defensive policy of interdiction to suppress the circulation of abolitionist publications.[29]

Of course, the memory of these foreign revolutions was kept alive by the near-success of several slave rebellions in the American South, but the assessment of their origins and of the agency of the enslaved was inseparable from the assessment of abolitionist publicity. When a copy of *The Liberator* was found on the person of one of Nat Turner's accomplices, Southern governors and legislatures named the abolitionist editor as a virtual accomplice and petitioned the mayor of Boston, Harrison Gray Otis, to stop the circulation of the newspaper at its source. Drawing on the precedent of international law, elected officials in both the North and South came to regard abolitionist publications as foreign agents that violated the territorial sovereignty of individual states, so that the appearance of a single copy of a newspaper across state lines could constitute a patently illegal attempt to foment insurrection among the enslaved.[30] By this overdetermined symbolism of the abolitionists' public sphere, the printed article was equal in agency and effect to a rebellious slave—and yet we should not regard this symbolism independently of the material conditions that produced abolitionist publications.

The dense network of printers, artisan societies, and egalitarian republican politics into which Garrison intertwined the abolitionist agenda
functioned as a historical medium, connecting the spread of abolitionist publicity and the threat of slave insurrection to the terrors, or
alternately, the blessings of an eighteenth-century democratic revolution. The abolitionists' print culture, in other words, served as a memory culture, instructing contemporaries in the historic significance of
their current struggle and establishing a system of analogies with distant events.

Garrison, always ready for the opportunity to make such comparisons, claimed in his letter to Wendell Philips that the distribution
of the abolitionists' newspapers, tracts, and pamphlets was enough to
"bring down the walls of the American Bastille." Each and every one of
the abolitionists' printed articles possessed a similarly overdetermined
historical significance; together, they lent the abolitionists a public
identity that coexisted with the memory of a people. The circulation of
the abolitionists' publications thus can be said to have represented the
New England abolition movement diachronically, or in relation to time,
rather than synchronically, or as a community sharing the same space.
It was responsible for giving the abolitionists' public sphere the "time
dimension" that J. G. A. Pocock has ascribed to the political discourse
of civic republicanism, and it ensured that the publicity for the cause
would produce a similar awareness of historical time.[31] The articles
and tokens of abolitionist publicity served the movement as a medium
of historicism perhaps even more than as a medium of sociality, and, as
such, distinguished the abolitionist public not just from the contemporary manifestation of the people but from any existing social formation.

How can we square these two dimensions of the abolitionists'
public sphere, the first promising the inclusion of politically disenfranchised Americans under the rubric of literate discussion and the second
seeming to forgo the prospect of its own realization for an imaginary
connection with a historically absent public? The competing attention that Garrison gave to the women's movement and "people of color"
and to the republican ideal of a white male citizenry does make the

abolitionists' political project seem logistically incompatible as well as ideologically contradictory, and therefore ripe for the criticism that many theorists and Americanist scholars have brought to Habermas's portrayal of the liberal public sphere. Presented as both a conceptual and at times even nostalgic premise for liberal democracy and as a culturally contingent, empirical institution, the public sphere has been the object of feminist revisions and post-Marxist deconstructions, many of which reveal its provisions for social and political exclusion. It has served just as well as the subject of eighteenth-century intellectual history and, alternately, of nineteenth-century cultural studies, which have done so much to transform the idealized space of rational discussion into a contested site of identity politics.[32]

My own use of these disparate methodologies and fields for the preceding exposition of the abolitionists' public sphere betrays my ambition for this book, which is to profit from the often fruitful dialectical tension that the category of the public sphere has introduced into American studies. A socially progressive cultural politics, after all, did coexist with an unblinking regard for the norms of republican citizenship in the abolitionists' discourse of publicity.[33] What is more, Garrison intended his appeals to the marginalized and to the normative to complement each other, so that a disinterested, rational public and a persecuted minority might be rendered in the image of each other. The insurgence of noncitizens in the discussion of the slavery question, he maintained, had to come from the past and to signal the uncanny return of a virtuous public. White male abolitionists were given the opportunity to surrender their contemporary designation as a people, disclaim their affinity with enfranchised white men, and become identified with an oppressed minority by representing themselves as equally dated remnants of another age. In other words, Garrison mediated between an ideologically restrictive version of the public sphere and a socially constituted counterpublic through an ironic relation to history. The distinction between citizen and noncitizen, he seemed to realize, could only be overcome through the past, or through the detour of a historical comparison. His conviction made the abolitionists' ideal of political equality contingent on a comparison between subjects who belonged to different times, not on an identity between subjects.

Garrison put the history of the American Revolution to this ironic use in his *Declaration of Sentiments*, which gave the oppressed of his time the leading roles that had belonged to a white male citizenry. With evident relish, he claimed that the "grievances [of revolutionary patriots], great as they were, were trifling in comparison with the wrongs and sufferings of those for whom we plead (4)" but his aspirations for the enslaved and disenfranchised compelled him to look favorably on the historical precedent and to retain the gendered designation that gave those patriots their exclusive claim to citizenship. By the end of the document, Garrison had pledged on behalf of the abolition movement "to secure to the colored population of the United States, all the rights and privileges which belong to them as men" (11), which was the same need voiced by Frederick Douglass and by many leaders of the black antislavery movement. As I show in a subsequent chapter, Garrison was appealing to and would continue to appeal to a free African American community that proudly maintained its republican lineage in the face of racism, social segregation, and colonizationist pressure from their supposed benefactors. The white abolitionist leader in turn incorporated its anti-colonizationist position into an abolitionist historiography that regarded the patriarchal traditions of the American republic as what Benjamin called "the tradition of the oppressed"—an endangered but potentially revolutionary legacy that had to be rescued from "a conformism that is about to overpower it."[34] The past of public virtue, civic engagement, and democratic resistance, Garrison argued, could not be idly commemorated by a slaveholding citizenry or folded into the nation's official historiography. It belonged to "the people of color," the oppressed of his day. He would establish the faculty of memory in the abolitionists' institution of the public sphere in order to pursue the revolutionary purpose Benjamin attributes to the historian and "blast a specific era out the homogeneous course of history."[35]

The abolitionists' public sphere thus served the same purpose as their historiography, which was to reverse the identities of citizen and noncitizen with a historical analogy and to appropriate the historical narrative of the American republic for the struggle of the disenfranchised. Of course, they demonstrated their own form of paternalism in this endeavor, extending their custody over the cause of the enslaved to the founding ideals of the nation, but for the disputants in the antislavery struggle, the abolitionists' consistent use of this mode of narration had the effect of transforming the normative and otherwise exclusive conventions of republican citizenship—the literate discussion of public affairs, the civic engagement in the life of the polity, the free association of an educated populace—into signifiers of oppression. The affliction of the emergent women's movement, for instance, was what precisely made abolitionist women worthy of an homage to the patriarchs of the American Revolution. With a deliberate use of irony, Garrison argued that a mob attack on a public meeting of the Boston Female Anti-Slavery Society threatened not only the survival of "the liberty of speech and of the press," the cause for which "our fathers shed their blood," but the legacy of their struggle, "THE PEOPLE OF THE UNITED STATES."[36] He heroized the contributions of Lydia Maria Child with a similar appeal to patriarchal tradition, deeming her "the first woman in the republic."

The many critics of abolition in antebellum Boston justified their opposition to the ascendance of abolitionist women with a counterrevolutionary discourse of social leveling and foreign insurrection that had determined the American reception of the French Revolution and then spurred the passage of the infamous Alien and Sedition Acts. Thomas Russell Sullivan, author of the widely read *Letters against the Immediate Abolition of Slavery*, looked to this precedent for the terms of his critique when he damned Garrison and the Massachusetts Anti-Slavery Society for "commenc[ing] the agitation of a legal, constitutional, and political reform . . . by measures adapted to inflame the passions of the multitude, inducing the women and children, the boarding school misses and factory girls . . . upon the avowed plan of turning the current of popular opinion."[37] For Sullivan, the pretense of these women threatened the "deliberate counsel of the experienced and judicious" with the same dangers that a member of the ruling elite would have found in the alleged excesses of democracy. Sounding as much like an eighteenth-century Federalist as a nineteenth-century antifeminist, Sullivan accused the abolitionists of summoning "the passions of the multitude" against the wisdom of the elected few; in like fashion, he accused the women's abolition movement of collaborating with an "Agitator and Foreign Agent"—the English abolitionist George Thompson, who took on the requisite role of jacobin spy and foreign subversive in accepting an invitation to appear before the Boston Female Anti-Slavery Society.[38] Synthesizing the brittle defensiveness against English cultural commentators (whose numbers included the women of letters Fanny Kemble, Harriet Martineau, and Frances Trollope) with an intense antifeminist local prejudice, Sullivan recreated a narrative of French-inspired insurrection on American soil that inflamed nationalist xenophobia in the 1790s. The New England abolition movement, he concluded, was guilty of a "public indictable offense" worthy of true jacobins: sedition against the government of Massachusetts (40).[39]

The same year that Sullivan leveled his charges against Boston's women's abolition movement, Harrison Gray Otis spoke from the steps of Faneuil Hall decrying the same seditious threat to the integrity of the Union. The spread of abolitionist publicity, Otis declared in memorable words, had converted "ladies' sewing parties" into "abolition clubs," ably connecting this new, domestic institution of the public sphere to the memory of organized subversion.[40] Shortly after that speech, a mob stormed a meeting of the Boston Female Anti-Slavery Society that had been advertised as featuring Thompson and systematically destroyed any and all evidence of publicity for the event. An anachronistic narrative of jacobin plots and internal sedition, in other words, was not just a paranoid invention or misplaced obsession but a condition of intelligibility for abolitionist agitation and a contemporary figure for women's public role. The very anachronism of this narrative, the fact that jacobins no longer prowled the shores of America and that the French Revolution had been concluded, made it essential to the cultural politics of the antebellum era, for the political participation of abolitionist women could be deemed marginal and subversive to the extent that it could be regarded as historically belated.

The postcolonial critic Homi Bhabha has argued that the only point of entry for the disenfranchised and the marginalized into the narrative of a progressive modernity is through the past, or through the "time-lag" implicit in the iteration of "epochal events."[41] They are outcasts, he says, not only from the discursive space of the nation but from the temporality of its narration, the "'empty homogenous time'" in which national subjects recognize a common origin and shared destiny, and thus are fated to appear as belated entrants in a historical spectacle already unfolded.[42] His foil for this critique of modernity is Benedict Anderson's concept of the "imagined community," which is premised on the mass distribution of printed articles among a nominally uniform body of literate subjects. For Anderson, the technologies of "print capitalism" hasten the mutual recognition of fellow subjects as existing in the same space and time precisely by "pirating" the events of distant and foreign revolution for contemporary uses.[43]

My own formulation of the abolitionists' public sphere thus pays tribute to Anderson's conception in assuming the mediation of print culture in any collective self-representation and particularly a historical one. However, I am also attempting to render the potential of Bhabha's critique of Anderson's nationalist model for a counternational direction of nineteenth-century American studies in suggesting the importance of a diachronic mode of representation to the critical role of a public. Garrison and the Massachusetts Anti-Slavery Society simply did not intend their campaign of mass distribution to foster the experience of simultaneity among literate subjects or produce the synchronized image of a national people. They maintained their resistance to both the nation-state and to the homogeneous consciousness of a white male citizenry precisely in failing to interpellate the members of their reading public in the same historical moment. Abolitionist publicity, they insisted, could posit the existence of a public only in relation to an event already occurred, a condition that ensured the belatedness and even the irrelevance of the abolition movement but that also gave them ample opportunity for what Bhabha calls the "performativity of discursive practice" and "the ethics of self-enactment."[44] The New England abolitionists, I would argue, indeed found the resources for this self-invention in the manifest irony of their historical comparisons and, by extension, in the conscious anachronism of their public sphere. The constitutive trope of their collective identity, an analogy between the oppressed of their own day and an atavistic ideal of a republican citizenry, helped to demonstrate not just the impossibility of any social realization for an "abolitionized" reading public but the discursive, generically imaginary structure of its representation. I will put a final point on the revision of Anderson's nationalist model by proposing that the inadequacy of this representation is precisely what made their public an imagined community.

Claude Lefort is a political theorist who has associated the limitations of the imaginary with the dissonance or antagonism of democratic society. He distinguishes the social imaginary of democracy from the ideological constructions of a popular will by the internal and external contradiction that keeps the space of the public open, the social identity of a public vacant.[45] Before we pass any judgment on the democratic or egalitarian value of the abolitionists' enterprise, however, I want to tease out the implications of the imagination as a distinctively aesthetic mode of interpellation. The imagination, according to Paul Ricoeur, is an inherently flawed mechanism for connecting the experience of otherwise distinct subjects, for "transferring 'my here' to 'your there.'" It is the faculty responsible for creating the fiction of social ties and yet it cannot do so without a "criterion of non-congruence" that reveals the futility and the artifice of the endeavor. Unlike ideology, which suppresses the effect of its operation in order to maintain the "non-transparency of our cultural codes," the imagination betrays its origin in the discourse of aestheticism with the "tense logic" of frankly improbable, provisional analogies. The "initial act" of the imagination, Ricoeur argues, is to represent the continuing existence of the subject by connecting one temporal moment to the next, but here too "the possibility of historical experience" is compromised by the imperfection of the comparison, the "effect of reverberation or echo."[46]

The ambivalence of the abolitionists' appeals to founding fathers, the anachronism of their historical model, and the awkwardness of their comparisons between the disenfranchised and the enfranchised of another time all can be said to have marked the abolitionists' public identity as a truly imaginary community. This reading of the imagination can help us distinguish the discursive structure of the abolitionists' public identity from the totalized image of a national people but it can also furnish the starting point for a critique of their political project. We can forecast the direction of this critique with the example of a proudly marginal abolitionist, Henry David Thoreau, who brought the abolitionists' method of self-fashioning to its logical conclusion when he staged his own exclusion and exile from the American polity. With forced comparisons between his own act of civil disobedience and the American Revolution and with half-hearted nostalgia for a lost civic tradition, Thoreau sought to present himself not just as the relic of another age but, above all, as a slave. His historical references might have served the same purpose that Garrison intended for abolitionist publicity, but in creating his own, self-referential version of an abolitionist utopia, he revealed the central conceit of their public sphere—an alliance with the disenfranchised and particularly with the enslaved—to share the structure of an aesthetic expression.

. The following chapters adopt the historical methodologies of American studies to recreate the abolitionists' material culture of print and publicity, but in doing so, they invariably document what Ricoeur would call the practical work of the imagination in the creation of a public sphere. The first chapter, "The Sedition of Nonresistance," describes the symbolic function of the abolitionists' printed articles, which was to represent their movement historically, or by a position in time. In committing his abolitionist agenda to a libertarian strategy of free speech and critical discussion, Garrison consciously dated abolition as an eighteenth-century movement whose every act of dissent bore the memory of a past revolutionary act. Chapter 2, "Garrisonism and the Public Sphere," chronicles Garrison's deliberate reconstruction of eighteenth-century republicanism in his management of *The Liberator*, which he meant to represent a corporate attempt on the part of the Massachusetts Anti-Slavery Society to conduct a rational, disinterested discussion of the slavery question. Together, these chapters argue that the germane historical setting for the antislavery agitation of the mid-1830s was in fact the 1790s, when the radical democratic politics of artisan republicanism looked back further still to the unfulfilled promise of the American Revolution and threatened to abrogate the constitutional order. The pamphleteer and publicist Thomas Paine serves in this overdetermined historical moment as Garrison's animating spirit, inspiring him toward seditious acts of dissent and an even more insurrectionist strategy of "disunion."

The success of his venture can be measured by the currency of his name, which, in the form of the appellation "Garrisonism," could be said to share the properties of *The Liberator* itself and signify nothing less than the promise of unlimited publicity. With chapter 3, "Frederick Douglass's Public Body," however, we can begin to test the possibility of rendering a public sphere in the analogical form that both Garrison and Douglass proposed. For Douglass, his own "colored" newspaper, *The North Star*, represented the best chance for literate African Americans to substantiate their claims not just on citizenship but on a recognizably republican representation of citizenship based on the quality of manliness. The slippage between this representation, which Douglass sought to provide for his black readers through the medium of the newspaper, and the public acclaim for Douglass's own "manly form" is testament to the "tense logic" of all the abolitionists' historical comparisons. A similar tension can be detected in the meaning of "Garrisonism," for although Garrison and his allies meant the term to have a public attribution closely associated with the value of literate discussion, it also designated Garrison himself as the man, or, as one rival put it, "abolition incarnate." The first part of the book thus circles back to the critical issues raised by the abolitionists' deference to the historical ideal of a white male citizenry and questions whether their institution of a public sphere could avoid reproducing the embodied attributes of race and gender that separated citizen from noncitizen. I am going to say in advance that it could not, but that both Garrison's and Douglass's representation of a public betrayed the faculty of the imagination in making those attributes, particularly that of color, the ideologically normative signs of virtue, civic engagement, and political progress.

Chapter 4, "Faneuil Hall: The Civic Institution of the Imaginary," turns the argument of the book toward a consideration of the public sphere in a more concrete form and urban context but only to elaborate more fully the discursive structure of the abolitionists' historical comparisons. As we have seen, the abolitionists' appeal to Faneuil Hall, the so-called Cradle of liberty, constituted one of their most fertile historical analogies for the representation of their movement. With their use of the name, they hoped to extract the tradition of public assembly and town meetings from Boston's civic authority and cede the historical role of a people to the city's most outcast, iconoclastic reform society. However, Garrison paid such explicit homage to the heroic exploits of the city's revolutionary forbears that the literary conventions of mourning and reverence that clustered around his evocation of Faneuil Hall ultimately can be said to have yielded the abolitionists' own trope of public space. Of course, a gothic language of commemoration might have given the figure of "abolition's public forum" a more patriarchal inflection than the historical associations of newspapers and pamphlets could give it, but Garrison and the Massachusetts Anti-Slavery Society meant their version of Faneuil Hall to separate their movement from the popular gatherings of the present and to indicate their own, hopelessly marginal place in Boston's civic life. The abolitionists' institution of the public sphere in this instance could rightly be called an imaginary public space, commensurate only with the place of outsiders.

The last two chapters, "Thoreau's Civic Imagination" and "Douglass's Sublime," are devoted to exploring the connection between the oppressed white male abolitionist and the marginalized black slave in relation to the abolitionists' method of historical comparison. The final chapter begins appropriately by presenting the famous speech by

Frederick Douglass, "What to the Slave Is the Fourth of July," as a rhetorical turn on an already ironic narrative of filial succession, but the penultimate chapter on Thoreau sets the stage for this intervention by teasing out the language of utopia that otherwise lay hidden within the structure of a historical analogy. Thoreau's own representation of utopia can be seen as recapitulating the formation of the abolitionists' public sphere in being a synthesis of incongruous and anachronistic utopias, all of which valorize life in the woods according to the virtues of the *civitas*, or civic space. At the same time, he operated as a critic of the abolitionists' political project in turning his attention to time, or by forcing a comparison between their mode of historical representation and a utopian narrative of progress. Thoreau offered his most extended commentary on the narrative construction of progress in *Walden*, which also represented his attempt to translate the signifiers of a progressive modernity into a language of the present, or what he called "the nick of time."

To the extent that Garrison and his allies maintained a historical connection with the idea of a citizenry and the agency of literate discussion, they betrayed their determination to create their own version of a progressive modernity for the waging of the antislavery struggle; they kept their faith with what Habermas has described as the uncompleted project of modernity.[47] After all, a historical ideal of the people did reemerge through the abolitionists' efforts and sanctify their antislavery agitation not just with the memory of a popular revolution but with the image of its perpetual progress. What is more, the remembrance of a democratic movement in its original context functioned like a guarantee of the abolitionists' cause and foretold its eventual victory over the political institutions of the present day. The most implacably ideological element of the abolitionists' mode of historical narration thus might not be found in the dialectical relation between citizen and noncitizen but in its unmistakably providential aspect, which celebrated the immanent arrival of liberty, equality, and, yes, the fraternity of the human species. This aspect might well be the one historical idiom of eighteenth-century political discourse that the New England abolitionists did not retrieve with their characteristic ironic, strategic awareness. On the contrary, their conviction in the inevitable progress of their movement helps to identity their political project as a true product of the Enlightenment.

In order to chart the alternative course laid out by Douglass, I want to spend the remainder of this introductory essay uncovering the Enlightenment narrative of modernity that lay beneath the anachronisms and disjunctions of the abolitionists' historical comparisons. This narrative can be reconstructed from Garrison's most perverse assessment of the abolition movement's prospects, which he offered to Philadelphia abolitionists whose meeting hall had been destroyed by fire:

> Your cause will not prosper here—the philosophy of reform forbids you to expect it—until it excites popular tumult, and brings down upon it a shower of brickbats and rotten eggs, and is threatened with a coat of tar and feathers. How was it in New England as the truth began to affect the consciousness of the people? Why, sir, that whole section of the country was racked to its every centre, and violence was everywhere awakened toward the active friends of the helpless. Then, sir, our cause began to make swift progress.[48]

For Garrison, the abolitionists' moment of crisis was not merely their finest hour but their utopian moment, the point at which the "active friends of the helpless" gained the role of principle actor in a grand political drama. In this narrative construction, all the signs of the abolition movement's disparity with the trends and temper of the time—the violent opposition to the discussion of abolition, the contrary disposition of popular opinion—obtained as evidence of an underlying continuity with a distant but sweeping historical movement synonymous with progress itself. Nearly ten years later, Garrison could see the same movement unfolding in the "mountain-load of indignities" that the abolition movement had endured. "Everything around us indicates that great events are at hand," he confidently reported to the Massachusetts Anti-Slavery Society in 1845. "A revolution is begun which never will—which never can—go backwards."[49]

In his historical assessments of the abolition movement, Garrison used the magical words of the Enlightenment—progress and revolution—with every intent of reproducing the "great events" of that historical epoch and their recognition thereof. The "popular tumult" that arose against the abolitionists would seem to indicate otherwise, but he seemed to assemble a narrative of progressive modernity from the very untimeliness of their political initiatives with the politics of their own era. The abolitionists, he seemed to be saying, were acting out a drama that had already been staged but was still so resonant in the minds of contemporaries that the failure of their efforts invoked its key acts. Moreover, he meant this judgment to betray the fragility of his own standpoint, which shared with the abolition movement the quality of being isolated, contrarian, and wholly dependent on the currency of obsolete values. Of course, there might have been an appeal to nostalgia in Garrison's narration of abolitionist progress, but the more obvious tone of militancy in his rhetoric suggests that he meant the anachronism of his judgment and that of the abolitionists' initiatives to overcome all considerations of their viability or relevance and to foretell the eventual victory of the cause. What Garrison retrieved from the Enlightenment, in other words, is what Kant called a "prophetic history," or a "history of future times," and with this mode of narration he betrayed his true plans for the abolition movement at its most besieged.[50]

We can infer these plans from Kant's own articulation of a progressive Enlightenment, which, like Garrison's, was strikingly candid about the untimeliness of its own conclusions. Here I am referring not to the manifesto-like "What Is Enlightenment?" but to the more self-referential determination of historical progress found in "The Contest of the Faculties." Writing during the unfolding saga of the French Revolution, Kant admitted that it if "a people's revolution or constitutional reform were ultimately to fail," its partisans would still retain their belief in the progress of democracy and the liberation of the oppressed. The key, he seemed to realize, was that they should have a belief to retain, which means they must have heard all this somewhere before:

For the occurrence in question is too momentous, too intimately inter-woven with the interests of humanity and too widespread in its influence upon all the parts of the world for nations not to be reminded of it when favorable circumstances present themselves, and to rise up and make renewed attempts of the same kind as before. After all, since it is of such an important concern of the human race, the intended constitution ... will not fail to instill the lessons of repeated experience into the hearts of everyone.[51]

This lucid and beautiful passage might serve as an epitaph for the aboli-tion movement precisely because it pays tribute to its historical predica-ment. The pamphleteering, the public meetings, the call for rational and disinterested discussion, and above all the providential belief in political progress all were too old, so to speak, for the antebellum anti-slavery struggle; they could not save the movement from the depreda-tions of the class-based, racially segregated, gender-exclusive slugfest of the Jacksonian public sphere, and the abolitionists came too late to deploy them. On the other hand, the abolitionists' symbols and articles of publicity were exactly like "the lessons of repeated experience" that were said to convince the onlookers to otherwise contingent events that they were witnessing the signature events of the Enlightenment. These printed articles told of the past triumphs of a revolutionary people and served to remind the interested observers of a succeeding age that they too were in the midst of an epochal period of human liberation even when all indications were against them. Kant's "prophetic history" of humanity, in other words, can help us place the New England abolition movement in the context of the Enlightenment because it holds that a pedagogy of incident and precedent would always intervene in the recog-nition of political progress. The immediate participants in the drama of the Enlightenment, like the abolitionists who came after them, were latecomers in this regard as well: they had to rely on the faculty of their memories in order to register the magnitude of a historic occasion.

Garrison wanted little else for the abolition movement than for it to have come too late. Although this would position the movement on the wrong side of contemporary politics, he seemed to understand that belatedness could be an epistemologically privileged position that put abolition on the side of progress, revolution, and popular democracy. He thus invoked the narrative of Enlightenment with the same intention that he betrayed in his historical representation of the abolitionist public sphere, which was to collapse the position of privilege with that of oppression so that the minority of his own day could operate as the history-making, sovereign people. But here we can anticipate the "No in thunder" from Frederick Douglass when we note that Garrison would secure this minority position for the largely white male abolition movement precisely by representing it historically, or by a position in time. Of course, the persecution of the abolition movement by mobs, laws, and government would do much to convince its members that they had much in common with both the free and enslaved victims of racism, and yet Garrison's rhetorical salute to these persecutions in the passages above reminds us that the position of the minority was to be understood in relation to a judgment of progress and therefore could be considered a feature of narrative. He described the abolitionists in the midst of their persecution as alienated, belated participants in a lapsed historical drama, and while this might have accorded with the potential for vulnerability and failure that Kant built into the narration of modernity, it did not put a stop to his own narration or prevent the abolitionists from adopting the role of protagonists. For Garrison, the difficulty of staging the epochal events of the Enlightenment in the present day seemed to generate a still more expansive vision of "swift progress" based specifically on the political agency of a people.

Garrison realized this vision in a speech in 1831 before a gathering of free African Americans. He directed their own antislavery efforts toward "the powerful energies of the press," without which "every cause must languish," and in return he would include the most oppressed members of the abolition movement within the most expansive possible historical drama: "It was this engine which produced and trimphantly effected the American Revolution, it has two times overthrown the despotism in France; it is fanning the flame of liberty in Poland; its power is shaking the government of Great Britain to its center."[52] The agency of the press, in other words, operated through history in accordance with the universal, worldwide progress of liberty. The political prospects of free African Americans were judged on this same basis, which made their subjectivity solely intelligible through and coextensive with the abolitionists' representation of their own publicity.

The fact that the New England abolitionists coded these articles of publicity with the "lessons of repeated experience" meant that Garrison did not assume an unbroken continuity between their current struggle and the unfolding of the Enlightenment. They seemed acutely aware that they had ransacked the past for the needs of the present and that their presumption of a public identity was due completely to the formal structure of their historical analogies—and yet they did not swerve from their conviction that the formalism, the disjunctions, and the ironies of their self-representation all served political ends and sustained the promise of former revolutions. Even the abolitionists' cultural politics was more political than cultural, at least in this ideological sense. Their signal expression of affinity with the oppressed, their insistence on the anachronism of their historical position, helped to reproduce a narrative of political modernity that guaranteed the appearance of a people.

A more critical possibility for the narration of modernity has been imagined in the postcolonial criticism of Bhabha, who would rewrite Kant's reflections on the "lessons of repeated experience" from the perspective of the oppressed:

> The sign of history does not consist in an essence of the event itself, nor exclusively in the *immediate consciousness* of its agents and actors, but in its form as a *spectacle*, spectacle that signifies *because of* the distanciation and displacement between the event and those who are its spectators. Modernity ... privileges those who "bear witness," those who are "subjected," or ... historically displaced. It gives them a representative position through the spatial distance, or the *time-lag* between the Great Event and its circulation as a historical sign of the "people" or an "epoch," that constitutes the memory and the moral of the event *as a narrative.*[53]

In Bhabha's version of Kant's formulation, the sense of alienation and belatedness experienced by the spectators of history is much more acute. It is also more causal, serving as a limiting but enabling condition that is not overcome by the mediation of signs, lessons, memory, or prophecy. Bhabha wants to maintain the "time-lag" between the "Great Event" and its symbolic recurrence, and while this position might have served as Garrison's premise for an alliance between the abolitionists, "those who bear witness," and the enslaved, "those who are subjected," it cannot generate another version of what the white abolitionist had called "swift progress." For Bhahba, the postcolonial perspective is a means to introduce the aesthetic effect of distanciation and to slow down or "dam up" the narration of political modernity in a way that is indicative of true alterity.

We can glimpse this effect in Bhabha's use of scare quotes around "people" and "epoch," stylistic additions to Kant's formulation that are intended to reflect the standing of these categories as being subject to their articulation. His further point is that the narration of modernity is a culturally inflected aesthetic act that might depend on the "lessons of repeated experience," or what he calls "the pedagogy of the symbols of progress, historicism, modernization, homogeneous empty time," but that also reveals them as arbitrary signifiers in a narrative construction of progress, contingent on the demands of that narration. The final irony for Bhabha is that Kant himself provided for this aesthetic dimension in his own exposition of the Enlightenment, an observation shared also by Foucault on the basis of his rereading of the seminal essay "What Is Enlightenment?"[54] Foucault regards modernity not as an attempt to date a historical moment but as an attempt to come to terms with the time of its own writing, as a "way out" from the serial narration of history itself. He follows Kant's route of escape straight to the aesthetic discourse of modernity, which he regards as the source of an "attitude" whereby one establishes not only "a mode of relationship . . . with oneself" but "a form of relationship to the present."[55]

In this book, the critical figures who would parse the abolitionists' language of past and future are also those who developed an aesthetic vocabulary for halting their narrative of progress. Both Thoreau and Douglass (the latter specifically in his oratory) in this sense saw anti-slavery as it is, not as it was or as it was supposed to be. They found a way out from the abolitionists' public sphere, adopting a critical position that displaced them from a historical representation of the people and situated them squarely in the present moment. The fact that this position kept Thoreau from affiliating himself with the abolition movement in any other way than to adopt the cause and persona of the fugitive slave is significant in itself, for it meant that he did not intend for his individualized acts of resistance to compose either the traces of citizenship or to reassemble the faculty of civic action. In overdetermining his own "sort of space," as he called his retreat at Walden Pond, with the tropes of the abolitionists' public sphere, he submitted them to the aesthetic effect of distanciation, which is exactly the effect that Douglass would attempt to produce with his oratory. "Your religion justifies our tyrants, and you are yourselves our enslavers. I see my enslavers here in Concord, and before my eyes," he declared before a public assembly of the Massachusetts Anti-Slavery Society, and with that accusation he sought to interrupt the formation of an abolitionist consensus within perhaps the most institutional boundary of the abolitionists' public sphere.[56] In a broader sense, he sought to forestall the formation of an abolitionist public with the force and fury of his rhetoric, which induced not only the thrilling experience of awe, wonder, and rational incapacity in many of his listeners but also the sublime experience of terror. Douglass's expression of the sublime, I will argue in the last chapter, indeed forced abolitionists to interrupt their analogical comparisons to the revolutionary struggles of another age. For the duration of his speeches, they had to surrender their historical consciousness as well as their invincible belief in abolitionist progress and keep their narrative representation of the movement subject to the temporality or time of his articulation. The aesthetic inflection of Douglass's oratory, like the former slave himself, proved totally inassimilable to the "time dimension" in which the abolitionists cast their public identity.

The last two chapters of the book in this sense stage a conflict between an aesthetic register of language and tropes and the utopian premise of the public sphere, which the abolitionists would recast as a position in time. As such, they are intended to dramatize the critical potential of aestheticism in the discourse of modernity, a potential that I have smuggled into my exposition of the abolition movement's public sphere by calling attention to its discursive structure and particularly to its narrative form. "The importance of the philosophy of the beautiful and the sublime," writes Lyotard, "lies both in the de-realisation of the object of aesthetic feelings, and in the absence of . . . the historico-political object, which as such has no reality, and . . . must remain in-existent.[57] Lyotard's conclusion—"Revolutionary politics is based on a transcendental illusion"—might appear to reduce the abolitionists' political project to nothing more than misprision, but his technical use of the term "transcendental" means that he is following a Kantian tradition of implicating the activity and techniques of the imagination in any cognition, especially one regarding the course or direction of history. He goes on to compile a list of aesthetic devices—the use of analogies, illustrative examples, and judgments of historical relation—that are essential to the redemptive narrative of modernity and by extension to the abolitionists' role as the people.

Was the abolitionists' public sphere thus nothing more than the product of their imagination, reducible to the inclination or need for a public to exist and wholly dependent on the historical signs that were furnished by their publications? By combining historicist, critical, and theoretical methologies in the foregoing discussion of abolitionist publicity, I do want to raise questions regarding the relation of aesthetics to politics, particularly in the context of a democratic self-representation. These questions, I hope, arise from the signature conceit of the abolitionists' public sphere—its symbolic standing as a historical institution—and become more pressing as my analysis uncovers their manipulation of historical signifiers. They originate in the historical inquiry of the first four chapters of the book, which, in sequence, depict a public that existed on the condition of its invisibility, the public attribution of an individual voice, the republican attributes of a black man's body, and, in chapter 4, the materialization of a trope of public space. The rest of the book can be said to be devoted to exploring the stakes raised by these imaginative transformations of the public sphere.

If we confronted Garrison and the New England abolitionists with the aesthetic dimension of their political project, with their use of metaphor, analogy, and irony, or with their determination to project themselves into the narrative of modernity on the basis of their distance from its signal events, they would never surrender their conviction of their historical place, of their relation to a former revolution. That uncertainty would have undermined the entire rationale for the discussion of abolition. With their publicity campaign, they wanted to establish objectively that place and resolve all questions regarding the destiny of their movement. Furthermore, they counted on the circulation of their printed articles to establish the objectivity of a historical ideal that had been transplanted from another era. Their public sphere, so dependent on the memory of lapsed political ideals and institutions, depended also on this physical evidence. The abolitionists' ambition for their publicity campaign indeed was to provide a historical, material basis for an imaginary public, and so it is with this unlikely objective that we begin.

CHAPTER 1

The Sedition of Nonresistance

From its inception in the early 1830s until the end of the decade, the New England abolitionists' publicity campaign circulated not only pamphlets and newspapers but the traces of a former revolutionary threat. The object of this campaign, the formation of a reading public composed of the enslaved, the free blacks of the North, and the women of the abolition movement, was decried by the enemies of abolition as the essence of jacobinism, or, alternately, hailed by the sympathizers of the cause as the resurgence of a people. The egalitarianism of the abolitionists' public sphere, I have previously argued, was intelligible as a political narrative that was all the more unsettling for being incongruous with its times.

Why then did Garrison's opponents fear the overthrow of constitutional government and the destruction of the social order at the very moment when he and his allies within the Massachusetts Anti-Slavery Society seemed to surrender the political objectives of their publicity campaign in favor of the possibility of collective political *inaction*? From 1838 until the end of the decade, Garrison and several of his closest allies publicly embraced nonresistance, a pacifist doctrine that enjoined its adherents to withdraw formally from the arena of electoral politics and to suspend all organized political activity. As articulated by its principle exponent, Adin Ballou, nonresistance imposed a blanket prohibition on its adherents—"We can neither fight for [government], legislate in it, hold its offices, vote at its elections, nor act any political part within its pale"—and in that spirit, abolitionists were asked to eschew all the conventional strategies that a reform movement could pursue.[1]

Scholars have typically attributed the ascension of nonresistance within the New England abolition movement to the moral idealism and Perfectionist spirituality that is said to have guided Garrison's more radical initiatives, but if the contemporary reaction to this strategy is any indication, the problem with nonresistance was that it was all too political and, in fact, dangerously revolutionary.[2] As the Reverend Joseph Tracy charged, the abolitionists' refusal to hold office, wage war, or vote challenged "the right of a nation to govern its individual members," a position that he insisted was "the very foundation principle of Jacobinism."[3] Calvin Colton, the colonizationist author of *Abolition a Sedition* who had detected the "machinery" of jacobinism in their publicity campaign, followed suit in contending that the revolutionary design of the abolition movement could be inferred from their latest heresy. "They," meaning the abolitionist supporters of nonresistance, "would deny that their 'doctrines are Jacobinical;' and why set up the defence before they are accused, except from the consciousness that all the world will pronounce them so."[4]

Nonresistance thus cannot be so easily squared with the ideological narrative of the reform era as a period of triumphant individualism and moral absolutism.[5] On the contrary, the currency of anachronisms and the mediation of historical tropes seemed to be as determinate in this seemingly apolitical phase of the antislavery struggle as they were in the abolitionists' institution of a public sphere. In this chapter I want to establish conclusively this continuity by proposing an alternative genealogy for nonresistance that starts with Garrison's investment in the historical value of abolitionist publicity and ends with the legal standing of printed dissent in the postrevolutionary American polity. My premise for this revisionary analysis is that the print culture of the antebellum era was not merely a material resource for the abolitionists' publicity campaign but a medium of historical awareness that lent every expression of dissent a diachronic, historically overdetermined significance.

Garrison had intended the discussion of abolition and, particularly, the distribution of the abolitionists' printed articles to circulate the memory of the nation's founding revolutionary struggle, but when he accepted an invitation from Abner Kneeland, Boston's spokesperson for the deist "First Society of Free Enquirers," to gather the nascent New England abolition movement in the society's public hall, he secured an alliance with a reform society that based its resistance on the arguably dim prospect of a continuing Enlightenment. Kneeland's society of Freethinkers was part of a loosely organized movement of latter-day deists that had advocated the progress of "mental liberty" and the continuation of a democratic, specifically French revolution for the benefit of the uneducated and working classes since the late eighteenth century. Within the Freethought movement, Tom Paine was venerated as the fearless author of the *Rights of Man* and *Age of Reason* but first and foremost as a printer who upheld the most egalitarian possibilities of the trade.[6]

If the name of Paine could instill the promise of an iconoclastic, artisan republicanism in subsequent generations of tradesmen and Freethinkers, it could also tar any self-declared republican society with the memories of past insurrections and socially destructive political revolutions. Still renowned and alternately reviled in the antebellum era for the allegedly seditious arguments of the *Rights of Man*, and particularly for the infidelity of *Age of Reason*, Paine brought Kneeland, and his counterpart in New York, Frances Wright, the opprobrium that earlier generations had given to the reputed jacobin turncoat.[7] Paine's infamy in turn brought the charges of infidelity and jacobinism to any contemporary movement or initiative that seemed to champion the social equality of classes, races, and genders, and that included the New England abolition movement, Wright's radical feminism, as well as the class politics of the Freethought movement.[8]

From 1830 to 1834, roughly the time that Garrison was gathering his forces, Kneeland offered listeners to his addresses and readers of his newspaper, the *Boston Investigator*, a steady dose of such radically republican measures as land reform, economic equality, and public education drawn from the political economy of the *Rights of Man* as well as what would turn out to be legally blasphemous attacks against the clergy.[9] In his early organizational efforts on behalf of the abolition movement, Garrison followed suit, agitating for the establishment of "free negro" schools and of voluntary associations of African American printers and laborers in the name of *Liberty and Equality Forever!* As if to found these societies under the infidel precepts of a disciple of Paine, he added, "I ask no church to grant me authority to speak . . . I am not careful to consult Martin Luther, or John Calvin, or his Holiness the Pope."[10] Garrison's connection with the Freethought movement, in other words, helped him to displace the stakes of the antislavery struggle from the political, social, and economic issues of the present day to the distant prospect of the Enlightenment. He also gained a particular historical reference for the abolitionists' political initiatives, I will argue, nonresistance included, that linked the public sphere of abolitionist discussion to the social equality, iconoclastic criticism, and, ultimately, universal liberation that Paine and subsequent generations of his followers had foreseen in the progress of reason.

Garrison gained still more by the 1834 trial of Kneeland for the crime of blasphemy: a rather detailed historical scenario that helped him to situate the abolition movement in the midst of a counterrevolutionary reaction against the ideals of the Enlightenment. The Commonwealth of Massachusetts had indicted Kneeland for reprinting several articles derogatory to the clergy. The prosecuting attorney for the commonwealth revealed his true object when he condemned the defendant for popularizing the works of Hume, Voltaire, and Volney et al. among "those who have no learning nor leisure to consider and refute its falsehoods."[11] Kneeland was found guilty, that is, of promoting an Enlightenment doctrine of rationalist free inquiry among an allegedly uneducated working class, a crime that had been attached to deism since the 1790s and specifically to the publication of *Age of Reason*. He assumed the same liability as its author for promoting Enlightenment-era radicalism among nineteenth-century Americans and even found himself prosecuted for the same crime Paine was found guilty of in absentia under English common law, the crime of seditious libel.[12] With the help of these historical precedents, the prosecutor argued that Kneeland's blasphemy in fact evinced the "the obvious tendency of a libel," its true object being "to disturb the public safety and tranquility," and "the subversion of all law and order in society."[13]

By invoking the law of seditious libel, the prosecuting attorney drew on the memory of past subversions and conjured still more parties to Kneeland's crime—the dangerously "self-created" "democratic-republican societies" of the 1790s and the emergent republican opposition press, both of which were held responsible for everything from jacobin collaboration to illicit conspiracies with secret European rationalist sects. In the contentious postrevolutionary politics of the era, republican printers eventually would be held legally accountable for their allegedly libelous criticism of the Federalist government and eventually were deemed threats to the security of the state under the Alien and Sedition Acts.[14] For his part, Kneeland recognized the charges as nothing more than leftover animus from another age, the repetition of "stale and often contradicted falsehoods about the 'illuminati'" and "the lies about . . . the *Age of Reason*."[15]

Garrison, on the other hand, regarded Kneeland's conviction under the spirit if not the letter of libel law as perfectly suited for their age. For the abolitionist editor, it proved that they were fighting for the progress of the Enlightenment against reactionary forces of church and state and that a source of free inquiry could still be prosecuted for spreading the word of democracy among the unlettered and uneducated. In an 1836 issue of *The Liberator*, he reprinted a call from the governor of New York for a second enactment of the Alien and Sedition Acts that would criminalize the abolitionists' condemnation of American slavery and prevent the circulation of abolitionist publications beyond the borders of Massachusetts.[16] Two years later, he printed a petition for the amnesty of Kneeland that sidestepped the charge of blasphemy in order to claim, as he put it, "free discussion as a principle." "The assumption by government of a right to proscribe and repress opinions," he wrote, with one eye on the fate of abolitionists' own publicity campaign, "has been the ground of the grossest depravation of religion, and of the most

grinding despotism."[17] Garrison defended Kneeland on classically libertarian grounds, posing the freedom of discussion as a time-honored
check on tyranny and as an essential defense against the corruption of
the polity. He looked backward not only to the legal persecution of a
republican press but to an eighteenth-century Anglo-American political discourse that helped to theorize the dissenting tradition of a parliamentary opposition and the critical inquiry of an unfettered press as
the cherished liberties of a free people.[18] Any strategy that championed
the right of free speech therefore associated the abolition movement
with a historic, ongoing struggle of a people against tyranny, and that
included nonresistance.

In the same year that he defended Kneeland, Garrison inaugurated
his campaign for nonresistance with the same libertarian principles.
Writing in 1838 to a dubious friend and colleague, Samuel May, Garrison claimed that nonresistance "denies to no man the right to think,
speak and act, except as his reason and conscience may dictate,"[19] and
thereafter publicized the controversial theory as if it vindicated nothing
more than the principles of free speech. Against the wishes of many
subscribers to *The Liberator*, he gave the subject of nonresistance its
own column, defending his decision in an editorial titled "Free Discussion."[20] At the first meeting of the newly formed New England Non-
Resistance Society in 1839, its members took their cue from Garrison
and adopted, with full attribution, the motto of the Massachusetts Anti-
Slavery Society: "Abolition thrives in actual proportion to the growth
of free discussion on all moral and political subjects." The next order of
business was to approve their primary resolution: "That the only basis
upon which a reformatory society can stand and effect its work in the
heart of men is a sacred respect for the right of opinion."[21] Nonresistance, then, did not compel abolitionists to abandon the object of their
publicity campaign or to forswear the formation of a public sphere. In
advocating the pacifist strategy, Garrison in fact was attempting to for-
malize his conviction that little else was required for the abolition of
slavery than free discussion, and he moved to exclude more purposive,
coordinated political action on that basis.

At the same meeting of the New England Non-Resistance Society, Garrison included an important proviso for this kind of free discussion: "This acknowledgment of the right of opinion does not forbid our interrogating others as to their opinion—endeavoring to change their opinions if we deem them erroneous, and protesting against their opinions. . . . There are times and places where those opinions which are not in our view just may be attacked." Although this imperative for dissent tended to prevent the social organization of the society's members and exacerbate the internecine warfare that already raged within the New England abolition movement, Garrison considered any expression of dissent to preserve the role of a critical public in an increasingly corrupt American polity and to extend the blessings of democracy to the enslaved.[22] He drew on the ideological narrative of eighteenth-century libertarianism and the historical precedent of postrevolutionary republicanism and concluded that the same dangers that had imperiled the progress of freedom of a people in former generations now endangered the abolitionists' cause. For Garrison, the tangible sign of this historical recurrence was the prosecution of editors and printers for seditious libel, which constituted not just a threat to an individual's right of free speech but the resurgence of state-sponsored tyranny from a former age. He regarded every obstacle to the discussion of abolition—the spontaneous mob attacks, the prohibitive postal regulations, the resolutions of state legislatures, and ultimately a congressional ban on the reading of abolitionist petitions—in light of this historical narrative and appealed to the principles of nonresistance on this basis. Garrison's advocacy of nonresistance in this sense presumed the freedom of a public sphere that did not exist in contemporary political culture, that belonged to the lore, so to speak, of liberal democracy. More specifically, it depended on the categorization of free speech and dissent under a lapsed, postrevolutionary standard of seditious libel in order to give the otherwise politically inert adherents to nonresistance the historic place of a revolutionary public.

In breaking the link between the free discussion of abolition and any contemporary definition of political agency, nonresistance might well be considered a signal manifestation of the abolitionists' imaginary public, an extension of their politics of anachronism. In like fashion, nonresistance extended a conceit of the abolitionists' political project and connected the abolition movement to the predicament of the disenfranchised by way of a historical comparison with a revolutionary people. However, the abolitionists' historical relation to the ideal of a people also can be said to have gained a new and distinctive dimension under the theory of nonresistance. That same relation, I will argue, placed the movement in a structural opposition or spatial relation to the state in a way that could have direct bearing on the disposition of power in the antebellum polity. The abolition movement, Garrison seemed to acknowledge, did have a place in contemporary political culture but it was outside the state, separate from the jurisdiction and control of its laws, and alienated from the entitlements of citizenship.

As one would expect, this representation of the abolition movement engaged Garrison's opponents in an often theoretical debate concerning "the right of a nation to govern its members," as the Reverend Tracy had put it. Elizur Wright, a founding member of the Massachusetts Anti-Slavery Society and one of the many abolitionist critics of nonresistance, found himself insisting on the place and role of the state in any antislavery initiative: "If you follow out your doctrine," he argued, "surely you must cease having anything to do with Congress and State legislatures. Our action upon them in the direction of humanity not only recognizes but tends to confirm their power, for human governments are never so strong as when the weakest enjoy their protection."[23] As Wright clearly saw, nonresistance displaced the struggle for liberty from the sphere of constitutionally guaranteed rights, juridical positivism, and legislative sovereignty circumscribed by the state to what he considered a no-man's land of political impotence. The 1838 *Declaration of Sentiments* that Garrison wrote for the New England Non-Resistance Society, on the other hand, was just as categorical:

> As every human government is upheld by physical strength, and its laws
> are enforced eventually at the point of the bayonet, we cannot hold any

office which imposes upon its incumbent the obligation to compel men to do right, on pain of imprisonment or death. We therefore voluntarily exclude ourselves from every legislative and judicial body, and repudiate all human politics, worldly honors, and stations of authority.[24]

As Garrison collected more evidence of the state's brute strength and the violence of its laws, he would attempt to conduct the antislavery struggle independently of the state and forgo the claims of the abolition movement to representation per se. Under the principles of nonresistance, the New England abolition movement, custodians and bearers of a public identity, would have to disavow the official recognition that a representative government would bestow on an enfranchised, sovereign people.

For critics like Wright and Tracy, the abolition movement might well have been invisible, and yet Garrison's determination to forbid the appearance of a people in any other form except through the faculty of perpetual dissent sustained a negative condition for democracy that contemporary theorists such as Tocqueville considered essential to the preservation of liberty. In *Democracy in America*, Tocqueville identified the distinction of democratic society as its "ceaseless agitation," its "restless and all-pervading activity," which, according to his modern expositor Claude Lefort, could be found in a public sphere of competing opinions and the free exchange of incompatible ideas. Whereas power had been embodied in a monarchical subject, which in turn gave society its own body, the public sphere of democracy ensures that the "social space of politics" will remain an "empty place . . . such that no individual and no group can be consubstantial with it."[25] The countervailing tendency that Tocqueville detected in democracies was for citizens to confuse their social or civil existence with the "absolute will of the majority" that prevailed under their political constitution and thereby give birth to a new form of tyranny, a "tyranny of the majority."[26]

Armed with the premises of a political theorist, Garrison could see the evidence of this tyranny in the popular opposition to abolitionist discussion, in the state-sponsored suppression of abolitionist petitions, and ultimately within the confines of the abolition movement itself. One loyal Massachusetts Anti-Slavery Society member who objected to Garrison's advocacy of nonresistance undoubtedly claimed to speak for the majority when he stated, "Republican liberty is only the liberty to say and do what the prevailing voice and will of the brotherhood will allow and protect."[27] To break the bond between society and state and to reinstate the agitation of a democratic society thus became Garrison's object in promoting nonresistance as an abolitionist initiative. For him, the pacifist strategy promised nothing less than a "renovated and purified form of political action" that would reveal the "kingdoms and governments of this world" in their "real deformity,"[28] and although this might have made him sound like a Perfectionist, it also made him a libertarian critic of the constitutional order, sensitive to the ever-present threat of corruption within the polity and to the need for a critical, autonomous people on principle.[29]

On the basis of that principle, Garrison criticized, libeled, and when possible blasphemed any opponent to abolition as a representative of the nation's "slaveholding despotism." His theorization of non-resistance in this sense emerged from his own practice as editor of *The Liberator*, and from his awareness of his legal liability as a contrarian editor. He had inaugurated his editorial mission with a libel against the slave trader Francis Todd—who, it turned out, was not a slave trader—and for the rest of the decade wore the charge of his "harsh language" as a badge of honor.[30] He levied memorable blasts against slaveholders and proslavery statesmen from the editorial pages of *The Liberator*, but he seemed to reserve his harshest language for the clerical leaders of evangelical reform, as if he what he wanted above all was to share Abner Kneeland's crime of blasphemy, the legacy of iconoclastic republicanism, and ultimately a political kinship with the seditious libeler Tom Paine. "I protest against this companionship," he declared, referring to the Protestant leadership of the reform movement, for "it is becoming more and more apparent, that they are nothing better than hirelings, in the bad sense of that term—that they are blind leaders of the blind, dumb dogs that cannot bark, spiritual popes."[31]

Although broadsides like this ensured the unpopularity of the abolition movement among the already converted advocates of reform, they were consistent with Garrison's object in provoking and exchanging criticism, which was to protect the abolition movement not only from its representation by the state but from its consolidation into a form of public opinion. In return, he would give abolitionists a strictly legal index of their public identity, the liability of their political dissent under the law of seditious libel, which acknowledged not just the historical precedent of a republican opposition but the contemporary conditions arrayed *against* the abolition movement. Garrison could look for and find these conditions in the protests of libeled ministers, the bureaucratic minutiae of postal regulations, the arson of a southern mob, and, ultimately, in the federal regulation against the discussion of abolition in the halls of Congress; for the abolitionist editor, they were all the instruments of a "slaveholding despotism" that bound the disposition of public opinion to the sovereignty of a state in way that precluded the discussion of abolition. Having conceived the abolition movement as a publicity campaign appealing to the opinion of "every man, every woman, and every child," he seemed to realize that the prospects for an abolitionist public sphere had diminished to the vanishing point. However, he conceived his most controversial strategy to date, a precursor of his more direct attack on the sovereignty of the constitutional state, by positing the agency and role of a critical public on the strength of a legal infraction, and with little else to go by other than that formal standard. Nonresistance thus stood for the public sphere of abolitionist discussion in the absence of a public.

Of course, Garrison's own efforts and those of other reform groups paid testimony to the opposite phenomenon, the creation of multiple, competing forms of public culture as well as new kinds of publicness. Even the evidence that Garrison concocted against the abolitionists' public sphere—the coordination of official and unofficial resistance to the discussion of abolition—bore witness to what Habermas would call the "political public sphere," the state-supervised realm of free speech and public discussion that arrives with the ascension of the liberal constitutional order.[32] Garrison's strategy of nonresistance, in other words, was part of a frankly utopian attempt to displace the abolitionists' public identity from any existing manifestation of the public sphere, or to represent the displacement of the abolition movement from the very boundaries of the antebellum polity. With this pacifist theory, he sought an outcast status for the abolition that corresponded to an anachronistic ideal of a critical public but that also identified them with and as the oppressed.

The racial politics of this ambition can be glimpsed in Garrison's defense of the abolitionists' publicity campaign that he submitted to the state legislature of Massachusetts in 1836. The legislature was then considering imposing its own ban on the distribution of abolitionist publications, setting up a confrontation between state power and the libertarian principles of free discussion that Garrison would soon dramatize in the theory of nonresistance. The object of abolition, he maintained, "is to rescue THE LIBERTY OF SPEECH from the grasp of that oppression, which now holds millions of our colored countrymen by their throats—a liberty which is becoming more and more abridged, for which gags and padlocks are now recommended, without which men are abject as brutes, and in defence of which our fathers poured out their blood like water."[33] In typical fashion, Garrison represented the public agency of the abolition movement with a narrative trope that linked the fate of abolitionist discussion to the late struggle of its revolutionary forbears. The New England abolitionists, he claimed, fought for an endangered legacy, the right of free speech, the cause for which the American Revolution was said to be fought and won. They were endangered to that same extent and occupied a position in the antebellum polity that was alternately idealized and dismissed.

Garrison's diachronic representation of the abolitionists' public sphere, however, had a more radical and transparent aim in this setting than he had allowed in previous articulations of their affliction. By his reckoning, slavery would end only when a tyrannical state ceased its persecution of the Massachusetts Anti-Slavery Society and freed abolitionists from their metaphoric gags and padlocks, a proposition that not only defied the difference between white male citizens and enslaved African Americans but also sought to reconcile the suffering and persecutions of slavery with a discursive, avowedly figurative version of the same. From the inception of the abolitionists' publicity campaign, Garrison had attempted to portray the critical position of an abolitionist public with and through the same comparisons, but as we observe his deepening conviction in a libertarian politics of dissent and his accompanying modulation of enslavement, we cannot help but regard the strategy of nonresistance as an initiative designed to institutionalize the fantasy of an abject, subaltern state for enfranchised citizens.

Garrison's Prosecution Complex

Garrison's rise as an institutional figure in the abolition movement suggests that an individual abolitionist could gain his or her credibility as a public voice when he or she was convicted of libel. Garrison's colleague David Lee Child was a casualty of prosecution for seditious libel in 1829, judged guilty of maliciously and wickedly intending to "injure and vilify the good name, the fame, credit, and reputation for honesty of one John Keyes, Esq., a member of the Honorable Senate of the General Court of Massachusetts ... and maliciously intending to deprive the said John Keyes of his offices aforesaid, and the confidence of the people of his senatorial district." With the help of a pamphlet reprinting the transcript of the case, Child presented his own aggrieved right as the bulwark of a free people, successfully reviving libertarian ideals for the nascent abolition movement. "The representatives of the people," Child's defense lawyer argued, "are mere servants of the people.... Their official conduct is liable to be scrutinized and canvassed at all times by those under whom and for whom they are acting."[34]

In 1829 Garrison claimed the same right in the name of the people, though he had to work harder for it. He was convicted under civil not criminal law for the libel of Francis Todd, the owner of a reputed slave ship, and had to represent himself as an enemy of the state. Writing from his prison cell in Baltimore, he declared, "Whatever relates to the freedom of the press is intimately connected with the rights of the people" but that with the "growing tendency in many courts, to stifle free inquiry, to dishearten every effort of reform, and to intimidate conductors of newspapers," he could be counted on to contest the law of the courts.[35] His career as an abolitionist editor indeed began in earnest when he was sprung from jail by Arthur Tappan, and even though the conviction had discredited his previous employer, William Ladd, editor of the *Genius of Emancipation*, Garrison made the defense of libelous criticism the subject of most of his editorials during the first year of *The Liberator*. For Garrison, the crime of libel established the libertarian credentials of his editorial mission and, by extension, the cause of the New England abolition movement, which he straightaway committed to the defense of free speech.

What put these two convicted editors at the forefront of the antislavery struggle? There is a story to be told here, and its origins are in the legal tradition of common law that American jurisprudence adopted nearly wholesale from England. The Anglo-American common law of seditious (or criminal) libel presumed to protect the good reputation of elected officials or other representatives of the state from malicious, unfounded printed criticism. It further decreed that their good reputation was necessary to the legitimacy of government, thereby forging an alliance between the stability of the state and the disposition of popular opinion. Despite the precedent of the Zenger case, the truth of printed criticism was only fitfully admitted in seditious libel cases (it was always allowed in civil cases) because the American jurists who enforced this common-law tradition implicitly accepted the English Whig libertarian argument for free speech, which had made popular opinion a necessary support for government. Any criticism of a public person designed to weaken that support thereby constituted the crime of sedition.[36]

In the postrevolutionary era, the American legislature formally recognized the vulnerability of the federal government to printed criticism with the passage of the Alien and Sedition Acts. The stated intention of the famous 1798 statute was to prevent "the publication of false, scandalous and malicious matter against the government," which, under the tenets of libel law, constituted, "false, scandalous, and malicious attempts to deprive the good people of the United States,"[37] but even after a Republican administration came to power and Jefferson cancelled the Alien and Sedition Acts, libel prosecution continued to put the burden of protecting and upholding the government on the opposition press. The lasting precedent to emerge from *People v. Croswell* in 1804 was that even admittedly truthful criticism "reflecting on government, magistracy, or individuals" could be published "with impunity" only if the criticism had "good motives" and "justifiable ends."[38]

These standards of seditious libel put a lasting stamp on the Federalist stronghold of Massachusetts, on its John Adams–authored constitution, and, of course, on its judiciary. In the face of mounting legislative pressure to allow verifiable criticism of public officials, the chief justices of the commonwealth upheld the English common-law tradition, which prevented them from considering the truth of printed criticism against a public official or standing government. The majority opinion of Chief Justice Parker, written in 1825, argued that the state was permanently injured by a criminal libel:

> The general principle decided is, that it is immaterial to the character of a libel as a public offense, whether the matter of it be true or false . . . because the interest of the public requires that men not invested with the authority of the laws, shall not usurp the power of public accusation, and arraign before the public, with malicious motives, their neighbors and fellow citizens. . . . The common law therefore is left unpaired by the constitution.[39]

As magistrates such as Parker were laying down the law, the Massachusetts legislature was pursuing a revision of criminal libel that would have separated the interests of the public from the interests of public officials. Although an 1827 statute, "An Act Relating to Prosecution for Libel and to Pleadings in Actions for Libel and Slander," stated that a defendant could furnish "evidence in his defense, the truth of the matter contained in the publications charged as libelous: Provided that . . . the matter charged as libelous was published with good motives and for justifiable ends," seditious libel cases continued to be prosecuted by the Massachusetts judiciary well into the 1840s.[40]

Given this history, Garrison would have been remiss not to be acutely aware of the standards for seditious libel, and so even though he had been convicted under civil law, he challenged his contemporaries to judge him by criminal standards. "Epithets may be rightly applied, it is true, and yet be uttered in a bad spirit, or with a malicious design," he wrote. "What then? Shall we discard all terms which are description of crime, because they are not always used with fairness and propriety?"[41] By invoking these legalistic standards, he evidently wanted abolitionist criticism to be seen as undermining the confidence of the people in their government. He wanted his own libel of Todd to have this criminal intent, and he straightaway admitted that the truth of his printed criticism was irrelevant. Introducing himself to his readers in 1831 in one of his first editorials for *The Liberator*, he attempted to prove that the reputed slave trader in fact represented the state:

> Slavery is legal. Yet if I charge an individual with following it, either occasionally or regularly, I am guilty of a "gross and malicious libel"—of defaming his good name, fame, and reputation—of "foul calumny and base innuendo"—with sundry other law phrases set forth as an indictment. . . . The trial, in fact, was not to ascertain whether my charges were true, but whether they contained anything disreputable to the character of the accused; and the verdict does not implicate or condemn me but the law.[42]

Since the state affirmed the law of slavery, Garrison argued, there could be no distinction between personal injury, or civil cases, and injuries to the state, which seditious libels supposedly inflicted. In Garrison's interpretation, his civil conviction betrayed the interest of the judiciary in nullifying an indictment of slavery. More importantly, the conflation of the civil and the seditious, or the private affairs of society and the public affairs of the state, was said to be directly attributable to the judiciary's defense of slaveholders.

Until mob violence peaked in 1835, Garrison routed much of his

understanding of the state, the law, and the opposition of the abolition movement through a deepening reading of his own libel conviction. As a newspaper editor with both civil and criminal liability for his
published criticism, he can be forgiven for making such a personal
interpretation, though one begins to suspect that his unrelenting self-
defense, his so-called paranoid style, was part of a more strategic, legalistic defense. Under the column carefully titled "Slander," Garrison
complained, "They have compassed me about also with words of hatred;
and fought against me without a cause."[43] His prosecution complex was
still at work in 1834, when, unwilling to let his readers forget that he
was a convicted libeler, he announced the reissue of "A Brief Sketch of
the Trial of William Lloyd Garrison for an Alleged Libel on Francis
Todd of Newburyport, Mass.," a pamphlet he had published five years
earlier upon his imprisonment. Writing in 1829, he had proclaimed that
"Every new prosecution for libel ... may be viewed as a test, how far
[the freedom of the press] has been restricted by power on the one hand,
or perverted by licentiousness on the other."[44] And yet there might even
have been more at stake for Garrison in 1834. His rationale for reissu-
ing the pamphlet warned of a further miscarriage of justice that was
threatening to stifle him yet again:

> I am not less denunciatory and fanatical in 1829 than I am in 1834....
> [But when I was first released from prison] I had not publicly impeached
> the character, nor deprecated the tendency of the American Colonization
> Society, but as soon as I began to do so, and its friends to consider me a
> formidable antagonist, then I was at once transformed into a blood-thirsty
> monster, then the most opprobrious epithets were too weak to describe
> my wickedness—then the southern mansealers were duly notified of my
> incendiary proceedings, and urged to offer bribes for my destruction—
> then the fury of the mob was steered up against me—than I became a
> lunatic, an incendiary, a calumniator, a fanatic, &c., &c.,!![45]

Although Garrison's defense—that the Protestant establishment's American Colonization Society was responsible for his own character assas-
sination—might have been intended to present himself as a victim of

slander, it also reminded his readers of his former crime. He had been guilty of libel for impugning Todd's character; now he was guilty for impugning the character of the colonizationists. Both convictions, one in the courts and the other in the court of public opinion, effectively subordinated the truth or falsity of published criticism to the effect on the reputation of the injured party. Garrison's battle with the American Colonization Society, in other words, was waged in the distorted image of his libel conviction, which had brought the criminal standards of sedition to bear on an essentially civil, or private, matter.

The war of words between Garrison and the society had begun in 1829 with the publication of "Thoughts on African Colonization," a scathing commentary on the racist and collaborationist tendencies of the prevailing antislavery initiative, but it seemed to reach a fever pitch in 1833, in the aftermath of Garrison's well-publicized trip to England. Before a sympathetic London audience, he argued that the purpose of the American Colonization Society was "To render the slave system secure and lucrative—and lastly, To remove from the country 'those mirrors which reflect the light of liberty into the dark bosoms of the slaves'—namely, the free people of color."[46] At home in Boston, members of the Colonizationist Society of Massachusetts were speechless. "I cannot but deplore," said Caleb Cushing in an oration before the faithful, "the misapprehensions of facts, delusions, or wickedness [with] which this [address] assails the objects and supporters of a public charity so generous in design as the Colonization Society."[47] R. R. Gurley, a founding spirit and leader of the American Colonization Society, had been exchanging public letters in genteel fashion with his counterpart in the American Anti-Slavery Society, Arthur Tappan, but he threw up his hands at Garrison's unsparing criticism, telling the friendly Boston *Recorder* that he had "long ago given up correcting [Garrison's] misrepresentations."[48] Ignoring the substance, or truth, of Garrison's charges, the colonizationists condemned him for the act of issuing them.

Gurley's comment, reprinted in *The Liberator*, prompted this revealing rejoinder from Garrison's ally Oliver Johnson, which was also printed in *The Liberator*:

This is tantamount to an assertion that the Editor of the Liberator is given to misrepresentation. Now, Mr. Editor, I pronounce this an unqualified slander. The columns of the Liberator are at his service, to point out any misrepresentation either of sentiment or fact; and he is challenged to show even the "shadow" of a foundation for this uncharitable assumption.[49]

For Johnson, Gurley's printed remarks had no substance either. They were judged only by their malicious attack on the character of Garrison, who had affronted the character of the American Colonization Society in his London address. Here was a slander for a slander, or a libel for a libel. Accordingly, the most pressing issue for Johnson and Garrison, Gurley and Cushing in their ongoing debate over immediate abolition and colonization could only be the public standing of their own reputations and characters, not the virtues of their respective antislavery positions. The debate over abolition in New England in this sense seemed conducted entirely within the standards set by seditious libel prosecution, chief of which was the protection of reputation and character at the expense of the truth.

Although the conflict between Garrison and the colonizationists might appear to have been needlessly, selfishly narrowed by their immersion in a litigious context of libel and slander, it acquired a grander scope with Kneeland's indictment for blasphemy, just as Garrison was returning from England to face equally intense criticism from the American Colonization Society. The two shared the distinction of being iconoclastic newspaper editors at war with the Protestant establishment, but when Garrison saw the spectacle of the Massachusetts judiciary rushing to defend the church against a minor but irreligious figure like Kneeland, he saw yet another opportunity for the abolition movement. Kneeland's trial gave Garrison the legal grounds for interpreting his escalating war with the Protestant colonizationists in the terms he had been trying to frame it: as unlawful but legal punishment from the state for otherwise truthful criticism. "It might have been expected," he wrote in Kneeland's defense, "that a church and a ministry which does not believe that it is safe to obey God by letting the oppressed go free would have so little faith in the power of christianity as to suppose that it stands in need of such auxiliaries for its protection as swords, constables, sheriffs and prisons."[50] Now it could be said: the church and the state were in league not against Kneeland but against abolition.

For his part, Kneeland was just as ready to attribute his persecution to the injustices of the printing trade. Writing on "misrepresentations and slanders" in 1835, he shot back at the "Pious journals." "You think you know something about the infidels in Boston," he wrote, "because you have read the misrepresentations and slanders that have been published in Boston papers, and offer this spurious commodity to your pious brethren cheap for cash."[51] The partisanship of an editor is certainly evident in Kneeland's defense of his infidelity, as is the struggle to compete in a commercial marketplace. Garrison, on the other hand, used the occasion of Kneeland's misfortune to rise above his war of words with the American Colonization Society, which had tired even loyal subscribers to *The Liberator*, and expose the reactionary forces of church and state that were determined to retard the progress of liberty. All Garrison had to do was pit one newspaper against another and impugn its editors with impunity. Writing less than two months after Kneeland's deprecation of "Pious journals" appeared in the Boston *Investigator*, Garrison delivered a blow to his clerical antagonists in a manner appropriate to an indicted infidel:

> Many of our religious newspapers are a disgrace to Christianity. They are filled with apologies for sin, and sinners of the worst class. Melancholy, disgust, indignation, and amazement are excited within us, as we peruse their vitiated columns. . . . And those which are pre-eminently corrupt and sterile at the North are the Boston Recorder, Vermont Chronicle, Christian Mirror, New York Observer, Cincinnati Journal, New Hampshire Observer.[52]

Of course, these newspapers committed no other sin other than having espoused colonization, but Garrison's criticism was intended to associate them with a corrupt and despotic state. *The Liberator* in turn was associated with the crime of sedition, to the extent that Garrison could approximate the blasphemy of Kneeland's anticlericalism.

Garrison did use the abolitionist press as a dangerous instrument in a developing abolitionist crusade against the state. It did not hurt his representation of this cause when Southern governors condemned the circulation of abolitionist publications within their borders and a Northern governor issued a call to revive the federal statute that had jailed the partisans of republicanism in the 1790s. Armed with this historical comparison, he declared that "the mingled outcries" of "'infidelity, incendiarism, treason, fanaticism'" that came from his clerical antagonists sounded "like strains of melody" that proved "the rectitude of my course."[53] Eventually, Garrison would complete the process begun by his own campaign of self-incrimination, dispense with the mediation of clerical criticism, and defy the state directly. Flaunting a crime that his civil conviction could only approximate, Garrison asked in an 1838 Fourth of July address, "Is this preaching sedition? Sedition against what?"[54]

Libels, Gags, and National Boundaries

When the members of the New England Non-Resistance Society adopted their constitution, they adopted the conventional arguments of pacifism in singling out the existence of a standing army and militia as evidence of government's abject dependency on force. However, the proposition that "no one, who professes to have the spirit of Christ, can consistently sue a man at law for redress of injuries" marks the constitution as the work of Garrison.[55] For Garrison, the strategy of nonresistance was a direct response to the most powerful oppression that he had felt, the very oppression he believed united him with the enslaved. This force was made manifest in the violence of mob attacks as well as in the imprecations of his colonizationist adversaries, but it was most effectively and consistently applied against him by the state through the means of libel law. In Garrison's reading of the abolitionists' persecution, the law that demonstrated the state's monopolization of this force was the Pinckney Gag Law, which, like the Alien and Sedition

Acts, depended to a surprising extent on the precedent and logic of libel prosecution.

As stated by Senator Henry Pinckney of South Carolina, the stated intent of the 1836 Gag Law was to prohibit the reading of abolitionist petitions within the halls of Congress:

> Resolved, that all petitions, memorials, resolutions, propositions, or papers, relating in any way, or to any extent, whatever, to the subject of slavery, or the abolition of slavery, shall, without being further printed or referred, be laid on the table, that no further action whatever shall be had thereon.[56]

The passage of this law did more than establish a procedural norm for the U.S. Congress, for in the course of researching and devising it, the national legislature defined its institutional boundaries, and, by extension, the boundaries of the nation in a way that was completely compatible with the common law of seditious libel. By this measure, the happiness, welfare, and harmony of society was judged integral to the interests of the state, which in turn was defined as a community of its own. The legal bonds between the people and the state were found in interlocking acts of self-defense that could come from either an embattled "vigilance committee" of a small Southern town or the embattled representatives of a sovereign people. Both were attempting to stanch a flood of abolitionist publications that was inundating their respective communities.

For the elected representatives of the nation-state, these publications were the countless petitions that had been submitted by abolitionists to the floor of the legislature. Many called for the suspension of trade between slaveholding and nonslaveholding states but most of them requested that the Congress abolish slavery in the District of Columbia.[57] The national government thus was forced to police its small federal protectorate just as the governments of several Southern states were defending their borders against the abolitionists' "direct-mail" publicity campaign. Legislatures in North Carolina and Louisiana, for example, petitioned the mayor of Boston to stop the spread of abolitionist publications at the source, which would have meant censoring, prosecuting, or imprisoning Garrison. A Washington city ordinance imitated their example in forbidding both slaves and freedmen from reading *The Liberator*, a law designed to prevent organized insurrection among the most dangerous members of the abolitionist reading public, the enslaved themselves.[58]

The 1836 case of *United States v. Reuben Crandall, M.D.* provided further proof that the federal government would take a similar stand to that of slaveholding communities against the spread of abolitionist publicity. Crandall had been convicted of seditious libel for circulating the publications of the American Anti-Slavery Society in the District of Columbia, the seat of national government and also slave territory. According to the prosecuting attorney in this case, Francis Scott Key, a particularly zealous libel prosecutor, there was no difference between the two. He charged that the purpose of Crandall's pamphlets was to "inflame and excite the people of the United States to resist and oppose and disregard the laws of a Government and the rights of the proprietors of slaves in said country," invoking "our right and the right of the whole slaveholding community to self-protection."[59] As the slaveholding community in question comprised the territory of representative government, Crandall's conviction for seditious libel under common law can be said to have protected the same symbolic space that the Gag Law protected from abolitionist petitions. The converse can also be asserted: the Gag Law literally covered the same territory that was threatened by the abolitionists' sedition.

In adopting the logic of libel prosecution, Pinckney's Gag Law also aspired to achieve the social purpose of common law, which was to fuse the authority of government with local customs and community interests. Of course, those customs and interests belonged to slaveholders, with whom the architects of the Gag Law openly identified. In sort of a dry run for the Gag Law, Senator John Calhoun had tried and failed to make it a federal crime *not* to destroy abolitionist publications when they were delivered in direct-mail fashion to the post offices of Southern communities. In his "Report from the Select Committee on the Circulation of Incendiary Publications" of February 1836, he rested his argument for the sovereignty of the federal government in this matter on the "great, primary, and inherent right of self-defense, which by the laws of nature, belongs to all communities."[60] He had in mind a recent mob attack on a federal post office in Charleston, South Carolina, which he attempted to enshrine as a model of proper conduct for the state.[61] His report would also legitimize slaveholders' fears of a "servile revolt" as the outcome, if not the intention, of abolitionist publications and hold local postmasters legally responsible for even receiving them.[62]

Although Calhoun's attempt to inscribe a community's "right of self-defense" into statutory law failed by a vote of "only," as Garrison complained, 19 to 25,[63] the Calhoun report had succeeded in adopting the model of the common law, the delicate compact between social norms and legal precedents, from the Southern states' slave code and applying it on a national scale.[64] The "law of slavery," as its apologists called it, brokered the intimate relationship between the state and the private interests of society that served as the basis of slaveholding seignorialism. As Eugene Genovese has shown, slave laws maintained a carefully erected order of precedents and customary privileges in the English common-law tradition, particularly in its provisions for "extralegal personal force" and its appeal to personal honor. As a result, Genovese argues, the jurisprudence of Southern communities never recognized the generically liberal distinction between the state and society, instead upholding the privileges and social standing of slaveholders as integral to the legitimacy of the state.[65]

One month after Calhoun issued his report on "incendiary publications," Congress passed the Pinckney Gag Law, formally equating the interests of the nation-state with the communal norms and common-law tradition of a slaveholding society. Although the report on which the bill was based was authored by Henry Pinckney, the true champion of the federal statute was none other than Calhoun—he framed the argument of the report for his fellow representatives and attempted to define national sovereignty in accord with a locality's defense of its borders. "Our true position," he declared, "that which is indispensable to our defense here, is, that Congress has no legitimate jurisdiction over the subject of slavery either here or elsewhere. The reception of this petition surrenders this commanding position. . . . For our right to reject these petitions is as clear and unquestionable as that Congress has no right to abolish slavery in the states."[66] With a proper show of deference to the common law of slavery, Calhoun argued that the most powerful assertion of federal sovereignty could only reinforce the "rights . . . which separate and distinct communities possess."[67] In this case, the community in question was both the U.S. Congress, whose right Calhoun defended, and Washington D.C., over which the Constitution had granted, Pinckney argued, "exclusive legislation." The Gag Law in this sense defined the boundaries of national sovereignty with the administrative terms of a modern state—that is, as a bureaucratic jurisdiction over a self-defined sphere—and at the same time on the model of a small town.

Calhoun's justification for the suppression of the abolitionist petitions proved just how provincial this nation-state could be. His rhetoric of the embattled "frontier" of Congress in his speech on behalf of the Gag Law presented a national legislative body as a community in itself, endowed with the same rights of self-defense and self-preservation that the people of Charleston had seized:

> There is but one way [to resist the threat of abolition]: we must meet the enemy on the frontier—on the question of receiving; we must secure that important pass—it is our Thermopylae. . . . In the present context, the question of receiving constitutes our frontier. It is the first, the exterior question, that covers and protects all the others. Let it be penetrated by receiving this petition, and not a point of resistance can be found within, as far as this government is concerned. If we cannot maintain ourselves there, we cannot on any interior position.[68]

The process that began with the determination of Southern communities to protect the private property of slaveholders and to maintain the legality of local custom had produced not just an expansive moment of nationalism but a martial concept of the national interest. Of course, this interest was invariably declared and exercised in the name of "the right of self-defense."

Whether the Gag Law constituted a step toward more perfect representative government or a wholesale adoption of the slave code was a question of some consequence for Garrison, his fellow abolitionists, and their abolition strategy. As the Calhoun and Pinckney Reports were being debated in the United States Congress, Garrison wrote that abolition had now become "emphatically a NATIONAL object, around which are clustering momentous consequences."[69] Reporting to the Massachusetts Anti-Slavery Society on the events of 1836, he could describe local incidents of antiabolitionist public sentiment on a suitably national scale:

> What are irresponsible mobs, what the robbing of the public mail, what the administration of lynch law by an infuriated rabble, compared to the act of trampling upon the right of petition by the representatives of a free people? . . . What have you gained by exchanging a monarchical government for a slaveholding despotism? And who are putting chains upon your bodies—a seal upon your lips—the brand of SLAVES upon your cheeks? Your own Senators and Representatives![70]

The passage of the Gag Law elicited Garrison's first direct criticism of the federal government and introduced the epithet "slaveholding despotism" to the abolitionists' lexicon. Under this regime, slaveholders served as the unelected representatives of the state, lending their interests, prerogatives, and customary rights to the national sovereign for the purpose of suppressing the discussion of abolition. In adopting the character of slaveholders, the American republic in turn amassed the absolutist power once enjoyed by European oligarchies, a comparison that no doubt did wonders for Garrison's narrative representation of the abolition movement.[71] In his reading, the Gag Law set the stage for a renewed clash between a time-honored form of tyranny and a liberty-loving people.

However, Garrison's condemnation also implied that any historical analogy or narrative representation of a public also made the abolitionists akin to the enslaved, a comparison that signaled his recognition
of the distinct terms for the Gag Law. The rationale for the Gag Law
had expressly defined abolitionist petitions as agents of sedition and
violent insurrection, similar in function and effect to that of African
American conspirators against their masters. Moreover, the Gag Law
defined the floor of Congress as a besieged but intact slave territory, a
categorization that placed those petitions under the same legal restrictions and civil jurisdiction that policed a presumably restless population of slaves. A central premise of the abolitionists' political project,
the bond between free white abolitionists and black slaves, thus took
shape under the pressure of a federal statute, and particularly through
the way that the statute represented the tokens of abolitionist discussion. As a result of this law, Garrison could view every subsequent
assault on the abolitionists' free speech as a positive application of state
sovereignty, which only intensified his argument regarding the abolitionists' vulnerability to the force of law. The Gag Law indeed furnished
the limiting but enabling condition for the abolitionists' public sphere
to the extent that it made citizens who upheld the freedom of discussion
in the name of a free people the persecuted victims of a "slaveholding
despotism."

In the aftermath of the Gag Law, the New England abolitionists
would define their public sphere by a structural opposition to the state
and conduct any further discussion of the slavery question in light of
this antagonism. As the first decade of his abolitionist initiative came to
a close, Garrison increasingly conceived the agency of abolitionist publicity in direct defiance of the legal-political order and as inherently
seditious—but did he also recognize the implications of the social representation that he, Calhoun, and Pinckney had given the abolition movement when they sought to describe the scope and force of the Gag Law?
What did it mean for Garrison and his fellow members of the Massachusetts Anti-Slavery Society to assume the identity of the enslaved,
especially given that the circulation of abolitionist petitions was due in

no small part to the efforts of abolitionist women? As feminist historians have shown, female abolitionist societies were largely responsible for the petition drive of the abolition movement, a fact that could have just as easily made the onslaught of petitions in Congress evidence of the mobilization of women in the public life of the nation.[72] Just one year earlier, Garrison had heroized the emergent women's movement as a crucial sponsor of the abolitionists' public sphere and decried an attack on a public gathering of the Boston Female Anti-Slavery as an assault on the freedom of discussion.[73] Now he seemed determined to shed the socially pluralistic, egalitarian identity that had accrued to the abolition movement by virtue of its publicity campaign in favor of a "national object" for abolition, one at odds with the statist logic of the Gag Law.

As his address to the Massachusetts legislature demonstrated, Garrison even determined the condition of slavery by this logic, shedding its social particularities and racial determinations in order to offer a libertarian representation of a besieged public. I argue here and in the next chapter that Garrison conceived this image of an enslaved people in accordance with his self-representation of an embattled, legally liable abolitionist editor who courted prosecution with each unprovable libel on slaveholders and colonizationists. Although the collaboration of the federal government with slaveholders might be even more unprovable, Garrison's intent in the ensuing years was to model the situation of the abolition movement on his own and make abolitionists not just outcasts from the domain of citizenship but the criminals of the state. As a convicted libeler, he had felt the power of law compel him to jail; as a self-declared victim of a "slaveholding despotism," he could observe this power alienating the political rights of every American.

The confidence and righteousness that Garrison gained from assuming the identity of a slave in turn gave his earliest formulation of nonresistance the axiomatic style of a political theory. Writing in an 1837 editorial under the pseudonym "Alethea," he warned that a new form of tyranny had been born, based on the representative function of liberal government:

Politicians and philosophers have sometimes foolishly speculated about
the best form of human government, . . . whether, for instance, the republican form of government is not better than the monarchical, and the
elective better than the hereditary, in all cases. But this is idle. What is
government but the express image of the moral character of a people? As
a general rule, in the nature of things, the deeper a nation is forsaken
in ignorance and depravity, the more arbitrary and cruel will be the government established.[74]

What made Garrison's "general rule" obtain? We should not discount
the role of seditious libel law in establishing the relation between the
government and the people as a binding contract against the unfettered
exercise of free speech. As enacted by the Pinckney Gag Law, this contract bound the private interests of slaveholders to the sovereignty of the
state in what Garrison called famously a "covenant with death, an agreement in hell." This covenant, he argued, was just as responsible for slavery as it was for the censorship of free discussion, and he would work
tirelessly to break the illicit connections of what Habermas has called a
"political public sphere"—the state-sponsored realm of civic rights and
participation—through the intervening faculty of critical dissent. In
the tradition of Anglo-American libertarianism, Garrison attributed
this faculty to an informed public, held criminally liable by a repressive
state under the standards of seditious libel, but in Garrison's latest modulation of the abolitionist cause, also a victim of slavery.

Violence and the Law of Government

In the aftermath of the Pinckney Gag Law, Garrison was free to develop
a trope of national tyranny that was based at once on isolated instances
of mob attacks and the local interests of a small town. One such attack,
on the abolitionist editor Elijah Lovejoy in Alton, Illinois, provided Garrison with a perfect image of a brutal government at work. Lovejoy had
been murdered in 1837 while defending his printing office with a rifle,
and though this spectacle might have tailored itself for Garrison's purposes, he made sure to present the events in accord with his developing

political theory of nonresistance. He took special interest in a resolution passed by the town council of Alton, which preceded the mob attack by a few days:[75]

> Resolved, That while there appears to be no disposition to prevent the liberty of free discussion through the medium of the press or otherwise, as a general thing, it is deemed a matter indispensable to the peace and harmony of this community that the labors and influence of the late Editor of the Observer be no longer identified with any establishment in this city.
>
> Resolved, That the discussion of the doctrines of immediate abolitionism, as they have been discussed in the columns of the Alton Observer, would be destructive of the peace and harmony of the citizens of Alton, and that, therefore, we cannot recommend the re-establishment of that paper, or any other of a similar character, and conducted with a like spirit.[75]

Here was Garrison's true interest in the Lovejoy murder: in identifying the interest of a representative government not just in "peace and harmony" of its citizens but in the legally seditious standing of an abolitionist publication, judged, like abolitionist petitions, as injurious to the rights of the community. The ensuing mob attack, in other words, was nothing more than the enactment of this resolution and a complementary expression of the Pinckney Gag Law.

In order to make this argument, Garrison had to pass up a golden opportunity to lionize Lovejoy and to condemn the lawless violence of mobs. In Garrison's mind, Lovejoy disqualified himself as an abolitionist martyr when he used a rifle in self-defense. The only lesson that he would take from Lovejoy's death was that "civil government—a government upheld by military power—is not justified."[76] With his prodding, the Massachusetts Anti-Slavery Society adopted a resolution at its 1838 meeting that affirmed the very "national object" he had found in the suppression of abolitionist petitions:

> That the guilt of this bloody tragedy is not local, nor confined exclusively to the immediate actors therein, but that it covers the land, inasmuch as

the tragedy itself is one of the natural and inevitable consequences of tolerating the execrable system of slavery in our midst . . . all who, for the last five years, have instigated riots or connived at the prostration of lawful government, or justified the enslavement of our colored countrymen,—do participate to a greater or less extent.[77]

The worst offenders, according to Garrison, were the national representatives of an unlawful government, and they shared the guilt that could be ascribed to the murderers of Lovejoy. In his annual report prepared for the 1838 meeting, Garrison took special pleasure in recording a warning given to a traveling abolitionist by a senator from South Carolina—"'WE WILL HANG HIM.'"—from the floor of the U.S. Congress. His annual report went on to mock President Van Buren for defending the Gag Law and then the Supreme Court for upholding slaveholders' property rights to a slave. With these three examples of anti-abolitionist sentiment, drawn from the three branches of government, Garrison wanted to demonstrate that violence was the literal law of the land and that the era of a slaveholding despotism had truly arrived.

In the same pages that he eulogized Lovejoy for the Massachusetts Anti-Slavery Society, Garrison imagined all abolitionists as the metaphoric prey of the lynching senator:

In vain shall he appeal to his unblemished character as a man, a citizen, and a christian; in vain claim the liberty of speech and of conscience, secured to him by the clearest constitutional provisions as an inalienable right; in vain protest that his heresy consists simply in a hearty subscription to the self-evident truths of the Declaration of Independence, in vain appeal for justice to the Supreme Court of his country; for there is none able to deliver him. Die he must; die ignobly; die upon the gallows.[78]

Forsaken by a government whose representatives made "no expression of surprise, or indignation, or horror" in response to the senator's promise, the victimized abolitionist would meet his end in a suitably violent execution under a representative government that had embraced, thanks to Calhoun, "the great, primary, and inherent right of self-defense, which by the laws of nature, belongs to all communities." The contrary claim of the victim to "the liberty of speech and of conscience" made it clear that the censorship of the state under the Gag Law was primarily on Garrison's mind when he dramatized the abolitionists' victimization and that he was determined to present statutory law as the basis for their enslavement.

In the weeks before he presented his annual report to the 1838 meeting of the society, Garrison printed a "Prospectus" for *The Liberator* in December 1837 that announced his editorial commitment to nonresistance. He deliberately introduced his decision as a publishing scandal that would elicit furious opposition to an unfettered, critical press such as *The Liberator*:

> To the bigoted, pharisaical, the time-serving, the selfish, the worshippers of expediency, the advocates of caste, the lovers of power, the enemies of liberty and equality, we make no appeal. It shall be our constant endeavor to make the Liberator so liberal in spirit, so straight-forward in its character, so disinterested in its object, so uncompromising in its principles, and so hostile to every form of prejudice and slavery, as to render it intolerable to them.[79]

Garrison looked forward to the opprobrium that nonresistance would elicit, for it would betray not just the illiberal, provincial spirit of press censorship but the insidious power of the state. His true enemy, he maintained in the "Prospectus," was "*human government, fashioned in the likeness and administered in the spirit of [men's] own disobedience.*" When he said that such governments were "founded on the assumed right to take human life at discretion," there was no doubt that he was already preparing his commentary on the state's endorsement of mob violence. As such, the power that Garrison expected to crush the discussion of non-resistance did not exist in any single party but consisted of the relation between the people and the state, or the representative function of government itself.

A dystopian portrait of political representation appeared prominently in a resolution passed at the first annual meeting of the New England Non-Resistance Society, held in September 1839:

> That every man thus consenting to the civil government of this country is responsible to God and man for the evils, and is accessory to the crimes, which are the necessary consequences of those false principles, when made the basis of legislative action, of which responsibility he can only divest himself by immediately repenting of his participation in this system from which these crimes and evils flow, and instantly abandoning it.[80]

Under this resolution, every American citizen and especially those who voted were accessory to a crime, the consensual agent of state-sponsored violence. The principle theorist of nonresistance, Adin Ballou, would have its adherents see their own behavior represented in the seemingly impersonal conduct of the state:

> If we may not inflict suffering and death on evil-doers for our own pleasure or advantage, we may not do this for the pleasure or advantage of 80,000, as a Marshal in the city of Boston; or of 600,000 as a Sheriff or Governor of Massachusetts; or of 15,000,000 as Chief Justice or President of the United States.[81]

Having adopted a pacifist opposition to war and armed force, the nonresistance theory went on to condemn all the codes with which society maintained order, redressed injury, and upheld justice. James Birney, one of Garrison's most stalwart and perceptive critics, surmised correctly that the application of the theory would not stop until the parental "power of personal chastisement" over disobedient children was revealed as the law of a brutal, proslavery regime.[82]

In the conception of Adin Ballou, the philosophy of nonresistance provided the abolitionist with a ready-made argument against slavery:

The fifteen million of human beings, combined and acting together as the United States, claim the right to separate husbands and wives, parents and children, and to make merchandise of the bodies and souls of men; but condemn and punish as the greatest villainies, these same acts in individuals.[83]

The participants at the New England Non-Resistance Society's 1839 annual meeting made a more deliberate invitation to abolitionists when they resolved that anyone who forsook the "law of violence in which the relation of master and slave originated" would be abiding by the principles of nonresistance; conversely, any show of violence was said to betray the "relation of master and slave." Abolitionists who were wary of this new theory thus could consider it "involved" in the antislavery struggle, as Garrison put it, "as the unit is included within the aggregate."[84]

However, this is as far as Garrison came to applying the principles of nonresistance to the reality of slavery. He simply refused to see the violence of slavery in any other form but the law, and this meant that he never saw slaveholding itself as anything more than a particularly illustrative example of the sins of "human government." In his 1837 "Prospectus," Garrison saw the "PRINCIPLE OF VIOLENCE" applied in the "naval and military power, penal enactments" of the state as well as in the conduct of "officers and servants" of popular government who "govern and [are] governed by that principle." In making special mention of the "appeal to the law of violence made in self-defense," he made an even more specific reference to Calhoun's arguments for the Pinckney Gag Law. Garrison's interest in nonresistance, in other words, was based on the countervailing possibility of an abolitionist public sphere that was free from the prosecution of the "law of violence" and the intervention of the state. Accordingly, he dedicated the new theory to "those who love FREE DISCUSSION, and an independent press which no party can bribe, and no sect can intimidate," as if the unfettered editorial freedom of *The Liberator* pertained directly to the prospects for nonresistance. For Garrison, there was no doubt that it did. His long-standing protest against his own libel conviction and his steady critique of state censorship had borne fruit in a theory that summarized the oppression of slaveholding America in a manner compatible with the legal and political predicament of an editor.

The many abolitionist critics of nonresistance, on the other hand, refused to recognize their movement from the perspective of a convicted libeler. The Massachusetts Anti-Slavery Society resolution in support of Lovejoy had appealed for the return of "lawful government" and solicited the rightful protection of American citizens under the law. Eventually, Garrison's opponents would abandon his antislavery enterprise in favor of a new abolitionist initiative based on the extension of the liberal constitutional order and of its legal provisions for citizenship—and yet Garrison could never imagine the abolition movement as anything other than afflicted by the law. The only basis for the abolitionists' public identity, he maintained, lay in the faculty and liability of criticism, and while this insistence might have drawn on a libertarian theory of political dissent and the postrevolutionary precedent of republican opposition, it also seemed to acknowledge that there really was no place for a critical public in the political public sphere of Jacksonian America and that no amount of literate discussion, not even the free discussion of nonresistance, could convene the members of the abolition movement as a public body. All the abolitionists could hope to do was to hold down the place of a public with the tokens or formal signs of their dissent, a strategy that rendered the anachronism of the abolitionists' position but that also effectively divorced their institution of the public sphere from the representation of a people. Under the principles of nonresistance, the abolitionists' public sphere only could conform to the space, or activity, of criticism.

Of Scale and Scope

Ironically, the initial gatherings for the New England Non-Resistance Society provided Garrison and his allies with the practical opportunities to establish a wholly negative position for the New England abolition movement in and through modes of sociality. The first meeting, in September 1839, seemed inspired by Garrison's condemnation of the "law of violence," producing resolutions that condemned the militarism of the American nation-state as "identical, in its principles and tendencies, with the armed establishments upon which all tyrannies and despotisms rest." The members of the society also resolved that since the Constitution furnished the state with "the exercise of certain of the sovereign powers of the people by servants of their own," that every American citizen was "responsible for its evils."[85] However, the participants in that first assembly paid remarkably close attention to libertarian principles that a defiant, disputatious editor would cherish, basing the very existence of their society on the pursuit of criticism as an end in itself.

The founding resolution of the New England Non-Resistance Society had been to maintain a "sacred respect for the right of opinion," and in support of this principle, Samuel May, its sponsor, would not allow a vote to be cast without an extended debate:

> It [is] better to spend days and weeks in their discussion than, by a hasty passage of [resolutions], to lay the foundation of future misunderstanding among ourselves. . . . I look back with pain and shame upon the history of another reform. . . . Some gave their assent to [its principles] without due consideration of their spirit and meaning. Let us take warning. I hope we shall have great length of discussion.[86]

May, Garrison's closest ally, advised that the controversy over the publicity for nonresistance in *The Liberator* be prolonged, though Garrison would not have needed to remind his fellow members that the sphere of free discussion sponsored by the New England Non-Resistance Society benefited also the liberty of the press. Starting with the "Prospectus," he had used *The Liberator* not only as his medium of publicity for the theory of nonresistance but as the model for public discussion that was conducted under its principles. H. C. Wright, Garrison's regular columnist for nonresistance, brought to bear his own favorable assessment of the editorial policy of *The Liberator* when he declared, "The man that is a non-resistant, whether an agent or member of the Society, let him discuss what subjects he pleases in his individual capacity."[87]

As promoted by Garrison, May, and Wright, nonresistance did seem to promise the atomization of the abolition movement into a collection of self-expressive, opinionated, dissenting individuals, and while this might be an accurate characterization of the dissent and public interchange that prevailed within the meetings of these reform societies, it does not capture the radical ambition that Garrison had for the abolitionists' public sphere.[88] In his 1838 annual report, he had argued that free speech was so thoroughly supervised by the "law of violence" that a public sphere demarcated the powers, parameters, and purview of the state, not the autonomy of a civil society. Accordingly, the principles of nonresistance assumed that the social intercourse of public discussion no longer took place within society but within the legal and political networks of the state. Only a "sacred respect for the right of opinion," expressed through their penchant for perpetual, disputatious discussion, could allow the members of the New England Non-Resistance Society to escape the false, illiberal public sphere that was found in political parties, representative government, public opinion, and, yes, even voluntary societies. All they had to do was to conduct their public discussion not just outside the jurisdiction of the state but independently of society.

According to Garrison, the nominally free expressions of dissent that characterized the discussion of nonresistance could displace the abolitionists' public sphere from the boundaries of society, for, strictly speaking, the New England Non-Resistance Society was not a society at all. At least, this was the unusual proposition he used to recruit his friend May:

> A word as to organizations. You know that my own mind is fetterless— that I abjure all creeds, all political and ecclesiastical organizations. How, then, can I approbate a non-resistance association? Freely enough, and with perfect consistency, because it destroys at a blow all the unnatural and artificial distinctions that obtain in society, and sunders, as by the touch of fire, all human cords by which the intellects and souls of men are bound. All ecclesiastical and political organizations are so constructed as to admit of rivalry, station, supremacy, domination, and caste; and it is

made a duty for men to join them, and be guided by their enactments. Our association places every men upon the dead level of equality. . . . It has no ranks, no titles, no honors, no emoluments, to hold out to men as an inducement to support it. On the contrary, it requires of every man a cheerful willingness to sacrifice all these, and count them as dung and dross. It denies to no man the right to think, speak and act, as his reason and conscience may dictate.[89]

Under the principles of nonresistance, the only common ground that the members of the New England Non-Resistance Society could share was a perfect state of freedom and equality in which no positive conditions were laid on each other and no positive actions were proffered. Garrison described this state as one that "contemplates nothing, repudiates nothing," the wholly negative condition under which he would attempt to institute the abolitionists' public sphere. The freedom of discussion, he insisted, was so endangered by the reign of a "slaveholding despotism" that any coordination of opinion or action by abolitionists would bring down the force of the law onto them and plunge them into slavery. His appeal to "the right of opinion" in this sense was intended to invert the ideological value of free speech within the liberal polity and to posit literate citizens as true victims of oppression in accord with what he called ominously a "dead level of equality."

As a sort of recompense for occupying this level, Garrison promised the adherents to nonresistance a public sphere of wider dimensions than abolitionists had imagined. In his 1837 "Prospectus," Garrison had claimed that the discussion of nonresistance in *The Liberator* would define the "cause of LIBERTY . . . upon a more extended scale" so that the motto of "UNIVERSAL EMANCIPATION" could be applied "in its widest latitude." The public sphere of abolitionist discussion would thereby attain a grander scale and deliver literate subjects from not only the civil bonds of a "slaveholding despotism" but from the tyranny of social intercourse itself—provided that abolitionists collectively demonstrated a "sacred respect for the right of opinion." For Garrison, the public agency of free speech had become a limiting case on social cohesion, a brake on the representation of a totalized society, and even more criti-cally for the abolition movement, a counterweight to the formation of a people. I will borrow again from Claude Lefort's rereading of *Democracy in America* and argue that his defense of the "right of opinion," like Tocqueville's defense of individual liberty, was intended to inaugurate a democratic society under a "new awareness of what cannot be known or mastered." The vision of democracy that Lefort attributes to Tocqueville "can only be reconciled with freedom if the representation of [its] realization in the real is held in check." In practical terms, this vision would preclude "a vision of the being of the social in which everyone is included."[90]

The minutes of the first annual meeting of the New England Non-Resistance Society seem to bear out Lefort's contention regarding a democratic society, for the members of the society expressed genuine indecision as to what kind of community the "right of opinion" had convened. After several failed attempts to describe how they would "combine together," they dispensed with any comparison to the Massachusetts Anti-Slavery Society and to religious denominations. All May could say was that "it is possible that the widest differences of opinion may exist with the utmost unions of heart, and the most uninterrupted affection."[91] Garrison's aspiration for unlimited discussion within the New England Non-Resistance Society was accompanied by a shared awareness that the abolitionists' publicity campaign, the manifold insti-tutions of their public life, and even the historical associations of their printed articles would never make them a public. Far from bemoan-ing their predicament, the abolitionist leader remained devoted to the freedom of speech and to a political imperative for fractious criticism in order to convince the members of the movement that they were not supposed to be a public body. A truly critical public, Garrison main-tained, performed its office precisely in antagonizing popular sentiment and upsetting social harmony, certifiably democratic acts of agitation that happened to answer to the standards of seditious libel.

In adopting the principles of nonresistance, Garrison thus did not expect the discussion of the slavery question to progress beyond the act of agitation. Rather than lamenting the limits of their enterprise, he wanted abolitionists to see that the public identity they had assumed for their movement was premised on its discrepancy with contemporary forms of the public, including that of a voluntary society, a religious denomination, public opinion, and, ultimately, the represented will of a popular sovereign. To reveal and to exacerbate further this discrepancy, he would confine the abolitionists' exercise of free speech to libelous criticism, a limitation that would give their public sphere the "extended scale" befitting the scope of their opposition. Nonresistance was "most critical and dangerous," Garrison told the members of the New England Non-Resistance Society in 1841, precisely because the "combat is so unequal." Although they would be judged "insane," he concluded triumphantly that "the non-resistant is the only one that feels the right to be bold in the conflict that has commenced." The waging of this conflict on unequal terms expressed Garrison's conviction that criticism—actionable, libelous criticism answering only to "the right of opinion"—could represent the public agency of democracy and, moreover, that only this agitation could creep between the increasingly closed relation between society and the state and enlarge the "latitude" and "scope" of the abolitionists' public discussion. "Let us remember," Garrison reminded his audience, "the philosophy of all reform is commotion—agitation."[92]

When we read Garrison's admonition to May, that adherents to nonresistance must "have long suffering toward those who may despitefully use and persecute us," we are reminded that the abolitionist leader never could imagine the public agency of the abolition movement without the presumption of its minority status, or, more precisely, its social isolation. His investment in the faculty of criticism further assumed that abolitionists were displaced historically from a progressive narrative of freedom and free inquiry and that they had only a legal infraction to underwrite their public identity, an assumption that authorized the "commotion" and "agitation" provoked by nonresistance in place of a historical protagonist. The libertarian theory that Garrison developed under the aegis of nonresistance and that would forestall the social realization of an abolitionist public, in other words, demanded the sly use of a declension narrative and a strategic use of nostalgia in order to give the abolition movement the role and agency of a public.

As I suggested in the introduction, Garrison conceived the abolitionist public identity through imaginative comparison to a historically absent public. His admonition to May, however, reminds us that any diachronic representation of a people also demanded a metaphoric comparison to the enslaved in order to render a belated, anachronistic position in time as a current state of persecution. The strategy of nonresistance thus posed the negative representation of democratic agency in ways that the abolitionists did not intend or expect—not in relation to a sovereign people but in relation to the enslaved. In attempting to vacate their public sphere of its social determination, Garrison and his allies in effect were institutionalizing the life of slavery as a repressed or absent cause, so to speak, for the political agency of the abolition movement—in the express absence of a "political part."

The problem of this negative representation is further complicated by Garrison's rather personal investment in the faculty of criticism. Indeed, what he did not consider was that he had chosen a medium for the formation of the abolitionists' public sphere to suit his editorial perspective. As a result, the abolitionists' public identity did not just take on an invisible form befitting their historical moment—it had taken also the far more accessible form of a particular libeler. Whether Garrison's editorial position can be reduced to his personal perspective or even, strictly speaking, to his person is a question that the next chapter will take up in detail, but our final analysis can only regard the ascension of nonresistance as having left the "scale" or "latitude" of the abolitionists' sphere of discussion in some doubt. Could Garrison use his editorial position to express the agency of the people or did the absence of any equivalent for a critical public mean that the role of editor would eventually assume its place, leaving the democratic ambition of the abolitionist agenda in the form of "Garrisonism"? Perhaps the strongest case we can make for the significance of libel law in this context is that it interposed a precedent and thus a past into the dialectic between personhood and its representation, and although this might have decreed the anachronism of the abolitionists' public identity, it also preserved something of the negative form that we associate not only with the liberal theory of democracy but with the historical ideal of republicanism.

CHAPTER 2

Garrisonism and the Public Sphere

Although the founding principles of nonresistance were acclaimed with a "sacred respect for the right of opinion," there was little doubt that the discussion of nonresistance in public venues and print media honored William Lloyd Garrison's right of opinion. It was his exercise of this right that gave nonresistance a regular column and columnist in *The Liberator*, the flagship abolitionist newspaper; it was his editorial policy that in turn set the agenda for the abolition movement and, his critics charged, turned it away from the singular object of freeing the slaves. Of course, Garrison claimed to publicize nonresistance for avowedly public ends—that is, exposing the tyranny of representative government, protecting the right of free speech from official and unofficial censorship, and, ultimately, freeing the abolition movement from the despotism of a proslavery state—but the expanded sphere of free discussion that he envisioned under the principles of nonresistance seemed to coincide in theory and practice with the editorial freedom he enjoyed. Writing in 1839, Amos Augustus Phelps, a former ally, admonished him directly: "You seem still to be possessed with the old idea that you and your paper are abolition incarnate, so that no man can dislike or reject either without disliking and rejecting abolition."[1]

For a large number of his contemporaries and for a generation of abolitionist scholars, Garrison was abolition's incarnation, and his editorial policies in turn embodied the movement. With the benefit of

Garrison's example, abolitionists are said to have assumed "the absolute necessity of freeing individuals from external restraints," all social, religious, or political institutions being considered the equal of slavery.[2] At his insistence, the New England abolition movement incorporated many more positions—nonresistance, anti-Sabbatarianism, and women's rights among them—than more single-minded advocates of the cause wanted to accommodate, but the culmination of Garrison's outsized influence might well be found in the doctrine of disunion, a principle and strategy that both the Massachusetts Anti-Slavery Society and the American Anti-Slavery Society adopted in the early 1840s. Disunion, in the words of one abolitionist scholar, held out "the possibility that a human being, not just a state, might secede from the Union" in order to speed the end of state-sponsored slavery, though once again it is impossible to mistake Garrison as the sovereign individual in question.[3]

Given this tradition of scholarship, it is little wonder that the New England abolitionists' agenda still can be appraised warily as little more than "Garrisonism," the contemporary appellation for all manner of abolitionist heresies but ultimately a synonym for a single person's undue influence over an otherwise promising political movement. In this reading of the abolition movement, Garrison himself represented an anarchic, excessively liberal form of individualism that made him a man for his times and his brand of abolition a sign of the times, provided one regards the reform movements of the Jacksonian era as governed by the moral dictates of the private subject.[4] For a consensus of abolitionist scholars, the historical lesson to be learned from the failure of his abolitionist enterprise to effect the liberation of slaves is, of course, the necessity of linking the heroic but inevitably fruitless displays of individual resistance to state-sponsored means of redress, such as the electoral system.[5]

However, a less ideologically restrictive and more historically overdetermined meaning of Garrisonism can be found in the commentary of one of its harshest critics, the historian Gilbert Barnes, who was determined to scale back the historical importance that late nineteenth- and early twentieth-century historians (many of them partisans of the abolitionist cause or their descendants) had bestowed on Garrison. Garrisonism, Barnes argued, paid tribute ultimately to Garrison's publicity for himself; his unequivocal pronouncements on behalf of immediate abolition, women's rights, nonresistance, and, eventually, disunion resulted in the "popular identification of the national movement with Garrison." Noting that few people actually read the newspaper in which he made these pronouncements but everybody seemed to know the scabrous reputation of its editor, he contended that "[Garrison] was simply a notorious name, a term of opprobrium, a grotesque of abolition fanaticism," a "figurehead" for an abolition movement that needed a "motto."[6]

Barnes may not have known how right he was. Garrison embodied the abolition movement precisely because he was a name whose currency bore witness to the structures of pamphleteering, newspaper publishing, and public discussion that abolitionists had put in place throughout the 1830s. As such, the true register in which Garrisonism obtained was not in the private sphere of moral influence and individual sovereignty but in a print culture of publicity and public discussion, where both his name and the newspaper that bore it could be said to circulate. In sharing the social structure of the abolitionists' public sphere, Garrisonism shared also its discursive structure and demonstrated their continuing investment in the historical associations of their printed articles. Garrisonism, nominally the signifier of the most liberal individualism, thus did not predicate an individual at all but stood for the prospect of a public sphere, reinstated under the ideological norms of a former political era. Far from signaling the embodiment of the abolition movement in the form of a single person, it symbolized the possibility of Garrison's disembodiment from himself in accord with the republican values of the abolitionists' print culture and its public standards of expression.[7]

We find these values and standards realized in, of all places, *The Liberator*, which can be said to have served as the signature press organ for the principles of Garrisonism from the moment it was published. In 1831 Garrison had inaugurated the newspaper with an almost satanic act of self-assertion—"I WILL BE HEARD," screamed the first editorial[8]—

and thereafter made it answerable to his editorial directives. However, the very category of the individual becomes ripe for reconsideration when we look more closely at *The Liberator* and discover that Garrison's editorial autonomy did not promise a model of freedom based on his self-realization or that of any other private subject. Instead, he devoted his most consistent effort to making sure that his editorial voice would be recognized as a voice of the public and that the newspaper would be seen as a public medium. To this end, he presented *The Liberator* as the rare press organ in which opposing viewpoints were "freely and impartially heard through its columns" according to an "example of fairness and magnanimity." Further distinguishing the newspaper from any other in the marketplace, he summoned the republican idioms of public virtue to describe a "FREE PRESS, in a comprehensive and manly sense . . . conducted in the spirit of absolute independence and entire impartiality."[9]

The "manly sense" to which Garrison referred also compelled him to demonstrate publicly a capacity for self-transcendence, in accord with the republican standards of citizenship that Michael Warner has memorably described.[10] He did so by refusing to take credit for the success of *The Liberator*, even as fellow members of the Massachusetts Anti-Slavery Society were acclaiming the newspaper as "the great pioneer in this cause" at their 1837 convention. He straightaway responded, "I think there has been too much said, and too frequent reference made, in applauding terms, respecting 'Garrison' and 'Garrisonism,'" before accepting a subsidy from the society for *The Liberator*.[11] Naturally wanting to appear unselfish, Garrison went beyond the demands of propriety and referred to himself as others did—as a name—while disclaiming ownership of that name. He did so in the name of *The Liberator*, through which he would stage the impartial, rational discussion of a public sphere, but also for the benefit his own name, which would become a certifiably public property through its association with the printed medium. As a result, Garrisonism would have all the public attributes that Garrison would seek to give *The Liberator*. Through his management of the newspaper, he would make sure that its editorial voice could not be reduced to him or to his individual expression; through calculated acts

of self-denial, he would present his own "example of fairness and magnanimity" as exemplary of the abolitionists' collective disinterest. First
gained and subsequently expanded through the medium of *The Liberator*, Garrison's symbolic role depended ultimately on the place of his
name in a republican economy that symbolized the presence of a people.

Who, then, spoke through *The Liberator*? For readers and participants in the antislavery struggle, the question of abolitionist subjectivity
raised by Garrison's influence invariably turned into a question of voice.
Of course, the signed editorials featured in the first column on the second page of every issue could be assigned easily to Garrison himself
but his editorial voice was detectable throughout the newspaper: in the
records of a Massachusetts Anti-Slavery Society meeting, in a nonresistance essay by Henry Clark Wright, in a derogatory newspaper editorial against "'no government' fanatics" reprinted in the column "Refuge
of Oppression," or in a few lines of abolitionist doggerel on the last
page. All of these could be considered examples of Garrisonism and yet
none of them was reducible to Garrison. *The Liberator* was so heterogeneous in its organization and content that it displaced his voice from a
single editorial or idea to any one of the printed items in its four pages.
As a result, articles on women's rights or penal reform bore his imprint
whether he authored them or not.[12]

In the midst of controversy, Garrison would attempt to lay claim
to a privately held opinion and to separate himself from the public outcry, but to no avail. The "right of opinion" he claimed as editor of *The
Liberator* underwrote the opinions of all others and allowed them to
be attributed to him. The free discussion that was conducted throughout the pages of *The Liberator* was so closely associated with Garrison's
influence that his name functioned effectively as a synonym, trope, or,
as Barnes said, a "motto" for a contentious, cacophonous collective
voice that could not be otherwise quantified. This was the true voice
of a people, Garrison claimed, whose discussion of the "'Peace question' . . . or any other unpopular question" would always be "marked by
liberality and disinterestedness," and it could only be heard in the newspaper he edited.[13] Constantly claiming his freedom as an editor while

simultaneously disowning his editorial voice, he wanted to make sure that the abolitionists themselves would share that advantage and demonstrate the qualities of a disinterested citizenry. As a result, nothing in print could truly be Garrison's own, and that included *The Liberator* itself, for unlike Horace Greeley, a rival voice of reform as editor and publisher of the *New York Tribune*, he never owned the newspaper. *The Liberator* merely bore the name of its editor.

What is an editor? In his attempt to understand the category of the author, Foucault referred to a text as a "discourse that possesses an author's name,"[14] and that may also be a good description of *The Liberator*'s contribution to Garrisonism. The editorial identity that Garrison assumed was so far from the model of possessive individualism that it can be said to signal the possibility of a lapse or gap in the ideology of liberal individualism that is supposed to have taken root in the antebellum era at the expense of the public discourse of republicanism and to have underwritten the authority of the nineteenth-century author.[15] Several studies of antebellum print culture suggest this possibility, and they are at their most persuasive in revising our understanding of nineteenth-century authorship and ownership. Meredith McGill's historical analysis of copyright law, for instance, argues that it actually perpetuated "the republican belief in the inherent publicity of print" and "stressed the interests of the polity over the property rights of individuals." In her study of Sarah Hall, the editor of *Godey's Magazine and Lady's Book*, Nicole Tonkovitch has argued that a historically overdetermined "institutional identity" maintained the public significance of printed discourse even while newspapers were assisting in the trend toward fictionalizing intimate, personal relations between readers.[16]

Garrison's authority as editor of *The Liberator* can be taken as another indication that an individual might still denominate his or her free speech as a public faculty and maintain the republican imperative for public life among nineteenth-century readers. His institutional identity bore all the tenets of eighteenth-century public discourse—the presumptions of interlocutors, the rational exchange of opinion, and the necessity for self-transcendence—from which abolitionists would fashion their public identity, and it thereby ensured that the abolition movement would maintain its characteristically ironic relation to historical tradition. The vestiges of republicanism and, by extension, the memory of an engaged, literate citizenry indeed coexisted with the influence of the individual voice through and in *The Liberator*, the signature article of the abolitionists' public sphere and therefore also a medium for their historical representation.

The republicanism of Garrison's editorial identity and its historical inflection, however, meant that it was no more able to convene a public body than the libertarian politics of nonresistance had been able to do. Like nonresistance, Garrisonism proposed only a model of public intercourse that ought to exist, that had to exist under the self-conception of a disinterested citizenry; the voice of *The Liberator* only could hold a place for the public where a public should be. The plurality of opinions and subjects that were featured in the newspaper can be said to have supplied the trace of a public while keeping the identity of its editorial voice latent, or, at best, leaving it a matter of inference. Garrisonism, in other words, demonstrated all the problems and possibilities that were posed by Garrison's relation to *The Liberator*, which is to say that it could not resolve the question of abolitionist subjectivity. It could only posit the bearer of a voice only through the act of attribution. Under the terms of Garrisonism, Garrison's own identity had to remain a matter of inference, as did the abolitionists' public identity.

The indeterminacy of Garrisonism was inscribed in the most radical aspects of the abolition agenda, which circumvented the question of a private or public subjectivity for the abolition movement by their connection to Garrison, or more specifically to his editorial voice. Owing much of their provisions to the publicity in *The Liberator*, nonresistance and disunion begged the more fundamental question of attribution: the relation of voice to subject. Like Garrisonism itself, they demonstrated the problems of referentiality that Lyotard has ascribed to a "regime of proper names" and in fact invited what he calls in one context "litigation" between competing parties. Lyotard's model of conflicted, intersubjective interpretation might be the most apt description of the abolitionists' public sphere in the form of Garrisonism. It represented the abolition movement in what Lyotard has called the manner of a proper name, which means that it prevented a collective body from appearing in any form that did not require the exercise and therefore the contingency of competing judgments. [17]

In the second decade of the New England abolition movement, the abolitionists' public identity and therefore the premise of their politics would be nearly completely routed through the problematic of Garrison's editorial identity. This is true especially in the cause of disunion, which might be said to have served as the essence of Garrisonism precisely because it institutionalized the question of attribution within the abolitionists' agenda. Nominally Garrison's own pet cause but hearkening toward the historical precedent of democratic revolution, the cause of disunion bore witness to the uncertain position of a revolutionary public in the postrevolutionary era. The publicity for disunion in *The Liberator* ensured that the larger question reflecting the abolitionists' historical predicament—who or what could be the agent of a perpetual democratic revolution in the absence of a liberty-loving people?—would be articulated as a problem of textual attribution: who or what was the subject declaring disunion?

A preliminary look at the "Anti-Slavery Declaration" that Garrison reprinted in *The Liberator* in the 1844 suggests that a disunion resolution could not help but restage the debate over the identity of his editorial voice. "We ... solemnly publish and declare," the resolution intoned, "that we are, and by right ought to be, FREE AND INDEPENDENT INDIVIDUALS, and that we are absolved from all religious and political allegiance and connection with the organized church and government of these United States,"[18] and while this might seem to demonstrate all the possibilities of individualism that Garrison is said to incarnate, it approximates more nearly the dynamics of textual attribution that Garrison's editorial identity imposed on the abolitionists' public identity. What if the closest either Garrisonism or disunion could bring the abolition movement to its self-realization was to present any form of identity, as "The Anti-Slavery Declaration" did, as a right, a declaration, an utterance, rather than as a priori subject? Then the bearer of the right, like the author of the declaration, would be determined through inference and attribution, implying deliberation among implied and actual interlocutors in a sphere of discussion. "The Anti-Slavery Declaration," after all, was undersigned by thirty-two members of local abolition societies and printed in the *Herald of Freedom*, an abolitionist newspaper edited by Nathaniel Rogers. Only when it was reprinted in *The Liberator* did it become a statement of Garrisonism.

In a more practical sense, the disunion "phase" of the abolition movement institutionalized the public sphere of contestation and debate as found in *The Liberator*, where every demonstration of Garrison's editorial freedom raised still more questions regarding the right of anyone to declare anything. Who had entitled Garrison to publicize the cause of disunion? and for whom was Garrison speaking? were the questions asked by the disputants in this public sphere, not, how did this position advance the cause of antislavery? For better or worse, the textual mediation of Garrisonism had become so central to the cause that it determined, or limited, the abolitionists' self-representation to an interrogative form. In the course of their interrogation, partisans could dispute Garrison's editorial authority or affirm it, but they could never establish definitively the grounds for this or that exercise of editorial autonomy. The authority for the right of free speech, Claude Lefort has argued, cannot be found within the boundaries of the subject or in what he calls "bourgeois egoism"; it arises solely from *"the legitimacy of a debate as to what is legitimate and what is illegitimate—*a debate which is necessarily without any guarantor and without any end." For Lefort, the public sphere of this debate has "the virtue of belonging to no one, of being large enough to accommodate only those who recognize one another within it and who give it a meaning, and of allowing the questioning of right to spread."[19]

The Liberator operated as the principle institution of the abolitionists' public sphere to this degree: it kept the identity of its editor vacant even while it made nearly every declaration of right synonymous with his name. Under the rubric of Garrisonism, the declaration and questioning of that right could seem to spread indefinitely—and yet we cannot ignore the specific terms of the criticism that was heaped on Garrison just as he was functioning in this capacity. What made the charge "abolition incarnate" suited for the influence of his editorial voice? More importantly, why did the most contentious and, by Lefort's reckoning, the most democratic phase of the abolitionist agenda demand a metaphor of embodiment to describe Garrison's sponsorship of public dispute in and through *The Liberator*? I will suggest an answer to this question and at the same time forecast the theme of the next chapter by proposing that Garrison intended to establish the newspaper as a historically recognizable, republican institution and incorporated, so to speak, the relation of the citizen to the body in the disposition of his own editorial voice. Of course, he would spare no effort to demonstrate his disinterest in his own authority, but the need for this demonstration, and the public attribution it was supposed to gain for his editorial voice, remind us that abolitionists' self-representation was almost wholly dependent on an ideology of republicanism that sought the abstraction of white male propertied persons into a rational citizenry while at the same time defining the identity of a public with the exclusive, physically particular attributes that belonged to those persons. The trouble with Garrisonism, in other words, is that it bore all too well the historical traces of a public, and as such it begs the nagging question of whether the abolitionists' public sphere was really free from its embodiment at all.

"The Organ of an Individual"

The first editorial that Garrison wrote for *The Liberator* prefigured the contested course for the abolition movement under the rubric of Garrisonism. "I will not equivocate—I will not excuse—I will not retreat a single inch," he promised, and like all previous and subsequent self-declarations, this one constituted not just an assertion of identity but an assertion of the right of declaration. In his first editorial post at the *Essex Courant* (whose name he changed to the *Newburyport Free Press*), he had declared himself "independent," "subservient to no party," and subject to "no man's patronage," ignoring the fact that the newspaper was in fact a Federalist party organ and subject to the control of the source of its patronage.[20] He pursued a similar course at his next post, as editor of the pacifist *Genius of Universal Emancipation*, exchanging its stated position on the gradual abolition of slavery for his own "immediatist" position and then landing himself in jail for printing a libel against a Baltimore shipowner. Garrison founded his abolitionist career, in other words, on declarations of editorial individuality that, strictly speaking, had no grounds of their own. With none of the privileges of genteel character that Protestant reform could lend him and without a newspaper of his own, he had nothing to underwrite his declarations except his assertion of right. He could not serve as the guarantor of that right, so he had to "take out a loan with himself" and assert the "I" on credit, conditions that Derrida has ascribed to the "declarative act which founds an institution" as well as to the modern autobiographical act.[21]

For at least one Protestant clergyman, Garrison was indeed a nonentity, a "low-lived, ignorant, insignificant mechanic . . . connected to no church and to nobody."[22] This dismissal, however, doubled as a deprecation of the urban artisan printer class, from which Garrison and several key members of the New England abolition movement emerged. The printer and editor William Goodell, for instance, addressed his appeals to "readers, farmers, mechanics, free laborers of the north," evidently seeking the same ground occupied by the Workingmen and Anti-Mason parties for the abolition movement and belying the abolitionists' reputation as a disaffected Whig gentry championing liberal ideals of humanitarian reform.[23] Garrison's colleague and the printer of *The Liberator*, Isaac Knapp, gained notoriety in his own right for publishing many of the lectures of George Thompson, the English abolitionist, to publicize his northeast tour; Elizur Wright, a founding member of the Massachusetts Anti-Slavery Society, started his career as a printer activist as well. The origins of the abolition movement in the antebellum era might well be traced through Garrison's printing career, through the pioneering accomplishments of the printer-editor Benjamin Lundy, and ultimately to a republican culture of printers and tradesmen that maintained the hostility of Thomas Paine to ecclesiastical prerogatives and that celebrated the progress of liberty in the achievement of civic equality.[24]

When Garrison proudly referred to himself at the height of his influence as a "poor, self-educated mechanic," it was clear that he welcomed the political association with the urban artisan printer class.[25] He dedicated a large portion of the resources of the abolition movement to the printing trade and sought to lend its egalitarian republicanism to the cause of abolition—and yet he can be said to have forsaken nearly all the paths for self-realization that either the artisan or bourgeois economies of the early nineteenth century laid open for the aspiring reform advocate with the freedom he demonstrated as editor of *The Liberator*.[26] That path belonged to Knapp, the printer and publisher of the newspaper, not to Garrison. Neither a man of property nor, strictly speaking, a man of the trade, he had nothing to his name except his name, which, unlike the names of so many other Protestant reformers, had no value as a family patronym. All he could do was to declare his name as if it were his inalienable right, an act that nonetheless proved critical to the fiscal survival of *The Liberator*.[27]

The abolitionists at the 1837 convention of the Massachusetts Anti-Slavery Society indeed acclaimed the newspaper as "the pioneer of this cause" precisely because Garrison had declared his editorial independence. They regarded Garrison's right of opinion as a signal asset of the abolition movement and were willing to underwrite the exercise of that right with a generous operating subsidy. Garrison in turn would make his strongest argument for the patronage of the society with yet another declaration:

> It will be seen at once, that the Liberator, if left to depend upon its subscription list alone, cannot maintain its ground, whilst *The Emancipator*, for instance, sustained by the funds of the Parent Society [the American Anti-Slavery Society], is issued on a much larger sheet, and afforded on the same terms. I do not wish the Liberator to be the organ either of this or any other Society, nor any body of men to be responsible for every

sentiment it may promulgate; and I am quite sure that I shall not permit any persons to control my pen, or establish a censorship over my writings.

Amasa Walker spoke for the members of the society when he admitted, "We do not all feel perfectly pleased with *all* Mr. G says," before voting to subsidize his right to say it. For his part, Garrison could not have been more clear: "It is neither my aim nor expectation to please every individual subscriber to *The Liberator*, in every particular: such a coincidence, while men differ so widely in their tastes and notions, on various subjects, is utterly impracticable."[28]

In procuring the financial support from the Massachusetts Anti-Slavery Society on these terms, Garrison had completed a most unconventional career trajectory for an aspiring printer-editor. He had achieved the artisan's touted goal of independence through his relation to an independent editorial voice that was identified closely with a certifiably public liberty, the right of free speech. To be sure, the editorial freedom was deemed Garrison's own—the resolution for the support of *The Liberator* made clear that the Massachusetts Anti-Slavery Society would be "leaving its editorial department in the hands of William Lloyd Garrison"—but the newspaper in which it appeared was not, so that *The Liberator* could and did prosper without Garrison's personal success. As a result, Garrison could claim that he took no personal interest in *The Liberator*, and, moreover, that he could not profit from its success. Having ensured the survival of the newspaper without incurring any personal liability or altering his material circumstances, he could differentiate himself from his editorial identity, which became in effect an institutional identity underwritten by the society. To further differentiate himself from that identity, Garrison claimed at the 1837 annual meeting that his freedom of speech could serve as an apt "motto" for the organization itself, since "those who are opposed to me in sentiment are always invited to occupy its pages."[29]

There was some truth to Garrison's claim that he pursued a corporate or collective end with his self-assertion, for accepting the Massachusetts Anti-Slavery Society's subsidy on these grounds, he was attempting to alter the self-image of the abolition movement so that it resembled more nearly a source or voice of critical inquiry, wholly unlike the editorial voices of so many other reform newspapers. In an early editorial, Garrison took on the profession to his own advantage, but also, he hoped, to the advantage of the readers of *The Liberator*:

> Our editors as a body—what are they? Measure their intelligence . . . it is as dwarfish as their subscription list. Examine their principles . . . they are as straws blown about by the wind—the breath of patronage, or the current of popular opinion. . . . Behold their independence! It is that of the miserable creature who begged pardon of mankind for having been born. It is that of the miserable creature who begged pardon of mankind for having been born into the world.[30]

By supporting Garrison, the New England movement was not just endorsing his vision of the vocation but freeing itself from the patronage, partisanship, and corruption of self-interest that, in his view, depreciated the value of antebellum newspapers. In a letter to his fellow editor David Lee Child, he dismissed even the official press organ of the American Anti-Slavery Society, avowing that "the [Anti-Slavery] Standard, being the organ of the whole society, cannot be a free paper in the same sense that *The Liberator*, the organ of an individual, is so."[31] An individual voice thus became central to the public sphere of abolitionist discussion and ultimately to the self-definition of the abolition movement as a free, disinterested public.

In order to sustain that public identity, Garrison needed to present his editorial privileges as if they were those of a society and to extend his editorial freedom to its members. And for these objectives he was dependent on the very institutional resources and connections that he decried. Patronage, subscription lists, popular opinion, and editorial dependence were, after all, the staples of antebellum journalism, without which no subscription newspaper or editor could survive. Before the advent of the penny press, nearly every newspaper in America was the press organ of a party, voluntary society, or religious denomination, which meant that their subscribers, their reading public, and hence their financial support came from the rolls of their respective subsidizing organizations, not from a free market of readers. So dependent were subscription newspapers on parties and organizations for their financial support that an 1850 census revealed that only 5 percent considered themselves as "neutral." The editors of these newspapers were not supposed to be neutral or independent either; the most strident of them took pride in publishing the opinions of a reading public that already subscribed to the political, religious, or moral principles for which the sponsoring organization stood.[32]

Even though *The Liberator* was a self-described "organ of an individual," it was also a subscription newspaper, and as such, operated under the same conditions as every other reform paper, whether it be abolitionist, colonizationist, temperance, or pacifist. Under these terms, some members of the Massachusetts Anti-Slavery Society might even be forgiven for assuming that their financial support made the newspaper answerable to the organization. Henry B. Stanton, soon to be among Garrison's principle critics, acknowledged that the realities of the market made it "utterly out of the question for a moral reform paper to be sustained by its subscription list."[33] At the 1837 convention, he made a motion for the subsidy under the conventional assumption that the patronage of the Massachusetts Anti-Slavery Society would make *The Liberator* the society's organ, just as *The Anti-Slavery Standard* served as the organ for the American Anti-Slavery Society. Garrison, however, had other ideas. He hoped to exploit the ambiguities of his arrangement with the Massachusetts society so that his exercise of free speech and even his editorial identity could obtain as the shared, distinctive property of abolitionists and, eventually, as the functional equivalent of the abolition society. He would use the example of his independence to preclude the prospect of partisan bonds and consensual opinion among abolitionists, but in order to realize this collective possibility, he had to maintain the very conventions of the subscriber newspaper marketplace that interpellated a reading public. His dependence on the customary calculus of the subscription newspaper marketplace could be measured by the question he asked at each abolitionist gathering: "Who takes the Liberator?"

Under these conditions, every subsequent statement of Garrison's editorial freedom further confused his identity with the collective identity of an organization, leading to the well-documented internecine warfare that rocked and then split the New England abolition movement. This warfare, I will argue, was conducive to Garrison's ambition for *The Liberator*, for in the midst of the so-called Clerical Appeals controversy of 1837 Garrison can be seen parlaying an anticlerical, antipatronage publicity campaign into a larger argument for the public, certifiably republican qualities of his editorial voice. Of course, the Massachusetts Anti-Slavery Society convention held in January of that same year had given his editorial identity the prerogatives and subsidies of patronage, but in the course of inciting and then resolving the "Clerical Appeals" controversy Garrison adapted these institutional conventions in such a way as to propose an alternative, undoubtedly anachronistic form for the society: that of a rational, virtuous public, shorn of partisan interests, self-interests, and destructive compromises. As editor of *The Liberator*, Garrison naturally would share in this distinction, which meant that his institutional identity served also as a historical institution of republicanism.

The seeds for the "Clerical Appeals" controversy were planted in 1829, when Garrison published a pamphlet called "Thoughts on African Colonization" purporting to expose the racism of the Protestant-led American Colonization Society, but with the advent of *The Liberator* in 1831, he undertook an even larger battle of more historical dimensions. With liberal use of the libelous invective we encountered in the previous chapter, he posed his self-declared editorial freedom not just as a refuge from a tacitly proslavery ecclesiastical establishment but as a remnant of the anticlerical, free inquiry heralded by the progress of the Enlightenment. "Our Country, the World, Our Countrymen, Mankind," proclaimed the masthead of *The Liberator*, and with the guidance of Tom Paine Garrison attempted to continue the struggle of true republicanism against the oppression of church and state.

In 1836 *The Liberator*'s campaign against the Protestant establishment intensified, as Garrison engaged the paterfamilias of reform, Samuel Ward Beecher, in a certified public relations disaster over the biblical authenticity of the Sabbath. Over the course of the next year, he printed a series of editorials disputing the moral authority of the clergy, cementing his reputation among Boston's clergy as a "low-lived mechanic" but, in Garrison's mind, securing the reputation of *The Liberator* as the last outpost of enlightened discussion in a society otherwise benighted by the church. In a July fourth address reprinted in *The Liberator*, he predicted that "the corruptions of the CHURCH, so called, are obviously more deap and incurable [than those of the nation] . . . and therefore . . . is first to be dashed to pieces."[34] Anticipating a drop in the subscription list from such sentiments, Garrison wrote to Samuel May, "Blessed be to God that I am not entangled with their yoke of bondage" but warned that a "mighty sectarian conspiracy is forming to crush me."[35]

The anticipated counterattack arrived in the form of a letter, "An Appeal of Clerical Abolitionists on Anti-Slavery Measures," from the Orthodox Congregational Churches of New England, which was reprinted in the denomination's organ, the *New England Spectator*, in August 1837. The five clergymen who authored the letter characterized Garrison's criticism as "wicked and base insinuations, the meanest and vilest form of lying" and inveighed against him for "heaping abuse upon ministers of the gospel and other excellent Christians, who do not feel prepared to enter fully into the efforts of anti-slavery societies."[36] The generally favorable reviews of the clergy's letter in the secular, commercial press confirmed the fear of Garrison partisans such as Lucretia Mott, who wrote that the "religious world, through all its various organs of communication with the universal public" was turning public opinion against Garrison and the Massachusetts Anti-Slavery Society and in favor of the American Anti-Slavery Society, most of whose members "chanced to be members also of sects which the appellants considered Orthodox." The average reader and the religiously observant member of the Massachusetts society would come to believe, Mott claimed, that "the object of the Liberator was to abolish the office of the ministry," an object that inspired the clergy "to induce men to cease to subscribe for the Liberator."[37]

At stake in the "Clerical Appeals" controversy was the momentous issue of whether the abolition movement was to have a religious or secular orientation. The recent conviction of Abner Kneeland for blasphemy and Garrison's own historical consciousness combined to give this question an even larger import concerning the very progress of the Enlightenment—and yet for all the combatants in this dispute, nothing seemed to be more critical than the status of *The Liberator*. The Reverend Charles Woodbury, a prominent member of the Massachusetts Anti-Slavery Society who had once stood by Garrison and denounced proslavery churches, seconded the sentiments of the "Clerical Appeal" when he wrote that the publicity for anti-Sabbatarianism, nonresistance, and women's rights had polluted *The Liberator* to the point where it was unserviceable to the abolition cause. "I once tried to like his paper—took it for one year and paid for it," he wrote in the *Spectator*, "and stopped it because that, though it did well on abolition on one page, it would say something on the other to injure it, which something, too, did not concern the point of abolishing slavery."[38] A second and then third "Clerical Appeal" appeared in the *Spectator* that advised prying Garrison from *The Liberator* and, failing that, making the *Spectator* the "new public organ" of the Massachusetts Anti-Slavery Society.[39]

Would the public organ of the New England abolition movement be answerable to the most well-endowed, august Protestant denomination in New England or to William Lloyd Garrison? There seemed to be little support for the latter from the American Anti-Slavery Society; its official comment, that the organization was "avowedly a Christian Society," indicated that the leaders of the national organization welcomed the return of the abolition movement to an evangelical, educational initiative.[40] In the face of this opposition, Garrison was able to keep *The Liberator* the "organ of an individual" precisely by submerging his own identity under his claims for the editorial independence of the newspaper. He accomplished this end in his "Layman's Reply" to the 'Clerical Appeals,'" which shrewdly presented his editorial voice as the antidote to the perils of patronage. After questioning whether the clergy's decision to print the clerical letters in the unfriendly *Spectator* and not in *The Liberator* was "manly or ingenuous," he dismissed its arguments as "the same dolorous cant which has so long characterized the Boston *Recorder*, Christian *Mirror*, Vermont *Chronicle*, &c. &c." The "Clerical Appeal," in other words, was nothing more than a conspiracy between publications and their patronage that would destroy the prospects for free discussion:

> All these [accusations in the "Appeal"] are merely the stale repetitions of what has been falsely iterated a thousand times over by pro-slavery advocates and mawkish apologists of slaveholders ever since my voice was first lifted up in the cause of my enslaved countrymen. They have not even the poor merit of originality—being most palpable plagiarisms from the columns of all the colonization press in the land.[41]

The press, the colonization movement, and the Protestant clergy all seemed to be saying the same thing because they were in fact bound together by the infrastructure and technologies of the subscriber newspaper market. In his "Layman's Reply," Garrison referred to this market as a "press-gang system" that enchained both unwary readers and the right of free speech to unthinking, partisan power. With this label, he believed he had identified the most coercive political apparatus in New England political society.

The alternative to both the *Spectator* and the "press-gang system" was, of course, *The Liberator*, though Garrison wanted to make sure that the survival of the self-described "organ of an individual" did not signal a personal triumph. He intended to install a recognizably public basis for the newspaper's editorial voice when he declared *The Liberator* free from any patronage whatsoever. To do this, he would have to give up the propitious financial arrangement to which the Massachusetts Anti-Slavery Society had agreed in January of that year. The society's subsidy, he wrote his brother-in-law after the publication of the first "Clerical Appeal," "gives the enemy some advantages in saying that the Society is responsible for all that I write and publish."[42] The "Prospectus of the Liberator," published in December 1837, thus announced, "The connection of the Liberator with the Massachusetts Anti-Slavery will cease, by our own choice, with the present year," and that its "pecuniary liabilities" would be "assumed by the publisher."[43] Freed from the obligations of patronage as well as from the burdens of ownership, Garrison seemed determined to use the "Clerical Appeals" controversy as an occasion to abstract his editorial identity from the conventions of the newspaper trade until all that remained of his relation to *The Liberator* was the freedom of its voice. Accordingly, the newspaper was left open to "those who love FREE DISCUSSION, and an independent press which no party can bribe, and no sect intimidate," the self-description of an enlightened public convened by abolitionist publications.

With *The Liberator*'s new status in 1838, Garrison's editorial freedom would enable its readers not just to escape the coercion of the press-gang system but to become a people. The "Prospectus" indeed was a republican strategy of negation that was designed to complicate Garrison's editorial freedom with a historical image of a public, constituted in the denial of its own interests. He could point to his habit of reprinting negative editorials from rival newspapers and announce, "I have laid before my readers thousands of columns of matter, strongly denunciatory of my sentiments, crowded with sweeping misrepresentations of my designs, and bitterly unjust in regard to the anti-slavery enterprise,"[44] and thereby demonstrate his own selflessness, but the basis for this self-presentation could be found in a republican political economy that Garrison sought to establish among readers and subscribers to *The Liberator*. In practical terms, his attempt entailed the creation of a print marketplace that was alternative in value and practice to both the subscriber marketplace and, as we will see, democratic market capitalism. Buying and selling *The Liberator* in this marketplace in turn would constitute the ennobling social discourse of a virtuous citizenry that could conduct all abolitionists toward the possibility of their own self-effacement and hence toward the full exercise of their reason. They would be relinquishing the opportunities for power and prestige offered by the "press-gang system," but by manipulating the conventions of the newspaper trade Garrison hoped to give the abolition movement opportunities for political influence that were not available in society, that were in fact antithetical to its realization as a society. With the success of *The Liberator*, abolitionists could recognize themselves in the historically distant image of a public.

We can see this utopian ambition at work in, of all places, the dreary work of fund-raising. Because he had refused the subsidy of the clergy and the Massachusetts Anti-Slavery Society, Garrison was obliged to ceaselessly solicit contributions, subscriptions, and gifts. He did so largely through private letters, resisting the growing custom in the antebellum economy to publicize business affairs and financial transactions in the public realm of newspapers while also contradicting the more comprehensive trend in antebellum print culture that placed letters within the purely private sphere of personal discourse.[45] Fund-raising for *The Liberator* thus allowed a private letter to a personal friend to signify an act of disinterested citizenship, such as the one that Garrison elicited from his friend and associate Edmund Quincy. According to Garrison, both they and their personal relations would be transcended in their transaction:

> I feel all the more unembarrassed in making the present appeal, as it is literally on behalf of the cause—and as it is not my wish or intention to have any exclusive personal interest in the contemplated purchase, beyond that of a fellow-soldier in the anti-slavery conflict. . . . True, it will in all probability be an outright gift to the cause; but it ceases to be a *personal* affair, and in case of personal dereliction, can at any time be claimed by the proprietors.[46]

Such an exchange would give Garrison a valuable commodity in this political economy, which was credit. To gain this credit, he had to empty himself of illicit concerns, motives, and interests so that prospective contributors would be contributing their money not for Garrison's personal use but for a public enterprise. When successful in these entreaties,

Garrison's character was proportionately esteemed, and others could extend their credit.[47]

Garrison was eager to maintain the value of his character in this fund-raising economy, for he knew that the political authority accorded to him was only as legitimate as the transactions that sustained *The Liberator*. A sign of hard times for both him and his newspaper came when he had to appeal directly to his abolitionist colleagues for a loan. "My public position," he confessed, "is such that I am specially anxious to maintain my credit for pecuniary punctuality in meeting my quarterly obligations, not having any credit at large for any antislavery labors."[48] For Garrison, a loan from his colleagues would maintain a "public position" that obtained solely in the sphere of social intercourse and through the probity of economic exchanges. A character that could be as perfectly and publicly demonstrated as this in turn would be entitled to all the rewards that republicanism could offer the exemplary individual. These included not just active commerce and prosperity but the possibility of his own self-effacement, from which ensued positive acts of virtue and the public good.[49] The success of *The Liberator* offered its subscribers, its patrons, and of course, its editor a similar opportunity, which would allow them all to escape the partisanship and self-interest of Jacksonian society and adopt a "public position."

One obvious difference remains between the republican political economy of the eighteenth century and the print marketplace that Garrison instituted on behalf of *The Liberator*. Much of his fund-raising redounded directly to him—not only did it subsidize his editorial control but in some cases it paid his household expenses. However, this can be said to have had the perverse effect of extracting Garrison's personal assets and liabilities from the purely private sphere and making them a public concern. As proof of this, we might note that patrons of the newspaper could just as easily contribute money for his personal use and be aware of no impropriety, while Garrison routinely recognized the most personal gesture of friendship or generosity as a disinterested statement of abolitionist principle. In a private letter of gratitude to Elizabeth Pease, one of his most faithful correspondents and patrons, he assured her, "My esteem for you is based upon the solid conviction, that you love truth, and justice and righteousness, for their own sake; that you are a fearless seeker after what is right and good; that you have a heart which deeply sympathizes with suffering humanity."[50] Apparently, even the personal sentiments of epistolary discourse could manifest public relevance when they were traded within the ersatz republican political economy of *The Liberator.* The financial success of *The Liberator* might even halt the ever-encroaching boundaries of the private sphere, depreciate the value of self-interest, and ultimately forestall the realization of a liberal capitalist society, at least among abolitionists.

Even when Garrison followed the example of Horace Greeley, the editor of the *New York Tribune,* and published a penny press, his brief foray into this new capitalist marketplace showed just how far his efforts on behalf of *The Liberator* had taken him:[51]

> Certainly, so cheap a paper leaves those persons without excuse, who have pleaded that they were too poor to take the Liberator. . . . It must not fail to be understood that the *Cradle of Liberty* will be made up of a portion of the anti-slavery articles contained in the Liberator, i.e. a transfer from the column of one paper to those of the other. It is thus only, that we shall be enabled to put this sheet at so cheap a rate. We feel and have no personal interest in its success, aside from the dissemination of light and truth.[52]

With this "transfer," Garrison was attempting also to adapt the republican political economy of *The Liberator* to a signature article of liberal capitalism. Refusing to take "personal interest in [the *Cradle of Liberty's*] success," he would renounce the rewards of the penny-press marketplace, just as he had refused the advantages of patronage that the subscriber newspaper marketplace offered. Of course, this would doom both *The Liberator* and the *Cradle of Liberty* to the economic privation that he imposed on himself, but he saw in the prospect of the newspaper's market failure the conditions for a public faculty of free speech, freed from private or particular determinations and rooted in the republican tradition of citizenship. [53]

Garrison promptly extended the symbolism of *The Liberator* to the social relations of his fellow abolitionists, which he celebrated in classically republican terms. Recollecting the spirit of a national abolitionist assembly, he wrote, "Such greetings and shaking of hands! such interchanges of thoughts and opinions! such *zeal and disinterestedness*" (my emphasis).[54] Combining the affective sentiment we associate with reform-era voluntary societies with the negative virtues of republicanism, Garrison's commendation of the abolitionists' "zeal and disinterestedness" was also a restatement of the economy he established for the editorial voice of *The Liberator*. Within the abolition movement, the passions felt by individuals could be reconciled with the reason exercised by a public; the most personal sentiments could demonstrate the possibility of self-transcendence that every citizen sought in the name of the public good. The financial success of *The Liberator* in this sense would turn back the clock on the nineteenth century and place the abolition movement in a distant time of the Enlightenment, of eighteenth-century civic life. The newspaper was the abolitionists' public sphere of free discussion as well as their historical institution, and all they had to do to assume their place in a historic struggle for liberty was to underwrite an "organ of an individual."

"Abolition Personified"

An avowedly public medium made answerable to a single editor's prerogatives, *The Liberator* was a hybrid, symbolically overdetermined institution that betrayed Garrison's ambition not just for the public attribution of his editorial voice but for the historical representation of the abolition movement. However, Garrison ensured that the abolition movement's sphere of free discussion would not surpass the boundaries set by the signification of Garrisonism by providing for the autonomy of the newspaper. For him and his allies, "Garrison" might obtain as a mere name, or as a token of the public discourse that maintained the prospect of an impersonal voice of public reason. His antagonists, on the other hand, were just as determined to refer the name to Garrison himself and to expose the fiction of the abolitionists' public identity with the traits of a personality.

This dispute informed the second internecine controversy of the New England abolition movement, the political party controversy that immediately followed the resolution of the "Clerical Appeals" controversy. After severing his connection with the Massachusetts Anti-Slavery Society, Garrison had indulged his editorial independence and committed *The Liberator* to publicizing such controversial causes as women's rights and nonresistance. In the 1837 "Prospectus," he was less prolix on the subject of women's rights—writing only that "we shall go for the RIGHTS OF WOMEN to their utmost extent"—than he was on nonresistance, but it is plain that he considered his own utterance of institutional freedom to sever the social and political relations that bound all abolitionists as surely as if they were enslaved. The result of his declaration was "an independent press which no party can bribe, and no sect intimidate," which also accorded with the self-image the abolition movement as a disinterested, autonomous public.

Garrison did accede to the suggestion of one of his chief fundraisers, Anne Warren Weston, that the New England Non-Resistance Society "should possess an organ of communication with the public other than the Liberator, and this as well on account of the one cause as the other."[55] However, a chorus of Massachusetts Anti-Slavery Society members, led by Henry Stanton, had already decided that Garrison's espousal of the cause of nonresistance had been too idiosyncratic, and that it made it made *The Liberator* unfit to conduct the abolitionists' free discussion. In an editorial titled "Watchman, What of the Night?" published in January 1839, Garrison warned of a second attempt to destroy the "organ of an individual":

> The design is . . . to throw the balance of power into the hands of a far different body of men, for the accomplishment of ulterior measures which are now in embryo. The next object is, to effect the establishment of a new weekly anti-slavery journal, to be the organ of the State Society, for the purpose, if not avowedly, yet designedly, to subvert *The Liberator*, and thus relieve the abolition cause in this State of the odium of countenancing such a paper. . . . The political necessity which is urged for another paper is ridiculous; and we know it is nothing but a hollow pretense.[56]

Garrison had in mind the recent results of a county abolitionist meeting at which two of his rivals from the "Clerical Appeals" controversy, Alanson St. Clair and Reverend Nathaniel Colver, persuaded the local society to reject the principles of nonresistance and to embrace the use of the vote. Their resolutions also argued "that a weekly and ably conducted anti-slavery paper, which shall take right, high, and consistent ground on this subject, and constantly urge abolitionists, as if duty bound, to use their political, as well as their moral and religious power and rights for the immediate overthrow of slavery, is now greatly needed in Massachusetts."[57] For St. Clair and Colver, a new press organ constituted a new organizational system for the Massachusetts Anti-Slavery Society that would produce consensual values and duties. Such a publication, "exclusively confined to slavery and abolition," would induce abolitionists to grasp collective ends and, more importantly, to organize themselves as a political movement.[58]

With competing versions of the abolitionist press corresponding to competing visions of the abolition movement, the stage was set for the 1839 annual meeting of the Massachusetts Anti-Slavery Society, where a larger group of Garrison's rivals attempted to convince the membership of the necessity for organized, partisan political activity. The meeting produced a heated exchange between Garrison and Stanton, which Mott recorded for posterity to Garrison's advantage. "Mr. Garrison!.," Stanton demanded, "Do you or do you not believe that it is a sin to go the polls?.," and to each repetition of the question, Garrison answered, "Sin for me!"[59] Garrison's proviso—"for me"—was still another declaration of editorial independence, an attempt to distinguish *The Liberator* from an "orthodox" press organ and to present it as an "organ of an individual." Stanton and his allies, on the other hand, were just as determined to collapse the distinction between Garrison's editorial voice and the Massachusetts Anti-Slavery Society so that *The Liberator* could be recognized for what they said it was: a perversion of a conventional press organ, in which a single person spoke for a society.

Unable to procure from the membership of the society either a censure of Garrison or the commitment to a new press organ, the dissenting group left to start the *Massachusetts Abolitionist*. Edited by Elizur Wright, John G. Whittier, and Stanton, the paper would be "devoted exclusively to the discussion of slavery" and to organizing the members of the newly formed Massachusetts Abolition Society on the model of a political party.[60] However, the more lasting challenge to the prominence of *The Liberator* was their charge that Garrison had not dismantled the "press-gang system," as he claimed, but in fact had become the gang. Even though Stanton's cited complaint against the newspaper at the 1839 convention suggested that the problem with *The Liberator* was that no printed opinion was allowed to become predominant or monolithic—"What accompanied this political matter [on abolition] on the other side of the paper? Discussions calculated to nullify its effect. Expressions of opposite opinion."[61]—he and his allies maintained that the editorial autonomy of *The Liberator* had reduced the abolition agenda to the most personal dimension. In Mott's rendition of this anti-Garrison sentiment, Garrison could be charged with having personalized the abolition agenda:

> "Garrison has too much influence," said one. "We must take it down little by little." "Have you got Garrison down yet?" said another; we are ready to come in when he is out of the way." "All the Massachusetts meetings are mere Garrison-glorifications," said a third; "they forget the *poor slave*." "Oh, the Massachusetts Society is the mere creature of Garrison," said a fourth. "So many abolitionists as there are in the State, opposed to him, why not get rid of him at once?" said the outside row. "All in good time—a newspaper first, as the organ of the Society."[62]

In response to Mott's tract, *Right and Wrong in Massachusetts*, Stanton and his fellow dissenters published *The True History of the Late Division in the Abolition Society*, in which they vehemently denied any secret designs to supplant *The Liberator* and, more importantly, any personal animus against Garrison. "It is not known that any of those," they insisted, "who have been prominent in the secession, have *ever* had the least personal difference with the individual, (Mr. Garrison,) out of hostility to whom it has been so often alleged the secession arose," even though the pamphlet considered the principle danger to the abolition movement to be "*personal and sectarian views on the subjects of Women's Rights, so called, Civil Government, the Church, the Ministry and the Sabbath.*"[63]

Reverend J. T. Woodbury, a leading schismatic at the 1839 convention, had once called Garrison "abolition personified and incarnate,"[64] and in the aftermath of the meeting these old charges resurfaced. Garrison's allies were accused henceforth of falling prey to idolatry while Garrison himself was given ambitions worthy of a Napoleon or, worse yet, a pope.[65] However, the blow that the abolitionist editor seemed to feel most keenly was to *The Liberator,* which stood condemned as his personal organ. Through the mediation of the newspaper, Garrison had sought to abstract his editorial voice and his published opinions from himself, but the ascension of *The Liberator* seemed to make him, in the eyes of his opponents, a monstrous parody of the public body he sought to institute within the abolition movement.

In response, Garrison sought to remind his fellow abolitionists that his most personal venture, the publicity on behalf of nonresistance, would maintain "even in the minds of your enemies, confidence in your disinterestedness." Without that display of editorial freedom, he reminded them, "there is reason to fear that you shall be regarded as those who have made the antislavery cause a hobby to ride into office."[66] Garrison, in other words, hoped to circumvent the question of his control over *The Liberator* by contrasting the medium of a disinterested public with the press organ of a political party, which held out only "mercenary rewards."

The failure of Garrison's antagonists to convince the Massachusetts Anti-Slavery Society to become a political party suggests that this distinction was itself sufficient to sustain the abolitionists' sense of their public identity and, by extension, of their anachronistic place in antebellum society. At the 1839 annual meeting, they repulsed a resolution that would have made voting compulsory, an attempt to institute among abolitionists an organizational unity precisely on the model of the "pressgang system."[67] As several commentators have noted, Garrison was able to defeat the resolution (or at least to have it tabled) by representing it as an obligation imposed by the society on the freedom of opinion.[68] His own resolution on the question of voting that was to carry the day portrayed a dystopian antislavery society that perpetuated the abuses of the ecclesiastical and political bodies that he endured as an editor:

> If specifications are essential in our constitution respecting the manner in which abolitionists shall act as members of the STATE, they are not less essential in relation to the manner in which they shall act as members of the CHURCH. We shall need, therefore, a clause to this effect—that members who are connected with any church, do pledge themselves that they will not hear any pro-slavery minister preacher; nor sit at the communion-table with those who proscribe their colored brother.... How apparent it is that, if we once begin in this manner to make specifications, we shall not know when to end! A huge volume would not suffice to contain them. This is to make a measure, instead of a principle, the basis of our organization. And is it not as essential that the CHURCH should be purified as the STATE should be reformed?

On the strength of these unflattering comparisons, Garrison was able to move the Massachusetts Anti-Slavery Society toward a negative version of itself: it may not "arraign either the political or religious views of its members. . . . All that a society or its organ may rightfully do is to entreat its members to abide by their principles."[69]

That *The Liberator* emerged not just unscathed but exemplary in the political party controversy gave Garrison the chance to represent his editorial identity according to the public self-image of the New England abolition movement. He seized the opportunity in the ensuing debate over the outcome of the 1839 annual meeting, which was transacted in the pages of *The Liberator*. An editorial titled "The Anti-Slavery Organization," coauthored by Francis Jackson, president of the Massachusetts Anti-Slavery Society, attempted to define the recently decided course for the abolition movement in a paragraph beginning, "Abolition is not 'the fulfilling of the law.'" Following was a series of five syntactically consistent negations that reached its climax in the conclusion that abolition was "not a theological controversy, nor a political crusade." Such an organization would seem to cancel any and all of its own initiatives, but for Garrison it contained unlimited prospects for the abolitionists' own freedom:

> As individuals, abolitionists may utter sentiments, which, in their associated capacity, they may not express. He who becomes an abolitionist, is under no obligation to change his views respecting the duty of going to the polls, or of belonging to a sect; they are those of an individual and are not binding at all upon any other member of the anti-slavery society. But if the society itself presumes to endorse those views as sound and obligatory upon all its member, then it violates the spirit of its own constitution. . . . This distinction between the liberty of an individual, and of an association composed of many elements, is important, and essential as much to the harmony of the whole body as to personal free agency.[70]

To exponents of an abolitionist political party, the logical and logistical precedence of "personal free agency" over an "associated capacity" was absolutely crippling, but Garrison held fast to the proposition that had governed his defenses of *The Liberator*: that any obstacle to the consolidation of opinion and to the pursuit of a collective interest gave abolitionists the far greater opportunity to convene themselves as a disinterested public. In this context, the generalized identity of the "whole body" was adumbrated in *preserving* the particularity of each part, and that required all abolitionists to recognize Garrison's editorial freedom as their common value.

The connection between Garrison's editorial independence and the prospective form of the abolition movement was explicitly argued in a pamphlet distributed by the newly formed "Friends of the Liberator" soon after the decisive meeting. A committee composed of loyal Massachusetts Anti-Slavery Society members to manage the newspaper, the "Friends" acknowledged "irreconcilable differences" among abolitionists "on questions of party politics" before celebrating the newspaper in terms that were reminiscent of the recently instituted society: *The Liberator* occupied "the only [ground] upon which any anti-slavery periodical can stand" because it encouraged the individual subject to pursue "*action consistent with his principles and his conscience.*"[71] The pamphlet's primary resolution confirmed that the analogue for this action was none other than Garrison:

> Resolved, so far from looking upon the expression of the peculiar views of its editor on other topics as a fault, or esteeming it a hindrance to the progress of the abolition cause, we value the Liberator for its fearless toleration and free discussion of all truth; and though we do not hold ourselves responsible for any sentiments uttered in its columns, we abhor that sectarian bigotry which would proscribe their free utterance, and clog its editor with the shackles of party or sect.

In the absence of an official organ for the Massachusetts Anti-Slavery Society, the "Friends" could present *The Liberator* not only as a libertarian institution but as a social institution in which a truly public discourse might thrive. Within the pages of the newspaper, the freedom of speech flourished, protected from the coercion of a political, ecclesiastical, or even abolitionist organization. Subscribing to *The Liberator* thus engaged the otherwise oppressed individual within a public sphere that was defunct everywhere else in society.

Unfortunately for the "Friends of the Liberator," subscribing to the newspaper also placed the abolitionist within the sphere of William Lloyd Garrison, which is exactly how James Birney, an established abolitionist editor from the rising "western" wing of the national abolition movement and soon to be the presidential candidate of the antislavery Liberty party, represented the Massachusetts Anti-Slavery Society. In a letter to *The Liberator,* he charged that the newspaper's ascendance had left abolitionists blindly following Garrison's lead, especially on the critical issue of voting. In his reply, Garrison attempted to separate his ideas from the platform of the society:

What I may have said and done, and what the Constitution [of the society] enjoins, are wholly distinct questions. . . . It is quite remarkable, that some of those who have been foremost in protesting against being reckoned my followers—who have been unwilling that I should be regarded as the mouth-piece of the Anti-Slavery Society, in any sense—who have repelled the slightest intimation from the enemies of abolition, that the Society is responsible for the sayings and doings of the Liberator—I say, it is quite remarkable, that, all at once, in the eyes of those persons, I have become an official organ, an unerring oracle, the Magnus Apollo of the whole land, whose speech and example are to followed implicitly.[72]

But it was true. Garrison had become an "official organ" of abolition during the struggle in which he and his allies spared no effort in distinguishing his editorial voice from the Massachusetts Anti-Slavery Society. Although he could maintain that he promoted ideas and opinions for which the society was not responsible, the outcome of the 1839 meeting showed that the abolition society conducted its business from principles for which Garrison was responsible. His refusal to cede control of *The Liberator* to a political party had been swiftly translated into the internal policy of the society, which saw in the full exercise of his editorial autonomy the promise of its own disembodiment into the form of a public.

Garrison's standing as "abolition personified and incarnate" in turn required him to demonstrate his individuality of opinion at the expense of the society so that his fellow abolitionists might recognize their public identity in him. He might be said to have become personified by his declarations of editorial independence but he would always have to distinguish this personification from himself if it was also to symbolize, or stand in for, the abolition movement. This was a ritual of self-denial that he performed with relish for the benefit of his antagonists, but particularly for Woodbury:

How has it happened that I have brought around me in a delightful association, men of all political parties and of all religious sects . . . ? It is a problem which has puzzled all the popularity hunters both in Church and State. . . . Now, sir, if I possess any influence, it has been obtained by being utterly regardless of the opinions of mankind; if I have acquired any popularity, it has been owing to my sturdy unwillingness to seek that honor which comes from men; . . . I have flattered no man, feared no man, bribed no man. Yet having made myself of no reputation, I have found a reputation.[73]

That this disclosure was made in a private letter and simultaneously published for all to read is indicative of Garrison's aspirations for *The Liberator*: that individual expressions might have the transparency of public reason, that with the success of the independent newspaper, private sentiments could have public relevance and supersede self-interests. And yet here we see a critical difference between the disinterested literate exchanges that Garrison sought to institute in the political economy of *The Liberator* and the closed economy of its editorial identity. By his own admission, his claim to disinterestedness was a constituent moment in the process of self-aggrandizement, which in turn entailed new shows of self-effacement. Having made his name synonymous with the abolition movement in its republican self-image, Garrison thus became committed to the task of asserting and annulling his own identity. Would the public identity that his fellow abolitionists recognized in the freedom of his editorial voice be likewise caught in the cycle of Garrisonism?

Revolution Incarnate

As the New England abolition movement entered its second decade, Garrisonism became still more determinate for the abolition agenda. From 1842, Garrison used *The Liberator* to publicize relentlessly the doctrine of disunion until it was adopted officially by the American Anti-Slavery Society and its Massachusetts counterpart at their 1844 annual conventions. At the meeting of the national society, of which Garrison was now president, the members formally adopted the resolution that since "political union in any form, between a slaveholding and free community, must necessarily involve the latter in the guilt of slavery . . . secession from the present United States government is the duty of every abolitionist."[74] A few weeks later, the Massachusetts Anti-Slavery Society declared its support for disunion by an even more resounding vote, announcing "that we deem it a first duty for [abolitionists] to agitate for a dissolution of the Union."[75] Supporters of these resolutions offered innumerable examples of the government's dedication to slavery, but the 1845 Massachusetts society's annual report clarified the true inspiration for disunion when it maintained that the abolitionists had adopted "this revolutionary policy . . . in virtue of the inherent right recognized in the Declaration of Independence . . . for a change in the form of their government, whenever it becomes intolerably oppressive or ceases to answer the end for which it was established."[76]

Garrison's own declaration of independence, "I WILL BE HEARD," can also be heard in the abolitionists' avowedly "revolutionary policy." The disunion resolutions that were moved at the 1844 annual conventions indeed could trace their origins directly to the editorial freedom that he had declared in the 1837 "Prospectus" for *The Liberator* and again in the aftermath of the 1839 annual meeting. Edited without organizational constraints or considerations, *The Liberator* made the most militant abolitionist strategy synonymous with Garrison's declaration of right, but as in the previous examples we have encountered, the publicity for disunion tended to confuse rather than to clarify the attribution of his editorial voice. His identity, like the identity of the bearer of the right of revolution, could only be inferred from the evidence of its declaration, which is why we might consider the abolitionists' most democratic self-representation the signal expression of Garrisonism. Without any authorization for their declaration of revolution and even without deciding who declaimed it, they took their bearings from the articulation of Garrison's editorial identity and committed themselves to reprising the revolutionary act of a people.

Strictly speaking, the issue of disunion had different authors: one was the Irish "Liberator," Daniel O'Connell, whose national tour in favor of the "Repeal of the Union" between Ireland and Britain generated extensive press coverage in *The Liberator*;[77] another was John Quincy Adams, who moved for the dissolution of the Union with a reading of the Declaration of Independence on the floor of the Congress.[78] However, neither of these declarations created as much confusion and controversy as Garrison's did when he publicized disunion, or repeal, as he first called it, in *The Liberator*. When he announced in the April 1842 issue of *The Liberator* (three weeks after he reported on Adam's disunion resolution) that the "REPEAL OF THE UNION" would be the "grand rallying point" of the upcoming annual convention of the American Anti-Slavery Society, a vicious storm of protest was unleashed in the press; the *New York Herald* declared that with *The Liberator*'s announcement, abolitionists had finally "flung off their masks."[79] Even the *Anti-Slavery Standard*, the press organ of the national society, featured an editorial wondering whether "the faith of many, who believed in [the] uprightness [of the abolition cause], will be shaken."[80]

In announcing the agenda for the 1842 annual convention, Garrison's own mask was "flung off," and the issue of repeal had ceased to be a nationalist or international cause and instead became Garrison's own. Of course, he sought to give the discussion of repeal the public attributes and public liberties that he gave all his demonstrations of editorial prerogative in addressing the "friends of liberty and republicanism" and summoning their "disinterestedness of purpose."[81] However, the "Executive Committee" of the society moved swiftly to assert jurisdictional authority over the abolition movement and to make Garrison personally responsible for any discussion of repeal. Antagonized by the presumptuousness of *The Liberator*, the committee took the unprecedented step of repudiating Garrison's announcement and issued a "Correction" in the *Anti-Slavery Standard*:

> Garrison's authority to bring the subject of a dissolution of the Union before the approaching session of the Abolition Society in this city, is distinctly disclaimed—the person having no right whatever to make such an annunciation. . . . This Committee deem it a duty to the Society which they represent, no less than to their fellow citizens, and to themselves

personally, to declare that they have not, at any time, either directly or impliedly, authorized such publications.[82]

Although the disclaimer briefly referred to the issue of repeal as "foreign to the purpose for which the American Anti-Slavery Society was organized," its primary intention was to assert the authority of the national organization over Garrison' editorial voice and to forestall its representation of the abolition movement. The official response of the society's executive committee reminded readers that the only political organization for which his newspaper spoke was himself. It did not consider the possibility that "the person having no right to make an annunciation" maintained an authority equal in kind and standing to that of "the Society."

Garrison was as eager as the executive committee to disavow his own authority, but for dramatically different purposes. Once again, he would use *The Liberator* to abstract the individuality of its editorial voice from himself so that his unauthorized "annunciation" might serve as an invitation to a more disinterested public discussion. To that end, he decided not to attend the upcoming meeting, dedicating his prospective absence to the prospect of morally redemptive social intercourse among abolitionists. Of course, he publicized the announcement of his absence in *The Liberator*:

> Under these circumstances, I am most anxious that a free and unbiassed opinion should be expressed by the society on the point, and that every appearance of personal anxiety on my part, as to its decision, should be avoided. I am determined not to allow it to be said, that the society was influenced by my presence and activity, to reverse the position of the Executive Committee—to disclaim the disclaimer.[83]

Disclaiming every declamation, Garrison sought to reproduce the republican economy of his editorial declamation in the public meeting of the abolitionists, so that the demonstration of his own disinterest could elevate the abolition movement itself above considerations of party and sect and consider political rights that accorded with the freedom of a people. The strategy worked, for his failure to attend the May 1842 meeting did lead to the consideration of the contraband issue, which was raised by proxy. Without his "presence and activity," the American Anti-Slavery Society conducted itself as a rational, deliberative public, making use of its liberty of speech to consider the more radical liberty of self-determination and democratic resistance. The right of "the person" to make an "annunciation" in this sense was affirmed without presenting Garrison as that person, which meant that *The Liberator* could and did speak for the collective body of abolitionists as the "organ of an individual." It was just that the authority of that individual, like that of "the person," required the absence of Garrison.

Was the official adoption of the doctrine of disunion by the abolition movement two years later then a victory for Garrison or for the cause of revolution? Perhaps all we can conclude with certainty is that it was a victory for *The Liberator*, whose announcement of repeal had triggered a discussion that had no authorization and could authorize no agent other than a disavowed, discredited editorial pronouncement. Given this precedent, the official, collective articulation of disunion could bear witness to the sovereignty of a revolutionary people only through the indeterminate authority and illegitimate "annunciations" that were associated with "the person." At the 1844 Massachusetts Anti-Slavery Society annual meeting, this condition was strikingly evident, particularly in the supposition that the right of declaration inhered solely within the articulation of that right and did not require the prior authorization of a sovereign agent or author. The right of Garrison's editorial voice to "make such an annunciation" had been ceded to all abolitionists, and in a nearly unanimous voice, the Massachusetts society formally severed its ties to the Union as easily as Garrison had disclaimed allegiance to the official bodies of the abolition movement: "For the reasons here enumerated, and others of similar import to which we might refer, we now publicly ABJURE OUR ALLEGIANCE TO THE CONSTITUTION OF THE UNITED STATES AND THE UNION, and ... declare its obligations, so far as they relate to ourselves, utterly null and void; and we now publicly pledge ourselves to seek, in all suitable ways, its peaceful dissolution."[84] Although this resolution was preceded by a statement of no less than twenty actuating reasons, it protested too much; there could be no mistaking that the society had taken its revolutionary agenda from Garrison's editorial voice and declared what could never be authorized conclusively.

Garrison's example was still more in evidence at the American Anti-Slavery Society's 1844 annual meeting, where the disunion resolution was passed with the acknowledgment that no one had been duly authorized to raise it. Not less than three protests, one authored by eight prominent members of the society, were read into the minutes; they composed almost as much of the reporting of the meeting as the disunion declarations themselves. Several counterarguments were offered in the course of debate, but the most telling protests recalled the earlier controversy that had greeted Garrison's unauthorized publicity for repeal and inveighed against the "presumptuousness" of the disunion cause, its injury to the "character and influence of the Society." Still another protest borrowed Garrison's customary self-defense and contended that the disunion resolution "virtually does away with my rights of conscience," which is why the entire contest over the declaration of disunion can be said to have assumed, and perhaps even endorsed, the institutional ascendance of the "organ of an individual" over the official, collective voice of an abolition society.[85] This is also why Garrison could afford to be sanguine about the opposition from the national society's members—"It was not to be expected, that a step so bold and revolutionary," he wrote in *The Liberator*, "would at first be adopted with perfect unanimity of its members"[86]—and looked forward to reprinting all the protests from individuals: the abolitionists' revolutionary destiny, after all, had started and ended with the self-determination that Garrison demonstrated in his own freedom of speech, in his editorial identity, and, ultimately, in his declarations of that identity. Those declarations, like the resolutions of disunion, were designed expressly to complicate the attribution of that identity and perhaps even to provoke a dispute cast in the most contentious image of a people. Disunion in this sense returned the abolitionist agenda to the point where Garrison originated: *ex nihilo,* in his declaration "I WILL BE HEARD."

By instituting this play of voice and identity within the national abolition movement, Garrison had made his editorial voice representative of the most insurrectionist abolitionist politics. His more strident declarations of disunion indeed could sound like restatements of his editorial policy, writ large:

> Man is superior to all political compacts, all governmental arrangements, all religious institutions. As means to an end, these may sometimes be useful, though they are never indispensable; but that end must always be the freedom and happiness of man, INDIVIDUAL MAN. It can never be true, that the public good requires the violent sacrifices of any, even the humblest citizen; for it is absolutely dependent on his preservation, not his destruction.[87]

The promise of disunion was that the liberties Garrison enjoyed as editor of *The Liberator* were ceded to all others as a political, even natural right, but that was also the promise of Garrisonism: that his institutional identity be detached from him and circulate among abolitionists as an easily obtainable, reproducible article of democracy. In practical terms, this meant that the success of the most ambitious abolitionist strategy depended on the circulation of *The Liberator* among an infinite number of readers, a condition that reminds us that disunion, like every other phase of the antislavery struggle, did more than institutionalize Garrison's editorial identity and make his name a byword: it entailed the creation of a public sphere.

Perhaps this is why the discourse of incarnation that Garrison's enemies threw back at him and his allies could not overturn their conviction in the meaning of his editorial freedom or reverse their self-representation as a critical public. The incarnation of the abolition movement in the image of Garrison had produced a collective identity for the abolition movement that only a press organ could have provided. The mediation of *The Liberator* in this incarnation in this sense did much to preserve what Lefort would call the "symbolic dimension" or "symbolic distinction" of a democratic body, even as the abolition movement seemed hell-bent on reducing itself to the image of "People-as-One."[88] The indispensability of print in this public self-recognition further ensured that Garrisonism would continue to embody the abolition movement in the discursive image of a disembodied citizenry. Garrison's incarnation, in other words, testified to the republican capacity of self-abstraction, which is to say that it might have approximated its historical model too precisely. The embodiment of the abolition movement became a matter of symbolic representation, or of collective self-abstraction, while Garrison's own corporeal existence became disembodied and technologically reproduced. The entire abolitionists' agenda seemed now crucially invested in obfuscating the difference between symbolization and embodiment in a manner redolent of the ideological mystification that was accomplished with the gendered category of republican "manliness." Whether this redounded to the benefit of those who were not men or designated as manly is a question the next chapter will address, but we should regard Garrisonism in this context as evidence of the abolitionists' determination to give their embodiment not just the physical dimensions of their public sphere but its figurative basis and expression. Garrison, after all, was said to be abolition incarnate *and* personified.

CHAPTER 3

Frederick Douglass's Public Body

As an abolitionist orator during the 1840s, Frederick Douglass confronted his audiences with the presence and power of a body that Garrison, in his capacity as editor of *The Liberator,* could have only approximated. It was Douglass who appeared as the representative of abolition principles through and in bodily form; it was Douglass's body that audiences acclaimed when they embraced abolitionist rhetoric. Standing before largely white audiences, the black orator composed a physical force, a corporeal reality that they sought to measure and put into words. James Russell Lowell spoke for others when he declared, "The very look and bearing of Douglass are an irresistible logic against the oppression of his race."[1]

What Douglass's looks and bearing demonstrated was the dramatic transformation of slave to man, an event that Thomas Wentworth Higginson claimed to witness in the course of a single lecture:

> And then there would perhaps come some man stumbling with his heavy slavery gait upon the platform, walking as if a hundred pounds ... were appended to each heal, and that man afterward, under the influence of freedom, developed into the superb stature and the distinguished bearing of Frederick Douglass.[2]

With an interest and intent equal to Higginson's, Douglass's audiences sharpened their observations of the black orator, whose every anatomical feature and gesture could signify the superiority of abolitionist principles. Such was their focus that his words, according to the abolitionist historian and editor John Blassingame, were not always reported faithfully or fully.[3] The reception of Douglass's oratory suggests that white abolitionists would abandon the promise of their own disembodiment into a historical image of the people and their investment in the articles of literate citizenship in order to identify their movement with the particularity of his body. Apparently, it had taken only the sight of a black man to incarnate the New England abolition movement in the form that Garrisonism had not been able to do.

Of course, the difference between these two institutions of the abolitionists' public sphere was that in identifying themselves with Garrison, they relied on the mediation of print to abstract all the qualities of a particular white man into those of a disinterested, literate citizenry. The fascination with Douglass's bodily properties, on the other hand, took place within the immediate confines of an oratorical performance that exposed the structural inequality of the public sphere. The disposition of the body, critics of Habermas's most utopian conception have said, and not the impersonal authority of reason marks the true boundary of the liberal public sphere, which historically separated propertied white men not only from the disenfranchised majority but from the materiality of their own bodies. "Modern citizenship," Robyn Weigman has stated succinctly, "functions as a disproportionate system in which the universalism ascribed to certain bodies (white male propertied) is protected and subtended by the infinite particularity assigned to others (black, female, unpropertied)."[4] In Douglass's reception, this distinction was dramatized and reenacted in a "visual sphere," wherein white audiences occupied the omnipotent, disembodied position of spectator and trained their eyes on the orator's black body.[5]

However, the distinction between these two versions of the public sphere becomes less clear when we attempt to reconstruct historically the standard of corporeality that was invoked in Douglass's reception. One of the sources for that standard can be said to be traced to Garrison, who not only sought to reinstate a republican expression of manhood in his own journalistic enterprise but acclaimed Douglass with the same expression. "There stood one," he recalled of his first sight of the future abolitionist orator, "in physical proportion and stature commanding and exact—in intellect richly endowed—in natural eloquence a prodigy." Together, these traits signaled the induction of the former slave "into the field of public usefulness, 'gave the world assurance of a MAN.'"[6] Douglass's transformation from slave to man, in other words, was symbolized by a republican political economy that had transformed the physical attribute of manhood into an ideological category of citizenship. His status as a richly endowed man would betray the inherent tension within the normative discourse of republicanism that in some sense kept it captive to the determinations of the body and that in turn defies a conclusive attribution.[7]

The other source for this standard of corporeality came from Douglass himself, or from his affiliation with a public culture of African American communities that shared many of Garrison's objectives and kept alive the obsolete norms and ideals of republicanism well into the antebellum era. For such black leaders as David Walker, Maria Stewart, Samuel Cornish, and James McCune, manhood indeed was a public property that signaled the usefulness of slaves and freemen to the growth of the American republic. Complementing this republican understanding of racial identity was a libertarian political agenda that considered a public usefulness proved in the establishment of "improvement" and relief organizations, in the emergence of literary societies, and especially in the success of so-called colored newspapers.[8] The trope of the body was no less operative in the statements of this agenda; looking forward to stimulating public intercourse between its African American readers, the freemen newspaper *Rights of All* declared that its purpose was to link together, "in one solid chain, the whole free population, so as to make them think, feel, and act, as one solid body, devoted to education and improvement." In the newspaper *Freedom's Journal*, Walker, author of the appeals to manhood in *Appeal to the Colored Citizens of the World*, would call on freemen "to form ourselves into a general body" through their literate social intercourse. The most vocal representatives of free African American communities, then, clearly saw a collective possibility in the corporeal category of the body that was directly in proportion to the prospects for an informed public. In his report to the 1847 National Convention of Colored People, McCune went so far as to declare that the creation of a freeman press organ was "the first step which will mark our certain advancement as a People."[9]

Together, these two contexts for Douglass's reception suggest that the standard of corporeality was as historically overdetermined as the abolitionists' public sphere and in fact could be traced to the various institutions of a black public sphere. As we will see, Douglass intended his body to manifest all the qualities of manhood that black leaders like Walker and McCune would ascribe to a people. Moreover, he presented those qualities through the same medium that African American free-men would use to embody themselves, which was through the attribution of a public faculty to the agency of a press organ. At first, Douglass appeared before audiences as an agent of *The Liberator*, which Garrison had called the organ of the free people of color. Later, he promoted his own newspapers, *The North Star* and the renamed *Frederick Douglass's Paper*, both of which were dedicated to the development of an African American civic culture on republican terms and standards. Douglass in turn dedicated his oratorical appearances to all these aforementioned newspapers, the success of which would create the "general body" to which Walker referred. The category of the body, in other words, might have been responsible for Douglass's unique standing as an orator and governed his audiences' responses to him but that was only because it originated in the public culture of newspapers and literary societies that Douglass represented. The "visual sphere" of oratory was linked in principle and practice to the print-mediated public sphere of the anti-slavery movement, and this ensured that Douglass's body would always be accorded the esteem of the colored press organ.

In the laudatory introduction that he wrote for *My Bondage and My Freedom*, McCune did not even have to alter his conviction in the util-ity of the press to acclaim Douglass as a physical specimen of black man-hood. On the contrary, Douglass was celebrated as the "Representative

American Man" and the type of his countrymen chiefly in his connection to *Frederick Douglass's Paper*, the latest incarnation of the newspaper Douglass founded in 1847. For McCune, there was little doubt that the former abolitionist orator had passed into "full grown manhood" in and through his capacity as editor of the paper. "Our editors," he pronounced, "rule the land," and so in publishing the freemen newspaper, Douglass "had raised himself by his own efforts to the highest position in society." As the editorial voice of the newspaper, Douglass had "won high mark in the public esteem" and suitable power, which was measured by the "very frequent mention" of his name in other newspapers.[10] Douglass's own manhood, in other words, was attributable to the circulation of his name and namesake, *Frederick Douglass's Paper*, among a reading public; under the terms of McCune's appraisal, he did not have any attributes of race or gender that the press organ did not have. This held true in his institutional role as editor: he seemed to embody the qualities that were ascribed alternately to a successful newspaper and to a virtuous, civic-minded people. "We must command the respect and admiration due men, who, against fearful odds, are struggling steadfastly for their rights," McCune had argued in his 1847 convention report. "This can only be done with a press of our own."[11]

The stakes of Douglass's own manhood are made clear in Robert Levine's analysis of the "politics of representative identity" within the black antislavery movement. As coeditors of *The North Star*, Douglass and Martin Delany developed influential and eventually incompatible positions on colonization and racial improvement that made them not just representatives but embodiments of their political positions.[12] After all, what was the physical demonstration of Douglass's manhood but an argument against the expatriation of African Americans to a foreign land, the living proof of the capacity of the race for republican virtue and public usefulness? I would argue that Douglass could embody this argument and become a "type" of his "countrymen" because he also assumed the privilege that Garrison procured through his connection to *The Liberator*, which was to speak as if his editorial voice was that of a public. As such, Douglass's connection to the press organ created more than a public attribution for his editorial voice. It offered a way for the putative embodiment of the race to serve as an index of literate social intercourse among a free people. When the name of *The North Star* was changed to *Frederick Douglass's Paper*, his embodiment, not to not to mention his manhood, depended still more on the circulation of the newspaper among an informed readership who would recognize the value of his name. Douglass's investment in the institution of the colored newspaper in this sense yielded a form of embodiment that was based on the structure and extent of publicity, and the same can be said of his racial identity: insofar as he gave off the "assurance of a MAN," Douglass took advantage of the political and cultural associations of the press organ to stipulate the existence of a black public.

So closely was Douglass's racial identity tied to African American institutions of publicity that Douglass himself found a way to invest the colored newspaper with the corporeality of the male body. He accomplished this in his fund-raising initiative for *Frederick Douglass's Paper*: a copy of the gift book *Autographs for Freedom* with each new subscription. Within *Autographs for Freedom* was the novella *The Heroic Slave*, where one could find a description of the black male body that equaled or surpassed the acclamations given to Douglass as a orator. Like the author, "Madison was of manly form. Tall, symmetrical, round, and strong. In his movements he seemed to combine with the strength of a lion, a lion's elasticity. His torn sleeves disclosed arms like polished iron. His face was 'black, but comely'."[13] Far from embodying chthonic matter, the black body seems consumed by its figural representation, ready-made as a figural icon of the antislavery cause—and yet Douglass had no other intention for his visual representation of the heroic slave than that it might serve practically as an article of publicity and hasten the development of a public culture among Northern freemen. The same was true of his own appearance in the visual sphere of oratory: as a contemporary expression of the corporeal, Douglass's body would betray the freemen's material investment in the public discourse of republicanism and demonstrate the qualities of the "general body" that black participants in the antislavery struggle saw at work in the annual "colored conventions," in

the efforts of various improvement societies, and of course in the success of the "colored newspaper."[14]

Nevertheless, we should not expect the public attribution of
Douglass's body to provide an essentialist categorization for the black
public sphere that could substitute for an essentialist categorization
of the racial subject. On the contrary, African American institutions
of publicity engaged a heterogeneous community of freemen in a fluid
process of combining and recombining with white abolitionists and
with each other, often leaving their collective identity in the provisional
form entailed by their public debate. In racially segregated Boston, for
example, black activists willingly dissolved the General Massachusetts
Colored Association in 1833 to merge with the nascent New England
Anti-Slavery Society (the forerunner of the Massachusetts Anti-Slavery
Society); the newly combined movement promptly recruited black orators like Charles Lenox Remond and black readers for *The Liberator*. By
the end of the decade, Boston's freemen leaders were meeting publicly
to consider severing their relationship with the Massachusetts Anti-
Slavery Society, but among the most prominent advocates of Garrison
and *The Liberator* was William C. Nell, a printer and organizer who had
worked for both Garrison's and Douglass's press organs.[15] The republican traditions extant in antebellum print culture, in conjunction with
the libertarian politics of the abolition movement, provided a genuinely
biracial, unstable ground for articulating a public identity that we can
associate with "black publicness."

According to Houston Baker, the black public sphere can be distinguished from a homogeneous community of subjects and the nostalgic connotations of the liberal public sphere by its facility for spelling out
contradictions, inviting comparisons, and recombining discordant cultural elements into "performative articulations of a public."[16] Taking up
the discursive model of "subaltern counter-publics" from Nancy Fraser,
Baker describes the public sphere as a zone of conflict that perversely
enables the constitution of racial identity, which is also in keeping with
the categorization of a counterpublic as "counter-concept" or a "category of negation" in the work of Negt and Kluge.[17] In her excursis on

"deterritorialized forms of publicity," Miriam Hansen has proposed that the promise of collective identity inherent in publicity is "grounded in a collective experience of marginalization and expropriation," so that the very boundary of the public can be said to change with these dynamic and, in some sense, hostile forces. As such, the counterpublic includes "difference and differentiation within its own borders," leading Hansen to conclude that a public in the destabilized form of public engagement incorporates "hegemonic efforts to suppress, fragment, delegitimate, or assimilate any [alternative] public formation."[18]

Together, Baker's and Hansen's arguments force us to look beyond personal conflicts between Garrison and Douglass and beyond the claim of the latter of an authentic racial identity.[19] The underlying conflict I want to set out from the beginning of this chapter is between a white male conception of the public sphere and the public sphere of disenfranchised free African Americans, who seem determined to acquire not just the civic benefits of republicanism but the symbolism of masculinity that underwrote them. There simply is no mistaking this regard— Garnet, Stewart, Walker, and McCune all made their claims on the collective possibility of black manhood—but there is also no mistaking the historical importance of artisanal republicanism to the self-determination of free black communities. Delany, for example, drew heavily on the tradition of freemasonry that had lionized Prince Hall, both father and son, as an embodiment of African American manhood; William Whipper, among the most effective organizers of the black public sphere, spoke before the 1835 National Convention of Colored Citizens of the need for "improving our general character, and embracing within our grasp the liberated slave for moral and mental culture." He was clear in saying that this mental culture originated in the "lucrative avocations, mechanic arts, and civil associations by which men acquire a knowledge of government" and that had been "suited only to the interest and use of a fairer complexion."[20] The republican culture of African American freemen was a zone of conflict that not only directed criticism against the enfranchised members of the "fairer complexion" but effectively made civic virtue into a matter of color. While this could not be mistaken as an essentialist basis for racial identity, it does suggest that color was something both less and more than skin deep in the racially charged politics of the antislavery struggle and that it would figure prominently in the most normative self-representation of a black people.

Douglass's own journey from abolitionist orator to editor of a freemen press organ suggests that he would contend simultaneously with the reality of color and the traditions of publicity that made it a such a politically potent signifier. We should note that he was led inexorably by his success as orator to the symbolism of the press organ, a reminder that the two phases of his career and the two institutions of his employ cannot be so easily separated. It was the white dominated Massachusetts Anti-Slavery Society, after all, that Douglass represented when he made his successful tour of Great Britain and conceived the need for a colored press. What is more, he devoted the press to both "the moral, social, religious, and intellectual elevation of a free colored people" and "the cause of liberty and progress," a cause that could be mistaken for Whipper's, Garrison's, or for that matter, Thomas Paine's.[21] For his speaking tour of Great Britain, he invoked the libertarian ideal of free social intercourse, which he adduced from the extent to which a "stranger" like him could "get fairly before the British public." Used to being told by Americans, "'We don't allow niggers in here,'" as he reported to readers of The Liberator, he enjoyed the full fruits of public life that were denied him in the United States. "On an equal footing with my white fellow citizens," he entered a more open English society that was fully conducive to the abolitionists' ideal of open discussion and debate.[22] Douglass was so moved by his success in "getting the question of slavery before the British public" that he resolved at the end of the tour to open American society to the discussion of slavery by circulating his opinions in a press organ. Once home, he embarked quickly on his journalistic enterprise, with his coeditor Delany serving as subscription agent/lecturer, just as he had formerly done for Garrison.

As we will see, Douglass never strayed far from the abolition movement's libertarian political agenda when he appeared to embody abolitionist principles on the platform and, in fact, projected the horizon of a black reading public from the immediacy of his physical appearance. While this might itself have symbolized his own seizure of the ideological prerogatives of republican manhood, it also reflected his determination to establish a public sphere on the basis of racial attributes that would otherwise disqualify him.[23] The epithet "nigger" was used principally as a bar on the black person's public life; the colored newspaper, on the other hand, was to be the passport of the black person to civic life in America. The operative categories of racial identity, in other words, were so deeply embedded in the self-definition of American public culture that Douglass's goal both in his oratory and in his journalism could only have been to convert the republican conditions of self-denial and self-abstraction into generic, perhaps even genetic racial characteristics that would manifest themselves publicly. The black public sphere in this sense resembled the "post-national" public body that Donald Pease has sought to deduce from the antimony between the disembodied category of the citizen and the subaltern category of the embodied subject. Democracy, Pease theorizes, is "recathected at the divide"—not as a resolution of real, racial contradiction or in the fiction of racial consensus but as an index of "permanent instability, an endless antagonism between figures integrated within ever changing social imaginaries and singularities forever external to them."[24]

How did African American institutions of publicity engender a category of racial identity that was synonymous with the embodied attributes of white manhood? Of course, Douglass was not the first to engage the republican ideal of citizenry for the benefit of the freemen community, but his efforts on behalf of *The North Star* helped to institutionalize the category of manhood as an arbiter of black progress and thus as a narrative trope of the Enlightenment. His strategy included embodying this category so that his own physical appearance could not be so easily distinguished from progress itself.

"The Race of Improvement"

When Douglass inaugurated *The North Star* in 1847 with a promise, "We shall stand in our paper as we have ever stood on the platform," he might not have known how closely the two enterprises would be inter-twined.[25] The new editor soon found out that he would be continuing the oratorical career that he began with the Massachusetts Anti-Slavery Society, touring the North as a subscription and publicity agent for the newspaper. What is more, the newspaper depended so much on its edi-tor's renown as an orator that what audiences, largely white audiences, saw was crucially related to what readers, specifically black readers, read. In their common perception of Douglass lay the real point of his enterprise.[26]

What did audiences see and readers read? In Douglass, they would have perceived a body and, in particular, a manly body. Garrison said famously that the appearance of the black orator on the platform "'gave the world assurance of a MAN,'" but the self-proclaimed "colored citi-zens of Boston" would not be outdone. When *Frederick Douglass's Paper* reported on Douglass's appearance before this group, it was said to be "anxious . . . to gaze upon [his] manly form."[27] The common assumption informing both his oratory and his journalism was that manhood needed to be demonstrated in and through public venues so that it might serve as a medium of civic identity for aspiring "colored citizens." As such, Douglass's enterprise depended not just on the slippage between the self-representation of African Americans and the republican ideal of the people but on the connection between the capacity for abstraction and the means of its embodiment.

In *My Bondage and My Freedom* Douglass stated that the purpose of publishing *The North Star* and the new focus of his antislavery enter-prise were to change the "low estimate . . . placed upon the negro, as a man" (237). He recognized chiefly the value of public appearances and of public opinion in raising this estimate and hoped that the success of *The North Star* would give all African Americans the quality of man-hood that observers inferred from his appearances on the platform. To this end, he committed the freemen communities of the North to appearing as he did, before a suspicious if not critical audience in pub-lic. Their character, like his own, would have to be manifested publicly, for the only way to remove the cause of prejudice and clear the way for emancipation was to demonstrate the involvement of the race in the public life of democracy.

With these criteria in mind, Douglass announced the publication of *The North Star* in December 1847 as the long-deferred entry of black people into the newspaper trade, the realm of free speech and public discussion where the manhood of the race finally would be established. The failure of Northern freemen to sustain a press organ had created such an insuperable obstacle to the presumption of equality that in his inaugural editorial he insisted, "Our race must be vindicated from the embarrassing imputations resulting from former non-successes." He emphasized the common predicament of the Northern freeman and the Southern slave—"We are one with you under the ban of prejudice and proscription—one with you under the slander of inferiority—one with you in social and political disenfranchisement"—while maintaining that only the emergence of a print culture within freemen communities could serve as a definitive demonstration of the true nature of the race and show black people as the equal to whites as they appeared in public. "In the grand struggle for liberty and equality now waging," Douglass concluded in his first editorial, "it is meet, right, and essential that there should arise in our ranks authors and editors, as well as orators."

With his plans for *The North Star*, Douglass sought to define inherent racial characteristics through and with the ideological symbolism of the press organ. In his second editorial, titled "Colored Newspapers," he reminded his readers that "facts are facts; white is not black, and black is not white" and advised his freemen readers to rise to the challenge. "The white man is superior to the black man," he wrote, "when he outstrips him in the race of improvement . . . we must take our stand side by side with our white fellow countrymen, in all the trades, arts, professions, and callings of the day."[28] For Douglass, racial characteristics were adjudged publicly, comparatively, and even competitively, reflecting his belief that the standard of political equality was inscribed on a scale that measured progress, or the lack thereof. In his introduction to the *Narrative of the Life of Frederick Douglass*, Garrison had sounded a comparatively racist note when he averred that the first-time orator "need[ed] nothing but a comparatively small amount of cultivation to make him an ornament to society and a blessing to his race,"[29] but Douglass seemed to agree that only such improvement, visible in the rise of editors, authors, and freemen newspapers, proved the fitness of the race.

With this conviction, Douglass seemed also to commit the position of freemen to a kind of racial science based on the comparison between avowedly civilized peoples and the manners and customs of nonwhite races. The standard of manhood that he developed through his apologias for *The North Star* was indeed derived from an Enlightenment ideology of human progress, but unlike his white predecessors in this field, Douglass would argue that the public life of democracy could dramatically change the standing of a race in this narrative of progress and that the institution of the press was a critical index of racial capabilities.[30] At the heart of this appeal was an egalitarian republicanism that stipulated an equal position and share for the artisan in the progress of the Enlightenment and that Whipper had invoked for the benefit of all black people. Just as Whipper had done at the 1835 colored convention, Douglass would see the promise of a "mental culture" realized in the work of artisans and specifically printers who would publish newspapers like his own. Interrupting his labor on behalf of *The North Star* to appear before the 1847 colored convention, he spoke as editor, printer, and most importantly as a republican advocate of learning when he declared, "this world is to be ruled, shaped, and guided by *the marvelous might of the mind.*"[31]

Until *The North Star* became a subscription newspaper of the Liberty Party, Douglass spoke as the taskmaster of the race who would spur its members in "the race of improvement" whether they wanted to be improved or not. In the startling editorial "What Are the Colored People Doing for Themselves," written in the middle of 1848, Douglass looked for and failed to find the signs of "manly self-reliance" in the freemen community, which had fallen victim to a "lazy, mean, and cowardly spirit." With an explicit comparison to European revolutions, he lamented the fact that while the "oppressed of the old world are ...

holding public meetings, putting forth addresses, passing resolutions, and in various other ways making their wishes known to the world," freemen were wasting time and money on "the weak and glittering follies of odd-fellowship and free masonry." These fraternal organizations, Douglass believed, constituted a false measure of manhood, for they did not present their public appearances as occasions and sites of democratic progress, and that was why white American enjoyed them: "The same persons who would puff such demonstrations in the newspapers, would mob us if we met to adopt measures for obtaining our just rights."[32]

Of course, Martin Delany and many of the most committed freemen leaders in Northern cities would not have been amused by Douglass's dismissal, especially since black Freemasonry had generated its own version of black republican manhood.[33] However, he was so determined to shift this designation to stipulate the education and development of black readers that he presented the success of *The North Star* as its only possible evidence. In "What Are the Colored People Doing for Themselves," he advised freemen to forsake the love of Masonic ceremony and even the comfort in the Christian religion in order to move themselves toward the goal of enlightenment. "Get wisdom—get understanding," he insisted and implied that the great Bethel Church of Philadelphia would provide true service to the cause only if "the pulpit would but speak the right word—the word for progress—the word for mental culture—[and] encourage reading." He concluded his editorial with a vision of racial elevation informed by the most progressive image of "mental culture" and the materiality of the body: "We may read and understand—we may speak and write—we may expose our wrongs ... we may at last wring from a reluctant public the all-important confession that we are men."

If only they would read *The North Star*, Douglass argued, freemen could appear in public as men. Unfortunately, that quality seemed to be reserved for "the two thousand [who] can be supposed to take any special interest in measures for our own elevation; and probably fifteen hundred [who] take, read and pay for an anti-slavery paper." In the same blistering editorial, he feared that the paucity of black newspaper subscribers would depress the estimate of the race in "the race of improvement":

> Unless we, the colored people of America, shall act about the work of our own regeneration and improvement, we are doomed to drag on in our present miserable and degraded condition for ages. Would that we could speak to every colored man, women and child in the land, and, with the help of Heaven, we would thunder into their ears their duties and responsibilities, until a spirit should be roused among them, never to be lulled till the last chain is broken.—But here we are mortified to think that we are now speaking to tens where would ought to speak to thousands.

The increased circulation of *The North Star*, Douglass implied, would demonstrate the racial characteristics of freemen in a way suited at once to the progress of the Enlightenment and to the entitlements of manhood. Manhood, after all, was the signal property of a reading public.

Douglass's jeremiad in "What Are the Colored People Doing for Themselves" had many precedents in African American antebellum culture. Maria Stewart's career was ended effectively by her derision of the manhood of the race, while Henry Highland Garnet broke into national prominence with an inflammatory appeal to slave rebellion based largely on the prerogatives of men.[34] In an 1848 address titled "The Slaves' Right to Revolt," Douglass showed that he was just as willing to warn white audiences of the mistake of misjudging the manhood of slaves:

> We are frequently taunted with cowardice for being slaves and for enduring such indignities and sufferings. The taunt comes with ill grace from you. You stand eighteen millions strong, united, educated, armed, ready to put us down; we are weak, ignorant, degraded, unarmed and three millions . . . I know how you will reply to this; you will say that I, and such as I are not *men*; you look upon us as beneath you; you look upon as naturally and necessarily degraded. But nevertheless we are MEN! You may pile up statutes against our manhood as high as heaven and still we are not changed thereby. WE ARE MEN.[35]

However, Douglass's attention to education and to its obverse, ignorance and degradation, testifies to his special, vested interest in black
manhood. Slave resistance seemed for him to follow closely from elevation and cultivation, the attributes of the Northern freemen communities who subscribed to *The North Star.*

Douglass's model in this regard was David Walker, who issued his
Appeal to the Colored Citizens of the World in 1829, nearly twenty years earlier. Although the *Appeal* was swiftly branded as "incendiary literature"
for its anticipated effect on the enslaved, its riveting question—"I ask
you, are we MEN?"[36]—showed it and Walker to be a product of a Boston
freemen culture that nourished not only vigorous institutions of publicity and occasions for public reading but an ideal of manhood rooted
in the ideal of "mental culture."[37] As such, much of the *Appeal* and his
speeches to the General Massachusetts Colored Association (of which
he was a founding member) were filled with arguments for the education,
cultivation, and elevation that freemen organizations and press organs
would provide. The *Appeal* concluded with the reminder, "You have to
prove to the Americans and to the world, that we are MEN, and not
brutes, as we have been represented, and by millions treated. Remember, to let the aim of your labors among your brethren and particularly
the youths, to be the dissemination of education and religion."[38] In the
hopes that black people might develop a literate self-awareness, he
charged his readers, *"go to work and enlighten your brethren."*[39]

As the Boston agent for *Freedom's Journal*, a New York–based press
organ that served as the unofficial anticolonizationist organ of the
freemen community, Walker was among the advocates of freemen newspapers who considered the development of "mental culture" to qualify
the members of the African race not only as enlightened but as men.
Writing in the first issue of *Freedom's Journal*, the editor Samuel Cornish
called forth an obsolete image of impartial newspaper readers when he
proclaimed his intention to "come boldly before an enlightened public"
and to correct the "misrepresentations" of free black people. While
acknowledging that "ignorance, poverty, and degradation has been our
lot," Cornish saw inevitable improvement in the condition of the race
in the progress of learning among a nascent reading public. Deploying

the most expansive language of the Enlightenment, *Freedom's Journal* proclaimed that "knowledge and civilization are shedding their enlivening rays over the rest of the human family," of which the black readers of the newspaper would soon be part.[40] *The Colored American*, publishing in the late 1830s, likewise offered itself as a "channel of communication for the interchange of thought . . . through which light and knowledge may flow to instruct, enliven, and fertilize all."[41]

Douglass's *North Star* should be included in this tradition of the colored newspaper, which perpetuated a narrative of Enlightenment progress in order to describe the inherent yet still latent qualities of the African race. In an 1848 speech, still filled with the optimism of his new venture, he foresaw the ascension of an African American reading public as a signature event of modernity: "The prospects are already brightening, the energies of all true hearts are with them in this struggle; improvements are visible in several northern states; colored men and women are becoming *readers* and *thinkers*."[42] As his enterprise foundered, however, he realized that colored men and women were not becoming enlightened in numbers sufficient to sustain *The North Star*. In 1849, the second year of *The North Star*, Douglass enlisted his readers in a subscription drive to do battle against the colonizationist movement and its sympathizers within the African American community. Colonization, he argued, was a retrograde, defeatist position that acknowledged the "distinct and peculiar condition" of the race, and so he exhorted his readers, "Let us keep pace with the wheels of American civilization, as the best means within our reach to prevent us from being crushed by it." More tangibly, he reminded them, "We have three newspaper in the hands of our own people. . . . Let us sustain our press, and keep our men in the field whose voices are never uplifted in our cause in vain."[43] By the end of 1849, there was no doubt that for Douglass the various positions on abolition, elevation, and colonization devolved on the representation of the African race and that its racial characteristics in turn devolved on the state of his newspaper.[44]

Douglass's investment in *The North Star*, the medium of enlightenment for "readers and thinkers," thus became a kind of racial science that sought to decide conclusively questions of fitness and of the capacity for self-perfection. Of course, Douglass deferred from measuring individual bodies, as practitioners of anthropometry would have done. On the other hand, he did entertain speculation on the ethnology of the race in a way that was compatible with the human sciences of the day. He schooled himself in the field for an important address titled "The Claims of the Negro Ethnologically Considered," in which he sought to affirm the common origin of humankind. The more "elementary claim," he admitted, "respects the manhood of the negro." Using the category at once as a synonym for humanity and of distinctively masculine achievement, Douglass attempted to describe "what constitutes a man" in a way favorable to the "humanity of the negro." The black man's "faculties and powers" were "uneducated and unimproved" but only when contrasted with "those of the highest cultivation," white men such as Clay, Webster, and Calhoun. By their standard, most white men would fail the test. With proportionate "cultivation," or with the right amount of "elevation," as Douglass had demanded from his readers, the freeman would be deemed to be just as manly, though he emphasized that "considering him possessing knowledge, or needing knowledge, his elevation or his degradation, his virtues, or his vices— . . . the negro is a man."[45]

Douglass's foray into ethnology did not take him far from the ideology of human self-perfection he adopted from the Enlightenment, which declaimed the manhood of the race in proportion to its rational faculties, its capacity for education, and the development of its "mental culture." As such, he transformed the category of black manhood from an object of scientific or biological study into an attribute of freemen public culture, realized in the existence of "readers and thinkers." And yet when we consider the importance of Douglass's own "manly form" to the freemen of Boston, we should also acknowledge that he was not averse to rendering the progress of modernity in embodied, gendered terms, or to proving the public attributes of freemen by seeming to fathom their innate racial qualities. We cannot disavow, in other words, the tendency to reembody the freemen's public identity according to the particularity of manhood and the essentialism of their race, which is why Douglass's body proved to be as necessary as *The North Star* to the freemen cause. "Black is not white," he had told his prospective readers, and he would not allow the representation of a reading public to be without color or to escape its racial embodiment. On the contrary, he saw in the colored newspaper something like the racial essence that exponents of racial morphology might deduce from the body.

Black Garrisonism

Why did Douglass return his political enterprise to the particularity of his body, relinquishing what Lauren Berlant has called the "privilege of abstraction" for the tortured, pseudoscientific task of adducing the manhood of the African race?[46] The short answer is that he wanted to prove that the promise of modernity belonged so nearly to the "persons of the despised race" that it could be considered an inherent racial endowment. From the inauguration of *The North Star*, Douglass had insisted that freemen would have to demonstrate their progress toward the ideal of "mental culture" in order to manifest their innate capacities. In the 1855 address "These Questions Cannot Be Answered by the White Race," he went on to define "certain duties, peculiarly the duties of the colored people" in a way that made the universal goal of enlightenment peculiar both to race and gender:

> Are they like other men? That's the question. Have they within themselves—enfolded within their organization, within their own brain—those germs of civilization, exalted character supposed to be within the reach of other men? These are questions being asked us as a colored race, by the world. It is asked us ... Can he rise from degradation to respectability, from ignorance to intelligence, from isolation to society ... from savagism and unrestrained life to a well-devised and well-organized civil government? The answer to these questions cannot be answered by the white race.[47]

On the one hand, Douglass's question endorsed both the Enlightenment ideal of universal humanity and the progressive narrative of modernity. On the other hand, a narrative of phylogenesis lurked within this human ontogenesis in the form of a distinctive, or peculiar, duty imposed on the members of a distinctive, or peculiar, race. Could they prove themselves? Could the so-called germs of civilization be found "within their . . . brain"? Seemingly for the benefit of "colored people," he rephrased the promise of Enlightenment, the abstraction of all particularities into a rational, universalized humanity, in biological terms.

Douglass pursued this political project through his connection with *The North Star*, his chosen medium for the reembodiment of citizenship and rationality. However, neither he nor his partner Delany could deny that the most public demonstration of black manhood needed the assistance of white abolitionists, or as Douglass said, "liberal donations from our and the slave's friends."[48] In an 1849 editorial, Delany was even more sanguine:

> Were there white subscribers sufficient . . . [for] this or any other paper, conducted by colored men, devoted to the elevation of their race, that would not reach the object aimed at, because the colored people themselves would still be deprived of its benefits, and occupying the same nonentical in different position, having others to think, act, read, and do for them.[49]

Delany believed that it was "morally impossible" for *The North Star* to become self-sustaining and hoped to elicit a permanent endowment from other thriving African American institutions. Douglass differed, holding fast to the belief that only the autonomy of a colored newspaper could allow black people to demonstrate "the germs of civilization" and "exalted character." These were the inherent endowments of the black race, he insisted, and unlike Delany, he confined himself to the ideology of the public sphere as the sphere in which racial properties were manifested.

The reason for Douglass's optimism was as peculiar as his self-declared cause: Garrison had already done exactly what he hoped his newspaper would accomplish, and with the support of black readers. They had made *The Liberator* nearly self-sustaining, particularly in its critical, most successful early years. The reading public that Douglass used to demonstrate the fitness of the race, in other words, already existed—but through the medium of a white-owned institution and the freedom of a white man's voice. Nothing could vindicate, and at the same time upset, his project for enlightenment and racial elevation more than this fact, the attachment of freemen readers to *The Liberator*. It spurred Douglass to present *The North Star* as the equivalent of a racial essence, a "colored" newspaper in almost essential form. This object in turn forced him to do anything to ensure the survival of *The North Star*, and that included, oddly enough, making the black press into a press organ for a white political party.

What made a newspaper "colored"? Although Douglass solicited black readers with what he thought was a simple fact—"white is not black; black is not white"—the facts were not so black and white. *The Liberator* proved that a newspaper could enjoy the favor of black readers, advance the agenda of a largely white organization, agitate on behalf of freemen and the enslaved, answer to the directives of a single white man, and still be recognized as colored. Douglass knew this possibility full well, for he proudly counted himself as one of those readers in the *Narrative of the Life of Frederick Douglass*. As he recorded in his first auto-biography, he discovered the cause of antislavery when he discovered *The Liberator*, from which he "got a pretty correct idea of the principles, measures, and spirit of the antislavery reform." More importantly, he seemed to "get" the critical role of the printed medium in disclaiming Garrison's editorial identity and thereby adumbrating the public identity of the abolition movement. In keeping with the self-image of the New England abolition movement, he deferred from naming Garrison as the editor and instead denominated *The Liberator* with an impersonal pronoun reserved for the working of democracy: "Its sympathy for my brethren in bonds—its scathing denunciations of slaveholders—its faithful exposures of slavery . . . sent a thrill of joy through my soul, such as I had never felt before."[50] Here was the disembodied agency of the press organ, articulated in accord with the condition for Garrisonism: that a reader could separate Garrison himself from the editorial voice of the newspaper, identify that voice with the disinterested principles of the abolition movement, and see the agency of liberty in their publication.

Douglass wrote the *Narrative* while serving as a subscription agent for *The Liberator*, which may explain his willingness to perpetuate the premise of Garrisonism. But in *My Bondage and My Freedom*, his former method of textual attribution was reversed so that Garrison's influence was duly noted. "His words were few, full of holy fire, and straight to the point," Douglass wrote, with deliberate attention to the editor's personal writing style, before making a suitably personal confession: "Learning to love him, through his paper, I was prepared to be pleased with his presence."[51] The credibility of Garrisonism thus would be reduced in proportion to the prominence of "his presence." On the other hand, *The North Star*, now called *Frederick Douglass's Paper*, was presented as the more suitable expression of antislavery principles. Whereas he had concluded his first autobiography with his discovery of *The Liberator*, he used the conclusion to *My Bondage and My Freedom* to describe his new ambition: to "disprove [African Americans'] alleged inferiority" with a "tolerably well conducted press, in the hands of the persons of the despised race."[52] His reference to the popular prejudice and scientific judgment of racial inferiority accorded with his interest in determining the essence of the race by *Frederick Douglass's Paper*, which is why he was intent on making the words and sentiments of *The Liberator* peculiar to Garrison. He hoped freemen would take a similar interest in the attribution of racial traits and read a newspaper peculiar to their own color and condition.

Many freemen did revere Garrison in personal terms; others resented him with equal intensity. Nonetheless, Douglass found it difficult to make his case against their misplaced "hero-worship" to which he pleaded guilty in *My Bondage and My Freedom* because, quite simply, there was something to Garrisonism, or to the assumption that a press organ could abstract a voice, a movement, a community, and indeed, a person from the particularities of their situation and render them as a free people. This assumption held true especially among free black communities of the North, for "colored" newspapers such as *Rights of All* and

Freedom's Journal had already synthesized the properties of the race with the political traditions and historical associations of eighteenth-century print culture. Douglass thus found it quite difficult to dislodge freemen from their attachment to Garrisonism and, more particularly, to *The Liberator.* Black readers identified their common cause, their common purpose, and even their common endowments in the same way that abolitionists detected the progress of democracy or the presence of a revolutionary people—that is, by inferring the disembodied, public agency of a press organ. The racial identity that freemen cultivated through their colored newspapers in fact shared many of the properties of Garrisonism, particularly in the overdetermination of the printed medium.

Garrison knew well the importance of the press organ to political interests and racial consciousness of freemen, for he gained the inspiration for his own antislavery enterprise from the tradition of colored newspaper, which included *Freedom's Journal* and the short-lived *Rights of All.* Deprived of any standing among Boston's Protestant reform establishment, he saw not only an untapped subscriber base but a libertarian tradition of critical, public dissent, both of which he might tap for the benefit of *The Liberator.* In doing so, he established Garrisonism as a public medium especially suited to the self-recognition of a black reading public. In the first issue of *The Liberator,* he included an open letter to "our free colored brethren," promising them that "your moral and intellectual elevation, the advancement of your rights, and the defense of your character will be a leading object of our paper."[53] Garrison thereafter would create a public signification of his abolition movement by retaining the attributes that a colored newspaper would bestow on its readers. In keeping with Cornish's and Walker's aims, he christened *The Liberator* by interpellating a freemen public—it is "their organ," Garrison claimed—and then exulted as the support of black readers made the newspaper self-sustaining, free from patronage. By 1834 he announced proudly that three quarters of the subscribers to *The Liberator* were black and, moreover, that he had nothing to do with its success. The discursive condition for Garrisonism—the self-denial of Garrison's authorial presence and its association with the historical image of a disinterested citizenry—had been met with the patronage of African American readers.

With the early success of *The Liberator*, the egalitarian republican tradition of freemen improvement societies and press organs also passed into Garrison's hands, or at least to organizations such as the Juvenile Garrison Independence Society. Under its auspices, young black men were taught mechanical arts and knowledge in accordance with the cherished freemen principle of self-improvement. In his 1835 speech to a colored convention, Whipper had said that it was imperative "to train the undisciplined youth in moral pursuits" so as "to impress on our people everywhere that in moral elevation true happiness consists," but throughout the 1830s the political project of Northern freemen was so closely related to the objectives and institutions of Garrisonism that it might be said to have served as the medium of racial identity, if not of black manhood. Garrisonism indeed could be considered "colored" to the extent that it constituted a whole set of public institutions and the attendant promise of civic participation, both of which were synonymous with Garrison's name.

In his notable 1831 "Address Delivered Before the Free People of Color," Garrison sought to develop not just a subscriber base for *The Liberator* but the republican institutions of "mental culture" among aspiring black printers. "Multiply periodicals among yourselves, to be conducted by men of your own color. The cause of emancipation demands at least 100 presses." Expanding his vision of limitless publicity to include the republican education of aspiring artisans, he advised, "Put your children to the trades; no master mechanic will [lack] colored with education."[54] In Garrison's appeal toward the egalitarian republicanism of the printing trade, the black audience would have recognized both the promise of the colored newspaper and the editorial voice of *The Liberator*, though still the advice must have stung. It had long been a subject of editorials in the black press that progress in this direction was inhibited by the "mean and shameful associations of white mechanics who refuse to work in the same shops" with "a colored man . . . [of] more than ordinary virtue and talent."[55]

For their part, African American patrons like James Forten gave Garrison's project its early seed money as well as his personal seal of approval: "May the 'Liberator' be the means . . . of raising up friends to the oppressed People of Color." Moreover, Forten encouraged Garrison to continue the virulent anticolonizationist editorials that were making the unknown abolitionist editor infamous among the North's Protestant reform establishment. "If the popular feeling [for colonization] was not so much in [the colonizationists'] favor," he assured Garrison, "your work would obtain a much greater circulation."[56] For his conversion from colonization to immediate abolition, the veritable first principle of Garrisonism, Garrison was also in debt to William Watkins, an African American minister from Baltimore, who convinced the aspiring editor to use *The Liberator* as an anticolonizationist organ in the tradition of the colored newspaper. No doubt recognizing a way to establish the patriotism, civic-mindedness, and civility of black people, Watkins paid lavish tribute to the Garrison's fledgling enterprise in a letter to the editor. "We recognize in *The Liberator*," he wrote in 1831, "the friend of bleeding humanity, the faithful representatives of our sentiments and interests, our uncompromising advocate of our . . . rights." In a gesture equally helpful to the republican pretensions of the New England abolition movement, he called the founding of the newspaper a "disinterested and generous undertaking" that could bring no favor to Garrison himself but that established the public-spiritedness, the public signification of Garrisonism at the very moment of its inception.[57] With Watkins's and Forten's endorsement, the editorial voice of *The Liberator* could speak as the disembodied voice of a reading public that also happened to fit perfectly the self-representation of the Northern freemen community.

This was unfortunate for Douglass, for it showed that both the colored newspaper and its attendant public body had a common, biracial heritage. They were the common property of both black and white abolitionists, which made it difficult, if not impossible to reconcile the essence of the race with the existence of a black reading public. In addressing the race as "readers and thinkers," Douglass thus could only be imitating the provisions of Garrisonism. So his only hope was that

Garrisonism would also be recognized as an imitation of the freemen's political agenda.[58] Some black abolitionists did just this—attempt to reestablish the lineage of the abolition movement so that they, rather than Garrison, appeared as its progenitors. In 1837 one Charles Gardner delivered an address in New York in which he regretted that Garrison had been "branded as the individual who turned the people of color against the colonization scheme."[59] The anticolonization movement, along with its public meetings, Gardner claimed, had been conceived by "people of color" when Garrison "was a schoolboy." More organized opposition to Garrisonism arose in 1839, when Garrison's espousal of nonresistance, the controversial strategy of political inaction, began to antagonize his freemen supporters as an insult to their republican manhood.[60] In the same year, "A Colored Man" published a letter in the newly formed *Massachusetts Abolitionist* that condemned Garrison for his betrayal of freemen interests and for his ambition to represent them. A public meeting of freemen in Boston's First Independent Baptist Church was necessary to affirm black support for *The Liberator* and to condemn the letter as "slander" and "wholesale falsehood."[61] By the end of the 1830s, Garrison was being assailed by several African American would-be publishers who found the marketplace for a black press in Boston controlled by him and his partisans.[62]

Douglass was a late entrant in this debate. Perhaps because *The Liberator* had descended from the tradition of the colored newspaper, he acknowledged its example and attempted to tread lightly in his departure from its principles. Even after he announced his commitment to the Liberty Party at the 1851 American Anti-Slavery Society convention, he continued to finesse fundamental differences on the issue of political antislavery movements, to provide publicity for the Massachusetts Anti-Slavery Society and the national society, and to extol *The Liberator* as the model for *Frederick Douglass's Paper.* As late as 1853, he lionized Garrison as the "veteran Editor" and acknowledged his former mentor's "noble example of truth, fairness, and fidelity" as impetus for his own efforts. After acclaiming *The Liberator* as "the pioneer sheet of our beneficent enterprise," Douglass went so far as to admit, "Differing from *The Liberator* as to the duty of voting, we desire nevertheless to imitate it, according to the measure of our ability."[63] But by the end of 1853, he could not contain his distaste for Garrisonism and attempted to render the ideal of black manhood in a way that no printer or editor had attempted. That is, he would denominate freemen by the particularity of their race and of their gender and forgo the disinterested, civic identity that the colored newspaper historically provided black readers. The trouble with Douglass's plan was that it still used and depended on the colored newspaper.

Although scholars typically regard the bitter schism between Garrison and Douglass in 1853 as the inevitable result of deeply held personal resentments or as the battle of two outsized egos, their battle can be understood in more contemporary terms as a publicity war between two rivals in the newspaper trade in which libels and personal depredations were the accepted means of attack. At stake for the combatants was the favor of a reading public and in particular of a black reading public, for both Garrison and Douglass had conceived their journalistic missions in the image of a colored newspaper. As veteran publicists, they did not consider any other locus or medium for racial identity; their common investment in the freemen tradition of libertarian politics had made their respective press organs synonymous at once with the spread of liberty and the capabilities of the race. Yet their fierce publicity war begs a critical question: could either newspaper have embodied a free colored people in accordance with this tradition? *The Liberator* had long enjoyed the support of black subscribers, but many black leaders such as Douglass were forsaking Garrisonism as the domain of white abolitionists. Douglass's press organs, on the other hand, had never gained the wholehearted support of black subscribers and survived only as the subsidized organ of the Liberty Party. Douglass and Garrison, in other words, were waging what Gramsci would call a war of position to establish the collective, or public, identity of the race.

The indeterminacy of that identity is suggested by the difficulty Douglass encountered in proving that *Frederick Douglass's Paper* was a colored newspaper. Since the second editorial of *The North Star*, he had invoked the "facts" of race on behalf of the newspaper, but as he departed publicly from the principles of Garrisonism, Garrison's partisans called his enterprise superfluous, fraudulent, even immoral. The editorial board of the *Pennsylvania Freemen* upbraided Douglass for his aspirations on behalf of *Frederick Douglass's Paper*:

> We think the facts indicate that Mr. Douglass was ambitious to become the exponent of the wrongs and demands of the colored people of this country, that he expected the Anti-Slavery sentiment to converge to his paper, the Anti-Slavery patronage to widen its circulation and increase its profits, that the eyes not only of America but of England and the world should be turned to him as the representative of the mighty movement which is convulsing this nation.[64]

In the midst of this publicity war, Douglass was often castigated for his "base ambition" and "ingratitude," character flaws that referred not so much to a personal deficiency but to *Frederick Douglass's Paper*. For Garrison's black and white partisans, Douglass's fault lay in his association with the colored newspaper, whose existence betrayed his ambition, his ingratitude, and ultimately, the *Freemen* contended, a defective "mental condition":

> If money has lifted the shackles from his limbs, their impress may linger on his spirit: if the lines of the lash have healed upon the back, its degrading influence may have penetrated his soul: if he has escaped the bondage of others, he may continue in frightful servitude to self. . . . He may be representative of the evils of slavery in the most fearful sense; for he may not only represent the manhood it degrades, but the degradation . . . the avarice it engenders, the love of dominion, the fierce impatience of opposition, the suspicion of motives, the jealousy of superiors, the interpretation of the highest thoughts through the lowest faculties.

Frederick Douglass's Paper thus attested to the degradation of the race, not to its elevation. In insisting that it represented "'the only newspaper devoted to the interests of the colored people,'" Douglass had wed the newspaper to the standard of black manhood he embodied, such that as that manhood was derogated, there was no reason for it to exist. Besides, the *Freemen* sniffed, "We had thought the Liberator devoted to 'the interests of the colored people.'"

Exactly. Douglass grasped the import of the harshest personal criticism against his manhood and realized that he incarnated the inferiority of the race so that *The Liberator* might have a clear field. In his exhaustive defense, "A Review of Anti-Slavery Relations," published in January 1854, he ruefully noted that his character had been good enough for white abolitionists until it became expedient to crush *Frederick Douglass's Paper*. Their interests, he warned, would be advanced by his "consenting to leave the field, giving up my mission in the world, abandoning my paper, flinging down my pen, shunning the platform."[65] The nominal cause for this public outcry was Douglass's refusal to deny the resurgent charge of infidelity that had been brought against several prominent abolitionists. He also alluded to his unexpected announcement of his political antislavery position at the 1851 American Anti-Slavery Society meeting, which he believed was still held against him. But for Douglass, no allegation against him, not even that definitive statement of an opposing principle, could obscure the true motivation of his enemies. In the "Review of Anti-Slavery Relations," he recalled that he had made his 1851 announcement while the society was drawing up its list of preferred newspapers, and from that moment his colored newspaper was "flung back upon me like falling leaves in autumn," taken off the preferred list, and starved of the abolition movement's institutional support. The relative fitness of Douglass's character and the "mental condition" of the race in this sense devolved on the competition for subscribers, specifically black subscribers, who were historically the original and most stalwart supporters of *The Liberator*.

In order to make a countervailing claim to a black reading public, Douglass had to expose *The Liberator* and Garrisonism as essentially white. For this purpose, he traveled into the very heart of Garrison's black subscriber base in August of 1853 to recommend *Frederick Douglass's Paper* to perhaps the most loyal subscribers to the rival newspaper. Douglass's appearance before the leading freemen of Boston set off a bitter exchange with William C. Nell, who was renowned in the New England reform community for having been hired by Garrison as a printer's apprentice over the objectives of the city's white artisans and as founder of the Massachusetts General Colored Association.[66] The author of *Colored Patriots of the American Revolution*, Nell foresaw the integration of the races on the grounds of equal citizenship, but to Douglass he was a "contemptible tool" for reminding his audience of Douglass's part in the recent infidelity controversy. Called to do a "'disagreeable duty'" on behalf of Garrisonism, Nell had become, in Douglass's words, one of the "practical enemies of the colored people" who "would, doubtless, be very happy to see my paper destroyed."[67]

For Douglass, who stood to inherit the black subscribers to *The Liberator*, the task was to sustain the public discourse that Garrisonism had established in Boston's African American community while separating Garrisonism from Garrison. He would do so by reminding his readers that Garrison was just a man, "grossly abused by his sycophantic followers," and, more importantly, a white man. Writing in "A Review of Anti-Slavery Relations," he would attempt to defy the transracial discourse of the New England abolition movement as well as the colored attributes of *The Liberator*:

> Abolitionism does not change the color of skin, so that while theoretically and abstractly, the cause of antislavery is the cause of universal man, it is practically and peculiarly the cause of the colored man—and any attempt ... on the part of Mr. Garrison ... to lift this holy cause into a sublimity, beyond the comprehension of the colored men, as a class, deserves to be branded by every colored man with the reprobation due to so stupendous an insult.

Here was a definitive blow to the colored properties of Garrisonism, the principle one being the public attribution of freemen. In theory, Douglass acknowledged, the cause of the freeborn and enslaved African

American was that of "universal man," but in the interest of *Frederick Douglass's Paper*, he was willing to destroy his constituency's pretensions of abstract citizenship and speak to them "peculiarly," or as "a class." In attempting to save the colored newspaper from its white editorial voice, he thus altered the promise of a public that had been lodged the image of the colored newspaper. The latter demonstrated the essential properties of the race that were all the more human for being, as he would say in his speech the next year, "ethnologically considered."

Douglass's attempt to introduce the fact or essence of color into the racially intertwined tradition of print culture would take him far from his original objective in printing *The North Star*, which had been to document the progress of the race with the growth of a reading public. As the newspaper became beholden to Gerritt Smith, answerable to the Liberty Party, and disconnected from the black subscriber base already claimed by *The Liberator*, he no longer could claim or pretend that the attributes of the colored newspaper belonged to black people at all. Instead, Douglass found the traits of the race in the fact of the colored newspaper, or in its sheer existence, which is why he was so eager and willing to use an engagement with the patronage system of subscription newspapers to save his journalistic enterprise. A newspaper such as *Frederick Douglass's Paper* was colored in the only sense that mattered. It embodied the properties of the race in itself and circulated them among an already organized readership that recognized on principle the capacity for active citizenship in African Americans. On the strength of this recognition, Douglass was able to present his eponymously named newspaper as the herald of what black people could become, the harbinger of a more permanent apparatus for the representation of his race on the order of the electoral system and military service. We might well measure the standing of the colored newspaper under Liberty Party patronage by the contemporary appeal of these exclusively male institutions to the freemen cause, especially since they perpetuated the masculine denomination that had inhered historically within the ideal of a black public.[68]

Douglass's dependence on the colored newspaper as both essence and symbol of color is one reason we return to his body more convinced than ever that its racial and masculine properties corresponded to the institution of the press organ. Douglass's determination to prove the "manly self-reliance" of the race with the success of *The North Star* and *Frederick Douglass's Paper* ended up giving the newspaper itself the attributes of color and manhood that his body was said to possess inherently. Print, in other words, had become an essential property in the manner of corporeality and designated the particularity of the race to the same degree. The republican associations of the colored newspaper in turn became dependent on their particular embodiment, and for this the freemen cause seemed to depend more than ever on the physical presence of the black man.

Physical Education

The difficulty Douglass had in attracting black subscribers for *Frederick Douglass's Paper*, combined with the appeal of his "manly form" among his Boston audience, indicates a subtle but unmistakable "structural transformation" of the freemen public sphere. The print-mediated republicanism of the 1820s and '30s seemed to pave the way for a corporeal designation of racial identity that, in the manner of the former tradition, identified reflexively the capacity for progress, improvement, and "mental culture" with the masculine qualities of the race. Of course, Douglass continued to present the colored newspaper as the crucial measure for determining them both, but he can be said to have played a part in this transformation precisely in failing, or refusing, to distinguish the attributes of black manhood that had been lodged in the press organ from their incarnation in the black male body. In doing so, the black editor would be forgoing the promise of disembodiment that Garrison, with the help of black subscribers, had realized in the editorial voice of *The Liberator*. However, Douglass's determination to lend his newspaper the essential attributes of the race led him to abandon the unsupportable pretense of abstraction and to offer the corporeality of the black male as a fittingly "peculiar" medium for the representation of a black reading public.

Shortly after the abortive trip to Boston, Douglass betrayed his determination to use the mediation of this "manly form" when he announced a "Liberal Offer to Subscribers." The stated goal of the offer was "to extend the circulation of our paper and to make . . . a better and more serviceable journal and advocate of the rights of humanity than ever before,"[69] but he implied also that its survival depended on placing the novella *The Heroic Slave* and, by extension, the hyperbolic representation of Madison Washington before the readers of the colored newspaper. Circulated in the manner and spirit of a press organ, Douglass intended his depiction to perform exactly the same task as the colored newspaper, which was to educate, improve, and enlighten a public. Readers would gape at "arms like polished iron," but they would also learn what a white victim of Washington's shipboard mutiny had to acknowledge:

> I confess gentlemen, I felt myself in the presence of a superior man; one who, had he been a white man, I would have followed willingly and gladly in any honorable enterprise. Our difference of color was the only ground for difference of action. It was not that his principles were wrong in the abstract; for they are the principles of 1776. But I could not bring myself to recognize their application to one whom I deemed my inferior. (163)

The abstract principles of the republic, Douglass would remind his less recalcitrant readers, did not remain intact despite their embodiment in the embruted slave. The heroism of Washington, coupled with the civic associations of his name, argued that the fulfillment of America's revolutionary legacy required nothing less than the "application" of the lessons of 1776 to the particular form of the black man.

If Douglass's description of Madison Washington imparted a didactic quality to the body of the heroic slave, then it also imitated the conventions of public art, which converted the putatively inert corporeality of the enslaved into a medium of civic pedagogy. As the art historian Michael Hutt has argued, the sculptural depictions of the seminude black male body belonged to a republican project of education and discipline that survived well into the postbellum era. The daunting form of the heroic slave rising from his chains, Hutt argues, communicated effectively the compressed force, the action in reserve, and, perhaps most importantly, the self-control that republicanism prized not only as a sign of manhood but as the effective guarantees of the public good.[70] As in *The Heroic Slave*, the statuesque body of the slave upheld nothing less than a republican tradition of citizenship, though we should note that the "application" of the "principles of 1776" to those who were considered chattel once again stipulated a corporeal representation of black manhood.

While this condition can be said to have been complicit with the ideological restrictions that kept African American men from entering the sphere of abstract citizenship and that denied African American women any civic representation at all, it also drew so nearly on republican standards of self-representation that it could not help but reproduce the normative identity of the citizen. The physicality of a Madison Washington or a Frederick Douglass indeed could be called uncanny representations of citizenship, especially when we consider that underwriting the didacticism of the slave's body was an educational regimen of civic republicanism that provided for the perfection of the body. From the example of the abolitionist and doctor Benjamin Rush, Ronald Takaki has argued that the Enlightenment project for the improvement of the human race, equated with the development of scientific knowledge, gave rise not only to a science of bodily purification and disease control but to a moral discourse of the body, centered on the triumph of self-governance over natural impulses and infirmities. Far from considering the body to be an obstacle to the progress and transcendence of reason, Rush's republicanism stipulated a refinement or an education of the body that was every bit as important to the body politic and the cultivation of its public manners as the education of its citizens. An ideal of civic virtue was implicit in the republican standards of physical and social hygiene, for the proper control of one's body was supposed to indicate both the spread of learning and the ability to participate disinterestedly in the affairs of the polity. By this same bodily standard, Rush avowed, Americans of African descent could attain their place in the republic and present themselves for consideration as citizens.[71]

Douglass indicated that he would adopt this same pedagogy for his own purposes in the same issue that he solicited subscribers with his "Liberal Offer." In an adjoining column titled "The Lecturer," he marveled at the "office" of the orator, the "distinguished and useful functionary" who could "perform the work of instruction on a grand, yet economical scale."[72] Offered at the height of the lyceum movement, Douglass's praise paid tribute not only to the contemporary prestige of the professional orator but to the ongoing transformation of oratory from a civic vocation into popular, mass entertainment.[73] However, Douglass might just as well have been invoking republican standards of self-discipline when he called the orator a "functionary" in the service of education. His regard for "instruction on a grand . . . scale" reminds us that the pedagogical imperative of the Enlightenment had not lapsed, especially among African American advocates of "mental culture," and that the properly trained orator could be charged with instituting the normative measures of republicanism among aspiring freemen. As a representative of *Frederick Douglass's Paper,* Douglass thus devoted his oratorical appearances to the very "mission" to which he dedicated the depiction of Madison Washington, and while this might have condemned him to appear in similarly statuesque form, the republican tradition that freemen sought to institute through the medium of the press included also provisions for the presentation of the body that were just as disciplinary and didactic. These provisions rendered his body the functional equivalent of a press organ, whereby every gesture and expression could be used to stipulate the existence, or at least the education, of a public.[74]

The orator's body could serve as a means of instruction because the same lessons that the colored press had sought to impart to black readers could be found in *The Columbian Orator,* the eloquence handbook Douglass discovered while still a slave. As its full title suggested, *The Columbian Orator: Containing a Variety of Selected Pieces; Together with Rules; Calculated to Improve Youth and Others in the Ornamental and Useful Art of Eloquence* was published as part of a republican pedagogy that compelled its students to submit every aspect of their vocal expression and bodily comportment to a disciplinary regimen. The properly trained orator then could manifest the laws and standards of public intercourse in his public conduct and thereby educate his observers in the same— and yet it was in its emphasis on the orator's physical comportment, even on the flesh, that *The Columbian Orator* betrayed its pedagogical function. "Emphasis" might be too mild a word—the operations of the body were expressly mandated and exhorted so that the orator "effects eye [and] ear." To this end, the handbook's countless guidelines for proper pronunciation, projection, cadence, inflection, and pacing were accompanied by rules for an apposite gesture, so that the public standards that governed the voice could be seen in "the motions of the countenance."[75]

Like Rush's moral discourse of the body, *The Columbian Orator* made corporeality not just an essential attribute but a medium of citizenship, for every bodily gesture and somatic expression told of the orator's voluntary submission to public standards recognized by all. This seemed to be in accord with the ersatz republicanism that handbooks like *The Columbian Orator* promoted into the nineteenth century. With the benefit of training in classical languages as well as civic virtues, taught through generous helpings of Cicero, Cato, and Coriolanus, these handbooks perpetuated the self-recognition of an increasingly fractious American public in the image of a disinterested citizenry.[76] The influence of this republicanism could still be felt in the 1857 *The Golden Age of the American Orator*, which addressed orators as latter-day "consuls and tribunes" who possessed "disinterested devotion to the cause of the people,"[77] but also in Douglass's body, which made available to his discerning audiences all the classical learning and republican pretensions they could want.

Nathaniel Rogers, the editor of the *Herald of Freedom*, showed himself to be among the pretentious when he said that Douglass's appearance on the platform called to mind "the port, the countenance, and heroic 'assurance' and almost the stature of the Roman Coriolanus."[78] This figural comparison had strategic importance for the majority of white male onlookers who were not classically educated or had not read *The Columbian Orator*. With his praise of the black male body, Rogers was interpellating an imaginary body of literate, disinterested citizens on the strength of a classical allusion, and while his gesture might have repro-duced the most restrictive conditions for white male citizenship, it also betrayed the complicity between the particularity of physical form and the abstraction of civic identity that prevailed within the disciplinary reg-imen of republicanism. The republican standards of citizenship seemed to demand their own embodiment, which meant that Douglass's self-presentation as an orator could do the same and signify either an imag-inary public body of white men or an actual black male body—or both.[79]

The slippage between these two bodies seemed to be forecast by the civic pedagogy of *The Columbian Orator,* which would institute a transparent relationship between the normativity of the printed medium and the embodied subject of republicanism.[80] This relationship was en-shrined not just in the handbook's grammatical regimen, which would teach its lessons for proper pronunciation through "the motions of the [orator's] countenance," but also in its selection of "Practical Pieces for Speaking . . . from the Pulpit, Pleadings at the Bar, Sublime Description, debates, declamations." Essays in *The Columbian Orator* were chosen not merely for their technical complexity but for the moral declamations and republican apologias that properly educated the citizen. The two pieces that Douglass mentioned in the *Narrative,* the "Dialogue between a Master and Slave" and "Part of Mr. O'Connor's Speech in the Irish House of Common" (misquoted as one of "Sheridan's mighty speeches"), were but two of the book's many lessons in natural rights theory and political liberalism of the Enlightenment. In the former, a runaway slave poses the pivotal question to his master, "I had lost the power, but how the right [of disposing of myself?]" (240). In the latter, O'Connor's argument for the liberation of Roman Catholics under Anglicanism invokes "the broad basis of immutable justice" and the "silken thread of reason" against the "ignorance, superstition, and want of concert in the people" (246). Practicing elocution with these essays ensured that the orator's bodily gestures would be governed by precisely those rules that governed a virtuous republic: justice, reason, and liberty.

With its selection of "practical pieces," *The Columbian Orator* clearly aimed at more than the orator's mindless obedience to rules of grammar.

It aimed beyond the prospective orator to a prospective reading public that knew of republican principles and regarded them as the basis of their common learning. However, the utility of oratory in this pedagogical endeavor also ensured that the creation of a white citizenry would not be accomplished any more directly than was the recruitment of a black reading public. The goal of *The Columbian Orator* was to create a "suitable conformity of the orator's voice and several parts of the body in speaking, to the subject matter of the discourse" (19), so that an orator, suitably conformed, could function effectively as a textual medium and teach the "principles of 1776" as surely as did Madison Washington's body. This was, as Douglass called it, "instruction on a grand, yet economical scale," and it meant that his own body could stand in for the corpus of writings that, if circulated publicly, would signal the spread of learning among a literate people. It might well have been the only corpus some of his audiences would ever know, but Douglass's most ambitious plans for his own newspapers never seemed to depart from the premise of this republican pedagogy and to consider the formation of a public sphere independently of his own body. It was his great accomplishment to collapse oratory's standards for the appearance of the body with the symbolic function of the printed medium in a way that reversed the process of self-abstraction and even its value in the political economy of republicanism.

The results of this reversal can be found in Douglass's journalistic enterprise, in which all the impersonal qualities that had been ascribed to a literate public became physical attributes, such as race and color. Even his editorial voice can be said to have taken on the essential characteristics of the body, in a manner consistent with the regimen of *The Columbian Orator*. As Fisher-Fishkin and Peterson have shown, Douglass learned from this handbook the "Enlightenment discourses of freedom and independence . . . the national principles of liberty, equality, and justice" and the "oratorical voices of national leaders"; combined, they would "greatly influence" the mission of *The North Star* and *Frederick Douglass's Paper.*[81] Yet if it is true that *The Columbian Orator* decreed that the grand sentiments of its printed documents were to be learned, articulated, and taught through the "motions of the countenance," and, moreover, that Douglass's oratorical appearances were devoted to the success of the colored newspaper, then his editorial voice can be said to have gained its agenda, its authority, and its representative function precisely by being reducible to the orator's most esteemed bodily features, especially his "manly form." The public medium of black manhood, defined by the facility for progress, improvement, and enlightenment, in this sense obtained materially, as a body. In its connection to the rhetoric and lessons of 1776, the same medium became still more manly and more colored until it could be considered the very nature to which Douglass appealed when he defended the nature and character of black people. His transformation of the public sphere thus ended with the printed medium, the vehicle for the self-abstraction of white people, manifesting the physical traits of race.

Embodying the Imaginary

Douglass's interest in this transformation can be inferred from the words of William Whipper, who had based his call for the development of "mental culture" among black artisans on the "spirit of that sacred instrument, the Declaration of Independence," the source of the nation's "first principles." A true believer in "pure, unmixed republicanism,"[82] Whipper reminds us that the earliest advocates of the colored newspaper meant their claim on public virtue to discredit the principle assumption of the Protestant colonizationist movement—that black people's African descent made them incompatible with the demands and rewards of full American citizenship—and to establish definitively the source of their own nativity. The putative manifesto of the colored convention movement, the 1834 "Declaration of Sentiments," confirms the fact that the free black population of the North felt itself under the obligation to prove an American descent. The presence of the document itself, produced on the historic occasion of a public gathering, indicates that freemen leaders would avail themselves of every symbolic gesture and venue in order to invest their cause with the patriotic lineage of the nation's founding revolution. Throwing down the gauntlet against colonization, the Declaration argued that the struggle for political equality fixed the origins of black people in America. "Let no man remove from his native country," it proclaimed, for "our principles are drawn from the book of divine revelation, and are incorporated in the Declaration of Independence."[83]

As the editor of a colored newspaper, Douglass still was waging this fight, which gained special urgency after the judgment of the Dred Scott case rendered an African lineage incompatible with constitutional protection on the presumption that African Americans were not parties to the founding of the republic.[84] His response drew on the anticolonizationist argument of the 1834 "Declaration of Sentiments," and particularly its insistence that the founding document of the American republic could prove the nationality of African Americans as surely as could their birthplace. In *The Heroic Slave* he lay claim to both "the principles of 1776" and the patriotic legend of the Old Dominion, expressing the freemen's belief that the founding principles of the American republic in fact were the equal of a birthright.

The fact that the novella was written and circulated on behalf of *Frederick Douglass's Paper* shows that Douglass also shared their interest in establishing the institutions of civic identity and that his intent was to construct a black public sphere on the basis of this genealogical trope. The colored newspaper, like the "Declaration of Sentiments," was invested with a genealogy, perhaps even a biological origin on this same basis, and that seemed to motivate Douglass to present the continuity of founding principles in a particular form. The body of Madison Washington, appreciated as a body, was said to give black manhood every "principle" contained in the Declaration of Independence, just as his own body, in "suitable conformity" with the essays of *The Columbian Orator*, articulated the republican principles of its "practical pieces." As the principle article of the black public sphere, the body of the black man became the focus of a paternity battle in which freemen argued that their lineage lay in printed documents and their political principles, not in the African lineage of their maternal line and not even in the whiteness of reputed slavemaster fathers.[85]

There is a short philological line between paternity and patriotism, but in *The Heroic Slave* Douglass attempted to sever the connection between actual white fathers and the names of the founding fathers so that he could establish the nationality of Africans under their republican principles. Although he began by feminizing the Commonwealth of Virginia as "the mother of statesmen," his more sustained argument was that the heroes of the early republic had the advantage of a historical record, which alone attested to the honor of their birthplace and, by extension, of their paternity. As a result, the lineage of "one of the truest, manliest, and bravest of her children" could be recovered only by reciting the story of the American republic. "There stands the fact," Douglass began, "that a man . . . loved liberty as much as Patrick Henry—deserved it as much as Thomas Jefferson,—and . . . fought for it with a valor as high . . . as he who led the armies of the American colonies through the great war for freedom and independence" (129). The publication of *The Heroic Slave* would make sure that the forgotten name of Madison Washington would resonate with those of Henry and Jefferson—and yet here was a nativist theory of national ancestry fully in keeping with the republican regimen of oratory, with the symbolism of the "colored newspaper," and, it must be added, with the conception of a displaced paternity. The manliness and heroic proportions of a slave were attributed to the legitimacy of a printed medium, which, in this case, was either the narrative record of American history or the novella itself. Despite being illegitimate himself, or perhaps because of that fact, Douglass affirmed a central premise of the freemen's civic identity in arguing that a discursive statement of founding principles was sufficient to establish the native properties and essence of the race.

In an address, "Slavery, the Slumbering Volcano," delivered in 1849, Douglass explicitly invoked "the example of the fathers of '76" to heroize the real Madison Washington, who had famously piloted the slave ship *Creole* to safe harbor in the British West Indies. The speech sought to trace Washington's origins to the displaced patrimony of American principles but only by describing the bodily features that were usually taken as a sign of barbarism, of racial inferiority, and, at the least, of African nativity. "[He was a] black man," Douglass proclaimed, beginning a catalog of negroid features, "with wooly head, high cheek bones, protruding lips, distended nostril, and retreating forehead, had the mastery of that ship." The methods of racial science buttressed a political argument for American citizenship, for Washington was said to be "inspired by the spirit of freedom." Indeed, "Slavery, the Slumbering Volcano" was not only an apologia for the manhood of the race after the example of Walker and Garnet but also an announcement that the most pure African slave was the most legitimately American. Consequently, the followers of Madison would "remain here," as Douglass advised, and stake his claim to their revolutionary lineage as they plotted rebellion.[86]

Douglass delved further into the nature of African features in "The Claims of the Negro Ethnologically Considered," delivered to the assembled scholars of Case Western Reserve but addressed in principle to the offending ethnologists and anthropologists who assigned black people a distinct, inferior human origin.[87] His counterargument was that the political and legal arguments for American citizenship could be established on the manhood of the black race, physically considered. After having established the claims of the "negro" to manhood—that is, a humanity capable of intellection and improvement—as the speech progressed he turned from this nominally Enlightenment standard of manhood in order to accept the racial comparisons that the disciplines of natural science, anatomy, and phrenology imposed on African Americans. The physical features that betokened racial inferiority, he claimed, were caused by the disproportion of cultivation, or "mental culture" that European races regarded as their exclusive inheritance, and that fated the "Irishmen ignorant and degraded" to share "the open uneducated mouth ... the shuffling gait—the retreating forehead and vacant expression" with the enslaved (515, 521). Pointing to "the heads of A. CRUMMEL, HENRY H. GARNET, SAM'L R. WARD, CHAS. LENOX REMOND [et al.]," he said in triumph that they "indicate the presence of intellect"; their anatomical features, like the manhood of the race, seemed to develop along with intelligence.[88] The heads of Garnet, Ward, and

Remond thus were in the "Websterian mold" (510), whose noble brow and physical bearing betokened his own great learning and the spread of further learning among all. Anatomical features and comportment, argued the student of *The Columbian Orator,* answered directly to education and cultivation, which made the progress of the black race according to republican principles traceable in physical form.

At the conclusion of his speech, Douglass composed these physical traces into a narrative of a triumphant American civilization:

> Colonization is out of the question. . . . Two hundred years have passed over him, his tears and blood have been mixed with the soil, and his attachment to the place of his birth is stronger than iron. . . . The history of the negro race proves them to be wonderfully adapted to all countries, all climates, all conditions . . . civilization cannot kill him. He accepts it—becomes part of it. In the Church, he is an Uncle Tom; in the State, he is the most abused and least offensive. All the facts in his history mark him out for a destiny, united to America and Americans. (524–25)

The task of the assembled anthropologists was to recognize a nationalist destiny in the history of the African race; the task of African Americans, on the other hand, was to accept this destiny and be improved by it. The origin of the "negro race," Douglass argued, could be found nowhere else than in its "blood mixed with the soil," and it was precisely by following this bloodline that white Americans could see the already developed African civilization in "this nation."[89] The physiological basis of American nationality would preclude the claims of racial inferiority, especially since Douglass made clear in an earlier speech, "A Nation in the Midst of the Nation," that "Our wrongs and outrages are as old as our country," and that since the founding of the republic, there has been "not a day, not an hour in any day—not a minute hour of the day, that the blood of my people does not gust forth at the call of the scourge."[90] This was a blood right of a different kind, though it was no less constitutive of American nationality for originating in oppression.

Although Douglass's narratives of American descent used a self-defensive displacement from a supposedly real, that is, African origin to maintain the fiction of a national paternity, his interest in the anatomical manifestation of rational progress, in the paternal lineage of a revolutionary spirit, and in the bodily expression of republican principles also shows that he could not abandon the standard of corporeality. On the contrary, he saw the success of the freemen cause in what Berlant calls the "suture of body and subjectivity to the public sphere of discourse."[91] Berlant describes this transformation as the basis for a postbellum constitutional order of enfranchised white and black men, but the signal institutions of the black public sphere—the artisan republicanism, the colored conventions, the "Declaration of Sentiments," and, of course, the colored newspaper—can be said to have been no less effective in converting the principles of "pure, unmixed republicanism" into the native attributes of race and ultimately into a blood right that black people possessed by virtue of being born in America. *The North Star* and *Frederick Douglass's Paper* thus would obtain in the black public sphere precisely like manhood and constitute biological evidence of a civic patrimony. As the inspiration of the colored newspaper, according to McCune and other advocates of the freemen cause, was the Declaration of Independence, the patriarch of this African American citizenry was none other than Thomas Jefferson, reputed father of Clotel, though the narrative of paternal descent that accounted for the values and even comportment of black manhood through the paternity of a seminal document also sustained the claims of African Americans to native-born citizenship in the express absence of white male paternity. As invoked in the apologias for the freemen's public sphere, the printed documents of the republic were imagined as the first seeds in a biological lineage that constituted, in Berlant's terms, a "national fantasy."

An uncanny descendent of the Freudian "family romance," the "national fantasy" or "National Symbolic" is said to generate a national lineage such as the one from which freemen claimed to descend while establishing the essential properties of citizenship in the corporeal, or the anatomical, facts of white manhood. As such, the "National Symbolic" is defined as the site where "constructs of law, defining and constricting citizenship" manifest themselves in the "regulation of desire and harnessing of affect to political life."[92] The black public sphere might be considered an institution of the symbolic to this same extent, especially when we consider the utility of its printed articles in proving a consanguineous, affective connection to a homeland and an equally consanguineous connection with the principles of founding fathers. By this measure, the direct offspring of this parentage, the "Declaration of Sentiments" and the colored newspaper, would be exactly what McCune had wanted them to be, which was "the first step which will mark our certain advancement as a People," and lend the representation of an African American public a narrative of bodily development, culminating in "full grown manhood." As the avowed "type of his countrymen" and most visible proponent of the colored newspaper, Douglass had helped to create to a national, or should we say republican fantasy that can be said to have given the public sphere of literate discussion a second life in the affective life of the body.

Unfortunately, Garrison depended on the same fantasy for the abolitionists' public sphere, which in turn had the same connection to the freemen community that Douglass wished for the colored newspaper. Garrison's largest debt to his black predecessors in this sense might be the historical structure of the abolitionists' public identity, which would possess an imagined paternity of founding fathers and thereby displace the white reformers from the assembled body of white male citizens who proclaimed their whiteness. For Garrison, the freemen's ideal of black manhood furthered the claim of abolitionists to the historical ideal of literate, disinterested citizenry, and while this might have demonstrated the interracial ancestry of the abolitionists' agenda, it also was critical in moving their collective self-representation beyond the boundaries of their white male bodies. At least, this seemed to be the result of Garrison's encomium to Douglass's manhood in his preface to the *Narrative*:

> As soon as he had taken his seat, filled with hope and admiration, I rose, and declared that PATRICK HENRY, of revolutionary fame, never made a

speech more eloquent in the cause of liberty.... I reminded the audience of the peril which surrounded this self-emancipated young man at the North—even in Massachusetts, on the soil of the Pilgrim Fathers, among the descendents of revolutionary sires; and I appealed to them, whether they would ever allow him to be carried back into slavery.... The response was unanimous and in thunder-tones—"NO!"[93]

With their acclaim for the "young man," the white members of the audience could be said to be affirming their own citizenship, ethnologically considered, for here was the same story that Douglass would tell on behalf of Madison Washington. However, Garrison's narrative of paternal descent could sustain only the most tenuous historical relation; he summoned the name and principles of Patrick Henry only to abstract the assembled white citizenry from its contemporary designation and place them under antislavery principles that may or may not have been shared by actual founding fathers. The imaginary public he convened in this instance at least shared this with the public body of free African Americans: a commemoration of dead white men that assumed and exploited the absence of their bodies.

CHAPTER 4

Faneuil Hall: The Civic Institution
of the Imaginary

Then, as now, a walk through Boston's streets could provide the historically minded citizen with memories not only of a successful revolution but of founding fathers—James Otis, John Hancock, Samuel Adams—whose names instilled a sense of reverence for the nation's founding principles. If that citizen was Henry Adams, his patriotism would be indistinguishable from his filiopiety, which he admitted was alive and well in the 1840s. Seeking to account for the "atmosphere" of Boston, Adams described his childhood as a "nest of associations so colonial—so troglodytic—as the first Church, the Boston State House, Beacon Hill, John Hancock and John Adams."[1] In this "nest," the name of Adams's paternal great-grandfather took its place alongside the place-names of eighteenth-century Boston and led young Henry inexorably to perhaps the city's greatest civic landmark, Faneuil Hall, where his paternal grandfather, John Quincy Adams, was mourned publicly. In that "official ceremony," Henry sensed not only the spirit of the former president but the "shadow of the War of 1812 ... the word Hartford Convention" (21) and nearly every other event of Boston's tumultuous political history in a demonstration of both civic and ancestral worship.

Not every Bostonian could claim Adams's paternal lineage but almost all harbored the conviction that had inspired the city's freemen community's regard for the corporeal dimension of black manhood: that they had descended from founding fathers whose declarations of freedom and equality constituted their lineage. Just as Adams did, they recognized their paternal descent in the spectacle of Faneuil Hall, where the official commemoration of statesmen, revolutionary heroes, and even "colored patriots" took place. William Nells, Garrison's protégé, Douglass's antagonist, and the author of *Colored Patriots of the American Revolution*, had deliberately chosen the site to honor the memory of Crispus Attucks, the first combatant, according to popular legend, killed in the historic struggle for liberty. Once enshrined in Faneuil Hall, Attucks's name, but more importantly his blood, could mix with that of the fallen heroes of the Boston Massacre, whose sacrifice had been honored there in a memorable public ceremony.[2] The commemorative festival for Attucks, attended by black, white, male, and female abolitionists, thus would honor the common descent of a liberty-loving people, though white nativist Bostonians, as one would expect, were just as eager to reserve this republican lineage for themselves.[3] The countervailing attempt by Boston's antiabolitionist forces to seize the historical memory of the American Revolution for their side centered as well on Faneuil Hall, for here was where Harrison Gray Otis gave his famous speech condemning the sedition of the abolition movement.[4] As a direct descendant of James Otis, another hero of the Revolution, he might have had special motivation for speaking from the steps of that ancestral hall to defend the integrity of the Union's family bonds. Faneuil Hall was the local address of what Berlant would call a national fantasy, the site in which the family romance of patrilinear citizenship was lived out as a reverence for founding fathers.[5]

William Lloyd Garrison, a newcomer to Boston with no family ties to the city, nonetheless showed himself to be a remarkably astute participant in a local political culture organized around the public act of commemoration and strategic acts of deference. After Otis's speech, Garrison professed his sorrow at the former mayor's indiscretion and then gave vent to the memories every Bostonian could claim to have of Faneuil Hall:

> I remember how intimately associated is the name of OTIS with the revolutionary struggle that emancipated this nation from the thraldom of the

mother country. You have dishonored that name—you have cast a stain of blood upon your reputation. You have presumed to lift your voice, even in the very Cradle of liberty, in panegyric of the vilest "brokers in the trade of blood."

Imagining Faneuil Hall as Otis's family mausoleum, Garrison went on to envision the macabre spectacle of a tombstone engraved with the most damning epitaph:

Here lies the body of

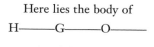

* * * *

Reader weep at human inconsistency and frailty!

The last public act of his life,

A life conspicuous for many honorable traits,

Was an earnest defense of

THE RIGHTS OF TYRANTS AND SLAVE-MONGERS

* * * *

This was made in

"THE OLD CRADLE OF LIBERTY"

To Garrison's "ecce homo" theatrics were added the conventions of gothic fiction, for he insisted that "THE FREE SPIRIT OF OUR FATHERS still walks unshackled, in pristine boldness and majesty, among us," alternately haunting and inspiring the current generation of Bostonians.[6]

Although Garrison showed a perfect fluency in the local conventions of filial homage, the overdetermined symbolism of Faneuil Hall ensured that he would not have to abandon the libertarian politics that had made the abolitionists the insurrectionists of their age. The hall, after all, was remembered as the site of revolutionary-era town meetings and public protests against the Stamp Act, so that in addition to the ghost of the fathers, the more disembodied "SPIRIT OF SEVENTY-SIX," or the spirit of revolution, would haunt Otis's errant progeny and remind them of the ringing declarations of principles that had made Faneuil

Hall such a monument to the democratic sovereignty of free speech. Paying tribute at once to this monument and to the agency of the abolitionists' free discussion, he promised Otis that "the cause of the bleeding slave shall yet be pleaded in Faneuil Hall, in tones as thrilling, in language as stirring, in eloquence as irresistible, as were ever heard within its walls!" Meanwhile, he said of the abolitionists, "We must, we will speak out, as often, as plainly, as loudly, as we choose."[7] Garrison, in other words, had found another name to honor among the patronyms already enshrined in Boston's civic memorial and it was the name of the people, which now belonged to the abolitionists by virtue of their unrelenting, iconoclastic free speech. In the "nest of associations" that centered on Faneuil Hall, he had discovered not just another historical reference for the abolitionists' anachronistic public identity but a certifiably historic institution for their public sphere.

What was Faneuil Hall without the names and historical associations that made it a site of civic memory? Before it became what Garrison had called fondly the "Old Cradle of Liberty," it was a colonial-era, city-owned marketplace that Boston's tradesmen left to rack and ruin. During the American Revolution, it served as the site of public protests and town meetings and, most famously, of the Stamp Act protest, but the renown of the building seemed to grow with its successive commemorations in a way that befit its later use as a cenotaph for revolutionary martyrs and memorial for founding fathers. Faneuil Hall's "power of place," to use the urban sociologist Dolores Hayden's term, was proportionate to its function as a "memory palace," which is distinguished by its ability to "encompass shared time in the form of shared territory."[8] As such, it helped to induce among Bostonians an awareness of their common history and to make Boston itself what M. Christine Boyer calls a "city of collective memory," sustained by its "memory system of public monuments and places, rearticulating these communal covenants and rehearsing their sovereign pledges in democracy: places where the rational voice of the people could be heard."[9] Faneuil Hall was a public space where the voice of the people could be heard, but more importantly remembered, and as such it gave nineteenth-century

Bostonians a fitting symbol of their self-proclaimed republican ancestry. An 1826 pamphlet paid tribute to Faneuil Hall, the "Cradle of Liberty," as the place where the "language which made a monarch tremble upon his throne for safety, and which inspired New England with confidence . . . against a royal bulwark of hereditary authority, had its origins." In true republican fashion, the deference for authority was both extinguished and preserved, for the pamphlet claimed that "no place was more distinguished for powerful eloquence than Faneuil Hall."[10]

As we will see, the narrative tropes of Faneuil Hall had such bearing on the actual public space of Faneuil Hall that Boston's foremost civic architect, Charles Bulfinch, was charged with ornamenting the previously Georgian structure with the neoclassical ornamentation of a republican institution. Not merely a semiotic code for "reading" the institution, the symbolism of a revolutionary origin proved to be monumental in itself, demonstrating all the attributes that Henri Lefebvre has ascribed to monumentality—its role in the self-recognition of the members of a society, its enshrining of their social relations, and especially its demarcation of the boundaries and space of social relations.[11] Lefebvre has declared his antipathy to the "priority-of-language-thesis" in order to recapture what he terms the material production of space, but if we consider the extent to which Bostonians actively involved the names of founding fathers and the utterance of those names in the conduct of their civic life, then we might see in the figurative and historical associations of Faneuil Hall a case in which language seemed to operate as a kind of "spatial practice" within a civic, indeed urban context.[12] At least, this was how the New England abolitionists made themselves at home in Boston—they reinstated the voice, agency, and ultimately the space of the people by restating the legend of the "Cradle of Liberty" and of all the other illustrious names of Boston's civic history that had gathered there. In doing so, they would gain a public space for their movement that situated them in a historic struggle for liberty but that existed solely in the iteration of the name of Faneuil Hall.

In his editorial against Otis's speech, Garrison paid such explicit homage to the name that he effectively reduced the historical institution to its discourse of patronyms and place-names. Summoning "the shades of Warren, of Hancock, of Otis, and of Adams," he went on to invoke the "martyrs at Lexington, Concord, and Bunker Hill," all of whom would defend Faneuil Hall from Otis's misuse. He made full use of its connection to the names of Boston's patriarchs in order to articulate an ironic narrative of paternal citizenship. "Nothing among all the dismal signs of the times," Garrison fumed from the pages of *The Liberator,* "more palpably exhibits the utter degeneracy of Bostonians from their parent stock than the occupancy of Faneuil Hall by a meeting called to palliate and support a system of slavery." Apostrophizing Boston's patri- archs, Garrison invited them to "Behold your unworthy descendents, obsequiously bowing under the whips of southern taskmasters," bring- ing "pollution and disgrace" to the hallowed "Old Cradle," now rechris- tened the "Coffin of liberty."[13] In Garrison's translation, the normative vocabulary for memorializing Faneuil Hall was turned into a language of metaphor, metonomy, and irony that could not help but affirm its standing as a trope, or an imaginary space.[14] Throughout the 1830s, he would modulate the patrilinear discourse of the "Old Cradle of Liberty" into a more avowedly figurative discourse that cleared the way for the self-determination of the abolition movement, though in doing so he would stay true to the memory of Faneuil Hall and perpetuate its rituals of commemoration.

The very first gathering of the New England abolition movement demonstrated the strength of the name of Faneuil Hall, which was suffi- cient to lend credibility to the nascent movement, to establish Garrison's civic credentials, and, above all, to convene the assembled abolitionists in the historic image of a public. Without a welcome from the city's Protestant establishment, Garrison looked for and found a place for the abolitionists' first gathering in the city's African American community, which was just as versed in the symbolism of a patrilinear descent as he would prove to be. Speaking from the confines of the African Meeting House and in the shadow of Boston's segregated "Nigger Hill," Garrison made clear that this new organization of abolitionists deserved a public space that befit its historical comparison with the people of revolutionary legend. "Faneuil Hall," he promised, invoking the hallowed name of the city's foremost civic institution, "shall ere long echo with the principles we have here set forth."[15] He can be said to have accomplished his aim in the 1850s, when the abolitionists' repeated appearances in the public space transformed Faneuil Hall, as James Brewer Stewart has written, from the ceremonial backdrop for Otis's defiance "into a temple of patriotic Bostonian resistance to slavecatchers and 'northern men with southern principles.'"[16]

Before they regularly occupied Faneuil Hall and made it their own, however, Garrison was more eager to echo the name of the abolition movement with the place-names and patronyms that constituted the civic discourse of Boston. He would take advantage of this civic ritual of reiteration in order to create a new chain of associations for Faneuil Hall and therefore a new conception of public space that corresponded to the marginal standing of the abolition movement and particularly to its alliance with the marginalized. As Lyotard has observed, "Names only designate landmarks which indicate procedures for reiteration, but which, in doing so, also allow the institution or attempted institution of new networks in which the given names will be included."[17] There would be a new "nest," in other words, to complement the already established symbolic discourse of Faneuil Hall, though like the normative vision that Otis articulated, it would recognize both the authority of the paternal name and the legitimacy of a paternal descent. Garrison's critical use of this historiography could be found in the transfer of the authority of the name to the despised abolition movement. By this metonymic act of substitution, he gave shape and dimension to the abolitionists' imaginary public space.[18]

In the mid-1830s, when the abolitionists' public identity depended at once on their exercise of free speech and their exclusion from the political public sphere, Garrison would render the abolitionists' claims to the public sphere in general and to Faneuil Hall in particular on these figurative grounds, or on the basis of language.[19] There might well be no better expression of what Castoriadis would call the radicalism of the imaginary, which is said to exceed and thereby disturb the very processes of social reproduction that created it.[20] To be sure, the abolitionists would put constant pressure on the municipal authorities of Boston to hold their meetings in Faneuil Hall, but as they contended with the official opposition and the separate and equal claims of an antiabolitionist white supremacist majority, they were more determined to claim the name of Faneuil Hall as an equivalent or even a substitute for the actual public space that Otis and his ilk had defamed.

An apt expression of their efforts could be found in a short-lived penny press, the *Cradle of Liberty*, whose name indicates what stock the abolitionists put in the most common metaphor for Faneuil Hall. The newspaper's carefully chosen motto, "Abolition's Public Forum," indicates still more the stock that they put in a figurative institution of public space. As self-declared outcasts from all the myriad public spheres of Boston's civic life, the abolitionists defied all other institutions, including the utopian conception that the majority of Bostonians recognized as their own. In doing so, they applied direct pressure to the utopian premise of public space itself, separating the name of Faneuil Hall and its historical associations from the brick and mortar institution until they could be said to stand alone. The attempt to create a public sphere from the circulation of Faneuil Hall's figurative appellation shows, if nothing else, that they considered this a practical object.[21]

In order to introduce a conceptual tension between an imaginary and concrete public space, the abolitionists had to sustain all the patriarchal associations of a "Cradle of Liberty," and Garrison did this every time he paid homage to the name. How, then, did the abolitionists expect to differentiate their public sphere from the practical and symbolic institutions of white male citizenship? What provisions for an imaginary Faneuil Hall were already present in the historical representation of Faneuil Hall, and which did they hope to exceed? In order to answer these questions, this chapter will have to examine the abolitionists' Faneuil Hall as one of a series of Faneuil Halls, all of them offering a public space in proportion to the meaning of the name and all of them part of the urban history of Boston. So closely were the discursive boundaries of this public space tied to the conditions of its material development that the medium of figurative representation that the abolitionists used for their own purposes can be said to have had its own history. By the end of the nineteenth century, the connection of the metaphor the "Cradle of Liberty" to the name of the people had given Bostonians not only a monumental symbol of their political heritage but a constitutive signifier in a language of freedom. Giving no less credence to its figurative meaning than the abolitionists, a civic-minded historian made use of the figure of metonymy to describe the magnitude of Faneuil Hall. "Wherever the name 'liberty' is spoken," he declared, "there Faneuil is known and the name honored."[22]

Given this institutional history, the abolitionists cannot be said to have deserted the realities of political struggle for the prison-house of a discursive form. The name of Faneuil Hall was an institution in itself, and the abolitionists did everything they could to preserve its monumentality. Moreover, the abolitionists interpolated themselves in a distinctively civic history when they attempted to attach its name to the name of the people and to denominate themselves as such. As I hope to show, the phases and events of Boston's city-building gave rise inevitably to new conceptions of public space, all of which were deemed to be so on the strength of new articulations of a public. The tropes of citizenship indeed shared a history with the material development of urban space, and no less can be said of the abolitionists' imaginary institution of Faneuil Hall. Their purchase on the name and all its figurative associations would remind us that a political act of self-fashioning that recreated a historic image of a public sphere was itself dependent on the historical conditions that shaped a city.

Public and Counterpublic Space

The concept of public space does sit at the crossroads between the ideological and the historical. It consistently reveals the difficulty of establishing its material dimensions without the interposition of moral discourses, political theory, and normative social values. Hannah Arendt's chronology of the devolution of the Greek polis into the private sphere of society is a case in point. Her account might be regarded as historical, but it has been of more permanent use in providing a narrative of liberal ideology that alternately celebrates and regrets the ascension of the capitalist order.[23] Another example of this conceptual slippage is provided by Habermas, who would remind us that his historical analysis of the liberal public sphere does not seek to describe empirically urban morphology, coffeehouse culture, or parliamentary structures. Instead, he seeks instead to uncover the "syndromes of meanings possessed of 'public' and 'publicity'" and thus the "essential sociological characteristics of various historical language strata."[24] With and without this provocation, many critics have utilized its ideological dimension to consign the bourgeois public sphere to narcissistic nostalgia and, alternately, to designate the possibility of multiple, provisional, or "counter"- publics. In the discourse of postmodernity, the clear-cut topographies of space have given way to cultural geographies of local, national, and international "flows" that describe the spatial structure of the vernacular, or the social practices, of marginalized groups.[25]

As a landmark to the democratic ideal of public assembly and the local ideal of a polis, Faneuil Hall provides us with a critical opportunity to see public space in its multiple roles: as a historical institution, as a moral premise of democracy, and perhaps most germane to our context, as a symbolic expression of civic life to be created and recreated in accordance with the needs of political argumentation. Faneuil Hall indeed could be considered nothing more or less than a material institution of ideology, especially in light of Lefebvre's question: "What is an ideology without a space to which it refers, a space which it describes? . . . Ideology per se might well be said to consist in a discourse upon social space."[26] And yet the alignment is never perfect, as the example of Faneuil Hall shows, and the social space is not closed. The distinction of public space might be that of democratic ideology, which is to say that it could never result in the production of a social or collective identity commensurate with the representation of its own borders. It has been the task of Laclau and Mouffe to clear the way for the end of an integral image of society, to subject the formation of society to the incommensurate and overdetermined articulations of the social while at the same time affirming the role of hegemony as the space of this conflict. Laclau has gone so far as to describe hegemony as a space, contingent on the plurality and incompleteness of meanings in democratic struggle, while Mouffe has looked forward to the regeneration of the public life of citizenship in the prospect of a "radical democratic hegemony."[27]

Faneuil Hall could be considered hegemonic, in the sense that it supplied the common expression and conditions for political struggle between combatants who nonetheless did not contend as equals. Their positions were asymmetrical and their resources unequal because their antagonism did not take place within an already circumscribed domain.[28] On the contrary, Laclau and Mouffe maintain that competing and incommensurate articulations of the social assume an exterior or marginal position, or what Mouffe calls a "constitutive outside." The "radical" element of hegemony is that heterogeneous acts of resistance corresponding to the diverse interests of marginalized groups will perpetually destabilize the space of the social in the image of their externality.[29] Indeed, this is how the New England abolitionists came to terms with the hegemony of public space in Boston. As such, their goal was not so much to enter Faneuil Hall as its rightful occupants as to use its symbolic dimensions, including its contradictory provisions for the historical representation of public dissent and the commemoration of a paternal ancestry, to equate their marginal standing with that of the people. They might have imitated the tactics of adversaries like Otis to this extent, but the claims and counterclaims to Faneuil Hall during the 1830s suggest that this public space served as both a site or arena for political conflicts of the antislavery struggle and a critical variable in them.

What was true of Boston's foremost civic monument was true of Boston itself, which played a similar role in the disputation of the slavery question. As James Brewer Stewart has insightfully argued, the civic consciousness of Boston, based not only on the interpretation of local monuments and tradition but on the theory and practice of free speech, created a surplus of publics, any one of which could be regarded as the properly local descendants of a revolutionary people. All it took was the slavery question to dislodge the lineal descendents of the Protestant establishment from their position of monopoly and open the discussion of reform first to the city's well-organized and civic-minded African American community and then to the equally civic-minded New England abolition movement. The ascent of Garrison and the Massachusetts Anti-Slavery Society opened up a contentious and all the more public sphere of debate that provoked the claims of various groups—dominant, emergent, residual, and even marginal—to the identity of the people, so that even as the discussion of abolition antagonized the lay and clerical supporters of African colonization, fomented divisions between the commercially attuned mercantile class and the liberal upper class of Brahmin reformers, opened up still more violent divisions between a politically ascendant class of artisans and working men and the free blacks who claimed the same mantle of republican manhood and virtue, and, finally, prompted an improbable alliance between the pro-Jacksonian working class and "gentlemen of property and standing" against the emergence of abolitionist women in public, the legitimacy of Boston's civic discourse was not in question. On the contrary, the divergent expressions of citizenship in antebellum Boston, answering to the multiplicity of reform organizations, to the complexities of urban politics, and to the heterogeneity of urban society, answered ultimately to a wholly normative conception of civic space as the site of free speech and dissent.[30]

As the memorial to filiopiety, civic memory, and public agitation, Faneuil Hall thus aroused all the conflicting conceptions of democracy that the political culture of Boston could be said to sustain. The institution itself seemed to obtain as what Laclau and Mouffe have called a "nodal point," or a necessarily provisional site of identification in a democratic struggle to articulate the identity of people, and to this extent the antagonism of Boston's public sphere might be said to have been localized at Faneuil Hall. As we can see in the controversy over the commemoration of Elijah Lovejoy, the murdered abolitionist editor, both marginal and dominant groups used the symbolism of this space not just to claim its public attributes for their cause but to redraw the boundaries of Faneuil Hall itself.

Although Lovejoy had been shot while defending his printing

office in Alton, Illinois, Garrison and the Massachusetts Anti-Slavery Society were determined to make his death an event in the civic life of Bostonians. Their first gesture in this direction was to argue that Lovejoy deserved the honor accorded the city's patriotic heroes and should be commemorated in Faneuil Hall, where the people of Boston could recognize their filial, even consanguineous bond with their ancestry. Their second gesture was more suited to the countervailing insurrectionist symbolism of the institution. Invoking the memory of contentious town meetings of the revolutionary era, the society proposed, in Garrison's words, a "spontaneous public meeting of the citizens of Boston" to be held in Faneuil Hall, where Bostonians could "express their alarm and horror in view of the prostration of civil liberty, and the murder of a christian minister for daring to maintain his inalienable and constitutional right." Casting the despised abolitionists as "the friends of free discussion and the liberty of the press," Garrison summoned the symbolism of the Stamp Act protest in order to make both Lovejoy and the defense of abolitionists' free speech native to Boston. Appealing at once to Bostonians' filial obligations and their zeal for discussion, he referred to the "'old Cradle of Liberty'" as "the most suitable building in which to hold the meeting."[31]

The death of Lovejoy gave Garrison the chance to complete the task he had initiated in the African Meeting House, which was to echo the name of Faneuil Hall with that of the abolition movement. Although he confessed the hope that the proposed Lovejoy protest would "atone" for the "disgraceful pro-slavery riot" that had victimized him two years earlier, he seemed at least as interested in using the Massachusetts Anti-Slavery Society's petition as something more than a rhetorical gesture and less than an outright demand. For Garrison, it was an occasion to interpellate the abolitionists in the language of Faneuil Hall. With a knowing reference to the "'old Cradle of Liberty,'" he would establish the place of the abolitionists in the public sphere of Boston through their familiarity with its traditions. On the basis of this iteration, the abolitionists then could speak as if they were the patriots of revolutionary legend—without having entered Faneuil Hall. As Garrison realized, the symbolic vocabulary of Faneuil Hall included not only a trope of public space but a signifier of the people, which in turn corresponded to the established role of free discussion in the city's political history. Carefully enveloping the proposal for the Lovejoy protest within this tradition, Garrison knew that the symbolic associations of Faneuil Hall were adequate to reproduce the normative ideal of a vocal citizenry and that the call for a "spontaneous public meeting" was sufficient to convene to the marginalized abolitionists as a public.

For this same reason, however, Boston's board of aldermen was equally qualified to articulate the historic dimensions of Faneuil Hall. Demonstrating the same fluency in the civic discourse of Boston as the abolitionists, the board considered itself, not the abolitionists, to have legal title to the public space of Faneuil Hall and, by extension, to the use of its name. Summarily dismissing the Massachusetts Anti-Slavery Society's proposal for a "spontaneous public meeting," the board found it "inexpedient" to "grant the prayer of said petition" in the name of Faneuil Hall and its venerable history. Its rebuttal put proportionate emphasis on the institution's symbolic importance as the site of public commemoration and filial loyalty, stating that a meeting to discuss Lovejoy's rights or wrongs "could only be a scene of confusion, which would be disreputable to the city, and injurious to the glory of that consecrated Hall."[32] The metaphor of consecration intensified the patriarchal connotations of the name to the point where we might recognize the board's objective as foreclosing the abolitionists' claim on Faneuil Hall with the excess use of its figuration. In keeping with its imagery of filial deference, the board devised a Federalist fantasy of disinterested legislative deliberation that never had any institutional connection to Faneuil Hall when it stated its preference for the "calm wisdom of public assemblies" over "the warmth of controversy engendered by public discussions." The board's refusal thus introduced a new meaning of its public space, as well as a new reference for the people, and both of them were articulated with the language of Faneuil Hall.

The contrary, competing articulations of Faneuil Hall—for the abolitionists, the "most suitable place" for a "spontaneous public meeting," and for the board of aldermen, a "consecrated Hall" for the "calm wisdom of public assemblies"—remind us that the hegemony of public space in Boston guaranteed an ongoing process of appropriation and reappropriation so that the name of Faneuil Hall could designate contradictory possibilities and expressions of democracy as well as incompatible forms of the people. Perhaps this is why the board of aldermen, which had tried to protect the hallowed ground of its ancestors, realized they had nothing to lose in reversing their decision regarding the society's petition and in filling Faneuil Hall with a largely antiabolitionist, procolonizationist, "colorphobic" public. In submitting to the city's tradition of civil liberties and acceding to the abolitionists' argument, the governing body knew that the exercise of free speech did not guarantee sympathy for abolition or convene a public in its opponents' image. The tumultuous public meeting that was held in Faneuil Hall to commemorate Lovejoy's death suggests instead that among the most important functions of the symbolism of public space was to bestow the name and ideal of the people upon any and all expressions of free speech. Thus James T. Austin, the attorney general of Massachusetts, could rely on the democratic tradition of Faneuil Hall to uphold his infamous sentiments:

> We have a menagerie here, with lions, tigers, hyenas, an elephant, a jackass or two, and monkeys in plenty. Suppose now, some new cosmopolite, some man of philanthropic feelings, not only towards man but animals, who believe that all are entitled to freedom as an inalienable right, should engage in the humane task of giving freedom to those wild beasts of the forest, some of whom are nobler than their keepers; or having discovered some new mode to reach their understanding, should try to induce them to break their cages and be free? The people of [a slaveholding state] had as much reason to be afraid of their slaves, as we should have of the wild beasts of the menagerie.[33]

Especially inspiring to the audience was the speaker's favorable comparison of Alton's homicidal mob to the patriots of Boston Tea Party fame, so that when the abolitionist speaker Wendell Phillips ascended the platform to declaim the cause of liberty, a duly appointed people who recognized the right of revolution could not help but find him unpopular, if not unpatriotic. He began his inaugural abolition address that night over boos and hisses.[34]

With the full force of public opinion empowered by a civic ritual of democracy to suppress the discussion of abolition, the abolitionists had cause to wonder: who were the people who had been born in the "Cradle of liberty"? Having seen the symbolism of Faneuil Hall accommodate hostile, seemingly antidemocratic sentiments in the name of the people, Garrison was more attuned than ever to the importance of the name and all its figurative associations. Speaking a few days after the abortive Lovejoy protest on the strategic occasion of Independence Day, Garrison lambasted the "time-honored, wine-honored, toast-drinking, powder-wasting" Fourth of July celebrations, but it soon became evident that the democratic ritual he most abhorred was the recent gathering in Faneuil Hall. Seeking to contrast that venerable institution with the public space of Marlboro Chapel, Garrison made note of the "beauty and convenience of the building in which we are now assembled" before launching into a defense of what he considered the true Faneuil Hall. Luridly describing the existing building as "decorated with whips and chains, and guarded by the Genius of tyranny," he used the hyperbole of his own rhetoric to intensify his listeners' regard for the name of Faneuil Hall. "The indwelling of a spirit, fierce and relentless as that of a tiger and hyena combined," Garrison said, was necessary "for a sworn officer of the law to stand up before all the people, in the old Cradle of liberty, and . . . commit rank perjury by justifying mobs."[35] Cast in the role as custodians of public memory, abolitionists would protect the "Cradle of liberty" from the defamations of its current denizens and particularly from Austin, called a "slanderer of the martyred dead." He castigated Austin's speech for committing the crime of "perjury" against Faneuil Hall, whose authenticity was made contingent on the truth of language. The same held true for the identity of the people—it was not found in the concatenation of public opinion in or the collective body of those who gathered in Faneuil Hall but in its metonymic association with the name of Faneuil Hall.

In the aftermath of this latest conflict with the popular will of Boston, the New England abolitionists seemed eager to identify themselves as a people who occupied a wholly imaginary space, the dimensions of a trope. For Garrison and the Massachusetts Anti-Slavery Society, Faneuil Hall indeed had to become nothing more or less than the "old Cradle of liberty"—that is, a figure for free speech rather than an actual locale for free speech; the language of Faneuil Hall would have to stand separate and apart from the concrete institution. As for the abolitionists, they would content themselves with saying the name, as Garrison did in Marlboro Chapel, and rely on the currency of place-names and patronyms in the civic discourse of Boston to constitute the public space of democracy wherever they stood.

Of course, this could not settle the question that had made Faneuil Hall the site and focus of political conflict, for it made the identity of the people who rightfully occupied the institution all the more contingent on the articulation of public space. And yet this same condition can be said to have held true from the moment the first brick of Faneuil Hall was laid. At every subsequent moment of its existence, throughout the material history of its development, we encounter what Lefebvre described as a "dialectical relationship between demand and command, along with its attendant questions: 'Who?' 'For Whom?' 'By whose agency?' 'Why and how?'" The founding of a monumental space, he argues, cannot be reduced to "the *command* that it be erected" or dated from the "moment when a particular social organization acceded to a pressing *demand* that it embody itself in a particular edifice." He designates instead a "creative capacity," which begs the question of its attribution while offering the indubitable evidence of "a community, or collectivity, of a group, of a faction, of a class in action, or an 'agent' (i.e., 'one who acts')."[36] No one, in other words, truly belonged in Faneuil Hall, but at the same time, everyone did. The production of public space created also the claims of successive generations of Bostonians to the identity of the public that founded it.

For this reason, we turn to the founding of Faneuil Hall to discover not just the conditions and occasions for the designation of a people but, more generally, the constitutive role of language in Boston's urban history. This role, I would argue, is different from the symbolic role played by the name of Faneuil Hall in the abolitionists' battle with civic authorities. My point in turning to the material development of the city's urban form in fact is to historicize the abolitionists' facility with the trope of public space and to place their faculty of the imagination in the larger context of urbanism. Of course, there is ample precedent for an analysis that would derive its formulation of a revolutionary people from the methods of urban history.[37] What the founding of Faneuil Hall reveals, however, is the more distinct process that attached the name of the people to a particular space and created an imaginary form.

The Concrete and the Imaginary

Let us begin with the name Faneuil. Through the gift of the eponymous hall and marketplace to the town of Boston in 1742, Peter Faneuil ensured that a family of internationally connected merchants, slave-holders, and, eventually, Loyalists would become synonymous with the name of the people. Answering a long-felt need for a centralized city marketplace, Faneuil turned to a family friend, the painter John Smibert, to design an arcaded structure in the high Georgian style that characterized much of Boston's colonial architecture. Not in the original proposal but included at Faneuil's behest was a second-floor assembly hall for town meetings. A rather stunned provincial government accept the building with a lasting show of gratitude, represented by the resolution of Thomas Hutchinson: that "to perpetuate [Peter Faneuil's] memory, the hall over the marketplace be named Faneuil Hall, and at all times thereafter be called and known by that name."[38]

Of course, Hutchinson and the committee of "wealthy and honored citizens" who named Faneuil Hall did not make use of the patronym with the intention of glorifying Faneuil or his family. Rather, they accepted the gift in the republican spirit in which it had been offered and intended the name to stand for the disinterested citizen who had subjected his interest to the public good. On making his gift, Faneuil had said, "I hope what I have done will be for the service to the whole country,"[39] thereby letting the committee regard him and his name as a monument to the people. By their resolution, the same status would flow to Faneuil Hall itself, which would stand for the moralized economic transactions that elevated citizens above their private interests and personal identities. Faneuil Hall, in other words, came into being as an article of the very republican political economy it was intended to stage.[40] The sponsors of this original, or republican, version of Faneuil Hall expected the building to promote an ennobling public life of commerce and virtue, but their plans for convening the people essentially took shape the moment they abstracted the name of Faneuil from its bearer and denominated a public space.

However, the civic ambition betrayed by the sponsors of the original Faneuil Hall was frustrated by an internal contradiction: it was pursued through a republican ideology that allowed as much for the self-denomination of citizens as for their self-perfection. Thus when Hutchinson and the sponsors of Faneuil Hall attempted to construct a public space in the name of the people, they were met with immediate resistance from the people of Boston, who would determine themselves. At a town meeting, the resolution to accept Faneuil Hall's purportedly disinterested gift passed by a vote of only 367 to 360, and then only with a proviso that "the market people should be at liberty to carry their marketing wheresoever they please about the town to dispose of it."[41]

Who were the "market people" whose "liberty" would be compromised by the creation of a public space? They were the people who made their living in the marketplace and they were not having any of Faneuil Hall and Marketplace. They were the urban mechanics, artisans, and farmers from Boston's outlying areas who literally carried the market on their backs, or on those of their horses. For them and their partners in commerce, the market could not be centralized because it could not be localized. The market was not a place at all but a political right of free trade and public assembly that market people could "dispose of" where they would. Without Faneuil Hall, they could exercise this right in the highways, byways, and alleyways of Boston, their market-place woven indistinguishably into what we would call the social fabric of urban life. To keep their marketplace public, the "market people" of Boston thus would have to fight against their acknowledgment as a people, which building Faneuil Hall would make. They would retain their identity as a free people by making sure that the marketplace in which they found their liberty could not be represented in concrete form.

The people who were determined that their public identity remain as invisible as their marketplace could be called a liberal people, who kept faith with the capitalist theory that an invisible hand guided the universal laws of a moral economy.[42] As Adam Smith had written, the presence of the public could only be inferred from the socially redemptive private transactions of the marketplace. Conceived in this economic role, the public was nothing more or less than the invisible spectator, or guarantor of capitalist exchanges that gave them their ultimately moral end.[43] How then could a "market people" accept their designation as a people through the construction of Faneuil Hall? The republican sponsors of the new marketplace were attempting to give the people of Boston their public identity through the very institution that forbid the realization of the public in any shape or form.

Faced with competition from an invisible marketplace and an invisible people, Faneuil Hall languished in disuse and was even frequently shuttered in the first decades of its existence. Nevertheless, the construction of the marketplace did create an entity that had not existed before: Boston itself, now a freeholder on the order of Peter Faneuil. Prior to Faneuil's gift, the town had neither legal standing as a property owner nor assets nor physical space to call its own. This is directly attributable to Boston's unique status among Atlantic port cities as an unchartered, unincorporated town, a status that meant Boston did not have a clearly demarcated commercial district or a clear role in the marketplace (though the business of the town could occasionally fall under the jurisdiction of the town's government when townspeople sought adjudication or improvements). A centralized marketplace that was part of a civic estate belonged in a provincially chartered city like

New York, with its corporate-owned markets, corporate-set prices, and corporate-granted vocational privileges, not a town of "market people."[44]

As the sustained opposition to Faneuil Hall suggests, Boston's new pseudo-corporate status made for more conflict than convenience. Standing empty and dignified in the first years after its construction, the hall stood for the divergence of interests between political officials and mercantile elites who sought to correspond their vision of the people to a civic estate and a "market people" who identified their autonomy and independence with the invisibility of the marketplace. In the ensuing decades, Faneuil Hall would be the focus of debates over the legal and physical development of Boston, but in its earliest years we can see that something even more fundamental was at stake in the conflict over Faneuil Hall. In imagining the institution through a republican political economy, the sponsors of the original building determined that the patronym Faneuil would signify the self-transcending capacities of the private person and thus the possibility of a people. The "market people" and their allies in commerce, on the other hand, would forestall the moment when the public could be known by any name.

However, it was not long before the commercial classes of Boston— the artisans, the merchants, international traders, and even the "market people"—discovered their own reasons for representing their interests as those of the public, and most of them would be found in the growing friction between the townspeople of Boston and England's provincial representatives. This friction had many causes and expressions, but it could be attributed to the structurally divided nature of Boston itself, which stipulated on the one hand a purely political sphere with no economic standing or function, and on the other, a heterogeneous commercial community that identified itself with the putative freedom of market exchanges. This division in turn actuated a classically liberal political awareness on the part of Boston's commercial classes that did provide for their self-representation as a people. With that awareness, an otherwise invisible marketplace suddenly became one of the stakes as well as the site of a political struggle, the public space of a free people.[45]

An unmistakable sign that the language of liberal democratic revolution had caught up to and claimed Faneuil Hall was the fact that the formerly reviled institution served as the site of the Stamp Act protest of 1765, an event that also secured its standing as the "Cradle of liberty." However, a single meeting could not have transformed the building from an unwanted and unused city-owned marketplace into a cherished symbol of democracy. Faneuil Hall first had to be recognized as a public space in keeping with the terms of political struggle in Boston, and for this to happen the institution's function as a centralized marketplace had to be forgotten and abandoned. A second, or liberal, version of Faneuil Hall owed its existence to the two institutions of the town that the market people had sought to preserve from the sponsors of the original Faneuil Hall: the decentralized marketplace and, as it turned out, the town meeting. Both these institutions sought to prevent the people from being represented in a concrete space or even as a people, but they would also provide the means for the self-representation of Boston's townspeople as an autonomous citizenry.

From the moment that the General Court of Massachusetts had founded Boston in 1632 with the declaration that it was "the fittest place for public meetings of any place in the Bay," the public realm of the town had been reserved for the deliberation of "political affairs" and particularly for institution of the town meeting.[46] Bostonians thereafter recognized their common citizenship not through a particular space or even through a Boston Common but primarily through the institution of public discussion, which could be found anywhere. As Gary Nash recounts, the famously contentious town meetings of colonial Boston yoked the governing selectmen to the interests of private propertyholders and even the propertyless—women, laborers, and African American freemen—into a discussion of the public good;[47] the public space of these meetings changed with circumstances and the demands of this debate. Faneuil Hall, for instance, could and did serve as public space for townspeople to express their dissent, but when over a thousand people gathered, that space would shift to the nearby Old South Church, also called, like all Congregational churches, a "meeting house."[48] With churches transformed into town halls and public spaces created at will, we might say that the only public domain that the people of Boston recognized as their own was public discussion itself. Faneuil Hall was esteemed or localized as public space only to the extent that it served this end.

While the townspeople of Boston were identifying the public space of Faneuil Hall with their right to gather and to determine themselves, the civic elites who had sponsored the original, or republican, Faneuil Hall set their sights on abolishing the institution of the town meeting. In successive plans, introduced in 1709, 1744, 1804, 1815, and successfully in 1821, to incorporate the town as the city of Boston, they sought to replace the friction of debate with a representative body governing the affairs of the people in their name. That these plans were defeated for as long as they were indicates that the people of Boston wanted to be neither incorporated nor represented. On the contrary, the town meeting with which they identified themselves often displayed the class antagonism that prevented a vigilant and disputatious citizenry from coalescing into a unified social body. The Stamp Act protest organized by Sam Adams, for example, condemned not only an unjust tax but the more clamorous, "unskilled" unrest not led by master artisans like Adams. Within this public realm took place a conflictual, ongoing, and open-ended process of political engagement, leading to temporary designations of public space and provisional formulations of the public.

That Adams and his fellow citizens gathered in Faneuil Hall in 1765 meant that a failed colonial institution had become a public space in accordance with this criterion, but in truth it could serve as the logical site for the town meeting only because it had been reconstructed according to the other institution with which the people of Boston circumscribed their public domain: the invisible, decentralized marketplace. This marketplace bore no relation to the stately structure that the sponsors of the original Faneuil Hall had misguidedly sponsored; it also differed significantly from the street marketplace of goods and services that the "market people" sought to protect. Faneuil Hall took on the liberal meaning of public space owing to the marketplace of print; it would comprise a public space coextensive with the exchanges of printed articles. Through this marketplace, the people of Boston not only recognized themselves as a public but circumscribed their public space.

For Faneuil Hall to become a public space, it had to take on the qualities of both the town meeting and the marketplace and become an invisible institution of the town. This condition was met in 1761, when it was destroyed by fire. Rising from the ashes of its disrepute was both a new Faneuil Hall and a new marketplace, the latter consisting of a lottery system to cover the costs of reconstruction. The currency in this marketplace was a paper scrip with the name of Faneuil Hall printed on it, as well as the unmistakable signature of Boston's merchant kingpin John Hancock.[49] Although it indemnified the lottery proceeds with Hancock's personal worth, this signature succeeded where Faneuil's name had failed—that is, in making the name of a wealthy sponsor of a city enterprise into the signifier of a resolutely public enterprise. Obviously, this would not be the last time that Hancock's signature performed this service in the name of the people, but in its connection with Faneuil Hall, his name operated exactly as currency and thereby held out the promise of a free and open marketplace in which even "market people" could participate.

The success of this new marketplace for Faneuil Hall required that the scrip be distributed throughout the town of Boston, a reminder of the special value that Michael Warner has attributed to the ubiquity of printed articles in America's public culture. The piece of paper that bore the patronyms of Hancock and Faneuil demonstrated a similar capacity: it abstracted a townspeople from their particular interests and private identities and pointed them toward an abstract conception of themselves.[50] In this case, the scrip bearing the name of Faneuil Hall succeeded not only in separating the patronym from Peter Faneuil himself but in making the name a common article of anyone who held the scrip. These Bostonians constituted an indiscriminately composed citizenry, linked not by kin, locale, or common practice but by the material possession of Faneuil's name, underwritten by Hancock's signature. The name itself signified their common bond, their common lineage, and ultimately, their common space, so that the chain of people holding the name could be said to possess a single name, synonymous with that of the people. The contiguity of printed articles in this sense had created what the construction of a civic estate emphatically had not: a public that recognized its commonality solely by its connection to Faneuil Hall.

Although the building itself was reopened in 1763, the paper scrip bearing the name and the newspaper advertisements for the lottery were still circulating in 1765, which meant that the value of print in this marketplace continued to determine both the form and function of public space. It is no wonder, then, that the townspeople of Boston who gathered in Faneuil Hall to protest the taxes imposed by the Stamp Act identified their popular resistance not just with the generically liberal right of trade but with the free circulation of printed articles.[51] They were using the same medium that had denominated Faneuil Hall as their public space to denominate themselves as a people, thereby ensuring that they would recognize themselves in the same form and in the same breath as the institution. The circulation of the name, underwritten by the social currency of the printed article, in turn became the foundation of a democratic order that regarded the freedom of speech and assembly on display at the Stamp Act protest as one of its signature expressions.

Faneuil Hall, already imbued with a symbolic function through the circulation of the name, gained still more renown by its association with the Boston Massacre commemoration, the tea tax protest, not to mention the patronyms of Adams, James Otis, and the other "Sons of Liberty." In the aftermath of the Revolution, these names and events became inseparably bound to the name of Faneuil Hall in a way that supported the legitimacy of this new democratic order. The institution served as the site of formal state dinners in honor of Washington, Lafayette, and Hancock, Massachusetts's first governor. On these official occasions, the name of Faneuil Hall continued to circulate in speeches, honorifics, and toasts that memorialized the building as the origin of the successful revolution.[52] In its new identity as the "Cradle of liberty," Faneuil Hall could be invoked in the same breath as the names of the venerated patriarchs and thereby serve as a trope for the ancestral home of democracy.

From the first transaction between the bearers of the lottery scrip, Faneuil Hall was an institution of democracy founded on the reproduction of the name, but by 1800 the result of this reiteration was to create "development pressure" to renovate the building according to the dimensions of the "Cradle of Liberty." No one less than Charles Bulfinch was given the job of making the Georgian-inspired structure into the architectural equivalent of this trope. The width of the building was doubled to accommodate a liberty-loving citizenry and a third story was added in order to raise the height of the assembly hall, now replete with neoclassical ornamentation befitting the glory of the new republic.[53] When Bulfinch finished in 1805, Faneuil Hall emerged in its most architecturally distinctive form, but we might regard his renovation as the culmination of the process that had founded public space through the symbolic function of a name and established the identity of the people from the possibility of its circulation.

However, neither the symbolic nor the material dimensions of the institution that Bostonians celebrated as the "Cradle of liberty" were exhausted in this second, or liberal, version of Faneuil Hall. By 1821, when Boston had finally incorporated itself as a city and gained an elected legislature, Faneuil Hall inevitably took on a new form and function in keeping with the contemporary articulation of the people. Although Bulfinch's renovation remained intact, the incorporation of Boston had created a new public space on the ground that Faneuil Hall stood, as the building and its environs had become part of the newly created city's newly acquired property. This new municipal district comprised six new streets around Faneuil Hall, a new granite structure called Quincy Marketplace, and Faneuil Hall itself.[54] Like the city streets, the institution had became the property of the city of Boston and so might be called municipal; and yet, as property, it could be said to have returned to its original form and become something private. This municipal, or private, version of Faneuil Hall was the very institution that Garrison and the New England abolitionists compared unfavorably to the "old 'Cradle of liberty,'" even though it demonstrated arguably the most unanswerable claim of any version to representing the people of Boston.

How could Faneuil Hall have retained its symbolic function as public space and continued to denominate the people while meeting the legal and political standards of private property? The short answer to this question is that the incorporation of Boston into a city created a new mode for designating both the people and their space when it abolished the town meeting, the institution of direct democracy that Bostonians had used to define their public space at will. In place of the town meeting were a city council and board of alderman, representative bodies empowered by the popular sovereignty of the commonwealth of Massachusetts to exercise its authority in the name of the people. One of the first official acts of this newly empowered city government was to make Faneuil Hall a daring and decisive demonstration of eminent domain. The protagonist of this enterprise was not a well-meaning but outflanked group of elite mercantilists and provincial selectmen who answered to the outcry of "market people" but the people themselves, legally represented by the city of Boston. On that authority, Mayor Josiah Quincy could constitutionally claim that seizing private property that abutted Faneuil Hall from the private people of Boston for the purpose of expansion not only served "the general interest of the citizens of Boston" but wielded the power of the public over the power of property privately held.[55] Of course, there was predicable opposition from three stubbornly private people, but after additional funds were acquired by the state legislature, the tax-levying strength of a government and its universally inclusive people finally overcame the resistance of personal wealth.

With the expansion of Faneuil Hall and Marketplace to include Quincy Market, the victory of both the municipal corporation and representative government was complete: the people had acted by constitutional mandate to secure a public estate, built for the express purpose of concentrating regional commerce in a small corner of Boston. To celebrate their victory, the people, the representative government of Boston, briefly moved its headquarters to Faneuil Hall. Henceforth, Faneuil Hall would always be occupied by the people through their popularly elected intermediaries, whether or not it was used for public meetings. It stood now in principle and in practice for the decision-making capacity of popular sovereignty, as well as its physical extension in property.

In 1837 Boston's board of aldermen exercised the power of popular sovereignty when it turned down the Massachusetts Anti-Slavery Society petition for Faneuil Hall, but even more importantly it offered a conception of public space fully consonant with the creation of a municipal corporation sixteen years earlier. That is, it considered the public estate of the city of Boston to have given its government a proprietary interest in public discussion:

> Resolved, That in the opinion of this Board [of aldermen], it is inexpedient to grant the prayer of said petition for the following reasons:—Resolutions and votes passed by a public meeting in Faneuil Hall, are often considered in other places as the expression of public opinion in this city; but it is believed by the board, that the resolution which would be likely to be sanctioned by the signers of this petition on this occasion, ought not to be regarded as the public voice of this city.[56]

In a bewildering appeal to the tradition of town meetings in Boston, the resolution decreed that precisely because the abolitionists had meant their meeting to be public, their request was invalid. If they had confined their invitation to only "one party," the "objection does not apply," but then they would not have sought out Faneuil Hall; a church or private lyceum hall would have sufficed. In a final show of deference to public opinion, the board based its decision on the fact that Faneuil Hall was deemed to be the site of the city's public voice "in other places."

The board thus would ensure that Faneuil Hall would remain public by closing it to public discussion, and with this decision it demonstrated the unexpected conclusion to the process of municipal incorporation: it made public space perversely private. Admittedly, it will confuse matters to say that the incorporation of Boston, the consolidation of its public estate, and the power of popular government over private property had ultimately a privatizing effect on Faneuil Hall, but some legal refinement can clarify matters. The sphere of governance and property that belonged to an incorporated city was constructed according to a category of law not always reducible to the constitutional, or statutory, law of representative government. This category of legal existence represented the sphere of the municipal corporation, one of the most complicated and mutable legal entities in the American corpus.

It would be oversimplifying the work of Oscar Handlin, Morton Horowitz, and Hendrick Hertog to propose a simple historical devolution from the public to the private municipal corporation. But the record of legal decisions that followed from *Trustees of Dartmouth College v. Woodward*, a landmark case that established the property rights of private corporation, did pave the way for a slow but steady transformation of the municipal corporation, chartered by the legislative sovereignty of the state, into a private entity, albeit one declaiming a public interest.[57] This transformation was accompanied by the steady cession of the authority, licenses, and capital for the development of public infrastructure to private corporations (though *Charles River Bridge Co. v. Warren Bridge Co.* was something of an exceptional decision in ensuring that their interests and profits would redound to the public benefit), so that any act of municipal government could only mimic the act of a private enterprise.

Such an act was undertaken by the city of Boston when it expanded the property around Faneuil Hall. Though purchased in the name of the people, Faneuil Hall had completed the cycle of its institutional history to return to the status of private property. The public function for this public space as well as its public financing was easily passed over. Instead, the committee charged with executing the plan for expanding Faneuil Hall and Marketplace to include Quincy Marketplace proudly announced that the expansion of public space had "augmented the real and productive property of the city." Whether the possession of property indeed made the city of Boston a private person on the order of Peter Faneuil is a question that the era's precedents of municipal corporate law only complicate, but when it distributed the stalls of newly constructed Quincy Market to private vendors, the city did function like a private person, that is, as owner and seller of property. And an un-successful *homo economicus* at that: though the Faneuil Hall committee claimed that the value "vested" in city property would more than make up for its debts, the city lost nearly $100,000 in the original transac-tions for the property surrounding Faneuil Hall.[58] At least here was one difference between Faneuil the private person and Boston, the munic-ipal person.

When it came time for the city government to demarcate public space, the board of aldermen borrowed freely from the private disposi-tion of a corporation and treated it as its private preserve. Thus the rejection of their petition for the Lovejoy protest is exactly what the abolitionists expected and perhaps even what they wanted. In the after-math of the board's decision, they would exploit the city's legal and political jurisdiction over public space to reveal the essentially personal nature of both public opinion and representative government. In fact, they argued, the assault on the discussion of abolition showed that the relationship between public opinion and the state had acquired an un-healthy intimacy that bordered on the pathological. Having debarred the abolitionists from Faneuil Hall, Boston's representative government was taking on the passions and prejudices of antiabolitionist mobs. Conversely, angry mobs such as the one at Alton acted with the law-making power of positive sovereignty. The conclusion that Garrison would draw from the controversy over Faneuil Hall was this: "The Board of Aldermen join with the mob in suppressing free discussion."[59]

In contrast to the public body that the board of aldermen claimed to represent, Garrison and the Massachusetts Anti-Slavery Society cel-ebrated a public unable to be privatized, personalized, or incorporated. They defined this indiscernible public by the defunct but still resonant institution of the town meeting, which attested not to a legally consti-tuted popular sovereign but to the incompatibility of the public with itself, an incompatibility clearly discernible in the perpetuity of debate regarding the public good.[60] Thus the stage was set for a contest between two conceptions of public space and two versions of Faneuil Hall. Ridi-culing the board's stewardship over the historical institution, Garrison argued that its true legacy was a public deducible only from the prolongation of indecision and the strength of agitation:

> And yet the Board have no objection to the use of the building by a "party," but when the occupancy of it is desired in the name of THE PEOPLE, for an object in support of which all are at least professedly agreed, then forsooth, it must not be granted, for fear of excitement! The fact constitutes the renown of Faneuil Hall, that it was built for the grand object of AGITATION—to keep up a perpetual EXCITEMENT—the excitement of free speech against gags and padlocks—the excitement of liberty in conflict with slavery—the excitement of equal rights against aristocratic usurpations. Its name, its history is EXCITEMENT! How it rocked during the "warmly contested questions" of the Revolution, when such "excited" disputants such as SAMUEL ADAMS, and JAMES OTIS, and JOHN HANCOCK, and JOSEPH WARREN, told what they thought about yokes for the necks, and chains for the limbs of the sons of the Pilgrims![61]

In Garrison's version of Boston's civic history, Faneuil Hall could represent the people neither officially nor metaphorically. Rather, the name stood for an inherently contentious, discordant public that could be known only by its metonymic association with other names: Adams, Otis, Hancock, Warren. Linking these revered patronyms to Faneuil Hall, he created a trope or figural space for the public in much the same way that Hancock and the sponsors of the lottery system had reconstructed the concrete institution: by using the currency of the name to constitute a common tie of citizenship that could not be reduced to common interests or social homogeneity.

Although Garrison made sure the name of Faneuil Hall retained the socially intelligible and historically resonant chain of associations—the town meeting, popular dissent, the freedom of speech, the declaration of political right—with which Bostonians established their claim to "the name of the PEOPLE," he also sought to prevent them or anyone else from recognizing themselves as such. He wanted Faneuil Hall and its associated names to signify not just the tropes of democracy but the figurative basis on which the identity of the people stood, so that the abolitionists' rhetorical appeals to the public space of free discussion might be seen as grounds in themselves. In this sense, we can say that Garrison was interested in Faneuil Hall as much for its role in authorizing the autonomy of language as for its role in authorizing the right of free speech; he seemed to hold the conviction that the distinguishing property of democracy, whether it be called "agitation" or "excitement," was its expression in language. Armed with the nomenclature of civic tradition, he could identify these words as merely synonyms for the otherwise unrepresentable agency of the public and still feel as if he were making good on the promise of civic life that the public space of Faneuil Hall held for the citizens of Boston. As a result, he did not have to argue that the name of Faneuil Hall predicated anything other than itself. "Its name," as Garrison insisted, "is excitement!"

What would become of Faneuil Hall when a city government seeking to administer its public estate and an insurgent movement that drew on the historical associations of democratic assembly both lay claim to a public space in the name of the people? The immediate effect of the controversy over the Lovejoy protest was to split Faneuil Hall into both a monumental symbol of popular sovereignty and the rhetorical expression of an imaginary public. The custodians of this monument, the governing body of Boston, would retrodetermine the founding of Faneuil Hall to coincide with the birth of the sovereign people they represented, which occurred when the elected legislature of Massachusetts incorporated the city of Boston and privatized its property. This was this date (including four years for the physical construction of Faneuil Hall and Quincy Marketplace) that the civic elites and scions of postbellum Boston observed when they staged a "semi-centennial" celebration for the building in 1876. With the inception of the "Cradle of liberty" dated from its reconstitution as city property, these celebrants honored Josiah Quincy as a civic patriarch, ensuring the continuing service of Faneuil Hall to the city's patrilinear discourse of citizenship.[62]

The abolitionists, on the other hand, would offer their own version of the "Cradle of liberty" and attempt to commandeer the symbolic dimension of Faneuil Hall for themselves. Rather than using the brick and mortar building or ultimately, the state as their medium of representation, Garrison and the Massachusetts Anti-Slavery Society would seek to make good on the expressive possibilities of language that the creation and recreation of Faneuil Hall had established in the civic life of Boston. That is, they would recognize the existence of the people solely in the utterance of the name and leave aside the official institutions, such as the electoral process, political parties, and, for the moment, public assemblies, that claimed to materialize it. With the inspiration of Faneuil Hall, they hoped to authorize nothing more or less than their own free speech as the proper locale of the public.

In Memory of Faneuil Hall

The Faneuil Hall that became known and loved as the "Cradle of liberty" can be considered the site where the signal expression of democracy, the utopian space of free speech and assembly, had not just a local address but a local history. As we have seen, its figurative representation of the people could be traced not only to the social exchanges of the print marketplace and the political institutions of town governance but to the material developments of city building. And yet the insurgent abolitionists were determined to introduce a dichotomy that had not previously existed: a distinction between a concrete Faneuil Hall and an imaginary Faneuil Hall, wholly commensurate with the figurative meaning of the "Cradle of liberty." In that distinction, they seemed to posit a radicalism, or autonomy of figurative expression, that they attempted still to equate with the public liberties and attributes of free speech.

The different phases of Faneuil Hall's institutional development in turn ensured that the abolitionists' trope of public space would be more than just words. Indeed, they could trace their innovation to the mediation of the print marketplace, which had given rise to the second, and arguably the definitive, incarnation of Faneuil Hall as well as to the other institutions of the abolitionists' public sphere. As such, they looked forward to the materialization of this public space solely in print, which is why Garrison drew attention to the trope of Faneuil Hall for the title of the movement's penny press. And yet the figurative appellation of Faneuil Hall seemed to operate also as a limit on the prospect of a historical recreation, or a break in the fiction of civic tradition that Faneuil Hall had come to symbolize. The effect of the verbal sophistication that was evident in the naming of the paper was to call attention to itself, or, more broadly, to the medium of the abolitionists' imagination.

The abolitionists' eponymous publishing venture could be distinguished further from the eighteenth-century lottery system that constituted the public space of Faneuil Hall by the fact that the name would circulate only among the small community of liberal reformers who read abolitionist publications like the *Cradle of Liberty* and *The Liberator* or who attended abolitionist meetings, not the indiscriminately composed citizenry who held the paper scrip. Consequently, the name of Faneuil Hall would never interpellate the people of Boston through the social exchanges of the print marketplace; their attempt to recreate a public sphere in the image of the "Cradle of liberty" would never reconcile the discursive structure of public space with the practical structures of civic life. On the contrary, Garrison and his Massachusetts Anti-Slavery Society allies hoped to make their language of Faneuil Hall an irreducible medium of citizenship, which would divorce the identity of the public from the social rituals and reproductions of democracy. They left unanswered the question of where the people could be convened or even who they were, but the abolitionists seemed to make their claim to Faneuil Hall under the assumption that an institution of democracy could be found anywhere language served the critical function of the public. This function, they believed, constituted both the enduring renown of Faneuil Hall and the role of self-declared outsiders to Boston's official public sphere.

New England abolitionists thus petitioned for the use of Faneuil Hall in 1837 under the assumption that their rhetorical appeal would have to suffice. Although their appeal was suffused with the legitimacy of democratic tradition, it also suited perfectly the abolitionists' sense of their minority status, their marginalization, and ultimately their dislocation from civic life. The imaginary public space that the abolitionists denominated for themselves in and with the name of Faneuil Hall in this sense had its origins in a fantasy of exclusion, which is also how they differentiated their movement from the institutions of citizenship; they seemed to develop their self-image as permanent exiles by bringing to fruition the figurative meaning of Faneuil Hall. For this same reason, the aldermen's reversal of their original decision should be counted as an anticlimax to their efforts. Never mind that the public assembly eventually held in the hall featured the notorious sentiments of Attorney General Austin and antiabolitionist public opinion. What made this public assembly not a public assembly was that it was held at all.

The triumphant Massachusetts Anti-Slavery Society resolution that finally opened the doors of Faneuil Hall made clear that the society's members regarded the concrete institution to be dead and buried whether they gained entry or not. All that remained of the former monument to democracy was the name:

> Whereas Faneuil Hall, belonging to us all, and consecrated to liberty and free discussion, has been denied to a portion of citizens who petitioned for leave to meet there ... Resolved, that the glory of the consecrated Hall, in which our fathers assembled to express their opinions on all occasion of an exciting character, is departed, and become desecrated to the idols and worshippers of despotism, if the fatal precedent is to be established by our rulers that Faneuil Hall shall be closed against citizens, be they many or be they few, who desire to assemble there in order to pledge themselves to the exertion of their whole influence for the suppression of mobs, for the discouragement of violence, for the vindication of the supremacy of the laws, and especially for the assertion and defense of the freedom the press.[63]

The death of Faneuil Hall is here mourned as part of a gothic narrative about the "departed" people. Yet its death at the hands of the board of aldermen was only the start of its afterlife as the spirit that haunted democracy, a spirit that could be summoned merely by saying the name.

The name of Faneuil Hall and its association with other names—the people, free speech, and liberty—composed the abolitionists' figurative language of Faneuil Hall, which the resolution presented, like Faneuil Hall itself, as "belonging to us all." Indeed, Faneuil Hall would forever be public through the independent existence of the name, proliferating without referent or object but always designating a place where the people should be. Secure in their possession of the name, the abolitionists left Faneuil Hall to the mockery of the present and hoped that it stayed dead. Without a place to go but already there, they placed their hopes for the resurgence of democracy in the belief that an imaginary Faneuil Hall existing only in their own rhetoric would displace the realities of public opinion with the experience of freedom found only in speech.

"Monumental history," Nietzsche writes, "is the masquerade costume in which the hatred of the great and powerful of their own age is disguised with satiated admiration for the great and powerful of past ages."[64] With much the same masquerade, Garrison and his allies within the Massachusetts Anti-Slavery Society moved the New England abolition movement farther than ever from the conventional venues of civic life such as voting and partisan organizing. In doing so, they could be secure in the knowledge that they stood rightly and rhetorically on the ground of Faneuil Hall wherever they exercised their freedom of speech. Its true place seemed to be nowhere else than in the language of commemoration and historical narrative that had given birth to both the figure of the "Cradle of liberty" and, as Nietzsche would have us intuit, the abolitionists' resistance. They maintained this conviction even if only one abolitionist stood up and spoke, for their exclusion from the public space of citizenship had given rise to a utopian public space that could exist nowhere in society but wherever speech was free. This was especially true for Garrison, who meant his protest against Boston's board of aldermen to stand on its own terms and stand in for the concrete institution of Faneuil Hall. The freedom of speech, he claimed, was nothing less than the rhetorical equivalent of public space, the "ground upon which all the citizens [of Boston] could amicably unite."[65]

He seemed to regale in the indeterminacy of language that made that ground either the abstract right of free speech or Faneuil Hall itself.

Nothing seemed to enrage Boston's critics of reform more than this imaginative claim on public space. According to Thomas Russell Sullivan, the author of *Letters against the Immediate Abolition of Slavery*, their pretense had debased public life in all of New England. "My mind was especially attracted to the manner in which public affairs are managed," he concluded from his observations, "where every man claims freedom to think, speak, and act for the public, and every other man admits his claim."[66] Like many Bostonians, Sullivan longed for the return of "public affairs" to duly elected public bodies, for the exclusion of abolitionists from the sphere of public discussion, for the reinstatement of official boundaries to public space. And yet the abolitionists were the ones with history on their side. By defending a venerated trope of Faneuil Hall from its contemporary denotation, they ensured that the discursive conditions for public space would survive its incarnation in brick and mortar and continue to underwrite the utopian dimension of language. To be sure, they might have projected the institutional development of Faneuil Hall well beyond the symbolic capacity that the civic history of Boston provided for it and utilized the city's normative representation of citizenship for the depiction of their exile. But by scrutinizing the successive versions of Faneuil Hall, we can place the abolitionists' political aspiration in the context of a larger, distinctively civic development that fixed the origins of public space in the signification of a name and ensured its future in the imagination.

CHAPTER 5

Thoreau's Civic Imagination

Henry David Thoreau's participation in the abolition movement was governed by the same principles that underwrote the New England abolitionists' public sphere, and that is why it should be considered to be marginal. With his "experiment in living," Thoreau expressed in dramatic and conclusive form the abolitionists' determination to separate their movement from the civil institutions of the political public sphere and from any positive representation of a people. His commitment to his own exclusion from the sphere of normative social relations led him to articulate a highly resonant discourse of social norms, which, like the abolitionists' discourse of publicity, could not disguise the sources of its historical reference. On the contrary, Thoreau's rhetoric consistently assumed the lapse of civil intercourse or the disappearance of an ennobling social space; moreover, it sought to reproduce the experience of this loss. In *Walden* he overlaid his description of life in the woods with elaborate metaphors of bourgeois commerce and analogies of civic enterprise, but just as in the abolitionists' petition for the use of Faneuil Hall, these spatial representations and tropes operated more as historical markers that surveyed, so to speak, an otherwise absent utopian space, whether it be the New England village, the independent family farm, or the *civitas* of republican political discourse.

At the same time, Thoreau meant his most imaginative use of language to bear testimony to the regeneration of civic life, if not to the regeneration of citizenship itself. At the least, he sought to authorize a kind of rhetoric that, like the abolitionists' invocation of Faneuil Hall, could induce its own sense of place. Indeed, we might consider his unlikely optimism, expressed at the end of *Walden* and articulated memorably in "Resistance for Civil Government," as the prospect of a "still more perfect and glorious State" that can be "imagined but not seen," as Thoreau's most generically abolitionist contribution to the various questions of reform he addressed.[1] His imagination of the perfect state or space of freedom built on the abolitionists' anachronistic vision of a public sphere, which was conceived as the place of outsiders or latecomers to the contemporary scene who otherwise had no place in Jacksonian political society. He would pursue an end similar to that of these more publicly engaged participants in the discussion of abolition and attempt to reconcile an expression of dissent from the smallest minority with the historical precedent of an informed public.

Thoreau's direct political response to the slavery question can be found in such essays as "Wendell Philips at the Lyceum," "Slavery in Massachusetts," "John Brown," and "Resistance to Civil Government" (subsequently retitled "Civil Disobedience"). In true abolitionist fashion, all of them call on the Anglo-American libertarian tradition of public dissent, and in "Resistance to Civil Government," Thoreau sought to equate his own expression of that right with the resistance of a people. His famous premise for his civil disobedience—"All men recognize the right of revolution"—drew its validity from the shared example of the American Revolution and led him to the conclusion that "it is not too soon for honest men to rebel and revolutionize" (227), but Thoreau seemed to know that he was positing the resurgence of a democratic revolution without accounting for the presence, or strictly speaking the place, of a democratic subjectivity in antebellum society. At the heart of "Resistance to Civil Government" is an allusiveness about the identity of a revolutionary agent that was more extensive than anything the abolitionists could have imagined for their own self-denomination. The closest he comes to a charge—"Action from principle—the perception and performance of right—changes things and relations; it is essentially revolutionary"—is so dependent on an invisible, self-performing agency that it leaves us wondering who is meant to do what. In the performance of this action, Thoreau seemed to imagine the inexorable process of atomization, not the totalization of subjectivity: "It not only divides states and churches, it divides families; aye, it divides the individual, separates the diabolical in him from the divine" (231).

The bearing of Thoreau's imagination on the abolitionists' political project becomes even more clear when we turn from his putatively abolitionist writings to the seemingly apolitical *Walden* and take our cue from the question he posed at the heart of his apologia for seclusion: "What sort of space is that which separates a man from his fellows and makes him solitary?"[2] In *Walden* Thoreau seemed to think through the imperative for revolutionary action he invoked in "Resistance to Civil Government" (the latter was delivered as an address in 1848, as he was writing the second and third drafts of the former) in relation to the formal expression of dissent and to ask himself whether there could be a space, place, or position for democracy if majorities were to be disbanded and the obligations of citizenship suspended. He claimed that the most individual expressions of free will were based on the memory of a revolutionary people, but in asking what "sort of space" was constituted by those expressions, he was indicating his willingness to test not just the utopian conception of active citizenship but the utility of any utopian representation at all.

As the last chapter showed, the New England abolitionists were careful to preserve the language if not the name of public space for the representation of their movement in the full knowledge that their claim on Faneuil Hall could never synthesize the abolition movement into the form or shape of the public. Using their connection to an imaginary Faneuil Hall, the one signified by the trope "'Cradle of liberty,'" and an equally historic ideal of the people, Garrison and the abolitionists took the sphere of abolitionist discussion so far from the conventional topography of the public sphere that the spatial dimension of democracy could be considered to have been suspended or abolished altogether—and yet it fell to Thoreau, the itinerant abolitionist and self-declared outsider to the movement, to force a contradiction between the abolitionists' political aspirations and the discursive medium of their self-representation. Although he coded his own expressions of free speech similarly, identifying them with the historic events of the revolutionary era, he could not invoke the names and traces of a revolutionary people without the expression of irony, or without subordinating them to the creative capacity of his imagination. Thoreau regarded language, in other words, as the enabling condition for political resistance but as no substitute for the public life of citizenship. Against the prospect of a public sphere reconstructed, so to speak, on the strength of the abolitionists' free speech, he would argue that the most historically inflected expression of dissent could reproduce only (to borrow Foucault's later characterization) the heterotopian aspect of language. A new and more troubling relation between words and things, according to Foucault, marks the end of an era in which "everything would be present in its proper place" through synchronic fictions of taxonomies, tables, and other discursive spaces. In evocative words with special resonance for the representation of Thoreau's exclusion, he describes the countervailing emergence of "a dimension of exteriority in which man appears as a finite, determined being, trapped in the density of what he does not think, and subject, in his very being, to the dispersion of time."[3]

The effects of time as well as a dimension of exteriority are evident in *Walden* in a way that the abolitionists' discourse of publicity could not make manifest. Although they sought to represent their resistance through the historical disjunction of their public sphere with the public sphere of the enfranchised citizen, they seemed to draw from the past a providential narrative of modernity that ensured the progress, if not the reinstatement, of the public agency of democracy in the antebellum era. As such, the abolitionists' measure of history and their assessment of time can be said to have originated in the same historical moment of Enlightenment they claimed to remember. Thoreau, on the other hand, committed the representation of his utopian space to the more disabling "dispersion" of time. That is, he drew directly the resources for his imagination from a historical process of modernization that stood separate and apart from the historical narrative of modernity.

In *Walden* he registered this process in the effects of urbanization, which is shown to have a determinate effect on the reference for his trope of utopia, the New England village. Addressing himself to "you who read these pages, who are said to live in New England," and even to the even smaller audience of Concord residents, he seemed prepared to address the prospects for the perfect state that he could only imagine as a local question, or as a question of locality; his description of what he called "your condition, especially your outward condition or circumstance in this world" was devoted expressly to "this town . . . as bad as it is" (2). Turning his attention to the effects of what historians call the "great transformation," he went on to chronicle the interpenetration of the capitalist marketplace into every sphere of Concord life, the growth of regional and national commercial networks that supplanted the autonomy of the town, the attenuation of traditional community ties, the influx of immigrants, and the rise of industrial urban settlements in nearby Lowell—all of which were made possible, as Charles Sellers would remind us, by the expansionist policies of the American state.[4] And yet for all his incisive criticism of this new political economy, Thoreau was seeking to elicit more than nostalgia for the loss of traditional village life. He was using *Walden* to assess what was lost and what was gained in the tragic calamities of the *gemeinschaft*, and, like Marshall Berman, he would conclude that once "everything solid had melted into air," an expressive or figural capacity for language remained behind that could not be reduced to any other purpose.[5] All he had to do to differentiate this capacity from another utopian prospect of modernity was to relate always the conditions for this very mode of representation to the material disposition of social space, and to make plain the connection of his own imaginative faculty to an unfolding historical process.

Thoreau's experience of urbanization can be differentiated from the urban history recounted in the previous chapter, which uncovered a symbolic representation of public space that the abolitionists both adopted and exceeded. Their trope of the "Cradle of liberty" had a history as concrete as that of the city, but it also relied on the uniquely expansive provincialism that let New Englanders confuse their local development and environs with a utopian space of citizenship, the "Athens of America," or, ultimately, the "city on a hill." Thoreau, on the other hand, had no trouble exposing the historical condition and contingencies for these discursive expressions, and he did so by invoking the most venerable of New England's spatial tropes. The traditional village, complete with town square, village green, and a necklace of family farms, as Joseph Woods has written, sustained an image of community perfectly compatible with the republican fantasies of antebellum New Englanders. This village ideal, however, did not even exist until it had been invented for the express purpose of articulating national principles. After having conducted a thorough revision of the development patterns of New England, Woods concludes that a local preference for the highly nucleated village form coincided with the development of the local historiography, which in turn was responsible for the many New England historical romances. *Walden* might be placed among the literary works—Catharine Maria Sedgwick's *New England Tales* and Henry Ward Beecher's *Norwood* among them—that memorialized, *Waverly*-style, the vanishing tradition of the New England village, or that, alternately, created the republic of letters known as "Virgilian Concord"[6]—except that Thoreau seemed more interested in describing the transformation of the village ideal into a prescription for living that could not be associated ultimately with any representation of place or even with a commemoration of it. In doing so, he would disable the civic consciousness the New England abolitionists demonstrated in their own historical references. He identified instead his "experiment in living" as a product, or casualty, of historical processes that could not preserve an absent place or interpellate an absent people.

Did any civic or political possibilities remain in Thoreau's sense of place? There is reason to believe that he conceived his retreat as a protest against the oppression of a proslavery state, particularly because he dedicated his own deprivation to the abolitionist cause. Warming to the subject in the company of his neighbor John Field, he says,

> The only true America is that country where you are at liberty to pursue
> such a mode of life that may enable you to do without [tea, coffee, and

meat everyday], and where the state does not endeavor to compel you to sustain the slavery and war and other superfluous expenses which directly or indirectly result from the use of such things. (137)

However, this rationale is only one of countless in *Walden* that subordinate every political stance to the value of self-containment. In return, Thoreau saw a golden opportunity to "carve and paint the very atmosphere through which we look, which morally we can do." In following this aesthetic prescription with the confession that his intent was "to live deep and suck out all the marrow of life . . . to rout out all that was not life, to cut a broad swath and shave close, to drive it into a corner, and reduce it to its lowest terms" (61), he provided so many figurative descriptions of the ideal of bourgeois autonomy that the nominal reference for all his normative prescription—the bourgeois space of civil or liberal society—is quite secondary to the enjoyment and expression of language.

Had the putative critic of capitalist modernization allied himself with its capacity for abstraction and sacrificed the intimacy of social relations and the concrete reality of social localities for, as Marx said famously, the "unreal universality" of an imaginary form?[7] In true Thoreau fashion, we should have to say that he used *Walden* to dodge a direct political response to this question. What he did instead was to reiterate the imperatives of bourgeois self-sufficiency and to parody the ethics of liberal capitalism until he had defamiliarized their ideological components. The first chapters of *Walden* show him compounding his apologia for classical liberalism with citations from eighteenth-century political economists such as Ricardo and Say. In doing so, he sought to draw attention to the origins of a civil society in the codification of economic principles, in the declaration of political rights, in the narration of the history of civilization and of its manners—in short, in the medium of its ideological representation. With his intellectual sophistication and wealth of historical allusions, he adopted Ferguson's, Smith's, and the Physiocrats' apologias for civil society in his paeans to independence and spiritual prosperity, but more importantly, he can be said to have adopted the self-consciously prescriptive features of modern liberalism that make it illegible in any other form but its most normative. Thoreau's parody of bourgeois self-sufficiency in this sense shared the distinction and conditions that modern theorists have ascribed to a liberal society: a willingness to date the moment of its emergence from the self-awareness of sociality; the reliance on an authoritative formulation for the sovereignty of avowedly inherent laws; the failure to reconcile the symbolic dimension of society with the totality of the social domain.[8] From the self-inscribed limits of bourgeois ideology, Claude Lefort has theorized a "social imaginary" that preserves "the space . . . between the enunciation and that that is enunciated," and that in turn maintains, through the incantatory power of its normative principles, "the fiction of a society which is, in principle, transparent to itself."[9]

In recommending Walden Pond for the civility of its squirrels, for the profits of bean growing, and for the joys of shack ownership, Thoreau might be said to have regaled in this fiction. That is, he presented his nominal settlement, a house in the woods, as the space of a social imaginary, relying on both the normative declamations of eighteenth-century political economy and the defamilarization of its representation to overcome the determinations of locale. In retrospect, none of the practical equivalents for Thoreau's "experiment in living"—the rustic retreat, the entrepreneurial enterprise, the naturalist observatory, the solitary excursion—could capture completely or exhaust all his allusive intentions. "I desire to speak somewhere without bounds," he confessed in the conclusion to *Walden*, and looked to his own rhetorical extravagance, "the volatile truth of our words," to "lay the foundation of a true expression" (214). In establishing his "sort of space" on this foundation, he thus restaged the genesis of a liberal society in a way that split off conclusively the political ideology from its respective spatial organization and promised to deterritorialize the space of social relations. Of course, this was the future Marx foresaw in the progress of liberal capitalism: whereas ancient kingdoms ruled from imperial cities and feudalism transferred power to the countryside, capitalism made the question of locale unnecessary and irrelevant.[10] In *Walden* the early modern conceptions of "town," "court," and "country" were similarly detached from their locale, so that what remained was Walden Pond—an amalgam of normative political, social, and economic principles that surpassed any single representation of place and betrayed consistently its own articulation.[11]

However, Thoreau did not want to cultivate his "sort of space" as a refuge from the historical process of modernization. Observing the changes to the town with a simultaneously mordant and mischievous tone, Thoreau was determined to show his "true expression" in diachronic, historical terms, as a development of history, in its relation to social-historical realities. He focused especially on the widespread process of modern urbanization, which was changing the built and unbuilt landscapes of Massachusetts into centers and subsidiaries of an emerging urban-industrial complex, and in doing so, he meant to document the emergence of the imagination, available not just as a compensatory sphere of self-determination but as a contemporary venue for civil relations.[12] Thoreau indeed hoped to reterritorialize the space of civil society as a set of activities—thinking, walking, writing, reading, observing—that together denominated the exercise of the imagination. True to the utopianism of the day, he wanted these activities to contain the possibility of a living space but he was quite clear in insisting that nothing in nature, in Brook Farm, or in Concord itself corresponded to the state of true freedom, which can be "imagined, but which cannot yet be anywhere seen." Precisely because of his commitment to the imagination, Thoreau made his "sort of space" sort of like a city—not the city of Boston or the urban-industrial city of Lowell but the city of the walker, the thinker, the observer, and especially the writer. What Thoreau imagined in Walden Pond, in other words, was the city of the flaneur, whose historical experience of urbanization is registered in individualized perception, in an idiosyncratic mode of expression, and, ultimately, in a self-conscious sense of place.

Walter Benjamin's reading of Baudelaire is my inspiration for re-reading *Walden* as a modern discourse of urbanism, for arguably the most provincial writer in New England literary culture was also the one most determined to create an experience of place that corresponded to the generically modern process of disorientation and dislocation. As it was for Baudelaire, this historical process is recorded subjectively, or in the emergence of an aesthetic consciousness whose "mission," as Benjamin describes it, is the "emancipation from experiences." Thus we read in the poetry of Baudelaire of the internal sensations, including the numbing absence of sensation, that the emergence of the modern city produced, rather than of the city itself. "He envisioned blank spaces," Benjamin says, "which he filled in with his poems. His work cannot merely be categorized as historical like anyone else's but it intended to be so and understood itself as so."[13] The history that this poetic representation recorded, Berman later argued, was in fact the destruction of medieval Paris by Napoleon III and Baron Hausmann, but so great is this loss that poems like "The Swan" can record the poet's appalled surprise at remembering, or perhaps at having forgotten, the experience of loss.[14]

In *Walden* Thoreau also sought to reproduce the modern process of urbanization in the contemplation of loss. Walking through the woods and recording the phases of his consciousness, he wanted the threatened extinction of traditional community life in a New England village to be registered as an irruption in the process of social reproduction that threatened to dislocate people from each other as well as from their locality. Yet as the flaneur of Walden Woods, Thoreau can be said also to have made himself at home in the distinctively urban experience of displacement. The increasing figuration of his prose at the end of *Walden* indicates his increasing distance from the town; he would explore the typically modern state of homelessness as a condition and equivalent for an aesthetic consciousness. This is why he was so ready to forgo the regeneration of Concord and to assign its community life to memory. He was already looking forward to its incarnation as a city.

Where could we expect to find this modern city? True to the modern discourse of urbanism, it exists not at Walden Pond but in *Walden*. There, Thoreau proliferated the signs or traces of an urban locale in a way that suggested the flaneur's mediated experience of place. For this same reason, the encroaching effects of industrial urbanization could be felt in Concord and its environs through its portents—the arrival of the railroad—and through its symptoms—the degeneration of "the manliest relations to men"—rather than as a concrete social form. As in the modern representation of city life, the material representation of urbanization is deferred and often displaced in the sensation of loss, anxiety, and disorientation, though these modern psychic structures, according to M. Caroline Boyer, can never correspond directly to the existing or emergent city. Instead, they entail what she calls the "city of collective memory": a lost or absent city that is preserved in "names of city streets and squares . . . its local monuments and celebration . . . as traces or ruins of their former selves."[15]

Like the flaneur, Thoreau marked the destruction of a cherished social space—in his case, the New England village—in the course of dramatizing the increasing sophistication, cultivation, and civilization of an individual self-consciousness. He looked forward to, in short, the arrival of cosmopolitanism in the wake of the town's destruction. In the "Conclusion" to *Walden*, he recommended the model of the "cosmopolite" over the life in the provincial village, whose residents would "think if rail-fences were pulled down, and stone-walls piled upon our farms, bounds are henceforth set to our lives and our fates decided" (211). He would mock their local attachment to Concord and even their nostalgia, for Thoreau posited the New England village as a social ideal in the full knowledge that it was already lost, or had never existed, or existed only in the minds of literate New Englanders.

Thoreau thus showed himself more ready than the abolitionists to abandon New England's local discourse of utopia and its attendant structure of commemoration. For Thoreau, the aesthetic consciousness of modern life held the possibility of the heterotopia of true citizenship, the critical position outside the public sphere where "the State," as he wrote in "Resistance to Civil Government," "places those who are not with her but against her" (231). In this position, he claimed to stand on "that more free but honorable ground," but unlike Garrison, he did not see this figure of space as the practical equivalent of a public space. Thoreau's submission "to the effects of time" was evident in his modulation of a civic identity and its modes of sociality into an urban consciousness that bore all the effects of social atomization and dispersion. Through the medium of his imagination, he would register nothing less than the modern experience of exile, and here we can foresee how he attempted to align his "sort of space" with the politics of the antislavery struggle: as the home of fugitive slaves, "men . . . with plantation manners, who listened from time to time, like the fox in the fable, as if they heard the hounds a-baying on their track, and looked at me beseechingly, as much as to say,—'O Christian, will you send me back?'" These were men, Thoreau claimed, "who had more wits than they knew what to do with" (102), and yet the same excess could be ascribed to him—he had too many conceits, too many rhymes, too much manner in his paean to the enslaved to reconstitute a civic language of political resistance and dissent. Thoreau's marginality depended on the incongruity of his aesthetic expression with any tradition or entitlement of citizenship and thereby challenged the abolitionists' claim to their utopian form of marginality.

The City That Never Was

We are confronted with the challenges of Thoreau's imagination as soon as we look again at *Walden* and discover that he went to the country to find the city. He admits that his retreat to the woods was motivated by necessity, since the opportunities for "beautiful living" once native to civilized society are now only found "out of doors, where there is no house and no housekeeper." Thus secluded, he finds "a good port" from which to conduct his "private business," a railroad line to link a "citizen of the world" to national and international marketplaces, a cosmopolitan alternative to Concord's unlettered, "provincial" culture, and with the help of Ellery Channing's companionship, even the bonhomie of Broadway in the woods. Perhaps most importantly, he determines that by cultivating Catonian civic virtue, he has reacquired the integrity to "sustain . . . the manliest relations to men" that his neighboring yeomen have forfeited.[16] In sum, every historic association of the city was present at Walden Pond—except, of course, the city.

The city is indeed both present and absent in *Walden*. It exists only through references and allusions to city life, which is to say it exists as the trope of metonomy. It has no geographical equivalent and, in fact, disclaims its status as locality, for Thoreau's intent is to use historically identified conventions of urbanism to conceive a space that corresponds to his imagination. Still retaining his sense of place or perhaps the conceit of a utopian reformer, he wants this space to be habitable and even to restore the sphere of civil relations to the most basic human activities, but above all he wants his urban references to demonstrate the enabling condition for an artistic sensibility: that the city is a construct of consciousness, commensurate with the awareness of individuality, if not alienation, that the process of modern urbanization engenders.[17] Thoreau's Walden Pond in this sense could take its place with Baudelaire's Paris, Whitman's New York, Crane's Bowery, and Dickens's London: that is, as urban spaces synonymous with an author's sense of place and thus with the extent of his subjective impressions.

The distinction of Walden Pond among these "unreal cities" is that Thoreau would force a contradiction between the aesthetically mediated experience of place and the actual place so that both the imaginative process and the means of representation are defamiliarized. In doing so, he was leaving behind the city itself as the implied referent, or site for his self-consciousness; more precisely, he was making an urban existence wholly contingent on the inferences, associations, and activities that he ascribed to his imagination. We might call Thoreau's representation of the city a "spatial practice" as Michel de Certeau describes it, particularly since *Walden*'s prescription for living seemed to designate the "walking rhetorics" and "pedestrian speech acts" that are said to compose a "*migrational,* or metaphorical, city." For Certeau, the "'city' founded by utopian and urbanistic discourse" is supplanted by "an immense social experience of lacking a place," which itself is known, in properly metaphorical fashion, only through the unexpected "'turns of phrase'" and inevitable "'wandering of the semantic'" that belong to the language of the everyday. Fredric Jameson's project of "cognitive mapping" likewise would appropriate an aesthetic mode of representation from the experience of urban life, though, once again, without being able to reproduce the spatial or ideological topographies of the modern city. In contrast to the centrality of the self-conscious subject and the utopianism of modernity, Jameson describes an ongoing process and quotidian struggle of situating the subject in a space that cannot be known in advance.[18]

Thoreau's method of orienting and surveying his domain at Walden Pond thus has in common with these two postmodern theorizations a willingness to divorce the image of the city from that of locale and to posit the space of his own subjectivity in accord with its figural representation.[19] He makes clear both these aims early on in *Walden*, when he designates a set of human activities that belong to his "mode of life" solely by their connection to the tropes of urban space. After berating his townsmen for their industriousness, he announces that his "purpose in going to Walden Pond was . . . to transact some private business" (13). Then he invites a comparison between his solitary life of rustic simplicity and that of the international mercantile trader, whose far-flung, multitudinous affairs elicit his unstinting praise and wonder. The worldliness of a cosmopolitan merchant, he writes, is a true test for the "faculties of a man—such problems as profit and loss, of interest, of tare and tret, and gauging of all kinds in it, as demand a universal knowledge" (13). This knowledge, Thoreau implies, could belong to anyone in Concord who desires the advantages of trade and civilization. He presents Walden Pond as "a good place for business" on account of its "good port and good foundation," as well as its ice trade and convenient railroad connection (14). In "Sounds," he writes that the railroad, transporting exotic goods from free and distant markets, makes him akin to the international merchant, a "citizen of the world" (80). He evidently wanted to build an Atlantic port city on his settlement at Walden Pond, "the germ," he calls it, "of something more" (175).

In representing his rural retreat with the normative values of urban mercantilism, Thoreau was seeking also to recover the potential for political autonomy inherent in a historical image of the city. According to Gary Nash, the eighteenth-century port city, including Boston,

Baltimore, Philadelphia, and Boston, was the center of liberalizing developments in government and trade as well as political movements for democracy. The international merchant commonly would have been a politically active Whig or Federalist allied with restive manufacturers and disenfranchised artisans. Together, they made the Atlantic commercial city the center of political resistance against monopolies, mercantilism, and colonialism.[20] Thoreau's self-comparison to the urban merchant thus perpetuates a vision of freedom wholly in keeping with the emergence of urban commercial classes in a postcolonial, laissez-faire economy. We may read his intention "to transact some private business with the fewest obstacles" as a homologous link between political and economic freedom but, more importantly, as an equally important link between liberalism's private space of freedom and a historical institution of urban space. This would have been compatible with his reigning ambition in *Walden* and in many of his political essays, which was to establish the prospects for revolution against resurgent tyranny, but his prescriptions for conducting "private business" can be said to have committed him also to building the locality for them.

In the spirit of urban Whigs, Thoreau envisioned Walden Pond as a free society of trade and commerce, politically and geographically external to the machinations of an intrusive state. He found these machinations everywhere in society, which is why his seemingly arbitrary protest against the poll tax can be regarded as an eighteenth-century version of an urban liberal's paranoia. As J. G. A. Pocock has said, the prevailing logic of corruption in Whig political discourse held that statist directives—whether they financed trade monopolies, the slave trade, or a system of railroads—were deforming the properly private affairs of civil society.[21] Likewise for Thoreau, a resurgent neomercantilist economy was responsible for the corruption of his fellow townspeople; the tyranny of the state, he seemed to say, was colonizing the separate sphere of civil society with its own space, the all-inclusive yet personalized space of the nation.[22] He saw the expansion of this space in the nationalist sentiments of citizens who "think it essential that the *Nation* have commerce, and export ice, and talk through a telegraph, and ride thirty miles an hour"; true to form—that is, to his reproduced urban form—he would counterdict the claims of the nation with an ideal of civil autonomy rooted in eighteenth-century urban liberalism. Applying with relish the liberal's standard of corruption to his patriotic towns-people, Thoreau mocked them for being "content to live baboons" (62).

Thoreau seemed well aware of the disparity between his settlement and the eighteenth-century commercial city but he was determined to let neither the location of Walden Pond nor the passage of time deprive him of the intelligence, freedom, and prosperity available to the period's urban bourgeoisie. He built his identification with this class by under-mining both the pastoral tradition of American letters and the nation-alist history it projected. When he did represent nature, it was not as an extension and progress of positive sovereignty but according to the self-negating provisions of civil society.[23] That is, he considered Walden Pond to be natural insofar as it was a completely commercial realm, free of superfluous obstacles and unconditioned by an intrusive alien power. Thoreau referred to this realm as "primitive and frontier life" not because it was wild but precisely because it was governed by "the essential laws of man's existence," which he found recorded in "the old day books of the merchants." Not surprisingly, these laws instructed Thoreau in the ways of bourgeois society: what is natural and necessary is "all that man obtains by his own exertions" (7). He thus disqualified the labor of his neighboring farmers, who work not for themselves but for the holders of their mortgages on their homes and farms; on the other hand, Thoreau recommended the virtue of the unencumbered wigwam, the profit of uncultivated fields, and the political economy of squirrels, all of which furnished him with his most explicitly self-justifying image of the urban bourgeoisie. He made special allowances when he added fuel and clothing to the necessities of food and shelter, but he consid-ered any life that followed intrinsic dictates of nature to be both a moral and material improvement over that of Concord townsmen. In the con-clusion, *Walden* recommends that the conscientious citizen devote him-self to "more sacred laws," but there can be no mistake that Thoreau's attachment to the equally invisible laws of the marketplace was intended to reproduce both the ideology of bourgeois commerce and its urban locale.

Thoreau's ironic references to the utopian discourse of the liberal marketplace linked *Walden* more directly to the Whig-Federalist project of city planning, which historically fused the republican politics of dis-interested virtue with an economically constituted social space. From the Revolution to the antebellum era, the commercial city was indeed the sphere in which the new nation's republican pretensions were given institutional form, often most effectively translated by the merchant classes who were spearheading the development of liberal capitalism. The lyceums, athenaeums, libraries, and salons that comprised the ante-bellum era's "republican institutions" were first developed in Atlantic port cities; with no attempt to disguise the city's principle indigenous activity, their wealthy patrons celebrated them as "cultural ornaments to mercantile society."[24] In conjunction with the ascension of French neoclassicism, these "cultural ornaments" fueled the Federalist city's comparisons to the classical polis, although this was more the case with Philadelphia and Boston than with single-mindedly mercantile New York.[25] Within the confines of this urban space, self-seeking burghers could transcend their interests in a manner consistent with their self-image as a disinterested citizenry.

This civic consciousness in turn put *Walden* at odds with the Jack-sonian project for liberal capitalism, which posited a rural form of eco-nomic society in the image of the enfranchised majority. For Thoreau, the moral advantages of commerce as well as the self-conception of a minority followed more closely from the Federalist city plan for virtuous citizenship. In "Reading" he proposed that Concord proper be developed along the lines of a classically Federalist city, replete with indigenous salons, galleries, libraries, lyceums, and other educational facilities. He exhorted the citizens of Concord not to adopt a "provincial" life but to "act collectively in the spirit of our [prospective] institutions" and "take the place of the noblemen in Europe" (74). The ambition to create "noble villages of men" was in keeping with an aristocratic tendency of Federalism, which would enshrine a tiny minority of educated men as the moral custodians of the new republic, though Thoreau seemed to provide for a more democratic distribution of civic virtue by proposing to revive Federalism's project of city planning. The New England village, he contended, could become a "noble village" by being transformed into a cosmopolitan center, capable of receiving information, influences, and goods from distant ports. The same held true for Walden Pond, or any place at all. "Reading" would attribute the Federalist civic ideal to any ennobling, self-directed activity and, in the process, resituate the moral discourse of republicanism in a liberal discourse of urbanism.[26]

Thoreau was so invested in the normative value of urban venues that he was ready to disregard the conventional association of republicanism with the pastoral. The best part about nature, he countered, was its resemblance to city life, which was the source and reference for a moralized discourse of enterprise he applied indiscriminately to the spaces of town, village, and country.[27] If the pastoral was celebrated at all, it was in accordance with the value of urban liberalism in New England, where agrarianism was promoted by the same Federalist urban merchants who were building the port city in their image of the *civitas*. A Boston group known as the Essex Junto was particularly determined to invest rural life with the same capacity for education for which the urban institutions were intended. The country seats and adjoining farms that dotted the eastern Massachusetts landscape were considered not as alternative pursuits in their own right but as necessary adjuncts to market exchanges that promoted scientific or horticultural learning, guaranteed their virtue, and signaled their contribution to the public good.[28]

In "Where I Lived, and What I Lived for," Thoreau confesses that he adopted the traditional land-use pattern of the urban capitalist, roaming the countryside as a self-appointed real-estate broker, financier, and landscape architect of imaginary country seats. He then reinterprets this conventional pattern of subdivision as the simple experience of sitting, though not without planning a manorial estate in his mind. Conspicuously omitting the farmer's field, he reports that "an afternoon sufficed to lay out the land into orchard, woodlot, and pasture, and to decide what fine oaks or pines should be left to stand before the door, and when each blasted tree could be seen to the best advantage." To further link his "*sedes*" to the styles and habits of the urban gentry, he speculates that "the future inhabitants of this region, wherever they may place their houses, may be sure that they had been anticipated" (55).

Like the urban capitalist, Thoreau did not mean to associate himself with the virtues of the yeomanry. His dedication to husbandry, on display in "The Bean Field," was inspired by an Anglo-American bourgeoisie that had adopted the Catonian ideal of an agrarian republic to represent the virtue of an urbanized commercial society. According to Pocock, "country" ideology originated in an attempt to base England's economy in nondependent land-holding, but as Britain evolved into an international trading empire, the signifier of place became the name of an opposition political party whose model republic was less associated with nature than with laissez-faire commerce. Against speculative, debt-inducing, and state-sponsored monopolies, the "country" exponents of a liberalized marketplace envisioned a public realm of free and equitable exchange in which the profits of commerce were in proportion to virtue.[29] To mitigate the power of the state, to recreate the space of civic virtue in the commercial city, *Cato's Letters* thus proposed "'agrarian law or something like it.'"[30]

In "The Bean Field" Thoreau seems also to have pursued agrarianism or something like it. What Robert Gross has revealed as the "great bean-field hoax" might have been played on the agricultural reformer,[31] but it can be considered also in the context of "country" ideology as an attempt to establish on ironic terms the republicanism of the commercial city. Thoreau notes the derision his bastardized husbandry elicited from locals but cannot disguise his pride for the $8.72 in his pocket, "the result of my experience in raising beans" (109). His narrowly economic assessment for the virtues of his toil might have been at variance with the cult of the noble yeoman, but Thoreau's interest in farming never strayed from the liberal apologia for civil commerce. In citing Cato's dictum—"the profits of agriculture are particularly pious or just"

(111)—he was casting his lot with the eighteenth-century Whig liberal, who endorsed such profits precisely because they shared the purported virtues of urban capitalism: they were obtained without excessive borrowing, without state capitalization, and perhaps most importantly to Thoreau, without submission to the brute force of the "slave-driver" within.

Politics and geography are often difficult to correspond, especially in the context of the "country" ideology Thoreau invoked. One appraisal of his overdetermined discourse—"Republican virtue and virtuous republicanism constitute the true polis, the republican city of 'country' orientation"—says much about the plastic nature of supposedly geographical signifiers.[32] Thoreau regaled in this confusion, creating a self-consciously figurative language that compared city to country and country to city without establishing either place as an actual referent. Horkheimer's judgment that Thoreau's "escape into the woods was conceived by a student of the Greek polis rather than by a peasant" rings true for this reason: the displays of erudition in "The Bean Field," first observed in the allusions to Virgil, Hector, Hercules, and finally to Cato's moral discourse on agriculture, lead us inexorably toward an awareness of language, which, Thoreau made sure to suggest, is the property of a cultivated city-dweller.[33]

Thoreau wanted to show off this cultivation in his self-comparison to other more conveniently situated aesthetes, remarking that "some of my contemporaries devoted to the fine arts in Boston or Rome . . . and others to trade in London and New York" would find him "devoted to husbandry" (108). It goes without saying that these contemporaries would find him devoted also to erudition, cultivation, and his own brand of cosmopolitanism in Walden Woods. *Walden* was his attempt at belles lettres, after all, and he would use its indeterminacy of setting and reference to establish the urbanity of his figural representation. In his allusive references to an eighteenth-century commercial city, a civic republican project of city planning, an antimercantilist country ideology, and, finally, the classical ideal of civic space, he seemed to be preparing for the future place of all these urban forms in the medium of his expression.

"The Nick of Time"

When Thoreau says in "The Bean Field" that he would plant "other crops than these ... a new generation of men" (110) and that he ploughed the ground "for the sake of tropes and expression" (108), we cannot help thinking that there was little in his description of Walden Pond that was not intended to be seen as a creation of language. In *Walden* he showed himself to be committed to the formal innovations that this entailed but he also meant the ceaseless play of language and the unexpected turns of phrase to project a lived sphere of activity, wherein the value of human, specifically civic, interactions obtained irrespective of social space. The "civic consciousness" he demonstrated on behalf of Concord's townspeople and the artistic formalism in this sense were false opposites for Thoreau. His determination to transplant the virtues of the *civitas* with life in the country was only his most dramatic show of irony.[34]

If only for this reason, we should not minimize Thoreau's growing investment in an explicitly figural discourse, which led him beyond his aptitude for political satire into a sophisticated philosophical playfulness before, according to one critic, finally reifying both language and his intellectual labor into unmarketable fetishes.[35] By the middle of *Walden*, Thoreau had assembled a Transcendentalist idiom of self-consciousness, full of extended metaphors of foundations, fathoming, and bottoms; in "The Pond," Walden Pond is inevitably apostrophized as a Cartesian subject. When he writes, "I am thankful that this pond was made deep and pure for a symbol" (189), we may read an ascending level of figuration, a meta-figural discourse that becomes his final horizon of experience. As *Walden* nears its end, Thoreau leaves behind any sense of place or spatial reference whatsoever and dissolves himself into this increasingly self-aware discourse. In the "Conclusion" he presents his "experiment in living" as the aspiration for hyperbole—"I fear chiefly lest my expression may not be *extra-vagant* enough" (214)—and then describes his efforts to exceed the limits of representation. He says he wants to awaken his contemporaries to the truth of an unsaid "residual statement," but the effect of this and the other figures of *Walden* is to make them a "literal monument"—that is, through such self-reflexive puns, to make language an irreducible experience and the ultimate promise of his retreat (215). In the end, he subordinates his preference for either city or country to the desire "to speak somewhere *without bounds*" (214).

The intensified consciousness of language in *Walden* does coincide with the displacement of Walden Pond as an actual locale, or with the abolition of space per se. However, it does not do away with the awareness and analysis of the historical conditions that produced it. As we have seen, Thoreau's elaborate use of tropes and figures effectively collapsed the respective spaces of distinct urban forms—the eighteenth-century commercial city, the Greek polis, the *civitas* of Catonian virtue—into each other, reproducing the likeness of the city in a form befitting the work of art in the age of mechanical reproduction. The foreshortening of distance and time in artistic representation in turn can be considered a historical process that is linked directly, Benjamin would tell us, to the modernization of society. Ejected from its original setting, the "uniqueness of every reality" is said to come into view "at very close range by way of its likeness, its reproduction," and the same can be said for Thoreau's imaginary city.[36] In its successive likenesses, all the historical permutations of the city are present, and at the same time, none of them are, for Thoreau truly welcomes the plenitude of language under the premise of declension that hangs over the opening chapters of *Walden*. As such, his intent in reproducing the city in the medium of language is not just to create a medium of historicism but to force a moment of historical awareness, to make us aware of time.

One way to reconstruct Thoreau's own historical awareness is by comparison with the pyschic structure of the urban flaneur, whose remembrance of a lost city links the emergence of aesthetic modernism to the traumatic emergence of modern consciousness. In Benjamin's reading of Baudelaire, this remembrance is a *memoire involuntaire* that permanently displaces the traumatic event from experience but leaves behind a memory trace, the point at which self-consciousness is said to come into being. The perception of these traces signifies a uniquely modern urban landscape of hidden events, former lives, and the signs of having forgotten, as well as an analogous landscape within the psyche, the space of the unconscious. This has been Jameson's interest in the Freudian language of memory traces and forgetfulness—in identifying the negative condition in the artistic discourse of modernism for representing the calamities and crises of historical experience. He looks for the "ultimate raw material" for the narrative unities, class allegories, and social fantasies of the artistic form and finds there a "symbolic enactment of the social" in which the real conditions of existence are present only as an "absent cause."[37]

In *Walden* the end of an independent yeomanry, the rise of a propertyless working class, the destruction of a local economy, and the triumph of the marketplace are all registered in the manner of "political unconscious"—they appear as the signs and occasions for Thoreau's heightened consciousness. We might be led to conclude that Thoreau's aesthetic self-consciousness shared the psychic structure of the modern neurotic—if he had not created the presumption of loss with a strategic intent. Unlike the flaneur, whose memory, or failure of memory is directed toward a lost city, Thoreau induced an awareness of historical distance by iterating the traces of a city that had never existed in Concord. Instead, the eighteenth-century port and the Federalist *civitas* are invoked with an attitude of what has been called "anticipatory nostalgia," which posits retroactively an originary site, or in the New England idiom, a "city on a hill," under the cloud of having done so too late.[38] Thoreau's excavation of Edward Johnson's "Wonder-Making Providence" was such an occasion for staging this nostalgia, an attempt to invoke a historical memory for an "experiment in living" that in truth defied all precedent. He went so far as to lend to his efforts the seal of approval from "the wealthy and principle men in New England" and perhaps even the former glory of their civilization, but with his pride reserved for his deep cellar, Thoreau seemed to be recalling the history of the region in order to present it, like his "sort of space," as an occasion for irony.[39]

A more subversive intent on Thoreau's part can be inferred from his commemoration of the New England village ideal, whose simple patterns of community life were being committed to memory in the face of modernization.[40] But with his stated preference for "tropes and expressions" and his creation of a figurative discourse of urbanism, Thoreau seemed to want to call a halt to the narrative structure of modernism and the neurotic longing of the flaneur, both of which would posit the inexorable passage of time and thus the inevitability of progress. At his most critical, he wanted to stop the flow of time, or, more precisely, to bring what Homi Bhabha has called the "temporal dimension in the inscription of [modernity]" to the level of awareness so that his contemporaries could see their histories being constructed for them.[41] To this end, he offered alternatives to calendrical time— the sidereal time of the seasons, in one instance—and a technological basis for clock time—the institution of the railroad schedule—all the while recommending that every person should follow his example and just stop and think. It was the only way to interrupt the narration of modern progress before it yielded a sense of inescapable time and fate. Thoreau posited his own iteration of this narrative in the "nick of time," which he was so "anxious to improve"; he situated himself in the "meeting of two eternities, the past and the future, which is pre-cisely the present moment." He apologized for "some obscurities," by which he meant his figurative expressions, but claimed to be resolute in his intention: he would "toe that line" and not slip off into memory or expectation (11).

At its most ambitious, Thoreau's retelling of this narrative could represent what Bhabha calls the "signifying space of iteration rather than a progressive, linear seriality," the outcome of which is either chronic longing or unfounded confidence.[42] In place of either sentiment, Thoreau looked forward to remembering so that he could interject the disjunctive moment of his own signification, stand still in the time of the present, and put history itself, as Benjamin provocatively describes it in his discourse on historicism, under arrest.[43] This very possibility is described in the "Conclusion" to *Walden*, where Thoreau describes the artist of the city of Kouroo who "made no compromise with Time"

(216). As an allegory of artistic creation, the story seems to capture the tendency of affirmative culture as a whole, which is to overcome the temporality of existence through the claims of eternal aesthetic value. However, Thoreau offers the allegory rather apologetically, as an interruption among his more concrete recommendations, or, better yet, as a distantiated figure, which means that its performative value could be differentiated from its pedagogical content. The performative, Bhahba has written, initiates a "shift in perspective" to an "enunciatory 'present' marked in the repetition and pulsation of its national sign."[44] We can substitute "civic" for "national" and conclude that Thoreau found himself in the "nick of time" at the moment when his own reiterations of urban utopias relinquished the modern historiography of progress and loss, of future and past in favor of the freedom of the "present moment."

Thoreau invoked the tradition of the *civitas* against the deformations of modern society; alternately, he looked forward to the arrival of more urbane civilization in the end of provincial village life. His conflicting attitudes toward the arrival of urbanization in Concord suggest that what we are reading in *Walden* is really the performance of a narrative of modernization that would record what Bhabha calls "a temporality of the 'in-between.'"[45] For Thoreau, this ironic representation of time entailed a new space, which corresponded to a life spent on the margins, and as such it served also as Thoreau's standpoint of resistance: not just the space of seclusion, though he conceived Walden Pond as such, but the state of being under arrest, which is where we discovered him in "Resistance to Civil Government" and where he made his stand against slavery. The disjunctive moment of his reiteration in this sense had its counterpart in the interregnum of imprisonment; together, they signified a critical potential for Thoreau that was tied directly to his ability to remain in the space between idealism and despair.

Having refused to place himself in a temporal narrative of modern progress, Thoreau chose a place that could be categorized only as a hiatus—"I am a sojourner in civilized life again," he admitted at the beginning of *Walden*—and true to form, he represented this marginal position from within the spatial tropes of utopia. He would be always on the boundary, which is where he said "the freer and less desponding spirits" who had been "put out and locked out of the State" (233) could be found. No matter that the social identity of these spirits—"the fugitive slave, and the Mexican prisoner on parole, and the Indian come to plead the wrongs of his race"—told of a marginality that extended well beyond Thoreau's sojourn. In the confines of prison, Thoreau reports in "Resistance to Civil Government," he had never felt so close to the institution of the town, admitting "I was fairly inside of it" (238).

Thoreau's determination to put conventional narratives of progress under arrest in this sense represented a "minority discourse," which, as Bhabha describes it, perpetuates an "insurmountable ambivalence" between normative and marginal positions.[46] Of course, this was Thoreau's intent—to appear as the exile who could still belong—but the discursive and logistical efforts he expended in order to remain on the boundary should remind us that there were others—the enslaved, the Mexican, the Indian—who endured the condition of marginality without metaphor or irony. His "minority discourse" might even be said to be for the majority, or for the white reformer who considered a hiatus preferable to either the privileges of enfranchisement or the subaltern existence of the disenfranchised, and if this sounds like an abolitionist position, it was. In *Walden* Thoreau made plain that he was passing up the chance to oppose the "gross and somewhat foreign servitude called Negro slavery" in favor of opposing the slave-driver within, a decision that gave his entire critique of modernization in Concord the same limits and potential as the abolitionist criticism of citizenship.

Thoreau's refinement, however, of this "gross" subject required a more overtly aesthetic comparison between the citizen and the slave than Garrison and the New England abolitionists had proposed for themselves. He offered a more radical version of this figurative comparison in that it precluded the detection of any and all political progress or any political agency. Thoreau would disable the political narrative of modernity no less than the historical narrative of modernization in order to interject "an otherness or alterity into the present," to use Bhabha's words again. It was by "toeing the line" and remaining under arrest that Thoreau staked his own claim to otherness, but in truth, this minority position was indecipherable without the play of meaning in all his figurative comparisons.

As part of his resistance to the language of progress, Thoreau refused to mount a eulogy for the impoverished farmer or even mourn for the loss of village life in Concord. He criticized their condition as he would slavery, but he was more interested in recounting the practices and customs of his contemporaries that served and reproduced the temporality of modernization. The daily grind of the laboring man, Thoreau argued, left him "no time to be anything but a machine" (3); with his labor, he had submitted the seasonal cycles of village life in Concord to the economic regimen and social organization required for capital-intensive industrial development. That Concord was fated never to be home to the manufacturing system that made eastern Massachusetts the site of America's first industrial cities did not matter to Thoreau.[47] With the everyday bustle of the town sounding to him "like the hammer laying the foundation of another Lowell,"[48] he focused his analysis on what one urban historian calls "industrial behaviours," which, like industrialization itself, are foundational for the work of city building.[49]

The arrival of the railroad, the iron link between the farmers of Concord and the ever-encroaching urban marketplace, indeed brought a quantification of time found in a factory. They "go and come with such regularity and precision ... that the farmers set their clocks by them, and thus one well conducted institution regulates a whole country" (80). This institution in turn governed all the time farmers spent on their labor, for Concord's local railroad was part of the heavily capitalized infrastructure and market reorganization that urban historians associated with a stage of "proto-industrialization."[50] With this development, family farms and local farmers became part of a more organized distribution system for the hungry people of Massachusetts's burgeoning cities. Native grains and corn were replaced with new cash crops such as fruits and vegetables that were transported along improved roads; with the arrival of the train, dairy products from the farthest reaches of

Massachusetts could be consumed in Boston. The farmers' patterns of land use and labor, Thoreau charged, corresponded exclusively to the desires and demands of remote nonresidents, not to those of their family or their community.[51]

The encumbered farmer now grew for a specialized agricultural market and brought his produce to a professional merchant or a centralized marketplace, such as the Middlesex Cattle Show, whose *"eclat"* Thoreau despised (22). Goods and services that might have produced by, between, or for local farmers thus came from elsewhere and were for sale, which is exactly what he saw with each arrival of the train:

> The whistle of the locomotive penetrates my woods summer and winter, . . . informing me that many restless city merchants are arriving within the circle of the town, or adventurous country traders from the other side. As they come under one horizon, they shout the warning to get off the track to the other, heard sometimes through the circles of two towns. Here come your groceries, country; your rations, countrymen! Nor is there any man so independent on his farm that he can say them nay. And here's your pay for them! screams the countryman's whistle. (78)

Specialized farming brought still more indignity to the farmer by propelling him into a monetary economy in which he could not compete, especially since cash tended to be a rather scarce commodity in communities like Concord. Its value depreciated that of plentiful agricultural goods and therefore could produce only diminishing returns:

> Every New Englander might easily raise all his own breadstuffs in this land of rye and Indian corn, and not depend on distant and fluctuating markets for them. . . . For the most part the farmer gives to his cattle and hogs the grain of his own producing, and buys flower, which is at least, no more wholesome, at a greater cost, at the store. (43)

The subservience of Concord's citizens to an urban mercantile exchange, Thoreau contended, had commodified not just the products of their labor but their labor itself, which was likewise "depreciated in the market" (3).

The impoverished farmer as much as the propertyless immigrant who roam through *Walden* thus were the denizens of a newly urbanized Concord. Thoreau intended his own shack, "bought and paid for," to contrast positively with the encumbered homes of his townsmen, who "for the most part have been toiling twenty, thirty, or forty years, that they may become the real owners of their farms." However, he also saw that the consolidation of capital in central lending institutions had created this pitiful fate for his neighbors. He gave eloquent testimony to the feudalizing effects of merchant capitalism when he described the subjugation of the Concord farmer to one of the most powerful instruments of urban capitalization.[52] "On applying to the assessors," he wrote, "I am surprised to learn that they cannot at once name a dozen in the town who own their farms free and clear. If you would know the history of these homesteads, inquire at the bank where they are mortgaged" (21). Under these conditions, Thoreau's neighbors were forced "to spend borrowed or stolen time, robbing your creditors of an hour" (4).

There was only one alternative to the progress of urbanization: Concord must become more like a commercial city of the eighteenth century. However, Thoreau could not propose this solution or any other without the figurative references and play of irony that he used to compose his imaginary urban space. He meant all his expressions to arrive "in the nick of time," but he would arrest or stop up the language of the reformer in order to keep himself suspended in the present moment. Indeed, he would not attempt to change anything but just wished "not to live in this restless, nervous, bustling, trivial Nineteenth Century, but stand or sit thoughtfully while it goes by" (218). In all likelihood, this was an impossible prospect without Thoreau's metaphors of sitting, standing, and the procession of time; it might have had its only equivalent in the experience of writing, or reading *Walden* itself. However, it was also perfectly consistent with the disjunctive commentary, the plays of language, and the subversive interjections of his critical commentary, all of which were intended to forestall a narrative representation of progress or nostalgic recollection of a precapitalist past.

To this end, Thoreau refused to create an arcadian fantasy of virtuous family farms; his conversations with George Minot, the stalwart yeoman farmer who inspired Thoreau with his claim that he had never sullied himself by participating in the market, furnished the image of an idealized economy more like the urban bourgeoisie's conception of a *civitas*.[53] A prerevolutionary agricultural economy, according to Betty Hobbes Pruitt's recasting of the Jeffersonian yeoman ideal, created cash crops and a regional marketplace, but above all a shared quest for self-sufficiency that allowed the pursuit of self-interest to serve the common good.[54] In an extended paean to the family farm in his *Journal*, Thoreau supplied still more dissonant references—it was said to be the model of "a state," of "separate principalities," or of a "confederacy"; it was "the older and more venerable state" and the seat of the "nobility of every country" who were "behind and prior and in some sense independent on [*sic*] the state."[55] The overdetermination of this representation confounded not only the description of space but the tropes of time, as the past of the independent farm seemed to have little to do with its future, which Thoreau seemed to see as a metaphor of resistance.

Still more ironies could be found in Thoreau's praise for the "very simplicity of man's life in the primitive ages," which made the native inhabitants of New England its only true landed gentry and their wigwams its only self-sustaining manors. He took pleasure in shifting geographical and temporal references and would do everything possible to prevent either the sylvan landscape or the prelapsarian past from being taken seriously as a starting point for a narrative of modernization. For Thoreau, however, the promise of this comic pastiche was not just to halt the narration of progress but to represent the ambiguity of his own position by reference to the native American, the truly other, and all the outcasts from the New England village ideal. That he did not converse or recall a conversation with such outcasts in *Walden* is beside the point; he would "conjure up the former occupants of these woods" in his imagination and "repeople the woods" in his dreams (175).

Indeed, this is the point of the aesthetic tour de force of "Winter Visitors," where Thoreau delivers a suitably equivocal eulogy for the African American inhabitants of the area by Walden Pond that was poised halfway between reverence and disparagement. Standing literally on their ground, he recalls "Cato Ingraham, slave of Duncan Ingraham," for his "half-obliterated cellar hole," now "filled with the smooth sumach . . . and one of the earliest species of goldenrod"; Brister Freeman, "'a handy Negro,'" is said to have his epitaph written "in the old Lincoln burying-ground, a little on one side, . . . where he is styled 'Sippio Brister—Scipio Africanus he had some title to be called'" (171–72). Having made typically playful use of civic republican conventions of commemoration, he evokes an entire civilization once extant in Walden Woods, but "cellar dents, like deserted fox burrows are all this is left where once were the stir and bustle of human life"; he confesses, "all I can learn . . . amounts to this, that 'Cato and Brister pulled wool'" (174–75). For Thoreau, life on the margins means menial labor long forgotten, and he refuses to offer a more grandiloquent commemoration for it. He remarks "how little does the memory of these human inhabitants enhance the landscape!" before he begins to imagine the future. The day-to-day existence of the marginalized, in other words, he recalls only in an elegiac interregnum, though it says much about Thoreau that he used such an interlude to interject himself in this same moment of time. He looked forward to having his house remembered as "the oldest in the hamlet," so that he might be recalled in the manner of Brister, whose name was given to Walden Pond's nearby spring.

If Thoreau meant to arrive between "the past and the future, which is precisely the present moment," he did so without suggesting clearly the relation between an abolitionist language of political resistance and the more disjunctive language of figurative comparisons with which he depicted his own resistance. To be sure, he sought to occupy a minority position that mimicked Garrison's own sense of exclusion, but his refusal to commemorate even Concord's own Crispus Attucks meant that he was relinquishing the abolitionists' hold on what Lyotard calls "the politics of forgetting," which creates a lost and therefore idealized community of fraternal citizens, or an equally revered tight-knit community of family farms.[56] The countervailing possibility that Thoreau foresaw in remembering, or in forgetting to remember, was that his retelling of the narrative of modernization could be seen as an artifact of the present and hence be taken as a sign of present realities. With this mode of historical awareness, it is true, he could offer little else than the figure of irony, the mode of a historical imagination, according to Hayden White, that comes closest to revealing its aesthetic dimension.[57] It was not long before Thoreau's apparent sympathy for the victims of urbanization and his longing for the bygone New England village gave way to an awareness of language in meditating his relation to these vestigial social forms. And yet in his signal use of irony, the overtly figurative comparison between the institution of slavery in the South and the circumstances of everyday life in Concord, Thoreau would attempt to cede to language a greater potential for resistance than abolitionists had seen in the discourse of citizenship. In his most self-referential, ironical, allusive modes of expression, he sought to reproduce not only his own displacement from the public sphere of citizenship but the displacement of all social outcasts, the Indian, the fugitive slave, and the Mexican, from even an imaginary institution of the public sphere.

The Exilic Imagination

Was it possible to reproduce a historic ideal of the public sphere, as the New England abolitionists conceived it, in the present moment? With the help of Thoreau's aesthetic critique of the narrative of modernity, we can consider this tenet of the abolitionists' political project as the source of a truly utopian aspiration. Everything about the agitation of the slavery question told Garrison and his allies that their republican discourse of citizenship, combined with their libertarian politics of publicity, had made them not merely civic pariahs but relics, the unwelcome remnants of a revolutionary age. They took pleasure in their reception and even posited their manifest anachronism as the sign of a resurgent public—and yet Thoreau would go one step further and argue that the absence of a people in space could not be rectified by the persistence of a people in time. He subjected, in other words, the historical representation of the abolition movement to the temporality of the present and would not reproduce the progressive narrative of modernity. He relied on contradictions of historical period—the classical *civitas* and the eighteenth-century commercial city were recalled simultaneously—and an indeterminacy of locale—city and country were represented in the likeness of each other—to demonstrate what Foucault calls the hetereotopia of language: that is, a stylized, formalized, truly aesthetic demonstration of the effects of time, a reenactment of the problem of orienting oneself in time.[58]

Thoreau was determined to go still further and posit an imaginary, or aesthetic, possibility for resistance that no abolitionist was quite ready to state out loud. That "separate, but more free and honorable ground" could be alternately the prison, the discursive space of citizenship, or the civic space of the commercial city, but it was always found in the medium of his representation, and the effect of that resistance could be detected imaginatively as well. With his invited comparisons to civic life, he evidently wanted the imagination to share a mode of articulation with the utopian discourse of the *civitas*, the historic realm of citizenship, but he seemed determined to reproduce this discourse in a way that told of the marginality of his aesthetic consciousness to Concord life, and, by extension, to the political life of the nation. "It is to the city that the migrants, the minorities, the diasporic come to change the history of the nation," Bhabha has written, and Thoreau saw the place for a similar urban form in the articulation of his critical standpoint. His determination to stop and find his own place in the homogeneous, empty time of modernity is part and parcel with "the imaginative geography of metropolitan space," where "emergent identifications . . . are played out . . . [and] the perplexity of the living is most acutely experienced."[59]

Just as Thoreau was offering the imagination in this metropolitan form, the civic elites of Concord were securing its future as an exclusive suburb by establishing educational and cultural institutions of enduring renown.[60] The author of *Walden*, on the other hand, was determined to have the troubles of the times on his side. Rather than attempting to develop an aesthetic sphere as a refuge from the indignities of urbanization or as a bourgeois fantasy of cultivation, he reserved the life of the imagination for the complexities of the present and even for the stagnation of his neighbors. "Cultivate poverty like a garden herb, like sage," he proposed in response to the ethic of progress that had afflicted his contemporaries, and "Do not seek so anxiously to be developed, to subject yourself to many influences to be played on; it is all dissipation" (217). The place for the imagination was in the indeterminacy of the present moment, when his contemporaries could not decide if the unfolding of progress was making their lives better or worse. Rather than impel them toward a decision, Thoreau counseled his readers to stand back from the pointless movement of "this nervous, restless, bustling Nineteenth Century" and "come to [their] own bearings," which is how they could live the life they imagined (218).

With this advice, Thoreau was also ceding the life of the imagination to the stagnant, marginal, itinerant neighbor—in other words, to himself—whose progress or regress could not be easily adduced. He would make the aesthetic consciousness of language into an incidence of marginality, or a cultivation of stagnation, which meant that the grounds for tropes and expression could be found always under one's feet. This marginal existence, Thoreau made sure his readers knew, only could be phrased figuratively—what did the injunctions to "Cultivate poverty like a garden herb," or to "Drive a nail home and clinch it so faithfully that you can wake up in the night and think of your own work with satisfaction" amount to but figures of speech?—and he appropriately said that at the end of the day, "you would not be ashamed to invoke the Muse" (219). With this advice, Thoreau showed that he was ready to settle himself nowhere else than in the poetry of his speech, or in the midst of language; he had found in his retreat the "interstice between word and thing," where, Benjamin says, "poetic excitation" can be found.[61] And yet Thoreau left no doubt that his own "excitation" left him in a marginal place in relation to society, for in cultivating expressions for poverty, he was rendering his language useless to society or for the ideological purpose of reproducing a society. In the formalism of his expression, he saw the opportunity to remain somewhere between a representation of social space and its actual or possible reference.

Thoreau thus wanted to pose the imagination as a critical dimension for resistance while devoting its aesthetic mode of expression—ironical, sophisticated, and allusive—to reproducing the experience of life on the margins. For Garrison and the New England abolitionists, this was the place from which all repudiation of social and political power could be made. In keeping with this conviction, they identified the public agency of abolition with the illicit political interventions of white women and black freemen in the public sphere of citizenship. And yet Thoreau might be said to have been even more true to this project in representing this place of marginality, the ground of abolitionist revolutionary action, in exact correspondence to its potential for displacement. That is, he situated the act of resistance on the margins where the abolitionists said it belonged and thereby deprived it of the utopian representation that made it akin to a civic act, a public faculty, and ultimately a restoration of citizenship.

This was part of the leap of Thoreau's imagination—he would make himself an outcast, an exile, the brother to the runaway slave—and he seemed to realize that this same leap deprived him of everything but the plenitude of its figurative expression. He staked everything on that leap—his political resistance, his critique of modernization, his aesthetic development, and his career as a writer—but his imagination was at once the means and the obstacle to his ambition. In *Walden*, where he bent semantically the meaning of slavery to denominate "the slave-driver within," he could only be a figurative slave, or a figurative witness to the oppression of other races. He could never be anything but a white and a male and a voter and therefore entitled to the rewards of what Marx called the "real conditions of existence." Writing almost a decade after his imprisonment, Thoreau knew that the closest he could ever get to the condition of servitude was through a "minority discourse" that layered the representations of social space on the tropes of figurative language, but it was precisely through the facility of the imagination that he attempted to repudiate the rewards of that existence and impoverish himself. His was truly, to use Adorno's phrase, an "exilic imagination" in that it saw the possibility of exile in a mode of figurative, specifically ironic expression that interchanged the position of citizen and slave, even self and other. It was to an act of the imagination, or particularly to the enjoyment of theatricality, that Thoreau had assigned the experience of this uncanniness, when he described himself as "the scene, so to speak, of thoughts and affections; and am sensible of a certain doubleness by which I can stand as remote from my self as from another" (91).

All Thoreau lacked in this ironic mode was "the wrongs of his race," perhaps even race itself, and that is why we must turn in the final chapter to the former slave, Frederick Douglass, to see through the translation of the political project of modernity into the representation of marginality. In Douglass's own awareness of language, we find the abolitionists' narrative of historical progress translated into a mode of irony that reenacts and restages the position of the exile as a "real condition of existence," or truly other condition. Thoreau's translation, on the other hand, depended solely on the tropes of spatial representation, try as he might to adopt the figure of the fugitive slave as his uncanny other. More precisely, it depended on the transformation of utopian space into a trope of displacement that could express the perplexity, the injustice, and ultimately the oppression of life for those with the determination to see it. In offering this marginal existence as an aesthetic potential, Thoreau was begging the very same question that the New England abolitionists raised in the representation of their public sphere and that Douglass addressed with his customary incisiveness, which was how to express the exteriority of the oppressed without offering a spatial representation of their position, or even a figural representation of space.

Thoreau's indisputable accomplishment in *Walden* thus would remain formal, or figural: it was to have transposed the normative ideal of citizenship—rooted at once in the ideal a classical *civitas*, the urban economy of the bourgeoisie, and the local tradition of village life—with life on the margins, or a life of "extravagance" that signaled the development of an aesthetic consciousness. In the process, he was laying out an unexpected but quite suggestive future for the utopian discourse of civic space in a species of cosmopolitanism reserved for and reproduced by the marginalized. For Thoreau, the signs of that cosmopolitanism were the figurative expressions and synchronic allusions to the urban form, but we might have to submit our final judgment of the political potential of this aesthetic development to, once again, the question of timing. Had Thoreau staked his claim to an imaginary exile too late to be included among the oppressed classes and races of his day? On the other hand, had he made his claim too early in the history of urbanism for an antebellum reformer to aspire to a fractured, disjointed modern consciousness, to operate as a political refugee from modern totalitarianism, or to claim kinship with the diasporic peoples of postmodern metropolitan space? He might have been both too early and too late for all these situations of exile, which is why in the final analysis Thoreau's determination to remain at home, or homeless in the present moment, ensures that the larger question of whether Thoreau's "sort of space" could be rephrased as a political position has to remain open. "The truth of our words," Thoreau himself had decreed, "is instantly translated" (215), if only so that it could not be rephrased in any other way and those words would remain, to our everlasting perplexity, a work of art.

CHAPTER 6

Douglass's Sublime:
The Art of the Slave

As a former slave, Frederick Douglass knew full well the challenge of translating the narrative of political modernity into the present moment. While Garrison and his white abolitionist colleagues could endorse the past and the future of the American republic as a reference for their public sphere, Douglass had to admit a "quailing sensation" when asked to celebrate the founding of the nation. That history belonged to a "branch of knowledge," he told his audience, "in which you feel, perhaps, a much deeper interest than your speaker."[1] Disowning the story of national origins, he called it "the staple of your national poetry and literature" before reiterating the familiar conventions and honorifics of filiopiety to ironic effect. Far from being recognized as heroes, the founding fathers, he told his audience, "were accounted in their day, plotters of mischief, agitators and rebels, dangerous men," so that to side with their struggle was "To side with the right, against the wrong, with the weak against the strong, and with the oppressed against the oppressor," he did not have to add, "in our day" (111). In his famous Fourth of July address, he took up the task of commemoration only to superimpose a contemporary perspective. "My business," he insisted, "is with the present" (114).[2]

As one of the oppressed, Douglass knew also what it meant to translate a narrative of political progress into an ironic language befitting the position of the outsider. In the same speech, Douglass assumed abruptly the identity of the slave and charged, "your celebration is a sham; your boasted liberty, an unholy license; your national greatness, swelling vanity; your sounds of rejoicing are empty and heartless; your denunciations of tyrants, brass fronted impudence" (109), and so on, until the nationalist tropes of oratory had been defamiliarized and their valences were reversed.[3] Above all, Douglass knew what it meant to produce the position of the outsider as a kind of performance, through a political rhetoric that was also an art. His infamous mimicry of venerable orators, his reiteration of civic pedagogy, and his inversion of political symbolism all betrayed a formal mastery of elocution that allied his mode of address not just with the present moment but with the expressive instant of enunciation—the critical juncture in his address in which he distinguished the language of his oration from the reified image of a national past. "This Fourth [of] July is yours, not mine. *You* may rejoice, *I* must mourn. . . . Do you mean, citizens, to mock me by asking to-day?" (116), Douglass asked his audience in the midst of his address, and with each rhetorical question, he interrupted the narrative representation of national identity with the reminder of his exclusion. His rhetoric announced itself with what Homi Bhabha calls the "suddenness of the signifier . . . which will not issue harmoniously into the present like the continuity of tradition."[4]

From the perspective of Walden Pond, Thoreau had foreseen a similar destiny for the narrative of political modernity, one which led also toward a "work of art." With the cultivation of tropes and expressions, he saw the opportunity to withdraw from the "nervous, bustling Nineteenth Century" and assume the position of an outcast minority. However, the "unexpected time signature" in which Douglass gave his address can be considered part of a "performance of racial identity" that did not require the work of the imagination.[5] His rhetorical art had more in common with the African American art of signifying, which would use the discordance of "black and white semantic fields" and "the free play of these associative rhetorical and semantic relations" to make known the presence of those whose very subjectivity was denied. Equating "liberty" with "license," "greatness" with "vanity," and, ultimately, freedom with slavery in an American republic, he constantly addressed his listeners in their self-image as "Americans" only to tell them that they claimed that title "while the whole political power of the nation . . . is solemnly pledged to support and perpetuate the enslavement of three millions of your countrymen" (125–26). Speaking in what Gates calls a "double-voiced language," Douglass would use the rhetorical reenactment of his exclusion to introduce "chaos," "unconscious associations," and, ultimately, the "Other of discourse" into the official language of national citizenship.[6]

Standing on the lecturer's platform, in the midst of an abolitionist assembly, Douglass could not help but speak from a no-man's land, or from "somewhere without bounds," which is where Thoreau wanted to go without leaving Concord. He had what the white minority lacked— a legal status as the other—and subsequently lived the itinerant, placeless existence that appeared in *Walden* as the endowment of figurative expression. He did so first as a runaway slave and then as a lecturer; he continued his life as a fugitive even after his life as a slave was ended. After escaping his Southern captivity, he toured the Northeast telling the story of his enslavement, eventually fleeing to Great Britain in order to retain his freedom. He toured England and Scotland without relinquishing his attachment to American nationality. On his return to the United States he attempted to set up a household and business in the African American community of Rochester, New York, but the lecturing profession had further designs on him, sending him on fund-raising missions to support his fledgling journalistic enterprise.[7] The institution of oratory, in other words, was an institution of homelessness for Douglass, and as such it gave him more than a platform for his rhetorical expression. It gave him the aesthetic consciousness that Thoreau had known as his sense of place but that Douglass experienced as the lifelong problem of the black man in America: the problem of knowing his place.

The orator's platform in this sense was both the venue and site for Douglass's sense of displacement, and with its expression he would establish the public sphere of oratory on strikingly different grounds from the public sphere of citizenship. In "What to the Slave Is the Fourth of July" he offered a glittering, cosmopolitan alternative to the space of the nation-state: "No nation can now shut itself up, from the surrounding world, and trot round in the same old path of its fathers without interference," he told his audience on the day of national commemoration. "Space is comparatively annihilated.—Thoughts expressed on one side of the Atlantic are distinctly heard on the other" (128–29). However, Douglass made sure in the same speech to define this utopian prospect as nothing less than the sentence imposed on the enslaved, the escaped slave, and the former slave in the land of their birth. As the victims of an "internal slave-trade," black Americans experienced a plight identical to that of Africans who suffered under the outlawed "foreign slave-trade"; Douglass deliberately adopted the "slave's point of view" in order to articulate an internally foreign condition. Savoring the rhetorical effect, he told his listeners, "I am not included within the pale of this glorious anniversary," reminding them that a discordant presence, an incommensurable other dwelled within their midst. He was determined, in other words, to translate the historical and spatial tropes of national identity into a foreign language that expressed not just the position of the outsider but what Houston Baker has called an "unknown land," the "'forms of things unknown,'" in an aesthetic idiom.[8]

Perhaps no abolitionist was more reliant on the medium of language to demonstrate the awareness of his predicament than Douglass, who spoke first as a self-described "American slave," then as a free man without citizenship, and finally, after the Fourteenth Amendment, as an American citizen without freedom. Accordingly, he used his oratory to occupy a rhetorical standpoint that could never be commensurate with the discursive borders of nationality or with the civic space of political resistance. Like Garrison and the afflicted members of the Massachusetts Anti-Slavery Society, he used his antislavery rhetoric to dramatize his own exclusion from these spatial tropes of citizenship. For the first few years of his career, he was part of a white-led abolitionist enterprise so eager to modulate the prerogatives of the white male with the oppression of the disenfranchised that it made his and other narrative accounts of enslavement a principle article of its public sphere. But unlike the New England abolitionists, he did not conceive his marginal position as the basis or equivalent of a public opposition; he would not use the expression of that marginality to constitute an imaginary space of citizenship or, in the case of Faneuil Hall, a trope of public space. He would sever the connection between language, space, and civic identity, the utopian premise underwriting the abolitionists' strategy of resistance, in order to indicate the limit of what language could represent.

In "What to the Slave Is the Fourth of July," Douglass meant to impose that limit and intervene decisively in the disputation of the slavery question by recreating the tropes of abolitionist resistance that he did not have the luxury of maintaining. He called his own existence, by which he meant the existence of slavery, the "antagonistic force in your government, the only thing that seriously disturbs and endangers your Union," and that disturbance, he insisted, could be experienced in the mode of his address. Slavery, he said, "fetters your progress; it is the enemy of improvement"; its ultimate effect was to make "your name a hissing, and a by-word to a mocking earth" (126–27), so that the progressive language of American republicanism could be phrased then and thereafter only with the figure of irony, if it could be phrased at all. In moving farther from the political function of abolitionist rhetoric, Douglass was introducing an aesthetic register into his oratory that could not reproduce the progress, and by extension the agency, of a democratic people in and through language. He would banish even the traces of a public from his language, but it was only by abandoning the facility of this representation that Douglass could establish his own relation to the historical moment of the Enlightenment and maintain his own place.[9]

What remained in Douglass's oratory was an expression of displacement that told also of the place of art in the rhetoric of antislavery. Eschewing at once the spatial representation of marginality and the narrative representation of a people, he situated himself on the boundary of expression, which is where, Houston Baker has argued, African American art originates and resides. "What exists on the antecedent line

of black modernity," he has written in relation to the Harlem Renaissance, "is a universe of enslavement," though clearly not a realm of
brutish suffering and inarticulate pain. On the contrary, the development of language, form, and rhetorical fluency in black aesthetics shows
at once "the black spokesperson's necessary task of employing audible
extant forms in ways that move clearly up, masterfully and re-soundingly
away from slavery"—without signifying the transcendence of the self-
conscious subject over the materiality of his or her conditions. On the
contrary, the attention to the sonority or sound of black expression,
which Baker finds demonstrated in the rhetorical fluency of black oratory, "summon[s] to view black sufferers of marginalization and dis-
possession" and thereby commits language to what the rational subject
cannot express.[10]

Douglass's own modulation of a political discourse of freedom and
progress toward an aesthetic expression took place in an institutional
venue that did not disguise the suffering and limitations of slavery. The
suspicion of his abilities, the outright hostility to his appearance in public, the indignity of racial segregation, and the persistence of his com-
modification in the nominally free states all accrued to Douglass also
and especially as an orator, the professional course taken by so many
former slaves. That course held that the suffering of the fugitive slave
was in direct proportion to his eloquence, clearing the way for the mis-
treatment and, alternately, his triumph as an orator. Appearing on behalf
of white organizations or to sell copies of his autobiography, the fugitive or former slave entered the public sphere of language, political
ideals, and citizenship fully in accordance with his former place in the
commercial economy of slavery, which is also to say that he did not enter.
He remained on the threshold of the public sphere, and so when he
ascended the platform and addressed his audience, he still seemed to be
dragging the long chain of slavery with him. Thomas Wentworth Higginson testified that he saw the famous black orator "stumbling with his
heavy slavery gait upon the platform, walking as if a hundred pounds . . .
of chains were appended to each heel" before "develop[ing] into the
superb status and the distinguished bearing of Frederick Douglass,"[11]

and that rendition might be said to describe the position of the former slave in the ideology of political modernity: somewhere between the objectification of the embruted slave and the transcendence of the rational citizen. For Baker, the crossroad is indeed the spatial trope for the black artist, who develops a language of aesthetic performance at the junction of freedom and oppression, always negotiating the possibility of liberation within "slavery's tight places."[12]

As one of the most successful orators of the antebellum era, Douglass found that he was in demand to perform his exclusion from the public sphere of citizenship, which in turn became his token of inclusion. He would always be on the boundary, with his rhetorical art serving as the sign of the limit of how far a literate former slave could go in the United States. Perhaps this is why Douglass as well as other prominent black orators such as William Wells Brown found a stage for their rhetoric on the geographical boundary of the nation. Speaking as literate noncitizens, they positioned themselves in a no-man's land or border zone between slaveholding America and the British dominion of Canada, the ultimate destination for so many fugitive slaves. To be sure, the entire region of central and western New York, the area including Seneca Falls and Douglass's own Rochester, was also the home of many fugitive slaves and thus represented the limit of American sovereignty, but as Russ Castronovo has shown, a visit to the New York–Canadian border at Niagara Falls became the black orators' ritual of observance, which, like so many others, did not disregard the dominant logic of American nationalism so much as it trumped it, or troped it for the purpose of rhetorical art.[13] (The remove of Boston's black community to Framingham, Massachusetts, on July 4 and its celebration of English emancipation on August 14 are other examples from the antebellum era.)[14] On that threshold between slaveholding America and a free British dominion, black orators restaged the logical quandary of their existence in a rhetoric that could never designate them as citizens but for which contemporary aestheticism had a name: the sublime, defined as the presentation of what cannot be imagined in space or time or universally shared among literate, rational subjects. With this transatlantic aesthetic idiom, Douglass established not just the marginality of his position in the American republic but the incompatibility of its rhetorical expression with the political discourse of citizenship. In doing so, his rhetoric questioned the very possibility of a community mediated by language, the ideological premise for the institution of the public sphere as well as for the abolitionists' public identity.

In his lecturing tours, Douglass discovered also a generically aesthetic representation of place with which to supplant the image of the public sphere: Niagara Falls, the locus classicus of the sublime. In the presence of this natural wonder, Douglass, like Brown, bore witness to the limits of American citizenship, appropriately enough, in a language that Americans had adopted wholesale from England.[15] In his report of his 1848 trip to western New York, the home of a rising African American antislavery movement, Douglass could not resist paying tribute to the spectacle of Niagara Falls with the conventions of a foreign literature:

> It is no part of our intention to attempt any description of the stupendous wonder. It is beyond the power of talent, poetry, or genius to describe it. The minute and descriptive pen of Scott would fail in such an attempt, while the widest, and grandest flight of Byron would be powerless, lifeless, and cold in comparison of the awful thunders of this eternal reality.[16]

Referring his avowedly feeble efforts to British models, Douglass expressed himself in a cosmopolitan gesture meant to betray not just his cultivation but the critical potential toward nationality and citizenship inherent in the modern discourse of aestheticism.[17] Extant from the first slave narrative, *The Interesting Narrative of the Life of Olaudah Equiano*, this potential has been held to have provided black expression with a transatlantic orientation that told of both Western civilization and the brutality of the slave trade, or "rationality and the practice of racial terror."[18] In the "counterculture" of the black Atlantic, the attempt to perpetuate the horror, pain, and particularly the memory of slavery creates an aesthetic translation of political discourse that begins with the

convention of an inexpressible, unrepeatable sensation—"It is beyond
the power of talent, genius, or poetry to describe," as Douglass said.

That same attempt, I will argue, also made the orator's platform a
permanent site of the sublime even when Douglass or Brown continued
their travels around the country and the world. The sublime in this
sense was an apt expression for the symbolic typography of the black
orator as well as an institutional feature of oratory itself. From his place
on the platform, Douglass could pose the challenge of aesthetics to
the political discourse of modernity, making use of the specialized message of the sublime to reveal the failure of language, and alternately,
the expression of that failure to fulfill the promise of communicability
among avowedly literate citizens. This admonitory message even found
its way into the inaugural issue of *The North Star*, which had been issued
in the image of black reading public. In the ode "To Niagara," one J. E.
Robinson commemorated the editor's recent visit to "the great wonder
of our western hemisphere."

> To-day I stand a pilgrim on thy verge,
> Old Niagara! and my willing ear
> Drinks in the deep base of thy wondrous voice—
> "The voice of many waters"!
>
> *   *   *   *   *
>
> Sublimity is thee; thou art sublimity;
> And the great seal of Deity is fixed
> Forever on thy brow! Tis no idolatry
> To Stand a mute-lipped worshipper at thy shrine,—
> To feel our weakness, while our spirit kneels[19]

The North Star, like Niagara Falls, served as an "inapt [*sic*] emblem of
the vast flood of light which Truth is now pouring upon the world," and
yet there was little doubt that "thy wondrous voice" belonged also to
Douglass, and that the force of the sublime, which reduced Robinson to
a "mute-lipped worshipper," made him the object of idolatry. In providing an aesthetic language for the former slave to indicate his marginal

position in the public sphere, the sublime served also as a means to hero-ize that position above and beyond the role of citizen. The aesthetic in-flection that Douglass's rhetoric would introduce into the public sphere in fact turned on the identification of the black orator himself with the inimitable scene and incomprehensible spectacle of Niagara Falls.

Of course, this identification meant that Douglass's most enthusi-astic reception could never signify his equality with his white audiences or, for that matter, his incipient citizenship. On the contrary, the sub-lime betrayed not just his marginal place in the community of literate citizens but the failure of oratory to overcome the structural imbalance, or asymmetry, of black and white subjects in the public sphere of citi-zenship. This asymmetry was best represented in the language of the aesthetic, so that when the most famous black orator of the day appeared on the platform, he was acclaimed by his largely white audiences as a superior force on the order of Niagara Falls: he was overpowering; he was inimitable; he was beyond their powers of comprehension; for some, he was "of no account." A report of an 1844 speech intended to pay him the ultimate compliment when it claimed that black oratory had surpassed the conventions of political discourse: "It was not what you would call oratory or eloquence; it was sterner, darker than these. It was the volcanic outbreak of human nature, long pent up in slavery and at last bursting its imprisonment."[20]

Douglass's aesthetic reception meant that the "racial gaze" of his white audiences operated fully within the public sphere of oratory but against the possibility of mutual self-recognition, reciprocal identifi-cation, and social equilibrium that oratory was supposed to engender among gathered citizens. The sublime, in other words, interjected the structure of racial discrimination into the public sphere of citizenship.[21] Indeed, the normative response to Douglass's oratory was not the ratio-nal consensus of assembled citizens but the aesthetic sensations of awe, fear, and wonder—any index of disequilibrium between the speaker and his audience. A typically "ferociously severe" oration was said to be accompanied by a "scornful expression" or a "contemptuous manner" of address. "Drawing himself up to his full height," as one account said,

Douglass seemed to tower over his listeners and command through fear.[22] No one less than Wendell Philips, probably the most formally trained abolitionist orator, made sure his audiences heard his words as if they were in the presence of a force that, like Niagara Falls, could take their own words away. "When such a man as Frederick Douglass tells you his story, the result of American prejudice—speaks the honest indignation of this race against the wrongs—when he tells you of your own conduct toward him—keep your hands by your sides," he advised. "Hush those echoing plaudits of yours; keep silent."[23]

In "What to the Slave Is the Fourth of July," Douglass showed his willingness to adopt the aesthetic representation that would make him respected, feared, but never equal:

> Oh! had I the ability, and could reach the nation's ear, I would today pour out a fiery stream of biting ridicule, blasting reproach, withering sarcasm, and stern rebuke. For it is not light that is needed, but fire; it is not the gentle shower, but thunder. We need the storm, the whirlwind and the earthquake. (287)

Audiences could feel the "storm, the whirlwind and the earthquake" unleashed at every Douglass lecture, for the rhetoric of the black orator seemed always to produce and reproduce a state of tension between the races, sometimes inverting but never transcending 'the relation of inequality that persisted within a democracy. Douglass's rhetorical expression of the sublime in this sense revealed a discrepancy between the political and aesthetic dimensions of oratory, which in turn maintained a foreign perspective within an ostensibly national institution. Coming to this country from an English discourse of "moral sense," the aesthetic conventions of the sublime in Douglass's rhetoric bore witness to the capacity for Americans to articulate an ethical or normative position for themselves from a position of exteriority, to judge themselves as if they were another.[24] That position reflected everything from the cultural influence and presumed superiority of English belles lettres to the suppressed influence and presumed inferiority of the African slave, their positions fused within a pedagogical regimen of oratory that sustained the necessity of a rule or admonition outside the ritual of consensus that oratory simultaneously sponsored. The aesthetic and particularly the sublime operated within the civic discourse of oratory in precisely this manner: they maintained the foreignness of putatively national ideals in presenting them as declamations or imperatives of citizenship that Americans themselves could not realize.

The classical theorization of the sublime, Longinus's "On the Sublime," used the heroization of the orator, who "can as it were consume by fire and carry away all before him," to posit both the failure of democratic self-determination and the heterogeneity of the orator with the public sphere.[25] But what was the place of the sublime in the civic discourse of American oratory, the source of the early republic's ersatz classical curriculum and its pedagogy of citizenship? The text credited with introducing Americans to the aesthetic category—the Englishman Hugh Blair's 1805 oratorical handbook, *Lectures on Rhetoric and Belles Lettres*—described the sublime according to its classical designation as a mode of rhetoric. Blair's *Lectures* belonged to the corpus of eloquence handbooks, *The Columbian Orator* among them, that articulated the republican self-image of the new nation, and yet as a foreign import, it also reaffirmed the potentially contradictory place of the aesthetic in the classical discourse of citizenship. It was the tenets of this English handbook, after all, that guided Americans' encounter with Niagara Falls, their nationalist icon, and that underwrote their sense of disequilibrium. The natural wonder, like the mountains of the Hudson Valley, acquired its humbling beauty through a "doctrine of association" that imbued such landscapes with a moral faculty appropriate to the remembrance of the nation's revolution or to the thrilling spectacle of national progress.[26] The vastness of time and space in turn was supposed to discipline or, better yet, oppress onlookers with their sense of insignificance, a disabling experience deemed necessary for the entitlement of citizenship.

In the literary discourse of American Transcendentalism, the sublime was used to transform the inimitable role model of the republic into an idealist subject whose power adumbrated the sovereignty of the nation. With this transformation, the aesthetic category became what Rob Wilson has called the "American sublime":

> If the Enlightenment sublime had represented the unrepresentable, confronted privation, and pushed language to the limits of imagining the vastness of nature and stellar infinitude as the subject's innermost ground, the Americanization of this sublime rhetoric represented, in effect, the interiorization of national claims as the Americanized self's inalienable ground. . . . The genre of the sublime helped to consolidate an American identity founded in representing a landscape of immensity and wildness ("power") open to multiple identifications ("use").[27]

As an account of Emerson's claim for the sovereignty of the subject, this is an able and insightful critique; Jehlen's rendition of the dialectical incarnation of self and landscape has this aesthetic reference as well.[28] However, Douglass's oratory presented the aesthetic figure in the express absence of idealism, sovereignty, and even subjectivity. His counter-American sublime took its inspiration from the position of the former slave, which, like Niagara Falls itself, comprised a foreign territory within a national space of citizens; he would use the same aesthetic expression to turn the historiography of the nation against itself. The signal declaration of "What to the Slave Is the Fourth of July"—"America is false to the past, false to the present, and solemnly binds herself to be false to the future" (117)—bore out all the contradictions that the aesthetic imposed on the civic institution of oratory and forbade the self-recognition of a people in either space or time.

As we will see, Douglass would become "the storm, the whirlwind and the earthquake" as often as was necessary. He made sure that his expression of the sublime was at the expense of oratory's putatively civic function. Moreover, he would establish his position among rational, disinterested citizens largely through the operation of incongruously aesthetic faculties, such as judgment, discrimination, and differentiation. In the rhetorical tradition of the sublime, he had found the asymmetrical structure of the aesthetic—the heterogeneity of the orator with his fellow citizens, the relation of inequality between the observer and the object of its gaze—and conducted transactions with his listeners that could never be assimilated to the model of sociality entailed by the faculty of citizenship—and yet he remained determined to articulate his place within an official scene of public self-recognition. Douglass, in other words, discovered the potential and disparity of the aesthetic within the civic discourse of oratory and never departed from the presumption that the conditions for his own aesthetic representation originated in a public sphere that only could reproduce the inequality of subjects.

In our time, historians such as Rogers M. Smith have made it impossible to regard the republican ideal of American citizenship without noting that foremost among its ideological purposes was to disenfranchise nonwhite and nonmale members of the American polity. However, we might regard oratory, which F. O. Matthiessen called the first art form of the new republic, as a more overt and specialized instrument of exclusion functioning within the discourse of republicanism that was allowed to coexist with the political ideal of equality.[29] As a contemporary institution of the aesthetic, oratory served as a medium of white male embodiment and, conversely, as a index of social intelligibility that established the limits of communicability and community among literate, self-designated citizens. Oratory convened a public afflicted, so to speak, with all these particularities, which is why it also served as a point of entry for the racial other into the discourse of modernity. As David Lloyd has written, the aesthetic culture of the Enlightenment supplanted the political representation of a popular will with the "merely logical" representation of a social totality that demanded the agreement of individual aesthetic judgments in principle, or equated it with the ethical principle of "common sense." Drawing on Kant's conception of the "*sensus communis*," Lloyd rephrases the political ideal of the people as "a subject formalized, if momentarily, into identity with 'everyone else,' that is, with the subject in general" so as to produce a "universal accord of a common, or public sense."[30] Accompanying the logical principle of unity was a narrative of interpellation that corresponded to a developmental narrative of aesthetic cultivation. The ideology of subject formation took this turn, Lloyd argues, precisely in order to deny the entrance of the African or the enslaved into the public sphere of citizenship. They were not as civilized or as cultivated and therefore their difference could be sustained in the midst of the ethical imperative for intersubjective self-recognition.

The challenge that aesthetics brings to the institution of the public sphere is attributed ultimately to Kant for this same reason. In *Critique of Judgment*, he derives the premise of a public sense—the belief in the universal communicability of individual expression and of the inevitability of consensus—from nothing more than the subjective enjoyment of taste among cultivated, properly prepared subjects. With full confidence in the narrative of cultivation, he concludes, "I can say that taste with more justice be called a *sensus communis* than can sound understanding; and that the aesthetic, rather than the intellectual judgment can be called the name of public sense."[31] However, his more pressing task is to establish the epistemological basis for the universality of taste, to discover "how the feeling [of universal communicability] in the judgment of taste comes to be exacted from every one as a sort of duty" (154). For critics like Eagleton, the indecipherable predisposition toward social concord represents an "ideology purified . . . raised to the second power" that leaves us "delighting in nothing but a universal solidarity beyond all vulgar utility."[32] He extends this critique of Kant to Habermas, whose concept of the "ideal speech community," given historical expression as the bourgeois public sphere, "proposes some deep spontaneous consensus built into our faculties, which the act of aesthetic taste most clearly exemplifies."[33]

Was the abolitionists' public identity, like Kant's "sensus communis," also a merely logical necessity that underwrote their judgment of themselves? Their pose as a latter-day people depended so much on the universal communicability of historical references and precedents that the social divisions within the movement itself could be subsumed within a historical narrative of inevitable progress. However, the abolitionists' narrative representation of a public can be said, in retrospect, to have lacked the temporality of the aesthetic, or the aesthetic mode of interpellation that Douglass's rhetoric would introduce into their public sphere. His rhetorical expression of the sublime would deconstruct a "public sense" into disparate, potentially incommensurate gestures that bespoke the subjectivity of their expression. As Luc Ferry has put it, the aesthetic forces us "how to think of bonds . . . in a society which pretends to begin with individuals in order to reconstruct the collective." Any articulation of the public thereby is troubled not only with the "problem of mediation between humans" but with the need to mediate between any single instance of social concord and the more distant, genuinely ethical horizon of a generalized, universal consensus.[34]

As the unlettered slave, the figure of incommensurable difference, Douglass was more than willing to pose all these challenges. In the name of the sublime, he would force his audiences to face the contingency of their existence as a people and, conversely, their need for an ideological totality through his mediation of their intersubjective transactions. His role as an orator in fact was to keep the public sphere subject to the terms and time of its articulation so that the institution that the abolitionists recognized as a sign of history, or of repeated experience, could become finally what Bhabha would call a sign of the present. For Douglass, the sublime was a truly contemporary form of the public sphere, divorced from the abolitionists' mode of memory and historical awareness but also, more chillingly, from the ideals of democracy. He seemed to grasp for his own sake what Jean-Luc Nancy has deduced philosophically from the modern discourse of the aesthetic: "that what was at stake in art was not the representation of the truth, but . . . to put it briefly, *the presentation of liberty*. It was this recognition that was engaged in and by the sublime."[35]

The Breakdown of the Public Sphere

According to Slavoj Žižek, the "most sublime image" in the recent history of democracy was the spectacle of newly liberated Romanians waving a Communist flag with its symbol of totalitarianism cut out. He saw in this moment a "unique intermediate state of passage," a "brief passing moment" when a "hole in the Big Other, the symbolic order became visible." Of course, the rebels' enthusiasm for this hole is said to pave the way for the reinstatement of a "Master-Signifier"—this time under the name of nationalism, democracy, or liberal capitalism; the image of a social totality will appear retroactively, Žižek promises, as a kind of "transcendental guarantee," or as compensation for the inability to realize the equivalency of subjects in the present moment or as a functioning social system.[36] With an economy of loss and gain unique to the sublime, Žižek thus depicts an ongoing crisis in the symbolic order that betrays not just the effect of social antagonism but the place of the alien figure, or what he calls the "hard kernel" that cannot be assimilated into an imagined community. As in the mutilated national standard, this place could be found within the symbolic representation of the community and even be integral to the perception of the whole— and yet the idealized social body represented by the sublime cannot disguise and in fact presumes the impossibility of establishing an identity between subjects. The sublime, Žižek says elsewhere, betrays "a certain fissure, an asymmetry, a certain 'pathological imbalance' which belies the universalism of bourgeois rights and duties."[37]

Douglass appeared as the sublime image of the public sphere at the same moment that enfranchised American citizens were seeking to idealize themselves on the basis of white manhood.[38] He would invoke this object at nearly every oratorical appearance in order to reveal the public sphere itself as a "pathological" institution, predicated on the failure to establish the equivalency between subjects that was necessary for its own operation. The breakdown of the public sphere in turn required the retroactive intervention of the law, and that is exactly what the former slave delivered in "What to the Slave Is the Fourth of July": nothing less than a dramatization of oratory as wholly, exclusively normative. In the course of his address, the invited speaker assumed the position of the excluded and dramatized the ravages of slavery on the self-description of an American citizenry—only to reinvite the rule of national sovereignty in the name of the Constitution in the final analysis. The standpoint of the noncitizen in this sense can hold the place for the law; it set the stage for the reinstatement of the law and revealed the necessity for the law within the supposedly autonomous operation of the public sphere. For its part, the audience of white male citizens was compelled to recognize its public identity in the form of an admonitory lesson or Master Signifier that did not, strictly speaking, belong among them.[39]

In "What to the Slave Is the Fourth of July" and in several other speeches in 1854 and 1855, Douglass united strategically his marginal position with that of the Constitution, articulating both as a foreign mandate, or an alien expression with regard to the people themselves. In defiance of Garrisonism, he increasingly saw his interests represented in a constitutional order that commanded the differentiation of the law with the people and based its rule on the manifest contradictions of the people with the ideal of democracy.[40] The founding rationale for the Constitution was transformed into a rather startling argument that equated the law of national sovereignty with the position of the noncitizen and the oppression of the slave, clearing the way for a political alliance between disenfranchised black abolitionists and the electoral system that lasted well into the postbellum period—and yet Douglass cannot be said to have made this argument within a public sphere that was coextensive with the constitutional order of the state or the jurisdiction of the law. The public sphere of his oratory featured instead the provisions for taste, criticism, and judgment that were found within the discourse of aestheticism and distinguished itself from any space or representation of citizenship.

Of course, the cultivation of taste and manners has been shown to have been essential to the theorization of the public discourse of Anglo-American libertarianism as well as to the apologia for bourgeois citizenship in the eighteenth century.[41] If scholars like Gordon Wood and David Shields are right, and the radicalism of American republicanism did devolve into a formalized system of comportment and social mannerism that guaranteed the mutual self-recognition of equals, then the aesthetic pedagogy of rhetoric, criticism, and belle lettres that laid down many of the tenets of this system was indeed internal to the rationale for American citizenship.[42] However, the civic ideal of the leisured, educated gentleman and the exclusive enfranchisement of the propertied classes remind us that the mode of social intercourse entailed by the discourse of aestheticism was not really compatible with and could even be foreign to the objective of republicanism, which was the formation of an equalized, informed citizenry. On the contrary, the aesthetic medium of sociality drew out the problem of establishing similitude between subjects to such an extent that the possibility of misrecognition, heterogeneity, and ultimately, otherness became endemic to the public sphere.

The mediation of aesthetics makes the need to establish social intelligibility that much greater, but the most confident exercise of aesthetic faculties never could reveal the ideal and standard of a common citizenry to be anything more than a need, an expectation, or a demand answering to the faculties themselves. What Lloyd has called the "circularity at the foundation of aesthetic judgment" presented the public in its most normative form—that is, as a necessary, if hypothetical reference point for every demonstration of taste and criticism—even while it showed the communicability and intersubjectivity of the public sphere to have an exclusively subjective basis, intelligible in the experience of pleasure and pain.[43] Feeling in this sense operated as law in accordance with the regulatory authority that was vested in the aesthetic in republican America and exposed the inability of the public sphere to police itself.[44]

We can begin to see the divergence of this aesthetic model of sociality from the public sphere of citizenship by recalling Douglass's invocation of the Constitution and noting that the rhetoric of the former slave took advantage of the mediation of a written text to establish an irreconcilable difference between the audience and its imagined social totality. Although this textual mediation was central to the institution and purpose of oratory as well as to the ideological reproduction of citizens, Douglass's rhetoric followed the example of "What to the Slave Is the Fourth of July" and invited unfavorable comparisons of his audience with the more formal requirements of civic pedagogy so that its members could never collapse the distinction between themselves and the rules for literate citizenship. A "scene of reading," as Brodhead would describe it, thus entered the public sphere of oratory as both the extension of its normative function and the ban on its political object.[45] The very existence of written rules for citizenship tended to forestall the completion of a republican pedagogy and to entail a gap or discrepancy between the orator and his audience and even between members of the audience, which neither the mediation of print nor an understanding of the rules could close. The formal provisions of rhetoric preserved the wholly formal conditions for a public sphere and posited the public itself as a mere abstract, hypothetical possibility.[46]

What was the written text that simultaneously prompted and forbade the self-realization of the people? In Douglass's case, it was *The Columbian Orator*, which subjected every expression and gesture of the orator to a formalized rule for self-presentation. As we saw in chapter 4, he sought to induce a "suitable conformity of the notions of the countenance ... to the subject matter of the discourse,"[47] but we should consider also that *The Columbian Orator* functioned like every other oratorical handbook in being first and foremost a social document that presumed that almost every audience member had read something like it and was likewise educated by its formal instruction. Such texts operated as an aesthetic medium of intersubjectivity in keeping the image of a uniformly educated consensus always before the members of the public sphere as both their civic ideal and their foreign mandate.

Douglass's reception does say much about his audiences' eagerness to follow the rules that were deemed necessary for their own consensus. Expressions of praise for the black orator tended to overlap with each other, as if the point was to demonstrate the equivalence of response. To this end, observers focused their attention on the "technical" qualities of his oratory, such as diction, pronunciation, and even grammar, which could be reproduced from speech to speech and from speaker to speaker. A typical judgment from a Massachusetts newspaper reporter termed Douglass a "remarkable man" on account of his "fluency in the use of language, choice and appropriate language, too";[48] in making this judgment, the observer thought to demonstrate his fluency in those same rules. The appraisal of Douglass's diction and word choice often made reference to a common education or common experience, as when one admirer recalled that "his language is classically chaste, not groaning under the flowery ornaments of school boy declamation, but terse yet eloquent . . . beautiful in its systemacity [*sic*] and unadorned simplicity."[49] The readers of this review could lay claim to this same education and experience in their appreciation of Douglass.

Douglass's oratory indeed gave every class of white male spectator the opportunity to imagine their commonality and thus their common citizenship insofar as they demonstrated their familiarity with the rules of oratory. This was in keeping with the ideological function of its civic pedagogy, which was to suture the gaps in learning and experience between the white male participants in a public sphere by articulating a formal standard of language. As William Charvat has shown, the need of civic elites in the postrevolutionary period was to codify avowedly general rules for both literate and oral expression from the motley agglomeration of regional dialects, ethnic and class accents, and dissenting opinions that threatened to undo the social order of the early American republic. Their goal was to unify a citizenry through their common knowledge of grammar, pronunciation, and diction, erasing all but the formal standards for inclusion in a public sphere and establishing the grounds for mutual recognition among fellow literate subjects on equally abstract terms[50]—and yet the imposition of these formal standards of language seemed to open up an arena for aesthetic expression and enjoyment that was at odds not only with the ideal of abstract, disinterested citizenship but with the attainment of social intelligibility, the precondition for a public sphere.

Douglass's admirers went so far as to compete with each other to show a superior knowledge of the rules, and, by extension, a refinement in learning and experience that might well have passed for the evidence of their cultivation. Their assessments of Douglass followed the same path, grading easily into discriminating judgments of taste. One civic-minded audience member meant to distinguish himself among his supposed equals when he stated that the black orator was "never declamatory, never placing himself in an oratorical attitude, and never making what are vulgarly called points." As if to affirm the fineness of his own perception, he concluded, "I don't know when I have listened to a more agreeable or instructive public speaker."[51] With yet another admirer showing off his good taste by declaring of Douglass, "his enunciation is quite elegant,"[52] each encomium seemed to beg the question of how to reconcile judgments that asserted the disparity of subjects into the consensual voice of an informed public.

Even more troubling for the formation of the public sphere were the distinctions drawn between the white male citizens who often composed Douglass's audience and the black orator—especially when those citizens appealed to the formal provisions of oratory to argue their equality with the former slave. In words that would haunt Douglass, a white abolitionist admirer opined that the ability of "the colored people [to] acquire the habit of thinking and speaking . . . may in great measure, accord for the self-possession of their manner, and the propriety and fluency of their language."[53] Apparently, oratory's formal standards for mutual recognition had not superseded racially encoded differences between subjects or rectified legal inconsistencies in citizenship in accordance with the aims of republicanism. On the contrary, the explicitly abstract conditions for the black orator's equality—"the habit of thinking and speaking"—assumed the *inability* of "the colored people" to equalize themselves in any other way except by learning proper grammar and pronunciation and thereby imposed a pedagogical narrative on the identity of citizenship that asserted the unequal development of an unlettered race. By this measure, even Douglass's most sympathetic listeners could not entertain the prospect of their similitude with the black orator in the present moment, but this was how the uniformity promised by the rules of oratory differed from the laws of the state as well as from the political ideal of democracy: it laid down formal standards for equality while leaving white male subjects free to judge, almost as a prerogative, or matter of taste.

Douglass himself did not seem to recognize any other terms under which to produce a consensus. On the contrary, he can be said to have opened up the public sphere to the exercise of aesthetic judgment when he demonstrated his mastery of the rules of oratory and imitated the famous orators of the day. In doing so, he defined himself as what Gates has called *"homo rhetoricus Africanus,"* an alien, incommensurate figure among literate subjects whose own literacy troubles the category of citizenship with the formal conditions for its validity.[54] From the inception of his oratorical career, Douglass was determined to bring a sophisticated self-awareness to an already formalized discourse; a staple of his early speeches was not heart-rending tales of his youth but the mimicry of Southern preachers and statesmen. According to one account, he could perform a mock debate between Calhoun, Clay, and Webster with such acute characterization that the members of the audience could easily identify each speaker.[55] To his fellow belletrist Thomas Wentworth Higginson, he was "the perfect mimic,"[56] but Douglass's facility could seem to work against him: white audiences often were so caught up in the display of his rhetorical dexterity that they could neglect or even dismiss the content of his speeches in favor of an aesthetic appreciation of a recognizable style. "Even when the subject matter wore thin," one observer reported, "the words came and arranged themselves so completely that they not only captivate but often deceive for ideas."[57]

Ephriam Peabody's survey of the emergent slave narrative genre, "Narration of Fugitive Slaves," represented an attempt to reconcile the aesthetic conditions of Douglass's reception with a progressive narrative of political modernity. Douglass's own narrative of escape in the *Narrative of the Life of Frederick Douglass* was said to offer "a vivid demonstration of the force and working of the native love of freedom in the individual mind," thereby "associating himself in no small part in the romance of the time." However, even Peabody's political allegory could not avoid a focus on Douglass's style. The essay took care to credit him with "a natural and ready eloquence, a delicacy of taste, a quick perception of proprieties, . . . and a felicity of expression, which are possessed by few among the more cultivated."[58] An exclusive attention to Douglass's language indeed held out the promise of incomparable aesthetic pleasure for the more cultivated. "He spoke calmly and deliberately at first," wrote one reporter, "but as he went on . . . his voice grew louder, clearer and deeper. His voice full and rich, and his enunciation, remarkably distinct and musical . . . occasionally his tones rolled out full and deep as those of an organ."[59]

Although we might consider Douglass's flaunting of his oratorical technique to be an entertaining digression from the main object of his talk and his audiences' fascination with his virtuosity to be evidence of their passing interest in antislavery, the republican discipline of oratory provided for such indulgences as taste, stylization, and pleasure to a degree we might not have imagined. *The Columbian Orator*, for example, instructed Douglass in the art of uniting an "address to the passions" with both political principles and grammatical standards of articulation; the subjective grounds for the expression and enjoyment of rhetoric thereby were united with its abstract rules for presentation. Each demonstration of taste in turn was indemnified by its conformity with a rule without proving its equality with other such demonstrations.[60]

Oratorical handbooks like *The Columbian Orator* created an American ideal of "judicial criticism," to use Charvat's phrase, which moralized every individual expression and adumbrated the possibility of a generalized consensus commensurate with the tendencies of all mankind.[61] However, the dependency of America's civic pedagogy on British aesthetics suggests that this ideal of a common sense or a universal humanity was not isomorphic with the ideal of a national people. The influence of British aesthetics on this civic pedagogy could be felt in the way that the latter tended to sidestep the civic goal of establishing the mutual recognition of literate subjects; both the correctness and the applicability of its formal standards instead were routed through the subjective medium of emotions. At least, this was the case in Blair's *Lectures on Rhetoric and Belles Lettres*. Although the book issued a mandate for discovering the universal principles of humanity in every single determination of taste, it did not look for a uniformity of perception in society. Instead, it attempted to identify immutable, inexorable principles of epistemology in the subjectivity of aesthetic judgments. Judgments of taste, Blair promised, were "found to be consonant to reason and to the principles of human nature, as to pass into established rules, and to be conveniently applied for the judging of the excellency of any perfor-mance."[62] Although he made sure that the mediation of his own text was necessary for the application of these rules to further examples, Blair did not hesitate to deduce the correctness of all aesthetic judgments on sub-jective grounds. "All the rules of genuine criticism," he concluded, "I have shown to be based ultimately on feeling; and taste and feeling are necessary to guide us in the application of these rules to every particu-lar instance" (28).

Blair's deduction was typical of the school of New Rhetoric, an Anglo-American pedagogy that dominated the theory and practice of oratory in the early national period but seemed to take Americans far from their political ideal of a disinterested, informed public in keeping with the dictates of taste.[63] However, the rules followed by Douglass and his audience make it clear that the provisions for taste and judgment that were most disruptive to the establishment of a national people could be found within the civic pedagogy of oratory and, furthermore, that they were intended to impose the limits, the fallibility, and as we will see, the temporality of a system of social intelligibility on the political ideal and agency of citizenship. To be sure, Blair had claimed that the universality of taste and emotion was discoverable in "every particular instance," but the role of taste in rhetorical practice was consonant with its critical function in the discourse of modernity, which was to incite deliberation, indecision, and even disagreement about the commonality of subjects and of their appraisals. In theory, a judgment of taste was not supposed to be proven by the actual accord of disparate subjects or by ref-erence to a particular object. Taste, Derrida has said, derives it legitimacy from "the formal conditions of possibility of . . . aesthetic objectivity in general" and could no longer render an aesthetic judgment if it "were in the least presupposed in favor of the real existence of the thing."[64]

The epistemology of an aesthetic discourse is evident in the seem-ingly uniform reception of Douglass's oratory, which was supposed to showcase the ability of each audience member to identify an example of the orator's rhetorical correctness from his or her own familiarity with the handbooks of oratory and, simultaneously, to invoke the rule of which Douglass's correctness was an example. In theory, the members of this public sphere would become aware of their common knowledge as well as the abstract rule or law that underwrote their consensus—and yet there would always be a hedge or check on that awareness that told them that they could not be too sure. The essence of aesthetic intersubjectivity, Ferry has argued, is that it is established in the absence of knowledge; the actual convergence of tastes can never be established merely by citing a universal rule. On the contrary, each member of Douglass's audiences was attempting always to relate his or her knowledge of a particular example to that rule in a way that depended on his or her own judgment of that relation and in fact on the subjectivity of that judgment.[65] The conformity of subjects with a universal rule was determined on the same grounds, delaying and effectively annulling the possibility of their identity. The beauty of an aesthetic intersubjectivity was that its purpose and design appeared spontaneously—Kant was ready to term the happy, unforced agreement of disparate judgments the condition for the experience of beauty[66]—and furthermore, that such agreement could originate only in a subject's expectation or desire for commonality with other subjects. But the law that enforced that agreement remained obscure and indeterminate, creating a public sphere based on nothing more than feeling.[67]

The differences in refinement and education that Douglass's admirers were so eager to demonstrate in this sense were symptomatic of a structural flaw in public sphere of oratory that made the individuality and disparity of subjects inevitable, even indicative of universal epistemological principles. Blair had gone so far as to posit the universality of those principles in the repeated exercise of taste and judgment, which in turn corresponded to a socially observable sense of distinction. This contradiction is elaborated in Mary Poovey's brilliant reading of eighteenth-century British aestheticism, which describes how its deduction of universal principles produced standards of gender and sexual identity that neither the republican discourse of political equality nor the liberal discourses of marketplace exchange could produce by themselves. The aesthetic ideal of universal communicability, argues Poovey, shows the readiness of such theorists as Burke, Addison, and Smith to rationalize the pleasure that the white male propertied subject takes in his own particularity by generating avowedly imaginary identifications between subjects. The aesthetic judgment of beauty allowed for and in turn demanded proportional kinds of particularity, which Poovey observes in the sexualizing of gender identities and in the discourse of heterosexual desire. In words that could apply to Douglass as well as to the eighteenth-century ideal woman, she writes, "The sexed body and its aestheticized excess—beauty—become the occasion and mandate for differentiation, for judgment—indeed for meaning itself."[68]

We need few other reminders of Douglass's aesthetic position in the public sphere than the lavish praise offered from men of taste regarding his manly beauty. With their judgments, they were applying the formal rules for taste and criticism that they learned from such sources as *The Columbian Orator* and *Lectures on Rhetoric and Belles Lettres*, but the pleasure they took in the application of these rules also suggests a particularity of expression that could not be generalized and that in turn made its way into individual desires. The most judicious assessments of one Ebenezer Basset betrayed as much when he recalled that Douglass's oratorical performance "left little to be desired":

> The tall and manly form of singular grace and vitality; the erect carriage that had something majestic about it; the searching but kindly eye; the whole cut of that strong, strange face, set off with the semblance of a certain scornful expression which told of the gall of the early trials to a proud and sensitive nature like his; the never to be forgotten flowing locks ... the perfect self-poise; the rare and happy blending of affability and modesty with dignity of bearing ... all this gave him a distinguished appearance, a truly imposing presence, which everywhere stamped him as a man of mark.[69]

This is an overdetermined vision of excess, simultaneously demanding concord with its unique sensibility and betraying the subjective basis for its articulation. In Bassett's vision indeed lay the demand, or what Bhahba calls the "scopic drive," for both beauty and otherness that subjects the scene of mutual recognition to a "trajectory of desire." Such fetishistic enjoyment, Bhabha argues, runs counter to the civic goal of cultural homogeneity and social intelligibility; it culminates in an "ambivalent, psychical process of identification" that orients the public sphere toward the object of discrimination, or toward the figure of beauty whose enjoyment could not be standardized.[70] Bhabha invokes Žižek in elaborating this point, which also might be the point at which Douglass's "manly form" passed from being beautiful to being sublime: "'We identify ourselves with the other at a point at which he is inimitable, at the point which eludes resemblance.'"[71]

Within the public sphere, the transaction between the empowered subject and the oppressed minority devolves upon a perverse longing for resemblance, and that is exactly what the aesthetic enjoyment of Douglass's oratory could not satisfy. The white abolitionist who observed that the "colored people" were demonstrating "self-possession of their manner, and the propriety and fluency of their language" no doubt wanted to recognize another white male citizen from the examples of Douglass's grammar and diction, but his appeal to a model of resemblance based on the formal criteria of rhetoric only intensified that longing and made their equality more difficult to determine. The iteration of rules and codes for mutual recognition functioned more like a mimicry that could be performed by either citizens or non-citizens. It complicated the already troubling indeterminacy of civic identity with what Bhabha calls the "figure of colonial [or racial] otherness—the white man's artifice imposed upon the black man's body." From this juxtaposition, a "'partial' presence" is said to emerge that bears the signs of citizenship—but not quite. The identity of white male citizenship is similarly compromised by a system that "must continually produce its slippage, its excess, its difference," if not its "strategic failure" in elaborating the criteria for civic identity.[72]

On these grounds, the formalist pedagogy of language and manners, the black orator and his white audiences met each other and constituted a public sphere that differed significantly from the "synchronic panoptical vision of domination." The task of staging and restaging racial and gender difference supplanted the spatial model of knowledge and power with a distinctively diachronic structure that could not reproduce the identity of citizenship in the image or shape of the subject, or from an analogy with any other subject.[73] This mode of interpellation seemed to take its bearings from, of all things, the facility of racial discrimination in establishing the terms of mutual recognition. For Lloyd, the "the insistence of a difference internal to the constitution of identity" is indeed the distinguishing attribute of an aesthetic standard of social intelligibility. The aesthetic ideal of *sensus communis* is said to base the similitude of subjects on the use of analogy, or, alternately, with the figure of metaphor, but a "narrative of representation" assumes and rectifies the failure of these spatial tropes with a "regulative principle" that commands both a hypothetical unity of subjects (or races) in the abstract image of humanity and their unequal development in time.[74]

That American citizens went so far as to provide positions of esteem in the public sphere for the black orator who met formal criteria for resemblance is perhaps the most dramatic example of the incoherence of a system that used the inequality of subjects to imagine their common identity. As the direct outcome of this system, Douglass's reception exposed the deficiency of knowledge, the temporality of self-understanding, and, ultimately, a historical structure of assimilation that the standards of taste and pleasure introduced into the scene of mutual recognition. According to Lloyd, these aesthetic standards are responsible for the "inexpungable melancholy of the pedagogical scene," which would complicate the self-awareness of a people with "the anxiety of an unattainable redemption" and "the idea of a fall." He localizes this scene in an "exemplary pedagogy," or a pedagogy of example, for "the example contains a historical structure, predicated on a historically necessary lapse from what looks like the natural immediacy of a historical culture to itself and projected forward as what must be reproduced, artificially or by way of pedagogical formalization, in a future state."[75]

We can easily recognize the influence of this pedagogy in the narrative of republicanism, which used countless examples of manners and conduct to envision the declension, and, alternately, the distant promise of a virtuous citizenry. But the same historical structure was extant in the public sphere of oratory, which would take a temporal, lapsarian form precisely when it was convened through the painstaking observation of examples. Of course, Douglass's admirers took obvious pleasure in noting every instance of his good grammar and diction, but their careful attention seemed to bring them no closer to assuming the identity to which their common knowledge entitled them or to recognizing that identity in the eloquence of the black orator. Instead, their exemplary pedagogy obliged them to accumulate still more examples to the point that the abstract identity of citizenship receded before them, appearing, in true aesthetic fashion, as a distant horizon or a destined future, never a present reality. Each citation of the black orator's good grammar moved this horizon from him as well, so that at the height of his renown, Douglass was forced to prove not just that a slave was capable of thinking and speaking but that he was capable of being a slave.

The familiar controversy incited by Douglass's oratory and its attendant expressions of racism thus had this aesthetic dimension: it demonstrated the "historically necessary lapse" of a formalist system that would use accumulated examples of language and manner to illustrate an otherwise unrepresentable ideal of civic identity. Not even the providential narrative of good grammar, which, Lloyd says, foretells and guarantees the congruence of the example with a universal rule, could repair this lapse. The "formal historicity" of that narrative imitates "the formally historical formation of its subjects," which would bar the equalization of subjects in the same time and create a pedagogical narrative of unequal development. "The sphere of common sense, properly one that establishes the identity and equality of all judging human subjects by way of formalization," Lloyd argues, is distinctive for posing the diachronic terms of that resemblance, and he draws attention to the failure of its realization for the same reason: the *sensus communis* can be manifested only through "the constant insistence on its instantiations," or, in other words, over time.[76]

The members of Douglass's audiences failed similarly in focusing their attention on each example of Douglass's conformity with the rules of oratory. An "exemplary pedagogy" made the standard of citizenship as difficult to fathom as the literacy of a slave and both of them as impossible to substantiate as a judgment of taste. Their fascination with the black man's good grammar served as an expression of aesthetic pleasure to this extent: it cast the formal basis of their commonality, the abstract ideal of citizenship, not only beyond the constituent transactions of their public sphere but beyond the sphere of knowledge. The idea of the citizen loomed above and behind them but it remained an idea, regulative and elusive, while each spectator remained white and male, captive to the particularity of his position and the limits of his judgment. In the final analysis, their judgments of Douglass can be said to have convened a public sphere according to the temporality of racial representation.

Even *The Liberator*, which represented the political promise of an inclusive public perhaps more than any other abolitionist forum, could not help but reproduce a narrative of unequal development when it celebrated his accomplishments:

> Many persons in the audience seemed unable to credit the statements which he gave of himself, and could not believe he was actually a slave. How a man, only six years out of bondage, and who had never gone to school in a day in his life, could speak with such eloquence—with such precision of language and power of thought—they were utterly at a loss to describe.[77]

The befuddlement is presented as consensual, as if the audience could furnish countless examples of the rules of oratory and still not know what those rules were supposed to underwrite. They were a people without knowing why; they ruled without knowledge of the rule by which they governed themselves. Their ignorance constituted the ritual of consensus at every Douglass lecture, subjecting the formation of the public sphere and the form of the people to the opacity of their aesthetic judgment.

The pleasure Douglass's audiences took in the spectacle of the black orator had to be qualified, for it meant that their chosen medium of mutual recognition could let them recognize nothing but the exception to the rule.

As this last comment suggests, the historical structure of the public sphere did more than just ensure the ignorance of white male citizens or the elusiveness of their civic identity. The pedagogy of examples operated as an aesthetic mode of sociality in reserving a position for the alien figure, or the uncanny other, in the ongoing negotiation of citizenship. Of course, this position was predicated on the operation of racism, manifested in "the difficulty of staging a human presence in the context of the African (American)'s commodified negation,"[78] but Robyn Weigman's hedge about the nationality of the subject only suggests the extent to which the aesthetic structure of the public sphere opened up American republicanism to the prospect of foreignness. It also foreshadows the extent to which Douglass, the ardent champion of anticolonization, would seize on that prospect as a sign of African presence in America. We thus should acknowledge the irony that Douglass's most ardent abolitionist supporters, such as Nathaniel Rogers, imposed on the civic ritual of consensus when he confessed his inability to understand how "such manly and lofty developments as he exhibits could have taken place under that unspeakable system."[79] Of course, the manly and lofty developments Douglass presented for his audiences took place under the unspeakable system of civic pedagogy, which means that the normative identity of the citizen and the predicament of the noncitizen could be easily confused and in fact interchanged through the mediation of aesthetic standards for the reception of oratory. Whether this mediation signaled the failure or the transcendence of the public sphere is a question that can be answered more completely after we investigate more fully the economy of the sublime, but we should note that the social transactions that took place under these standards never allowed the citizen to be equal with the noncitizen, only that the latter might appear in the unequal form of the law.

Economies of Race and Gender

For Rogers, who found it "truly astonishing" for a slave to have emerged from that "unspeakable system" as a literate subject, and for nearly everyone else who felt that his oratory was, as one observer put it, "a matter of wonder,"[80] Douglass's rhetoric was truly useless for the determination of citizenship. The supposedly rational calculus of examples dissolved into what Peter Fenves describes as a "rhetoric of astonishment," in keeping with the power and persuasion of the orator's rhetoric but "incommensurable with the language of measurement, schematization, counting, cognition, and representational thought in general" and therefore a "'pathology' in the original sense of the term."[81] Douglass's admirers recognized him on these same pathological terms, which means that they could not use the examples of his perfect diction to calculate the extent of their similitude with the black orator. The aesthetic pleasure that Douglass's audiences took in his eloquence consisted in the surrender of all but the purely formal conditions for determining his resemblance to a white man, and there again lay the limits of their pleasure.

According to Žižek, misrecognition, misprision, and the mortifying awareness of social antagonism are the "price to be paid for coming to terms with fantasy." The fantasy of the public sphere, of course, was the fiction of an equal citizenry, if not a universal human equality, and the price Douglass's audiences paid was the failure of their interpellation. Indeed, the former slave could never resemble just another enfranchised citizen; his superior eloquence made him a representative of the law, an object of emulation for others to follow, and above or beyond the examples of good grammar from which the white male members of Douglass's audiences would abstract their identity. They could not reconcile themselves with the overarching ideal of their totality, and at that moment the black orator passed from being beautiful into the sublime. The sublime represents force and power beyond comprehension, and yet "far from hindering the full submission of the subject to the ideological command," Žižek writes, "it is precisely this non-integrated surplus of senseless traumatism which confers on the law its unconditional authority."[82]

However, there is more to the symbolization of the sublime than the mystified image of authority, and Douglass's audiences felt more than the sovereignty of their own unconditional law. There was in Douglass's rhetoric an excessive force of presentation that seemed well beyond this economy of loss and gain; there was a species of "traumatism" that truly disarmed and panicked white people. The sublime, in other words, was as close a representation of race as could be found in the discourse of modernity, as evidenced by Burke's infamous example of terror—the sight of a black woman. Even Derrida's seemingly neutral observation that "the sublime exists by overspilling" contains many of the presumptions of racial science that made the African truly other: "it is no longer proportioned to man and his determinations" and "will be announced at the level of raw nature, a nature which no final or formal contour can frame."[83] Douglass, in other words, should have just stopped trying to fit the measure of African Americans to either white manhood or its formalization. No pathological system of resemblances, not even the most attenuated historical timeline of unequal development, could foretell his equalization with the white male subject. As the sublime, he became the very image of the deformation that Kant had ascribed to the African race. Even Kant's technical definition of the sublime in the *Critique of Judgment*—it appears "in point of form to contravene the ends of our power of judgment, to be ill-suited to our faculty of presentation, and to be, as it were, an outrage on the imagination" (91)—could sound remarkably like an expression of disgust that could render any black person irrecoverably contrary, ill-suited, or outrageous.

Of course, it was an indispensable part of Douglass's rhetorical art for him to appear as all three. He seemed to relish the most fearsome excesses of racism and used them to prevent his bewildered audiences from ever recognizing themselves in him. In an 1853 speech, "A Nation in the Midst of the Nation," in which he declared, "America has neither justice, mercy nor religion," he made sure to add, "She has no scales in which to weigh our wrongs—she has no standard by which to measure our wrongs," and with that claim, he joined his rhetoric with the fate of his people at the point at which they became immeasurable. He then showed off his command of language in a way that suggested there were no limits to his oratory, that it might keep building until it unleashed the true force of art:

> The outspread wing of American Christianity—apparently broad enough to give shelter to a perishing world—refuses to cover us. To us its bones are brass and its feathers iron. In running thither for shelter and succor, we have only fled from the hungry bloodhound to the devouring wolf— from a corrupt and selfish world to a hollow and hypocritical church; and may I not add, from the agonies of earth to the flames of hell!

Douglass meant to exceed every rule that could be found in *The Columbian Orator* for the propriety of expression and make his denunciation "extravagantly strong"—and yet he admitted that any rhetoric could represent the horrors of slavery "as the shadow to the substance." Using the idiom of the sublime, he described "my poor people" as "blasted and ruined," and he would not depart from the consequences of his damning proposition: "American humanity hates us, scorns us, disowns and denies our personality."[84]

If Douglass believed that the presence of the African race in America was denied and disowned, then he also believed that Madison Washington, his protagonist from *The Heroic Slave*, was also sublime. Of course, Washington could also be called beautiful; Douglass's paean to his "manly form" seemed to be a re-creation of the aesthetic standpoint from which he was judged. However, this standpoint was so "ill-adapted" to the intelligibility of civic discourse that Douglass had no trouble modulating his representation of Washington to reprise the formation of the public sphere from the outside in. That is, he would take the perspective of the disowned American, the heroic slave, and remind his readers from the outset that it was not merely a misprision of their aesthetic judgment but slavery that had erased the name of Madison Washington from the rolls of national history; it was slavery, not the failure of a subject's cognition, that provided only the "glimpses of this great character." His subsequent symbolization of the sublime thus

contained more than the aesthetic viewpoint that Douglass's own spectators enjoyed: "Like a guiding star on a stormy night, he is seen through
the parted clouds and howling tempests; or, like the gray peak of a men-
acing rock on a perilous coast, he is seen by the quivering flash of angry
lightning, and he again disappears covered with mystery."[85] Having
already assumed "the storm, the whirlwind and the earthquake" for his
oratory, Douglass left little doubt that the frightening storm surrounding Washington was nothing less than the storm of slave insurrection,
and that soon Americans would know not just the obscurity of the sublime but its terror.

Douglass's own position on slave insurrection could be hard to
determine, but there was little doubt that his oratory inspired similar
misgivings in proportion to its fury and excess. Peabody's criticism of
Douglass—that the black orator was "apt to mistake violence and extravagance of expression and denunciation for eloquence"[86]—was similar
in this respect to the admirer who sought to capture the distinction of
Douglass's rhetoric: "It was not what you could describe as oratory or
eloquence. It was sterner—darker—than these." The violence and the
darkness belonged to what the latter called "that terrible voice of his,"
in which could be felt nothing less than "the storm of insurrection."
Douglass himself had meant to adumbrate the irresistible force of the
heroic slave with "the quivering flash of angry lightning," and here we
might see the conclusive difference between the sublime and the beautiful. The sublime, as Žižek describes it, presents "suprasensible moral
Law" in its "superego dimension," commensurate with "purposeless
raging" and the "expenditure of forces" that do not serve the ends of
morality. Beauty, on the other hand, "is the symbol of the Good, i. e.
of the moral law as the pacifying agency which reins in our egotism
and renders possible harmonious social coexistence."[87] The difference
between the sublime and the beautiful, in other words, originates in
contrary representations of the law, and the "raging" and "expenditure"
of Douglass's rhetoric seemed to capture both the severity of an over-
bearing paternal principle and the putative "purposelessness" of a slave's
resistance.

Douglass gave expression to the affinity between this principle and the resistance of Madison Washington in giving his heroic slave the patrilinear descent of American statesmen. The fearsome spectacle of his resistance could just as easily constitute the imaginary law of their common paternity, the symbolic order of republicanism; the fury of Douglass's own rhetoric could be represented just as easily within the terms of an economy of masculinity, whereby the invisible white father and the excluded racial other battle and exchange places. Douglass, after all, had concluded from his battle with the overseer Covey that "A man without force, is without the essential dignity of humanity" (151), and he seemed determined to introduce the idioms of the sublime into the civic discourse of oratory through the measure of that manhood, a violent struggle against white patriarchy. The philosophical representation of the sublime, an allegory of reason disclosed and the law revealed through what Derrida calls an act of "sacrificial violence," indeed restages Douglass's own account of his transformation into a man.[88]

The masculinist allegory of the sublime translates easily into the philosophical terms of the master-slave complex, especially given David Brion Davis's contention regarding antislavery discourse. Slavery, he concludes, was recognized as an ideological problem for modernity and as an inherent antagonism within a modern subjectivity, which, under antislavery discourse, was reintegrated in strikingly paternalistic form.[89] However, Douglass could also shift the axis of racial relations in the symbolization of the sublime onto the dichotomies of gender relations and thereby complicate his already conflicted identification with the invisible white father.[90] Even in *The Heroic Slave*, he could supplant the patriarchal image of the law by commemorating and authorizing the maternal: Virginia, after all, has been "dignified by some the mother of statesmen" but suffers egregious indignities for being the mother of slaves (132). For this same reason, Lyotard's avowedly tortured analogy of domestic violence is perhaps most able to explain the force of the sublime: it relies so patently on sexism and on a final subjugation of allegorized femininity at the hands of the paternal principle. The sublime, he avows, is the result of an unhappy marriage of the faculty of imagination,

its "mother," with the uncompromising authority of reason and therefore can provide "the joy of seeing or of almost seeing the law" only
through "the mediation of its violence."[91] Whether that law belonged
ultimately to white male American citizens is the question at the heart
of much of Douglass's oratory, particularly to the disputed patrimony of
"What to the Slave Is the Fourth of July," and would largely determine
its representation of nationality. However, his countless depictions of
slave masters' sexual violence against black women can be considered as
apt an expression of the sublime—Barrett has called the black female
slave the "ultimate figure" in the "narrative representation of the tortured or injured body"[92]—precisely because they composed a metanarrative of subject formation commensurate with the pathologies of unequal
gender relations and sexualized violence.

For Douglass, time could not heal the effects of this violence or
dissipate its memory. It seemed to grow more inadmissible, even un-
mentionable in his accounts of enslavement. In early speeches and the
Narrative, the whipping of Aunt Hester was remembered as the "blood-
stained gate, the entrance to the hell of slavery (258)" and furnished all
the guilty pleasures that white male readers would be expected to seek
in a narrative of bodily pain. In *My Bondage and My Freedom*, however,
Douglass denies if not complicates those pleasures by placing the whipping scene of "Esther" in the more respectful context of a moral commentary on the injustices of slavery for black women. He lingered on
the scene of violence long enough to call it "revolting and shocking" but
the transformation of even qualified pleasure into the experience of pain
seemed to be accompanied by a prohibition of the kind furnished by the
sublime: "when the motives of this brutal castigation are considered,
language has no power to convey a just sense of its awful criminality."[93]
This categorical prohibition, replacing the earlier, stock confession in
the *Narrative*—"I wish I could commit to paper the feelings with which
I beheld [this terrible spectacle]" (258)—can be considered the crown-
ing moment in a long disquisition on the invisible wretchedness of his
mother and suggests a new, feminized iconography for the sublime.

The anthropomorphisms of domination, violence, and even rape cannot fail to impress themselves on us in Kant's philosophical accounts of the sublime, many of which suggest a feminized discourse of beauty despoiled. "Charms are repugnant to it," he warns, and unlike the frivolous, playful, and ultimately harmless interplay of faculties that attend both the company of women and the exercise of taste, there "seems to be no sport" in the presentation of the sublime; it is an occasion for "dead earnest in the affairs of the imagination" (91). The seriousness of this spectacle is implied in an extended passage that does not allow the authority of reason to appear except in the consciousness of being overpowered:

> Reason inevitably steps forward, as the faculty concerned with the independence of the absolute totality, and calls forth the effort of the mind, unavailing though it be, to make the representation of sense adequate to this totality. This feeling, and the feeling of the unattainability of the idea by means of the imagination, is itself a presentation of the subjective finality of our mind . . . and compels us subjectively to think nature itself in its totality as a presentation of something supersensible, without our being to effectuate this presentation objectively. (119)

Although DeMan has scoffed at the notion of any submission or loss in the phenomenology of the sublime, Kant seemed to introduce irredeemable suffering and inequality in the constitution of the subject.[94] More than a slave/master struggle that magically resolves itself through the transference of manhood, the sublime economy uses the destruction of the beautiful, here recounted in the submission of the "unavailing" imagination, in exactly the way that Douglass used narratives of sexualized violence: to preserve the memory of an "awful criminality," or what Kant had called appositely an "outrage on the imagination." All expression, even sympathy, is held in check, so to speak, by the difficulty of conceiving any purpose for this violence.

In the passage above, Kant implied the tragic fate of beauty not just in his reference to the "maternal" faculty of the imagination but in his description of the pressure "to think nature itself in its totality as a presentation of something supersensible in its totality." The damage done here is to the calm enjoyment of beauty, which presumed a harmonious universe in which each particular object had its place, and hence to the formation of the public sphere, which depended on the premise of universality inherent in every demonstration of taste and judgment. Because aesthetic pleasure, as Kant would remind us, ensues largely from the awareness that these premises are formalist, regulative, and therefore unprovable, the enjoyment of the beautiful never requires the subject to form its perceptions in this universal form, or to conceive an "absolute totality" of the moments of nature—but the sublime can and does. Potentially beautiful objects become sublime, Lyotard writes,

> when the imagination is asked to have an aesthetic comprehension of all the units included by composition in the progression. For then, if all the parts composed successively cannot be comprehended in a single moment (which is necessarily the case as the series increases by composition) . . . then the power of presentation of the imagination finds itself literally overwhelmed.[95]

Kant's examples of the Egyptian pyramid and basilica of St. Peter's are illustrative in this regard; he relies also on the concept of the mathematical sublime, which can be likened to the syntagmatic, consecutive motion that DeMan allegorizes as reading.[96] We proceed happily, confident that each word or number belongs to a larger totality, until this teleology is ruined, to use Lyotard's explication again, by "the aesthetic comprehension of the whole (at one time) of a larger or infinite series."[97] Calculation is useless, for we are not talking about even the largest quantity at all but the very idea of a whole, the absolute and pure reference of our judgments, in the "here and now." Indeed, Lyotard's exposition could not make it more clear that the infinite magnitude of the sublime is not a function of space but of time, or rather of "the inability to synthesize the givens by containing them within a 'single moment.'"[98]

Douglass's rhetoric thus became sublime when it offered its examples of eloquence to his auditors "all at once." In this form, it was ill adapted to the temporality of understanding, to the "formal historicity" of an exemplary pedagogy, and, ultimately, to the historical structure of assimilation put in place by the modern discourse of aestheticism. The distinct moments of subject-formation were collapsed, as were the distinctions between subjects, and in their place was an idea of commonality so immense that it could have gone only by the name of the people. Democracy itself, Žižek has observed, is a sublime object; it depends so much on acts such as voting, which signals the disarticulation of the people into atomized individuals, and the civic rituals of consensus, which, in the public sphere of oratory, linked the idea of a people to a historical, temporal mode of interpellation, that anything less than failure could destroy the conditions for democratic self-reflection altogether.[99] The narcissistic politics of the public sphere in this sense is the casualty in the sublime; the white male citizens of the republic would have liked to see in the literate black orator a former version of themselves, or a promise of what they could become, in accord with the orderly progress of liberty. But the presentation of Douglass's pedagogy "all at once" denied his audiences this pleasure and took from the mediation of history in detecting the alienated image of themselves. Of course, there was always the utopian promise of a restored unity, coincident with the arrival of the law; Douglass's audiences might well have expected to see the regeneration of the popular will in the destructive terms that political theorists from Rousseau on have imagined it. However, the public sphere of oratory was not exactly like the public sphere of citizenship, which meant that the idea of the people remained stubbornly dsytopian, perhaps even heterotopian, captive to the pointless raging and ungraspable motives of male violence. It goes without saying that this was its form, or formlessness as *Douglass* imagined it.

The sublime might further be considered the slave's point of view, for it substituted a corresponding metanarrative of subject formation that starts with the experience of slavery and treats *white male citizenship* as its negative moment. Perhaps this is why Douglass was so committed to the aesthetic conditions for his oratory and to the aesthetic imbalance of the public sphere: it meant that the temporality of assimilation was not overcome, and that the tragic story of beauty would not be forgotten. On the contrary, Douglass's sublime subjected the self-realization of the people to the assimilative, accumulative narrative of aesthetic enjoyment and the mediation of aesthetic pleasure in order to prevent the identification of a white man with a black man, which otherwise would have signaled the recuperation of power. The intersubjectivity of the public sphere was preserved in this manner, as was a public discourse of race, and Douglass seemed to make both contingent on the ineluctability of a female principle in the allegory of aesthetic pleasure. What was sacrificed was the reappearance of the paternal, the authority of the symbolic order, and Douglass seemed willing either to keep that space vacant or to vacate it himself in the name of beauty, or in the memory of beauty, which had been sacrificed without reason or the possibility of recovery. The sublime in this sense shifted the moral or political economies of bourgeois manhood to the reenactment of pointless, open-ended violence or irrecoverable loss, which is also what animated Douglass's vision of retribution. "I would blister [the conscience of the American public] all over, from center to circumference, until it gives signs of a purer and better life than it is now manifesting in the world," he promised, leaving little doubt that he meant to deliver a full measure of pain for all that he had received.[100]

The ritual sacrifice of aesthetic pleasure, never more threatening than when it had been destroyed, thus proved central to the rhetorical standpoint Douglass occupied in his oratory. Although he "identified with the American bondsman, making his wrongs mine," his iterations of female submission, sexualized violence, and senseless male rage equated his antagonism to slavery with his antagonism to the masculine tropes of national identity and lent that position an ambiguity of gender. Of course, Douglass espoused few antislavery principles on behalf of the Massachusetts Anti-Slavery Society, *The North Star,* or the Liberty/Republican Party that did not support ideologically restrictive institutions of manhood, whether they be American electoral politics, constitutional enfranchisement, or military conscription. On the other hand, the orientation of his career toward women's rights in the antebellum era and even more strikingly in the postbellum era were presaged by his elaboration of the narrative of the sublime in his oratory, which super-imposed racial inequality on the questions of gender and of female sex-uality in a way that skirted questions of citizenship and male equality. Perhaps this is a case in which the political objects of his oratory had caught up with its aesthetic modulation and established his struggle for freedom in the field of art.[101]

The Future of the Public Sphere

As an abolitionist orator, Douglass did occupy an uncertain position within the public discourse of antislavery. He refused to leave the site, so to speak, of the public sphere of oratory, just as he refused to relin-quish the memory of suffering; he maintained the difference of the "slave's point of view" from within the republic's rituals of consensus. Perhaps that is also why he could never represent the foreignness of his position to the satisfaction of Martin Delany, or, for that matter, with-out the feminized discourse of moralized suffering in *Uncle Tom's Cabin*. Fully engaged in the intersubjective transactions that alternately com-posed and deformed the public sphere, he sought to represent the het-erogeneity of his position as a black orator without any spatial measure whatsoever, especially as it regarded the representation of nationality.[102] Never a colonizationist or emigrationist, he chose instead to solicit the respect that white Americans extended toward foreign revolutionaries as well as the sympathy that they extended for the foreign victims of the African slave in a typically liminal expression of difference.

Douglass could find no better place for his opposition than on the border, and that is what made the speech he delivered on the occasion of his departure for America, on the very shores of Britain, an appro-priately antagonistic expression of the sublime. "I cannot speak well of her," he told the members of his British audience, "I cannot be loud in her praise, or pour forth warm eulogisms [*sic*] upon her name or insti-tutions." With these confessions of incapacity, taken straight from the English vocabulary of aestheticism, he betrayed the pride of place of an exile who still belonged:

America presents to the world an anomaly, such as no other nation ever did or can present before mankind. The people of the United States are the boldest in their professions to freedom, and the loudest in their professions of their love of liberty; yet no nation upon the face of the globe can exhibit a statute book so full of all that is as cruel, malicious, and infernal, as the American code of laws. We are a nation of inconsistencies, completely made up of inconsistencies.[103]

The repetition of dichotomy, so typical of Douglass's rhetoric, stopped the articulation of national identity at the point of contradiction and allowed the black orator to adopt the standpoint of his foreign audience. With the aesthetic modulation of his rhetoric, he might have abandoned the determinate category of citizenship, identified with his English cultural influences, and slipped out of his subaltern position in America—and yet his final reference to a "we" reminds us that he would stage and restage the failures of American civic discourse in order to keep his place on the border of the nation. Douglass, it seemed, was too interested in "exposing the damning deeds of slavery" in the medium of his oratory to progress beyond the limits imposed by art.

The sublime has been described by Lyotard as being "transcendentally 'localized' in two facultary realms," or between the ability to conceive of an unimaginable spectacle and the ability to represent it, and Douglass tried to fix likewise his position in the medium of his oratory.[104] In doing so, he was trying to arrest the consciousness of his audiences in the paralyzing spectacle of senseless, specifically male violence against helpless, often female slaves. Even when forced to consider the future and development of the antislavery struggle, he could not reconcile this sense of outrage, or the "outrage to the imagination," with the agency of citizenship or the progress of liberty. He admitted only that "the work is to be done by exposing the damning deeds of slavery, the abominations of the church, in short by Agitation," expressing memorably the distinction of an antislavery enterprise that could not offer anything more than the experience of tension. He would rise above that moment only to state the necessity for even more tension—"Agitate,

agitate. This is the grand instrumentality,"[105] he revealed to audiences—and thereby displace his rhetoric from the narrative representation of the abolitionists' public sphere. Douglass's form of agitation did not stipulate the existence of a public, the commemoration of a people, or the progress of democracy through time. His rhetoric laid down the law, in accordance with the sublime prohibition against representation, and decreed that a people could not be recreated or even imagined in the medium of history.

Time, Douglass seemed to recognize, was friendly to the development of taste and the refinement of manners, not to the attainment of democracy, and to prove it, he would never dislodge himself from the rule-bound transactions that formed and alternately deformed the public sphere. The truly foreign element of the aesthetic indeed lay in the dimension of time, which is also how Douglass would articulate his marginal position as a black orator in the antislavery struggle. He disabled a historically mediated civic consciousness and prevented the articulation of an abolitionist utopian future in exactly the way that the sublime ruined the happy teleology installed by the enjoyment of beauty. To sense and elucidate the inequality of races within an aesthetic discourse of cultivation and development; to make that inequality plain through formal conditions of oratory; and, finally, to expose the wrongs done to his race in the phenomenal experience of the sublime hence became the imperatives of an abolitionist discourse that seemed to have a future only in the renewed experience of tension. He seemed to put the narrative of modernity at the crossroads with art, where he kept the emergence of the people waiting on the determination of his judgment.

Of course, the abolitionists' public sphere would share the same fate and become subject to Douglass's judgment, which, like its aesthetic expression, could be alternately severe and seemingly pointless. [106] He served this notice when he faced down the most friendly audience imaginable, a gathering of the New England abolitionists, in the most symbolic setting imaginable, the home of the American Revolution: "I see my enslavers here in Concord."[107] The abolitionists' presumption of racial equality, their ironic use of localisms, and ultimately their historical comparison with a revolutionary people all would have to weather the withering scrutiny of a rhetorical whirlwind. But this was the condition that Douglass imposed on their public identity and particularly on their self-description as anachronistic outcasts. The sublime, after all, was really a story about the limits of the imagination.

A Cosmopolitan Point of View

In his most forceful abolitionist speeches, Douglass foresaw little future for the antislavery struggle other than a face-to-face encounter with racism. He meant the rhetorical enactment of still more "agitation" within the abolitionists' public sphere to signal the incompatibility of the present with a narrative construction of progress and of unseen continuity with the past. Garrison, on the other hand, was so determined to put time on the abolitionists' side that he actually looked forward to this state of antagonism. In his first public appearance on behalf of the cause, he presented the inevitable outcome of antislavery agitation—the virulent opposition of a white male American citizenry—as nothing less than the premise for his narrative of abolitionist progress, the first cause for a public identity. Speaking from Boston's Park Street Church in 1829, Garrison dispensed with the religious-typological prophecies of the city's Puritan ancestors, reminding his listeners that "'our fate ... is not foretold by signs and wonders: the meteors do not indeed glare in the form of types, and print it legibly in the sky.'" The signs and wonders of the abolition movement were to be found instead in the haphazard events, unforeseen needs, and embarrassing contingencies of the present moment, "unless," he noted, "the age of miracles return." Until then, the abolition of slavery, the millennial event of the age, was to be announced by the most unlikely sign imaginable, "a struggle with the worst passions of human nature."[1]

With this distinctive historiography, Garrison set the tone for an abolitionist political project that allied the agency of the people with a force of antagonism, or as Douglass had called it, an "antagonistic force within the nation." In doing so, he meant to reserve a minority status for the New England abolition movement, and throughout the coming decade he pursued alliances with the disenfranchised members of American society—women, free African Americans, and escaped slaves—in order to cement, so to speak, its unstable position within the polity. He maintained a warfare with the Protestant establishment, until then the leading advocate of antislavery, with a freemen-inspired anticolonizationist movement; he upset the already precarious balance of Jacksonian political culture with his appeals to the race- and gender-inclusive discussion of abolition. The result of all his efforts was to transform the public sphere of literate citizens and the image of public space itself into the space of outsiders and the refuge of the oppressed—and yet Garrison can be said to have relied ultimately on the axis of temporality to resolve his attenuated movement into a historical ideal of the people and to denominate the marginalized as such. The point of his cultural politics in fact was to bind together the disparate and incommensurate identities of citizen and noncitizen by a relation to time, or through the memory of a historic ideal, an objective that might have distinguished the abolitionists' public sphere from the ideological model of the nation but that was also designed to nullify the effect of racial and gender difference on their collective self-recognition.[2]

For Garrison, the key to resolving social incongruity was a mode of historical narration that guaranteed historical progress and therefore the agency of a people while finding social dissension and political conflict at every turn. By this reckoning, neither unanimity nor social homogeneity could be required of the abolitionist public. On the contrary, the outright opposition of an American populace to the discussion of abolition, the destruction of abolitionist publications, and trampling on the abolitionists' right of public assembly were for Garrison as telling an index of abolitionist progress as the "abolitionizing" of a reading public. Abolitionists' publicity, I would argue, demanded an ironic, detached, and perhaps even formalized historical awareness that looked for and found the signs of democracy in the worst of times, that prized even the worst incidence of racial antagonism as prophetic in its own right. The belief in an abolitionist subjectivity required no less, which meant that it required a capacity for irony and, by extension, an aesthetic awareness quite at odds with the belief in political progress.

But not quite. What Garrison relied on and what Douglass subsequently exploited was an aesthetic means of historical narration that originated within Kant's theorization of a progressive Enlightenment. For this reason, Kant's essays remain a starting point for both critical theory and the political ideology of liberalism, for the aesthetic deconstruction of modern subjectivity, and for the conception of a public. In "The Idea for a Universal History with a Cosmopolitan Purpose," Kant shows that he is willing to consider all the signs of social disintegration— human suffering, civil unrest, and, of course, war—as evidence of an "unsocial sociability," detectable only from a "cosmopolitan point of view." He makes no reference and therefore no apologies for the African slave trade, and so we might consider his own racism yet another of the incidents of a "continual antagonism." Unsurprisingly, the end of this supposedly universal history can only be a "pathologically enforced social union," something that Douglass surely would have recognized when he surveyed the state of the postbellum Union or perhaps even a sympathetic audience of covertly "color-phobic" white abolitionists.[3]

From this "cosmopolitan point of view," Kant did not foresee a glittering spectacle of human improvement or the epic march of a free people through time. He needed an extra, or outside, perspective in order to justify his vision of a progressive Enlightenment, and he found it in the realm of aesthetics. He admits cheerfully that a narration of political progress is really a self-fulfilling prophecy that demonstrates first and foremost the imagination of the subject and, more specifically, the need for imposing a narrative form.[4] In order to "perceive the hidden mechanism of nature's scheme" and project an end to discordant events, a contemporary observer has to start from that end, look backward on his or her own time, and reflect in retrospect on events that were transpiring in his or her era. In a striking admission, Kant admits that he derives this possibility from the experience of reading a novel, whose "otherwise planless *aggregate* of human actions" can be seen, also in retrospect, to have contained a providential narrative of epic proportion. The articulation of a universal history, in other words, required the facility of a comic imagination, if not a comic sense of timing that came with a cosmopolitan point of view.

In retrospect, the same aesthetic capacity can be said to have informed Garrison's original estimation of abolitionist progress and represented the agency of a people in the midst of a season of discord. The abolitionists' mode of self-fashioning could be considered novelistic to this extent, particularly when it is placed in a generic relation to the epic structure of history. In place of protagonists who reside in and shape their own time, the abolitionists' historiography featured quixotic or picaresque figures and seemingly misplaced acts of heroism. With jarring historical references to democratic revolutions and belated historical allusions to a revolutionary people, Garrison would represent the progress of the abolition movement with a similarly creative imagination and from a similarly anachronistic vision of progress.[5] Having borrowed his representation of abolitionist subjectivity from the epic literature of other times, he seemed to realize that there would be an almost comic incongruity between the world-changing, epochal events of modernity and the circumstances of the present moment—and yet Garrison would always make sure to commit the faculty of the imagination and the aesthetic awareness of its use to the abolitionists' political project in a way that confirmed and reproduced the agency of a people, or the historic ideal of citizenry. All the besieged, outnumbered abolitionists needed to be a citizenry or people was an ironic detachment that told them that their belatedness was a sign of their inevitable progress. The abolitionists' appeals to a forsaken but recoverable republican patrimony, the strategic repetition of civic rituals of commemoration, and the abject deference to historical figures and localities that had been transformed into proper names in this sense were all the elements of an aesthetic awareness that would make up for lapses in their political self-representation.

Thoreau's commentary on this political project was to seize on the utopian trope of citizenship—the separate ground of democratic resistance—and redeploy it as an aesthetic figure that could not compose a historical narrative. He would refuse to write a nationalist epic of individual progress or a gothic melodrama of filial mourning; the self-awareness of that expression was supposed to lead Americans away from any historical representation of a people and to deliver them from their manifest destiny. For Thoreau, the use or life of the imagination was inseparable from the reversals, stagnation, indeed the "unsocial sociability" of life in the present—which is also how Paul Ricoeur categorizes the meaning of utopia. According to Ricoeur, utopia betrays its origin in the modern discourse of aestheticism precisely in failing to represent historically the subject in time. "'Nowhere,'" he admits, translating literally its meaning, "may or *may not* give us a new orientation with respect to the 'here and now,'":

> But who knows whether this or that errant mode of existence is not a prophecy concerning man to come? Who knows even whether a certain amount of individual pathology is not the condition for social change, inasmuch as this pathology brings to light the sclerosis of worn out institutions? . . . Who knows whether the disease is not at the same time the remedy?[6]

We are faced with the question Thoreau addressed throughout *Walden*, which was how to cure the sufferer from his or her own impoverished standards for well-being. All that is needed, Ricoeur seems to suggest, is a sense of irony to turn a state of affliction into a utopian state, and that is what Thoreau—and Garrison—relied on to transform his present condition of affliction into a prescription for happiness. For Garrison, this ironic transformation told a historical narrative of inevitable progress, inseparable from the depiction of democracy at work. It constituted, in other words, a historical imagination, which is how he represented the public agency of the abolition movement when a "popular tumult" was turned against it.

Garrison thus would not have been surprised to find the enjoyment of irony and even a tendency toward black humor in the modern narrative of political progress. For Kant, an almost comic disjunction between the prophecy of human improvement and the conditions of the present was what inspired the belief in a redemptive enlightenment. He dedicated his essay "The Contest of the Faculties" to answering the signature question of his age, "is the human race continually improving?," but before he had finished, he had played a nasty little joke on its political allegory:

> A doctor who used to console his patients from day to day with hopes of imminent recovery, telling one that his pulse was better, and others that their faeces or perspiration heralded an improvement, etc. received a visit from one of his friends. "How are you my friend, and how is your illness?" was the first question. "How do you think," was the reply. "*I am dying of sheer recovery!*"[7]

Who knew that the philosopher of impenetrable transcendental deductions could be so sanguine about the answer to the signature question of his age? The determination of historical progress, Kant seems to argue, concerns nothing more than the constitution of the subject, and he apparently means that in both its etiological and hygenic senses. It is a self-made diagnosis, answering to a breakdown in subjectivity, but also a self-serving exercise with little to justify it but a clearly groundless expectation of improvement. The utopian narrative of historical progress in this sense was connected deeply to an aesthetic mode of self-awareness that seemed to feature not just an active imagination but a talent for thinking the worst.[8]

Garrison demonstrated this talent from the very first. He was so determined to lend the abolitionists' political project the benefits of the imagination that he would find in the worst sicknesses of his age, a pathology gripping the nation, not just the end of slavery but the momentous event of human liberation; from the most dire symptoms of disorder in the social life of the proslavery American polity, he announced the reappearance of a people from a revolutionary past and the completion of an unfulfilled republican mandate. He seemed to regale in the reversals and afflictions of the abolition movement, not so much as the paranoid, *pace* Hofstadter, but as Kant's hypochondriac, and foretold its historical progress with a sufferer's intimate knowledge of his symptoms. So acute was his perception—he felt the "willful defamation, lawless violence, . . . personal outrage . . . cruel persecution"[9] inflicted on the New England abolition movement to be historical trends—that he might be said to have created a symptomology of progress commensurate with an aesthetic state of agitation.

For his address in front of Park Street Church, Garrison affected the literary guise of a dissipated gothic hero, admitting that his prophecy of doom for the republic sounded like "the phantasm of a diseased imagination." "But a nation of infatuated freemen," he insisted, "take[s] no warning from history. . . . To their vision, the signs of the times are always ominous of good." Under these circumstances, a "diseased imagination" served the ends of American republicanism:

> I know, too, it is easy to persuade ourselves that we shall escape these maladies, which have destroyed other nations. But, how closely soever a republic may resemble the human body in its liability to disease and death, the instance is not on record, where a people expired on account of excessive watchfulness over their own health, or of any premature apprehension of decay; and there is no national epitaph which says "they were well, they wished to be better, they took physic, and died." (47–48)

For the editor who penned "Watchman, What of the Night?," there was no doubt that an uncomfortable state of watchfulness brought on by a "diseased imagination" had direct bearing on the existence of citizenry. It preserved for his afflicted contemporaries the memory of a truly virtuous republic and thereby rescued the republican ideal of a people from the past—the effect of antislavery agitation being not unlike a sickness. Writing in 1845, Garrison would judge the abolitionists' progress on the basis of a "sensation of uneasiness" and conclude, "A revolution is begun which never will—which never can—go backwards."[10] For Garrison, this state of agitation was the irreducible register of the abolitionists' historical agency, the source of their prophetic, distinctively cosmopolitan version of national history.[11] In this historical narrative, Jacksonian America, in the full bloom of its egalitarian capitalist experiment and at the same time willing itself backward toward race-based feudalism, was indeed dying of sheer recovery.

How did Douglass, the victim of this disease, interpret the signs that for Garrison spelled the end and the beginning of the American republic? Although he admitted to a "quailing sensation" similar to Garrison's while delivering his Fourth of July address, his oratory made his own injuries and insults seem too severe to merit a hypochondriac's attention to his symptoms, too severe for a comic imagination. He was so determined to shift the abolitionists' "cosmopolitan perspective" toward his own experience of "unsocial sociability" that he would preclude the determination of health or sickness or any representation of political progress. As an orator, he seemed to realize that the public sphere originated in and with his rhetorical art, and as such, it could serve as nothing but an occasion for pleasure, if not for the enjoyment of beauty. The most radical vision of American republicanism, promising equality and liberty for all, did seem to promote its political objectives as a thing of beauty, smoothing out all the gaps and disparities in the here and now with a providential narrative of unaccountable, spontaneously created social concord, but Douglass, as the physical object of beauty for white abolitionists, saw that he could take back this experience of pleasure as easily as he provided it. He wanted especially to take away any measure of time that could be derived from the experience of affliction. In his reenactment of the sublime was the radical and perhaps even democratic possibility of truly incongruous self-images, corresponding to incongruous grounds for historical judgment. The black abolitionist orator indeed was determined to speak from another history, another sense of time.[12]

In doing so, Douglass was rendering a verdict on the abolitionists' historical narration that was also a judgment on their constitution of themselves. He was as critical of the American republic as Garrison was, but he could never let his condemnations generate the self-fulfilling prophecy of human improvement that told of the agency of a people. He seemed to enjoy rendering judgments for their own sake, and left any conclusions to be drawn from them to the unsettling sensations of racial difference they produced in his white audiences. He exercised the faculty of judgment within the social space of the aesthetic, or within an intersubjective discourse of cases and rules, while Garrison used his judgment to measure the political progress of democracy according to a narrative construction of the subject. The faculty of judgment, Douglass seemed to realize, could be turned against the subject and demonstrate the fallibility, if not falseness, of all its determinations, which is also the lesson Lyotard draws from the Kantian discourse of aestheticism. None of the phenomenological reflections of modernity, he asserts, whether they be agitation, well-being, or the most perverse confidence in improvement, can ever signify the direction or agency of history. Taking his cue from Kant's own hypochondria, Lyotard concludes that the only cure for a "critical condition" is more of the same: "How should we judge? Often and intensely. Since it makes for a long life, we should judge a great deal. For the more we judge, the better we judge,"[13] and with this advice he might have been endorsing Douglass's prescription for the "better life" of the republic.

Douglass's route out of the abolitionists' political project thus was a way out of their historiography as well, for he would render his criticism of the American republic without offering it as a historical sign or reproducing a historical agency. He simply forbade his expression of free speech from begging comparisons with the image of a literate citizenry. His mode of judgment foreshadowed a life of democracy without a representation of the people, and in the interim he seized on the chance to release the language of antislavery from a connection to its name. For Douglass, the abolition movement had the opportunity to operate its public sphere as a truly contemporary, autonomous institution of criticism in which the authority for their judgments was taken out of the hands of the Otises, the Adamses, and all the founding fathers who served as signatories for a people in absentia and handed over to the voice of the oppressed.

The countervailing ambition of Garrison and the New England abolition movement was to render materially the traces of an absent people in their newspapers, in their pamphlets, and in their exercise of free speech so that an abolitionist public sphere could count as an institution of republican America. This was the goal of their publicity campaign, the founding abolitionist strategy of the 1830s, and as such it made every article of abolitionist literature conducive to the memory of a people. The circulation of abolitionist publications and the "abolitionizing" of the nation would perform a pedagogical function, instructing contemporaries in what Kant had called "the lessons of repeated experience"—*assuming* that a "people's revolution or constitutional reform ultimately were to fail." The agency of a people, Garrison seemed to recognize, was not manifest in the steady march of an epic protagonist or the magisterial unfolding of epochal events but in the intelligibility of the idea of progress among a receptive public, and for that they needed the evidence of abolitionist publicity.

The most practical purpose served by the abolitionists' publications might well have been in establishing the communicability of that idea, or in serving as a means of intersubjective awareness. They supplied the material conditions for a historical reception of the New England abolition movement and told of its inevitable progress despite the existence of a public that refused to read, that would retard the progress of liberty. Abolitionist publicity in this sense was the medium for the abolitionists' ironic mode of historical narration. It underwrote all the determinations of political agency—the unsettling encounter with racism, the perverse assessment of their oppression, and the hypochondriacal attention to national pathology—that could be ascribed to a diseased imagination and thereby made that aesthetic sense of agitation the best evidence of democracy.

Notes

Introduction

    1. William Lloyd Garrison, *Declaration of Sentiments and Constitution of the American Anti-Slavery Society* (New York, 1833), 9. All further citations are from this edition. The number of abolitionist publications distributed in 1837 is cited in W. Sherman Savage, *The Controversy over the Distribution of Abolitionist Literature, 1830–80* (Washington, D.C.: Association of Negro Life and History, 1938), 92. Garrison's predecessors in the antislavery movement, the organizations of the Protestant evangelical movement, were equally adept in publishing and circulation. For the precise dimensions of this publicity campaign, see Charles C. Cole, *The Social Ideas of the Northern Evangelists* (New York: Octogon, 1966), 9–14; Clifford S. Griffin, "The Abolitionists and the Benevolent Societies, 1831–1861," *Journal of Negro History* 4 (1959): 195–99; Griffin, *Their Brothers' Keeper: Moral Stewardship in the United States, 1800–1865* (New Brunswick: Rutgers University Press, 1960), 24–29; and Jon Butler, *Awash in a Sea of Faith: Christianizing the American People* (Cambridge: Harvard University Press, 1990), 277–80.

    2. William Lloyd Garrison to Wendell Phillips, June 4, 1839, in *A House Divided against Itself*, vol. 2 of *The Letters of William Lloyd Garrison*, ed. Walter Merrill and Louis Ruchames (Cambridge: Belknap-Harvard University Press, 1971), 488.

    3. In that same year, $1448 of the Massachusetts Anti-Slavery Society budget was devoted to printing, by far the largest expenditure. See *Proceedings of the Annual Meeting of the Massachusetts Anti-Slavery Society at its Annual Meeting,*

in *Annual Report of the Massachusetts Anti-Slavery Society,* 1837 (1831–53; reprint, Westport, Conn.: Negro Universities Press, 1970), 1: xiv (hereafter cited as *Proceedings* with year).

4. For the use of the term "abolitionize," see Maria Weston Chapman, *Right and Wrong in Boston* (Boston, 1839), frontispiece. The formation of antebellum reading publics in relation to political reform is discussed critically in Alexander Saxton, *The Rise and Fall of the White Republic: Class Politics and Mass Culture in Nineteenth-Century America* (London: Verso, 1990); Richard D. Brown, *The Strength of a People: The Idea of an Informed Citizenry in America, 1650–1870* (Chapel Hill: University of North Carolina Press, 1996); Ronald Zboray, *A Fictive People: Antebellum Economic Development and the American Reading Public* (New York: Oxford University Press, 1993); Lewis Perry, *Boats against the Current: American Culture between Revolution and Modernity, 1820–1860* (New York: Oxford University Press, 1993).

5. See Jürgen Habermas, *The Structural Transformation of the Public Sphere: An Inquiry into a Category of Bourgeois Society* (Cambridge: MIT Press, 1989), 24–89.

6. Garrison, "Prospectus," *The Liberator,* May 28, 1831, 3.

7. For a full account of the reading community created by Walker's pamphlet and Garrison's decision to reprint it, see Peter D. Hinks, *To Awaken My Afflicted Brethren: David Walker and the Problem of Antebellum Slave Resistance* (University Park: Pennsylvania State University Press, 1997).

8. Over the past decade, feminist scholarship has been responsible largely for reconstructing the abolition movement as a subject of critical inquiry, and I can assemble only a selective survey of its major contributions. See Karen Sánchez-Eppler, *Touching Liberty: Abolition, Feminism, and the Politics of the Body* (Berkeley: University of California Press, 1993); Mary Ryan, *Women in Public: Between Banners and Ballots, 1825–1880* (Baltimore: The Johns Hopkins University Press, 1990); Carolyn Karcher, *The First Women in the Republic: A Cultural Biography of Lydia Maria Child* (Durham: Duke University Press, 1994); Jean Fagin Yellin and John C. Van Horne, eds., *Abolitionist Sisterhood: Women's Political Culture in Antebellum America* (Ithaca: Cornell University Press, 1994); Jean Fagin Yellin, *Women and Sisters: The Antislavery Feminists in American Culture* (New Haven: Yale University Press, 1989), 29–44. Yellin's analysis has been particularly suggestive for this study in positing a link between the publicity of emblems and texts and the intervention of abolitionist women.

9. Lydia Maria Child, *An Appeal in Favor of that Class of Americans Called Africans* (Amherst: University of Massachusetts Press, 1996), 5.

10. Angelina Grimké, "Letters to Catharine Beecher," in *The Public Years of Sarah and Angelina Grimké: Selected Writings, 1835–1839,* ed. Larry Ceplair (New York: Columbia University Press, 1989), 164.

11. My use of Berlant's phrase is meant to comment critically on the republican economy of self-abstraction that Michael Warner ascribed to eighteenth-century print culture. See Lauren Berlant, *The Anatomy of National Fantasy: Hawthorne, Utopia, and Everyday Life* (Chicago: University of Chicago Press, 1991), 34; Michael Warner, *The Letters of the Republic: Publicity and the Public Sphere in Eighteenth-Century America* (Cambridge: Harvard University Press, 1990). Warner has explored the counterpotential of his own conception for the embodiment of subjects in "The Mass Public and the Mass Subject," in *Habermas and the Public Sphere,* ed. Craig Calhoun (Cambridge: MIT Press, 1992), 377–401.

12. For an account of this episode, see John Thomas, *The Liberator: William Lloyd Garrison* (Boston: Little, Brown, 1963), 188.

13. The short history and rationale for this penny-press newspaper can be found in "Cradle of Liberty," *The Liberator* April 5, 1839, 3; Wendell Phillips Garrison and Francis Jackson Garrison, *William Lloyd Garrison: The Story of His Life, Told by His Children,* vol. 2 (Boston, 1885–89; reprint, New York: Negro Universities Press, 1969), 284.

14. The socially stratified public culture of Jacksonian America receives enlightening analysis in Saxton, *Rise and Fall*; Mary Ryan, *Civic Wars: Democracy and Public Life in the American City during the Nineteenth Century* (Berkeley: University of California Press, 1997); Michael Schudson "Was There Ever a Public Sphere? If So, When? Reflections on the American Case," in *Habermas and the Public Sphere,* ed. Calhoun, 143–63; David Waldstreicher, *In the Midst of Perpetual Fetes: The Making of American Nationalism, 1776–1820* (Chapel Hill: University of North Carolina Press, 1997), 294–348. My thesis regarding the "untimeliness" of the abolitionists' public sphere, however, also draws on the theoretical explorations of history and historiography found in Hayden White, *The Content of the Form: Narrative Discourse and Historical Representation* (Baltimore: The Johns Hopkins University Press, 1987), 4–55; White, *Metahistory: The Historical Imagination of Nineteenth-Century Europe* (Baltimore: The Johns Hopkins University Press, 1973), 48–69 and 330–74; J. G. A. Pocock, "Modes of Political and

Historical Time in Eighteenth-Century England," in *Virtue, Commerce, and History: Essays on Political Thought and History, Chiefly in the Eighteenth Century,* by Pocock (Cambridge: Cambridge University Press, 1985), 89–119; and, of course, Friedrich Nietzsche, "On the Uses and Disadvantages of History for Life," in *Untimely Meditations,* trans. R. J. Hollingdale (Cambridge: Cambridge University Press, 1983), 59–123.

15. Jacques Derrida, *Specters of Marx: The State of Debt, the Work of Mourning, and the New International* (London: Routledge, 1994), 50.

16. Garrison, "Vindication of the Liberator," in *Selections from the Writings and Speeches of William Lloyd Garrison* (1852; reprint, New York: Negro Universities Press, 1968), 188.

17. Two seminal studies that describe the equivocal appeal of the Enlightenment in eighteenth-century America remain Louis Hartz, *The Liberal Tradition in America: An Interpretation of American Political Thought since the Revolution* (New York: Harcourt, Brace, and World, 1955), 36–76; and Henry May, *The Enlightenment in America* (New York: Oxford University Press, 1976), 109–68. A selective survey of scholarship of this "great transformation" of Jacksonian society would include Robert H. Wiebe, *The Opening of American Society: From the Adoption of the Constitution to the Eve of Disunion* (New York: Knopf, 1984), 194–320; Rogers M. Smith, *Civic Ideals: Conflicting Visions of Citizenship in U.S. History* (New Haven: Yale University Press, 1997), 115–242; Charles Sellers, *The Market Revolution: Jacksonian America, 1815–1846* (New York: Oxford University Press, 1991); Lawrence Frederick Kohl, *The Politics of Individualism: Parties and the American Character in the Jacksonian Era* (New York: Oxford University Press, 1989); George Thomas, *Revivalism and Cultural Change: Christianity, Nation-Building and the Market in Nineteenth-Century United States* (Chicago: University of Chicago Press, 1989); Jonathan Glickstein, *Concepts of Free Labor in Antebellum America* (New Haven: Yale University Press, 1991).

18. Derrida, *Specters of Marx,* 112, 109.

19. The rich archive of scholarship committed to republican America's discovery of history is represented by Russ Castronovo, *Fathering the Nation: American Genealogies of Slavery and Freedom* (Berkeley: University of California Press, 1995); Fred Somkin, *Unquiet Eagle: Memory and Desire in the Idea of American Freedom, 1815–1860* (Ithaca: Cornell University Press, 1967); Michael Kammen, *A Season of Youth: The American Revolution and the Historical Imagination* (New York: Knopf, 1978); Eric Sundquist, "Slavery, Revolution, and the American Renaissance," in *The American Renaissance Reconsidered,* ed. Walter

Benn Michaels and Donald E. Pease (Baltimore: The Johns Hopkins University Press, 1985), 1–33. For my citation of "fractures," see Sundquist, "Slavery, Revolution, and the American Renaissance," 9.

20. This portrait of the republicanism of the antebellum printing trade is drawn from Saxton, *Rise and Fall,* 95–108; Daniel Schiller, *Objectivity and the News: The Public and the Rise of Commercial Journalism* (Philadelphia: University of Pennsylvania Press, 1981), 45–50; Sean Wilentz, *Chants Democratic: New York City and the Rise of the American Working Class, 1788–1850* (New York: Oxford University Press, 1984), 77–87 and 153–211. A close examination of working-class partisan organizations and their newspapers is offered in Garry J. Kornblith, "Becoming Joseph Buckingham: The Struggle for Independence in Early Nineteenth-Century Boston," in *American Artisans: Crafting Social Identity, 1750–1850,* ed. Howard Rock, et al. (Baltimore: The Johns Hopkins University Press, 1995), 123–34; Ronald P. Formisano, *The Transformation of Political Culture: Massachusetts Parties, 1790s–1840s* (New York: Oxford University Press, 1983), 198–231; Edward Pessen, "The Working Men's Party Revisited," in *New Perspectives on Jacksonian Parties and Politics,* ed. Pessen (New York: Allyn and Bacon, 1969), 182–99.

21. A highly selective survey of this initiative would include Christopher Newfield, *The Emerson Effect: Individualism and Submission in America* (Chicago: University of Chicago Press, 1996); David F. Ericson, *The Shaping of American Liberalism: The Politics over Nullification and Slavery* (Chicago: University of Chicago Press, 1993), 1–26; James Henretta, "The Slow Triumph of Individualism: Law and Politics in New York, 1780–1860," in *American Chameleon: Individualism in a Trans-National Context,* ed. Richard O. Curry and Laurence Goodheart (Akron, Ohio: Kent State University Press, 1991), 87–106; Bruce Burgett, *Sentimental Bodies: Sex, Gender, and Citizenship in the Early Republic* (Princeton: Princeton University Press, 1998); Glenn Hendler, *Public Sentiments: Structures of Feeling in Nineteenth-Century American Literature* (Chapel Hill: University of North Carolina Press, 2001). The simultaneity of liberalism and republicanism is discussed more broadly as a problem of ideology and history in Joyce Appleby, *Liberalism and Republicanism in the Historical Imagination* (Cambridge: Harvard University Press, 1992).

22. A good account of Paine's significance within the artisnal community of postrevolutionary America remains Eric Foner, *Tom Paine and Revolutionary America* (New York: Oxford University Press, 1976), which also accounts for his influence on antebellum reform. The history of the Freethought movement

and its origins in Paine commemorative societies is found in Albert Post, *Popular Freethought in America, 1825–1850* (New York: Columbia University Press, 1943), 76; Wilenz, *Chants Democratic*, 153–57. A brilliant reading of Freethought in relation to antebellum gender politics is found in Lori Ginzburg, "'The Hearts of Your Readers Will Shudder': Fanny Wright, Infidelity, and American Freethought," *American Quarterly* 46 (1994): 195–226.

23. Garrison, "Free Speech and Free Inquiry," *Selections*, 239.

24. W. L. Sleigh, *Abolition Exposed!* (Philadelphia, 1838), 14.

25. Garrison to Erasmus D. Hudson, September 8, 1838, *A House Divided against Itself*, 384. A classic account of the rise of the Protestant "benevolent empire" and its repudiation of Garrison remains Gilbert Barnes, *The Anti-Slavery Impulse, 1830–44* (New York: Harcourt, Brace and World, 1961), 35–98. Also revealing of this antagonism is Robert H. Abzug, *Cosmos Crumbling: Reform and the Religious Imagination* (New York: Oxford University Press, 1994), 136–52. For an overview of Protestant evangelical reform in America, see Richard Cawardine, *Evangelicals and Politics in Antebellum America* (New Haven: Yale University Press, 1993).

26. Garrison devoted many of his early editorials in *The Liberator* to the progress of emancipation bills through Parliament. On the passage of the bill, he declared that an "auspicious" time had arrived for the formation of an American antislavery movement. See Garrison, "National Anti-Slavery Society," *The Liberator*, 5 October 1833, 3. The English origins and liberal ideology of abolition are recalled in David Brion Davis, *The Age of Slavery in the Age of Revolution, 1770–1823* (Ithaca: Cornell University Press, 1975), 84–163.

27. *Abolition a Sedition, by a Northern Man* (Philadelphia, 1839), 44.

28. My overly compressed version of postrevolutionary discord in the 1790s is drawn from Jerry Knudson, "The Rage around Tom Paine: Newspaper Reaction to His Homecoming," *New York Historical Society Quarterly* 53 (1969): 34–63; Marshall Smelzer, "The Jacobin Phrenzy: Federalism and the Menace of Liberty, Equality, and Fraternity," *Review of Politics* 13 (1951): 457–82; Vernon Stauffer, *New England and the Bavarian Illuminati* (New York: Columbia University Press, 1918), 108–34; Eugene P. Link, *Democratic Republican Societies, 1790–1800* (New York: Octagon, 1965), 114–35; David Brion Davis, *Revolutions: Reflections on American Equality and Foreign Liberations* (Cambridge: Harvard University Press, 1990); Joyce Appleby, *Capitalism and a New Social Order: The Republican Vision of the 1790s* (New York: New York University Press, 1984).

29. The popular reception of abolitionist publications as conducive to slave rebellion and the official measures taken to suppress their circulation are recounted in Leonard Richards, *Gentlemen of Property and Standing: Anti-Abolition Mobs in Jacksonian America* (New York: Oxford University Press, 1970); Lorman Ratner, *Powder Keg: Northern Opposition to the Antislavery Movement, 1831–1840* (New York: Basic Books, 1968); Savage, *Controversy over Distribution*, 34–46.

30. For the legislative enactments against abolitionist publications, see Savage, *Controversy over Distribution*, 34–46.

31. For this concept of "time dimension" inherent to republican ideology, see Pocock, "Modes of Political and Historical Time in Eighteenth-Century England," and *The Machiavellian Moment: Florentine Political Thought and the Atlantic Republican Tradition* (Princeton: Princeton University Press 1975), 3–9. A related conception is found in Jürgen Habermas, "Modernity's Consciousness of Time and Its Need for Self-Reassurance," in *The Philosophical Discourse of Modernity: Twelve Lectures*, trans. Frederick Lawrence (Cambridge: MIT Press, 1987), 1–22.

32. My foray into the critical literature of the liberal public sphere takes its cues from two familiar sources, Nancy Fraser, "Rethinking the Public Sphere: A Contribution to the Critique of Actually Existing Democracy," in *Habermas and the Public Sphere*, ed. Calhoun, 109–43; and Houston Baker, "Critical Memory and the Black Public Sphere," in *Public Culture* 7 (1994): 1–22. Of crucial service in articulating the ideological dimension of Habermas's conception has been Benjamin Lee, "Textuality, Mediation, and Public Discourse," in *Habermas and the Public Sphere*, 402–18; and Frederick Dolan, *Allegories of America: Narratives, Metaphysics, Politics* (Ithaca: Cornell University Press, 1994): 31–54. The prospect of a "counter-public sphere" is explored lucidly in Miriam Hansen, foreword, *Public Sphere and Experience: Toward an Analysis of the Bourgeois and Proletarian Public Sphere*, by Oskar Negt and Alexander Kluge (Minneapolis: University of Minnesota Press, 1993), xxxv–vi. Habermas's own response to the critical reception of his work makes clear his intention to explore the potential of "the normative theory of democracy" as both "counterfactual entity" and historical artifact. See Habermas, "Further Reflections on the Public Sphere," in *Habermas and the Public Sphere*, 439–40. My reference to nineteenth-century identity politics addresses points made in Ryan, *Civic Wars*.

33. Some recent investigations into the critical potential of republicanism are Chantal Mouffe, "Democratic Citizenship and the Political Community,"

in *Community at Loose Ends*, ed. Miami Theory Collective (Minneapolis: University of Minnesota Press, 1991), 70–82; John Brenkman, "Extreme Criticism," in *What's Left of Theory? New Work on the Politics of Literary Theory*, ed. Judith Butler and John Guillory (New York: Routledge, 2000), 114–36.

34. Walter Benjamin, "Theses on the Philosophy of History," in *Illuminations*, ed. Hannah Arendt (New York: Schocken Books, 1969), 255. The ironic relation between republican manhood, African American identity, and patriarchal narrative is, of course, the subject of Castronovo, *Fathering the Nation*. Of equally critical use in exploring the interlocking bonds between Garrison, civic republicanism, and African American communities has been Paul Goodman, *Of One Blood: Abolitionists and the Origin of Racial Equality* (Berkeley: University of California Press, 1998).

35. Benjamin, "Theses on the Philosophy of History," 263.

36. Garrison, "The Triumph of Mobocracy," in *Selections*, 380.

37. Thomas Russell Sullivan, *Letters against the Immediate Abolition of Slavery* (Boston, 1835), 4.

38. See Angelina Grimké's defense of the Boston society's association with Thompson in Angelina Grimké, "An Appeal to the Christian Women of the South," *The Public Years of Sarah and Angelina Grimké: Selected Writings, 1835–1839*, ed. Larry Ceplair (New York: Columbia University Press, 1989), 76–77.

39. My reading of Sullivan as antifeminist and xenophobe is informed by the analysis of Ratner, *Powder Keg*, 29–39. A similar commentary on foreign influence is found in James Kirke Paulding, *Slavery in the United States* (New York, 1836), 135. For an analysis on foreignness and gender representation in relation to Thompson, see Philip Lapansky, "Graphic Discord: Abolitionist and Anti-Abolitionist Images," in *The Abolitionist Sisterhood*, ed. Yellin and Van Horne, 201–30. For a gendered reading of the political conflicts of the 1790s, see Shirley Samuels, *Romances of the Republic: Women, the Family, and Violence in the Literature of the Early American Nation* (New York: Oxford University Press, 1996), 23–43.

40. Otis quoted in "Mr. Otis's Speech at Faneuil Hall," *The Liberator*, September 5, 1835, 4.

41. See Homi Bhabha, "Conclusion: 'Race,' Time, and the Revision of Modernity," in *Location of Culture* (London: Routledge, 1994), 245.

42. For this rereading of the "imagined community," see Bhabha, "Dissemination," in *Location of Culture*, 157–61.

43. See Benedict Anderson, *Imagined Communities: Reflections on the Origin and Spread of Nationalism* (London: Verso, 1991), 22–46 and 70–81.

44. Bhabha, "Conclusion: 'Race,' Time, and the Revision of Modernity," 243.

45. See Claude Lefort, "The Question of Democracy," in *Democracy and Political Theory* (Minneapolis: University of Minnesota Press, 1988), 9–20. The incongruity of the imaginary with the socializing function of ideology is also the subject of Cornelius Castoriadis, *The Imaginary Institution of Society*, trans. Kathleen Birney (Cambridge: MIT Press, 1987); and Castoriadis, "Radical Imagination the Social Instituting Imaginary," in *Rethinking Imagination: Culture and Creativity*, ed. Gillian Robinson and John Rundell (London: Routledge, 1994), 87–117.

46. Paul Ricoeur, "Imagination in Discourse and Action," in *Rethinking Imagination*, ed. Robinson and Rundell, 122–29.

47. Habermas describes an "unfinished project of modernity" and the attendant pressure to realize itself in "Hegel's Concept of Modernity," in *The Philosophical Discourse of Modernity*, 23–50.

48. Garrison quoted in Garrison and Garrison, *William Lloyd Garrison*, 2: 215 n. 2.

49. *Annual Report of the Massachusetts Anti-Slavery Society*, 1845 (1831–53; reprint, Westport, Conn.: Negro University Press, 1970) 2: 62. Hereafter cited as *Annual Report* with year.

50. See Immanuel Kant, "The Contest of the Faculties," in *Kant: Political Writings*, ed. Hans Reiss (Cambridge: Cambridge University Press, 1991), 177. In citing Kant in an Americanist context, I am following an unorthodox but promising course laid out in Robert Ferguson, *The American Enlightenment, 1750–1820* (Cambridge: Harvard University Press, 1997), 25–41.

51. Kant, "The Contest of the Faculties," 185.

52. Garrison, *An Address Delivered before the Free People of Color in Philadelphia* (Boston, 1831), 9.

53. Bhabha, "Conclusion: 'Race,' Time, and the Revision of Modernity," 243.

54. Ibid., 245–48.

55. Michel Foucault, "What Is Enlightenment?," in *Interpretive Social Science: A Second Look*, ed. Paul Rabinow and William M. Sullivan (Berkeley: University of California Press, 1987), 159 and 164.

56. Frederick Douglass, "Southern Slavery and Northern Religion," in *Speeches, Debates, and Interviews, 1841–1846*, vol. 1, The Frederick Douglass Papers, Ser. 1, ed. John Blassingame (New Haven: Yale University Press, 1979), 24.

57. Jean François Lyotard, "The Sign of History," in *Post-Structuralism and the Question of History*, ed. Derek Attridge et al. (Cambridge: Cambridge University Press, 1987), 168. An important investigation into the aesthetic nature of historical interpretation is Peter Fenves, *A Peculiar Fate: Metaphysics and World-History in Kant* (Ithaca: Cornell University Press, 1991).

1. The Sedition of Nonresistance

1. Adin Ballou, *Non-Resistance in Relation to Human Government* (Boston, 1839), 8.

2. Scholarly opinion of nonresistance as a Perfectionist movement is represented by Lewis Perry, *Radical Abolitionism: Anarchy and the Government of God in Antislavery Thought* (Ithaca: Cornell University Press, 1973), 68–118; John Thomas, *The Liberator: William Lloyd Garrison* (Boston: Little, Brown, 1963), 219–31; Ronald Walters, *The Antislavery Appeal: American Abolition after 1830* (New York: Hill and Wang, 1978), 55–68; Peter Brock, *Radical Pacifists in Antebellum America* (Princeton: Princeton University Press, 1968), 55–142. A pivotal exchange of letters between Garrison and the Perfectionist J. H. P. Noyes, said to be responsible for his "conversion" to nonresistance, is reprinted in Garrison and Garrison, *William Lloyd Garrison*, 2: 144–50.

3. Tracy quoted in "New England Non-Resistance Society," *The Liberator*, 19 October 1838, 4.

4. *Abolition a Sedition*, by a Northern Man (Philadelphia, 1839), 74.

5. A general statement of the influence of the individual in the context of traditional American studies historiography of the reform movement is found in George Frederickson, *The Inner Civil War: Northern Intellectuals and the Crisis of the Union* (New York: Harper and Row, 1965), 7–22. The critique of individualism and private morality as an artifact of apolitical liberalism can be traced to Carl Schmitt, *The Concept of the Political* (New Brunswick: Rutgers University Press, 1976); Reinhart Koselleck, *Critique and Crisis: Enlightenment and the Pathogenesis of Modern Society* (Cambridge: MIT Press, 1988); Hannah Arendt, *The Human Condition* (New York: Doubleday-Anchor Books, 1959), and "What Is Freedom?," in *Between Past and Future: Eight Exercises in Political Thought* (New York: Penguin Books, 1977), 143–76.

6. For the cultural transformation of deism under artisan republicanism, see James Turner, *Without God, Without Creed: The Origins of Unbelief in America* (Baltimore: The Johns Hopkins University Press, 1985), 35–52; G. Alfred Koch, *Republican Religion: The American Revolution and the Cult of Reason* (New York: Henry Holt, 1933), 54–90; May, *The Enlightenment in America*, 109–68.

7. Paine's infamy among late eighteenth- and early nineteenth-century Americans is recalled in Knudson, "The Rage around Tom Paine"; and Gary B. Nash, "The American Clergy and the French Revolution," *William and Mary Quarterly* 22 (1965): 392–412.

8. My reading of Paine's infamy as interpreted through antebellum gender and racial politics is informed by Samuels, *Romances of the Republic*, 23–43; and Ginzburg, "'The Hearts of Your Readers Will Shudder.'"

9. Kneeland's career is recalled in Post, *Popular Freethought in America*, 103–06.

10. Garrison, *An Address Delivered before the Free People of Color* (Boston, 1831), 1, 4.

11. *Report of the Arguments of the Attorney of the Commonwealth, at the Trials of Abner Kneeland* (Boston, 1834), 12, 16, and 19.

12. The dimensions of the counter-Enlightenment movement in America and its focus on Paine are described in Knudson, "The Rage around Tom Paine"; Nash, "The American Clergy and the French Revolution"; and Stauffer, *New England and the Bavarian Illuminati*. Paine's prosecution is recalled in Foner, *Tom Paine and Revolutionary America*, 228–30.

13. *Report of the Arguments*, 16 and 19.

14. The rise of the republican opposition press and its prosecution under a Federalist government are recalled in Link, *Democratic-Republican Societies*. The instrumentality of libel law to the Alien and Sedition Acts is argued in Leonard Levy, *Emergence of a Free Press* (New York: Oxford University Press), 210–98; Bernard Bailyn, "The Freedom of the Press in Revolutionary Libertarianism, 1760–1820," in *The Press and the American Revolution*, ed. John Hench Jr. (Worcester, Mass.: American Antiquarian Society, 1980), 56–96; and Norman Rosenberg, *Protecting the Best Men: An Interpretive History of the Law of Libel* (Chapel Hill: University of North Carolina Press, 1986), 71–100.

15. Abner Kneeland, "Misrepresentations and Slanders of the Editors and Other Writers of Pious Journals," *Boston Investigator*, August 7, 1835, 1.

16. Governor William Marcy of New York was quoted as issuing this

charge in "Proposition for the Passage of Another Alien and Sedition Law," *The Liberator*, January 30, 1836, 1.

17. William Lloyd Garrison, "Petition for the Pardon of Abner Kneeland," *The Liberator*, July 6, 1838, 4.

18. This condensed history of libertarianism is drawn from Brown, *The Strength of a People*, 1–118; Pocock, *The Machiavellian Moment*, 333–422; David Norbrook, "*Areopagitica*, Censorship, and the Early Modern Public Sphere," in *The Administration of Aesthetics: Censorship, Political Criticism, and the Public Sphere*, ed. Richard Burt (Minneapolis: University of Minnesota Press, 1994), 3–33; Roger Smith, *Liberalism and Constitutional Law* (Cambridge: Harvard, 1985), 94–96; David L. Jacobsen, ed., *The English Libertarian Heritage* (Indianapolis: Bobbs-Merrill Company, 1965); Bailyn, "The Freedom of the Press in Revolutionary Libertarianism." The recovery of a liberal political tradition can be said to counter the thesis of apoliticism in Hartz, *The Liberal Tradition in America*.

19. Garrison to Samuel May, September 24, 1838, *A House Divided against Itself*, 402.

20. Garrison, "Free Discussion," *The Liberator*, November 30, 1838, 4.

21. "Annual Meeting of the New England Non-Resistance Society," *The Liberator*, November 1, 1839, 4.

22. On the internecine struggles over the inclusion of nonresistance and women's rights within the abolitionist agenda, see Aileen Kraditor, *Means and Ends in American Abolitionism: Garrison and His Critics on Strategy and Tactics, 1834–1850* (New York: Pantheon, 1969); and Ronald G. Walters, *The Antislavery Appeal: American Abolition after 1830* (New York: Norton, 1978).

23. Wright quoted in Garrison and Garrison, *William Lloyd Garrison*, 2: 179.

24. "Declaration of Sentiments, Adopted by the Peace Convention, Held in Boston," *The Liberator*, September 28, 1838, 2.

25. Claude Lefort, "The Question of Democracy," in *Democracy and Political Theory*, 17.

26. For the implications of Toqueville's thesis with regard to the liberal polity, see Claude Lefort, "From Equality to Freedom: Fragments of an Interpretation of *Democracy in America*," in *Democracy and Political Theory*, 183–209.

27. One Hubbard Winslow quoted in *Proceedings* of 1838, 6.

28. Garrison, "Reply to James G. Birney," *The Liberator*, June 28, 1839, 2.

29. In Pocock's rendering of civic republicanism, the independence of

the private affairs of society from the depredations of the state is the first article of public virtue. See *The Machiavellian Moment*, 401–505.

30. For a self-defense of his libelous criticism, see William Lloyd Garrison, "Harsh Language—Retarding the Cause," in *Selections*, 121–34.

31. Garrison, "A Layman's Reply to a 'Clerical Appeal,'" *The Liberator*, September 18, 1837, 2.

32. The slippage between state and society as a feature of post-Enlightenment political public sphere is theorized in Habermas, *The Structural Transformation of the Public Sphere*, 80–84.

33. William Lloyd Garrison to the president of the Anti-Slavery Convention, January 30, 1836, in *A House Divided against Itself*, 29.

34. Trial of the case of *Commonwealth v. D. L. Child* (Boston, 1829), 3 and 22.

35. Garrison, "A Brief Sketch of the Trial of William Lloyd Garrison for an Alleged Libel on Francis Todd," in *Slave Rebels, Abolitionists, and Southern Courts: The Pamphlet Literature*, vol. 1, *Slavery, Race, and the American Legal System, 1700–1872*, ser. 4 (New York: Garland Publishing, 1988), 205.

36. My conception of the tradition and function of common law here and hereafter derives largely from William E. Nelson, *Americanization of the Common Law: The Impact of Legal Change on Massachusetts Society, 1760–1830* (Cambridge: Harvard University Press, 1975); and Morton J. Horwitz, *The Transformation of American Law, 1780–1860* (New York: Oxford University Press, 1992). A more narrow genealogy of libel law can be gleaned from Rosenberg, *Protecting the Best Men*, 71–100; and Frank Thayer, *Legal Control of the Press: Concerning Libel, Privacy, Contempt, Copyright, and Regulation of Advertising and Postal Laws* (Brooklyn: Foundation Press, 1962), 228–233. A lucid contemporary exposition of libel appears in Thomas Cooper, *A Treatise on the Law of Libel and the Liberty of the Press* (1830; reprint, New York: Arno Press, 1970).

37. Alien and Sedition Acts quoted in Smelser, "The Jacobin Phrenzy," 480.

38. *People v. Croswell* quoted in Thayer, *Legal Control of the Press*, 235. The significance of this statute for American libertarian theory is argued in Levy, *Emergence of a Free Press*, 340.

39. Parker quoted in Clyde Augustus Duniway, *The Development of Freedom of the Press in Massachusetts* (New York: Longmans, Green, and Company, 1906), 157. My account of libel prosecution in Massachusetts is heavily indebted to this source.

40. Quoted in Duniway, *The Development of the Freedom of the Press,* 159.

41. Garrison, "Harsh Language," 121.

42. Garrison, "The Libel Suit," *The Liberator,* January 15, 1831, 1.

43. Garrison, "Slander," *The Liberator,* July 16, 1833, 2. My revision of paranoia in this case pays homage to the characterization of antebellum reform in Richard Hofstadter, *The Paranoid Style in American Politics* (New York: Knopf, 1965), 14–30.

44. Garrison, "A Sketch of the Trial of William Lloyd Garrison," 205.

45. Garrison, "Trial of the Editor," *The Liberator,* February 22, 1834, 3.

46. *Speeches Delivered at the Anti-Colonization Meeting in Exeter Hall, London, July 13, 1833* (Boston, 1833), 7.

47. Caleb Cushing, *An Oration Pronounced at Boston before the Colonization Society of Massachusetts* (Boston, 1833), 13.

48. Gurley quoted in Oliver Johnson, "Boston Recorder," *The Liberator,* August 17, 1833, 3. Gurley's career and influence over the colonizationist movement in America is recounted in Early Fox, "The American Colonization Society," *Johns Hopkins Studies in History and Political Science* 37 (1919): 313–544; and John R. Bodo, *The Protestant Clergy and Public Issues, 1812–1848* (Princeton: Princeton University Press, 1954), 120–33.

49. Johnson, "Boston Recorder."

50. Garrison, "Imprisonment of Abner Kneeland," *The Liberator,* January 6, 1838, 3.

51. Kneeland, "Misrepresentations and Slanders," 2.

52. Garrison, "Religious Newspapers—The Clergy," *The Liberator,* 26 September 1835, 3.

53. Garrison, "Vindication of the Liberator," *Selections,* 187.

54. Garrison, *An Address Delivered in Marlboro Chapel, Boston* (Boston, 1838), 9.

55. "Constitution of the New England Non-Resistance Society," *The Liberator,* September 28, 1838, 2.

56. Henry Pinckney quoted in the *Annual Report* of 1837, 1: 22.

57. Not less than 1,412,000 petition signatures were filed before Congress in 1837–38, according to W. Sherman Savage, *Controversy over Distribution,* 92 n. 52. Garrison gave the figure of "probably not less than 500 memorials . . . containing not less than 75,000 or 100,000 signatures" presented at a single

session of Congress. See *Annual Report* of 1837, 17. The annual report of the Executive Committee of the American Anti-Slavery Society reported that from January 21 to May 1, 1837, 414,471 petitions were forwarded to Congress in opposition to slavery and the recently passed Gag Law. See *The Liberator,* May 18, 1838, 2.

58. The efforts of state legislatures and of the District of Columbia to suppress the circulation of these abolitionist petitions, newspapers, and pamphlets are recounted in Savage, *Controversy over Distribution,* 34–56; and Thomas, *The Liberator: William Lloyd Garrison,* 136–87.

59. Francis Scott Key, "A Part of the Speech Pronounced by F. S. Key on the Trial of Reuben Crandall, M.D.," in *Slave Rebels, Abolitionists, and Southern Courts,* 429 and 431.

60. John C. Calhoun, "Report from the Select Committee on the Circulation of Incendiary Publications," *The Papers of John C. Calhoun,* ed. Clyde Wilson (Columbia: University of South Carolina Press, 1980), 13: 59.

61. The attack of a Charleston mob on a local post office and the approving response of Postmaster General Amos Kendall are recounted in Leonard Richards, *Gentlemen of Property and Standing: Anti-Abolitionist Mobs in Jacksonian America* (New York: Oxford University Press, 1970), 73–77. The postmaster's efforts are analyzed insightfully in Richard B. Kielbowicz, *News in the Mail: The Press, the Post Office, and Public Information, 1700–1860s* (New York: Greenwood Press, 1989), 66–71. The rise of Kendall, a former newspaper editor, within the Jackson administration and the role of the partisan press in its initiatives is discussed at length in Sellers, *The Market Revolution,* 298–326.

62. Calhoun, "Report from the Select Committee," *Papers,* 13: 69.

63. Garrison made his criticism of the Calhoun Report in the *Annual Report* of 1837, 25–37.

64. Contradictory appraisals of this legal corpus by contemporaries can be found in Jacob D. Wheeler, *A Practical Treatise on the Law of Slavery* (1837; reprint, New York: Negro Universities Press, 1967), and William Goodell, *The American Slave Code* (1853; reprint, New York: Arno Press, 1969).

65. Genovese's analysis finds in Southern slave law an anomalous unity of custom with law that at times required paternal Southerners to wield the law against themselves if they desired to maintain their moral legitimacy. See *Roll, Jordon, Roll: The World the Slaves Made* (New York: Vintage Books, 1976), 25–49.

66. John C. Calhoun, "Speech on Abolition Petitions," in *The Works of John C. Calhoun*, ed. Richard Cralle (New York: D. Appleton and Company, 1851), 2: 483.

67. Calhoun, "Speech on Abolition Petitions," *Works*, 483.

68. Ibid., 484.

69. Garrison to Francis Jackson, January 20, 1836, in *A House Divided against Itself*, 30.

70. *Annual Report* of 1837, 22.

71. My discussion of the relation of a ruling class to the formation of the state has been informed by the theoretical and historical investigation of Anthony Giddens, *The Nation-State and Violence*, vol. 2 of *A Contemporary Critique of Historical Materialism* (Berkeley: University of California Press, 1987), 61–116.

72. The insurgency of abolitionist women in the petition campaign is recounted in Deborah Bingham Van Broekhoven, "'Let Your Names Be Enrolled': Method and Ideology in Women's Antislavery Petitioning," in *The Abolitionist Sisterhood*, ed. Yellin and Van Horne, 180–99.

73. The violence against women has been argued as an actuating cause of Garrison's conversion to non-resistance in Margaret Hope Bacon, "Antislavery Women and Non-Resistance," in *The Abolitionist Sisterhood*, ed. Jean Fagin Yellin and John C. Van Horne, 275–97.

74. Garrison, "Human Government," *The Liberator*, June 23, 1837, 3.

75. Resolution quoted in *Annual Report* of 1838, 33.

76. Garrison expressed his reservations about Lovejoy's act of self-defense in a letter to his colleague Samuel May. In the same letter, he named what he considered the true lesson of the incident. Garrison to Samuel J. May, December 30, 1837, *A House Divided against Itself*, 362.

77. *Proceedings*, 1838, 1: 37.

78. *Annual Report* of 1838, 10.

79. Garrison, "Prospectus of The Liberator," *The Liberator*, December 15, 1837, 3.

80. "Annual Meeting of the New England Non-Resistance Society."

81. Adin Ballou, *National Organizations; Prepared for the New England Non-Resistance Society* (Boston, 1839), 14.

82. Birney's objections appear in "View of the American Anti-Slavery Society as Connected with the 'No-Government' Question," *The Liberator*, June 28, 1839, 1.

83. Ballou, *National Organizations*, 4.

84. "Annual Meeting of the New England Non-Resistance Society."

85. "Annual Meeting of the New England Non-Resistance Society."

86. "First Annual Meeting of the New England Non-Resistance Society," *The Liberator*, October 11, 1839, 4.

87. "First Annual Meeting of the New England Non-Resistance Society."

88. This rendition of the abolition movement under the principles of nonresistance can be seen in Walters, *The Antislavery Appeal*, 55; and Gilbert Barnes, *The Anti-Slavery Impulse, 1830–44* (New York: Harcourt, Brace, and World, 1961), 28.

89. Garrison to Samuel May, September 24, 1838, *A House Divided against Itself*, 402.

90. Lefort, "Reversibility: Political Freedom and the Freedom of the Individual," in *Democracy and Political Theory*, 176–78.

91. "First Annual Meeting of the New England Non-Resistance Society."

92. "Annual Meeting of the New England Non-Resistance Society."

2. Garrisonism and the Public Sphere

1. Phelps quoted in Garrison and Garrison, *William Lloyd Garrison*, 2: 270.

2. Walters, *The Antislavery Appeal*, 55.

3. Ibid., 130. The depiction of Garrison and his allies as moral absolutists, committed to obtaining freedom from any kind of restraint and to adding "extraneous" issues to the discussion of abolition, has a long tradition in American studies. See, for example, Lawrence J. Friedman, *Gregarious Saints: Self and Community in American Abolitionism, 1830–70* (New York: Cambridge University Press, 1982), 63–65; Richard H. Sewell, *Ballots for Freedom: Anti-Slavery Politics in the United States, 1837–1860* (New York: Oxford University Press, 1976), 25–36; Dwight Lowell Dumond, *Antislavery: The Crusade for Freedom in America* (Ann Arbor: University of Michigan Press, 1961), 174; Walter M. Merrill, *Against Wind and Tide: A Biography of William Lloyd Garrison* (Cambridge: Harvard University Press, 1963); Perry, *Boats against the Current*, 234–59; and Barnes, *The Anti-Slavery Impulse, 1830–44*. The most damning criticism of Garrison and his allies might be found in Barnes's charge that the Massachusetts Anti-Slavery Society was "primarily an association of independent abolitionists for mutual self-expression" (88).

4. For a survey of the influence of individualism in the New England abolition movement, see the works listed under chapter 1, note 1.

5. The limits of Garrison's radicalism and the rise of the abolitionist political party system is chronicled in Sewell, *Ballots for Freedom*; Eric Foner, *Free Soil, Free Labor, Free Men: The Ideology the Republican Party before the Civil War* (New York: Oxford University Press, 1970).

6. Gilbert Barnes, *The Anti-Slavery Impulse*, 55, 58, and 51

7. My point here is drawn from Warner's conceptualization of print and of the textual attribution of the people, turned in this case to the representation of Garrison. See Warner, *Letters of the Republic.*

8. Garrison, "Commencement of the Liberator," in *Selections*, 63.

9. "Vindication of the Liberator," in *Selections*, 184.

10. My use of manliness is derived from Warner's argument regarding print culture, citizenship, and self-abstraction in the republican discourse of letters. See Warner, *Letters of the Republic*, 40–72.

11. *Proceedings* of 1837, 1: xxxiv.

12. For a discussion of this plurality in relation to the antebellum ideal of a voluntary society, see David Paul Nord, "Toqueville, Garrison, and the Perfection of Journalism," *Journalism History* 13 (1986): 56–63.

13. Garrison, "Free Discussion," *The Liberator*, November 30, 1838, 4.

14. Michel Foucault, "What Is an Author?" in *Language, Counter-Memory, Practice: Selected Essays and Interviews by Michel Foucault*, ed. Donald F. Bouchard (Ithaca: Cornell University Press, 1977), 123.

15. A selective survey of sources that address the formation of the American author on the model of individual sovereignty or ownership would include Wai-Chee Dimock, *Empire for Liberty: Melville and the Poetics of Individualism* (Princeton: Princeton University Press, 1989); William Charvat, *The Profession of Authorship in America: The Papers of William Charvat*, ed. Matthew J. Bruccoli (Columbus: Ohio State University Press, 1968), 5–48; Nina Baym, *Novels, Readers, and Reviewers: Responses to Fiction in Antebellum America* (Ithaca: Cornell University Press, 1984), 13–29; and Cathy Davidson, *Revolution and the Word: The Rise of the Novel in America* (New York: Oxford University Press, 1989), 83–91. The tradition has some of its most current practitioners in comparativist studies, represented by Mark Rose, *Authors and Owners: The Invention of Copyright* (Cambridge: Harvard University Press, 1993); and Martha Woodmansee, *The Author, Art, and the Market: Rereading the History of Aesthetics* (New York: Columbia University Press, 1994). A contrasting perspective emphasizing the mediation of the state and its insulation of authorship from the marketplace is found

in Carla Hesse, "Enlightenment Epistemology and the Laws of Authorship in Revolutionary France, 1777–1793," in *Law and the Order of Culture*, ed. Robert Post (Berkeley: University of California Press, 1991), 109–38.

16. Meredith McGill, "The Matter of the Text: Commerce, Print Culture, and the Authority of the State in American Copyright Law," *American Literary History* 9 (1997): 21–59; Nicole Tonkovitch, "Rhetorical Power in the Victorian Parlor: *Godey's Lady's Book* and the Gendering of Nineteenth Century Rhetoric," in *Oratorical Culture in Nineteenth-Century America: Transformations in the Theory and Practice of Rhetoric*, ed. Gregory Clark and S. Michael Halloran (Carbondale: Southern Illinois University Press, 1993), 158–83. A third example of this trend toward the disputed nature of the authorial voice and the horizon of public culture in antebellum America is Nancy Ruttenberg, *Democratic Personality: Popular Voice and the Trial of American Authorship* (Stanford: Stanford University Press, 1998).

17. See Jean-François Lyotard, "Judicious in Dispute, or Kant after Marx," in *The Aims of Representation: Subject/Text/History*, ed. Murray Krieger (Stanford: Stanford University Press, 1987), 46–57.

18. "Antislavery Declaration of Independence," *The Liberator*, June 7, 1844, 1.

19. Claude Lefort, "Human Rights and the Welfare State," in *Democracy and Political Theory*, 39, 41.

20. The early history of Garrison's presumption of editorial freedom is recounted in James Brewer Stewart, *William Lloyd Garrison and the Challenge of Emancipation* (Arlington Heights, Ill.: Harlan Davidson, 1992), 26–28; and Robert Abzug, *Cosmos Crumbling: American Reform and the Religious Imagination* (New York: Oxford University Press, 1994), 135–47.

21. Derrida derives the problem of autobiography in the context of philosophy from the indeterminate status of the signatory in Nietzsche's *Ecce Homo*. See Jacques Derrida, "Otobiographs: The Teaching of Nietzsche and the Politics of the Proper Name," in *The Ear of the Other: Otobiography, Transference, Translation*, ed. Christie V. McDonald (New York: Schocken Books, 1985), 3–38.

22. Quoted in Truman Nelson, introduction to Garrison, *Selections*, xiii.

23. William Goodell, *Anti-Slavery Lectures* (Utica, 1839) 4. A range of complimentary and unflattering portraits of the abolitionists as liberal elitist reformers can be found in Perry, *Boats against the Current*, 234; and Linda Kerber,

Federalists in Dissent: Imagery and Ideology in Jeffersonian America (Ithaca: Cornell University Press, 1970).

24. I construct this alternative, artisan-republican genealogy for Garrison's political biography and abolition in general from Stewart, *William Lloyd Garrison and the Challenge of Emancipation*, 13–43; and Abzug, *Cosmos Crumbling*, 136–52. Lundy's significance to Protestant reform is argued in Clifford S. Griffin, *Their Brothers' Keeper: Moral Stewardship in the United States, 1800–1865* (New Brunswick: Rutgers University Press, 1960), 20–25. For the anticlerical orientation and republican aspirations of printers and tradesmen, see Pessen, "The Working Men's Party Revisited"; Formisano, *The Transformation of Political Culture*, 198–231; and Wilenz, *Chants Democratic*, 153–57.

25. Garrison's self-representation is from Garrison to James T. Woodbury, 28 August 1837, *A House Divided against Itself*, 296.

26. For a revealing excavation of the professional narrative of the aspiring artisan, see Kornblith, "Becoming Joseph Buckingham," 123–34.

27. The fate of *The Liberator* depended so much on Garrison's name that he was able to wrest the newspaper away from its first publisher, his partner Isaac Knapp. Garrison described the circumstances behind the split and the doubling of the paper in a letter to his confidant, Elizabeth Pease. See William Lloyd Garrison to Elizabeth Pease, May 15, 1842, *No Union with Slaveholders*, vol. 3 of *The Letters of William Lloyd Garrison*, ed. Walter Merrill and Louis Ruchames (Cambridge: Belknap Press of Harvard University Press, 1971), 79. Knapp in turn mounted a challenge to Garrison in the form of a new newspaper, *Knapp's Liberator*. For a brief description of Knapp's ill-fated venture, see Garrison and Garrison, *William Lloyd Garrison*, 3: 38–40.

28. *Proceedings* of 1837, xxxvi.

29. Ibid.

30. Garrison, "Editors and Newspapers," *The Liberator*, November 30, 1833, 3.

31. Garrison to David Lee Child, June 12, 1842, in *No Union with Slaveholders*, 161.

32. The classic account of the antebellum partisan press remains Michael Schudson, *Discovering the News: A Social History of American Newspapers* (New York: Basic Books, 1978), 11–28; see also Frank Luther Mott, *American Journalism: A History* (New York: Macmillan, 1962), 114–252. For an unusually detailed account of the mutually beneficial relationship between government printing

contracts, political parties, and newspapers, see Culver Smith, *The Press, Politics, and Patronage: The American Government's Use of Newspapers, 1789–1875* (Athens: University of Georgia Press, 1977) 39–144. The figure of 5 percent of newspapers claiming neutrality is found in Mott, *American Journalism*, 215 n. 2.

33. *Proceedings* of 1837, xxxiv.

34. Garrison quoted in *The True History of the Late Division of the Anti-Slavery Society, Being Part of the Second Annual Report of the Massachusetts Abolition Society* (Boston, 1841), 8.

35. Garrison quoted in Garrison and Garrison, *William Lloyd Garrison*, 2: 108.

36. "An Appeal of Clerical Abolitionists" reprinted in *The Liberator*, August 18, 1837, 1.

37. Lucretia Mott, *Right and Wrong in Massachusetts* (Boston, 1839), 37 and 50.

38. Woodbury quoted in Garrison and Garrison, *William Lloyd Garrison*, 2: 143.

39. The arguments of the second and third clerical letter are synthesized in Garrison and Garrison, *William Lloyd Garrison*, 2: 156–58.

40. The response of American Anti-Slavery Society to Garrison's dispute with the clergy and the Protestant sympathies within the national abolition movement are recorded in John McKivigan, *The War against Pro-Slavery Religion: Abolition and the Northern Churches, 1830–65* (Ithaca: Cornell University Press, 1984), 58–62.

41. "A Layman's Reply to a 'Clerical Appeal,'" *The Liberator*, August 18, 1837, 2.

42. Garrison to George W. Benson, 26 August 1837, *A House Divided against Itself*, 291.

43. "Prospectus of the Liberator," *The Liberator*, December 15, 1837, 2.

44. Garrison, "Vindication of The Liberator," 186 and 185.

45. These developments are analyzed subtly in Richard D. Brown, *Knowledge Is Power: The Diffusion of Information in Early America, 1770–1865* (New York: Oxford University Press, 1989), 230.

46. Garrison to Edmund Quincy, December 14, 1844, *No Union with Slaveholders*, 271.

47. The intended affinity here is between Garrison and Franklin, as his self-invention is explored in Warner, *Letters of the Republic*, 73–96. For some

biographical connections between these graduates of the printing trade, see Stewart, *William Lloyd Garrison*, 15–18.

48. Garrison to the Financial Committee of *The Liberator*, September 28, 1849, *No Union with Slaveholders*, 667.

49. The accounts of republican political economy are legion, but my characterization relies on J. E. Crowley, *This Sheba, Self: The Conceptualization of Economic Life in Eighteenth-Century America* (Baltimore: The Johns Hopkins University Press, 1974); Drew McCoy, *The Elusive Republic: Political Economy in Jeffersonian America* (Chapel Hill: University of North Carolina Press, 1980); Albert O. Hirschman, *The Passions and the Interests: Political Arguments for Capitalism before Its Triumph* (Princeton: Princeton University Press, 1977); and Ralph Lerner, *The Thinking Revolutionary: Principle and Practice in the New Republic* (Ithaca: Cornell University Press, 1987), 195–221.

50. Garrison to Elizabeth Pease, October 25, 1846, *No Union with Slaveholders*, 444.

51. Greeley's rise as the editor of the New York *Tribune* and as a spokesman for liberal ideology of capitalism is described in Eric Foner, *Free Soil, Free Labor, Free Men*, 14–39.

52. Garrison, "The Cradle of Liberty," *The Liberator*, April 5, 1839, 3.

53. In 1837, one year after Greeley's penny press's first year, *The Liberator* reported the number of its subscribers at 3,000, its highest amount; it declined thereafter. See Garrison and Garrison, *William Lloyd Garrison*, 2: 123 n.

54. Garrison to Oliver Johnson," May 12, 1840, *A House Divided*, 607.

55. Weston's letter of November 11, 1838, to Garrison quoted in Garrison and Garrison, *William Lloyd Garrison*, 2: 240. The paper, whose motto was "Resist not Evil—Jesus Christ," published its first issue in January 1839 and its last in June 1842. See Garrison and Garrison, *William Lloyd Garrison*, 2: 326; and Margaret Hope Bacon, "Antislavery Women and Non-Resistance," in *Abolitionist Sisterhood*, ed. Yellin and Van Horne, 275–97.

56. "Watchman, What of the Night?" *The Liberator*, January 11, 1839, 3.

57. Resolutions of country meeting are reprinted in Garrison and Garrison, *William Lloyd Garrison*, 2: 267–68.

58. The enthusiasm of abolitionists for electoral politics and the success of their bloc voting strategy is argued in Sewell, *Ballots for Freedom*, 12–20.

59. Mott, *Right and Wrong in Massachusetts*, 102.

60. The first issue of the *Massachusetts Abolitionist* appeared on February

2, 1839. For an account of the founding of this newspaper and its parent society, see Garrison and Garrison, *William Lloyd Garrison*, 2: 276–80 and 280 n. 2. One strategy to avert the takeover of *The Liberator* that Garrison considered but never enacted was to start his own version of an abolitionist society organ. *The Abolitionist* was to be edited by himself, Edmund Quincy, and Wendell Phillips. See Garrison to Samuel May, January 4, 1839, *A House Divided*, 415.

61. Stanton quoted in Mott, *Right and Wrong in Massachusetts*, 100.

62. Mott, *Right and Wrong in Massachusetts*, 64–65.

63. *The True History of the Late Division of the Anti-Slavery Societies*, 6 and 4.

64. Phelps quoted in Garrison and Garrison, *William Lloyd Garrison*, 2: 270.

65. John LeBosquet reminded Garrison's followers that "IDOLATRY is the worship of another being besides 'JEHOVAH . . .'" while William Goodell accused Garrison of Napoleonic ambitions. Quoted in Garrison and Garrison, *William Lloyd Garrison*, 2: 271 and 277. Joseph Tracy ("of Boston *Recorder* variety") and Goodell were also deemed responsible for quoting Vide's *Natural History of Spiritual Despotism* on "How to Make a Pope." Their comments were reprinted in "Abolition and Non-Resistance," *The Liberator*, May 15, 1840, 1.

66. Garrison, "Address to the Anti-Slavery Electors of Massachusetts," *The Liberator*, October 25, 1839, 2.

67. Resolution quoted in Garrison and Garrison, *William Lloyd Garrison*, 2: 273.

68. Aileen Kraditor has persuasively presented Garrison's resistance to voting as a gesture of pluralism, designed to secure the diversity of abolitionist opinion. See *Means and Ends in American Abolitionism*, 103–22.

69. Resolution reprinted in Garrison and Garrison, *William Lloyd Garrison*, 2: 275.

70. Garrison and Francis Jackson, "The Anti-Slavery Organization," *The Liberator*, April 5, 1839, 3.

71. Pamphlet from the "Friends of The Liberator" quoted in Garrison and Garrison, *William Lloyd Garrison*, 2: 278. The authors of this pamphlet were George Thompson, Amasa Walker, Maria Chapman, and Nathaniel Rogers.

72. "Reply to James G. Birney," *The Liberator*, June 28, 1839, 2.

73. Garrison to James T. Woodbury, August 28, 1837, *A House Divided*, 296–97. This letter was simultaneously published in *The Liberator*, September 1, 1837, 2.

74. The resolution was moved by Wendell Phillips, although Garrison was quick to follow it up with a well-prepared and enumerated discussion of its merits. See "Business Meetings of the American Anti-Slavery Society for 1844," *The Liberator*, May 24, 1844, 2.

75. The Massachusetts society's resolution is recorded in "No Union with Slaveholders," *The Liberator*, June 14, 1844, 2.

76. *Annual Report* of 1845, 29–30.

77. "Daniel O'Connell versus American Slavery" *The Liberator*, March 25, 1842. Almost the entire issue is devoted to the Irish nationalist's tour. The Boston-based Irish Repeal Association, however, did not appreciate Garrison's affiliation with the cause of Irish repeal and refused to support the petition, "An Address of the Irish People to Their Countrymen and Countrywomen in America," signed by the mayor of Dublin, that the abolitionist editor Charles Lenox Remond had brought triumphantly home from his own lecture tour of Ireland. See Garrison and Garrison, *William Lloyd Garrison*, 3: 43–44. Garrison's incredulity at the Irish-American association's antagonism to the abolitionist argument for repeal is found in a letter to Abel Brown, March 18, 1842, *No Union with Slaveholders*, 56.

78. Adams's reading of his resolution is reported in *The Liberator*, April 1, 1842, 3, and received the full endorsement of the Massachusetts Anti-Slavery Society in the *Annual Report* of 1843, 4.

79. The *New York Herald* remark was reprinted in "Daring Abolition Movement," *The Liberator*, May 20, 1842, 2. Garrison chronicled the response of the press to the issue of repeal in the *Annual Report* of 1843, 53.

80. Garrison's announcement of the agenda of the American Anti-Slavery Society meeting appears in "The Annual Meeting in New York," *The Liberator*, April 22, 1842, 3. The *Antislavery Standard* editorial is reprinted in "From the Anti-Slavery Standard," *The Liberator*, May 13, 1842, 1.

81. Garrison, "The Annual Meeting in New York."

82. "Extraordinary Disclaimer," *The Liberator*, May 6, 1842, 3.

83. "To the Executive Committee of the American A. S. Society," *The Liberator*, May 27, 1842, 2.

84. "The Twelfth Annual Meeting of the Massachusetts Anti-Slavery Society," *The Liberator*, February 2, 1844, 3.

85. Protests signed by David Lee Child, Ellis Gray Loring, and William White are found in "Business Meeting of the American Anti-Slavery Society."

86. Garrison, "The Protests," *The Liberator*, May 24, 1844, 2.

87. Garrison, "The American Union," *Selections*, 117.

88. Claude Lefort, "The Image of the Body and Totalitarianism," in *The Political Forms of Modern Society: Bureaucracy, Democracy, Totalitarianism*, ed. John B. Thompson (Cambridge: MIT Press, 1986), 304.

3. Frederick Douglass's Public Body

1. James Russell Lowell quoted in Robert T. Oliver, *The History of Public Speaking in America* (Boston: Allyn and Bacon, 1965), 248.

2. Thomas Wentworth Higginson, *American Orators and Oratory* (Cleveland, 1901), 76.

3. Blassingame reports this tendency of contemporary reportage in his introduction to Douglass's edited speeches. See *The Frederick Douglass Papers: Series one, Speeches, Debates, and Interviews*, vol. 1, *1841–1846*, ed. John W. Blassingame (New Haven, Conn.: Yale University Press, 1979), lxvii.

4. Robyn Weigman, *American Anatomies: Theorizing Race and Gender* (Durham: Duke University Press, 1995), 6. Weigman also describes the visuality of the public sphere in its racist deformation, 22–39. For Sánchez-Eppler, the asymmetry of abstract citizenship foregrounds the problem of representation inherent to both political constitutions and political subjectivity. See *Touching Liberty*, 5–10. A cogent critique of the Enlightenment tropes of universality as founded on racial discrimination remains Henry Louis Gates Jr., "Writing Race and the Difference It Makes," *Race, Writing, and Difference*, ed. Gates (Chicago: University of Chicago Press, 1986), 1–20; also see Anthony Appiah and Amy Gutman, *Color Conscious: The Political Morality of Race* (Princeton: Princeton University Press, 1996). The same hierarchical distinction has been shown to originate in the representation of the degrading effects of slavery. See Dana D. Nelson, *The Word in Black and White: Reading "Race" in American Literature, 1863–67* (New York: Oxford University Press, 1992), 6–11.

5. Herman Beavers, "The Blind Leading the Blind: The Racial Gaze in *Benito Cereno* and *The Heroic Slave*," *Criticism and the Color Line: Desegregating American Studies* (New Brunswick: Rutgers University Press, 1996), 206. The material culture of this visual spectacle and its capacity for exploitation is described in Benjamin Reiss, "P. T. Barnum, Joice Heth, and Antebellum Spectacles of Race," *American Quarterly* 51 (1999): 78–107. The Foucauldian model of institutionalized power relations as inherent to the concept of visuality and the

possibility of corporeal knowledge is explored in Jonathan Crary, *Techniques of the Observer: On Vision and Modernity in the Nineteenth Century* (Cambridge: MIT Press, 1990).

6. William Lloyd Garrison, introduction to *Narrative of the Life of Frederick Douglass, Fugitive Slave*, by Frederick Douglass, in *Classic Slave Narratives*, ed. Henry Louis Gates Jr. (New York: New American Library, 1987), 246.

7. My allusion here is to a capacity for debate and dissension within the representation of the body, which is discussed in Burgett, *Sentimental Bodies*, 11–20.

8. My re-creation of the public culture of antebellum African Americans draws here and elsewhere on James Oliver Horton, *Free People of Color: Inside the African-American Community* (Washington, D.C.: Smithsonian Institution Press, 1993); James Oliver Horton and Lois E. Horton, *In Hope of Liberty: Culture, Community, and Protest among Northern Free Blacks, 1700–1860* (New York: Oxford University Press, 1997); Horton and Horton, *Black Bostonians: Family Life and Community Struggle in the Antebellum North* (New York: Holmes and Meier, 1979); Gary B. Nash, *Forging Freedom: The Formation of Philadelphia's Black Community, 1720–1840* (Cambridge: Harvard University Press, 1988); and Leonard Curry, *Free Blacks in Urban America, 1800–1850: The Shadow of the Dream* (Chicago: University of Chicago Press, 1981). I am contrasting this masculine dimension of African American culture with the female orientation of other black antislavery societies. See Julie Winch, "'You Have Talents—Only Cultivate Them': Philadelphia Black Female Literary Societies and the Abolitionist Crusade," in *The Abolitionist Sisterhood*, ed. Yellin and Van Horne, 107–18; and Dorothy Sterling and Mary Helen Washington, eds., *We Are Your Sisters: Black Women of the Nineteenth Century* (New York: Norton, 1997).

9. *Rights of All* quoted in Hinks, *To Awaken My Afflicted Brethren*, 92. Walker quoted in Hinks, *To Awaken*, 105. James McCune Smith, "Report of the Committee on a National Press," in *Proceedings of the National Convention of Colored People and Their Friends, Minutes of the Proceedings of the National Negro Conventions, The American Negro: His History and Literature* (New York: Arno and New York Times, 1969), 19.

10. McCune, introduction to *My Bondage and My Freedom*, by Frederick Douglass, ed. William L. Andrews (Urbana: University of Illinois Press, 1987), 17.

11. James Smith McCune, "Report of the Committee on a National Press," 20.

12. See Robert S. Levine, *Martin Delany, Frederick Douglass, and the Politics of Representative Identity* (Chapel Hill: University of North Carolina Press, 1997), 2–7. Levine's emphasis on the dialectical relation between the two publishing partners is intended to displace the issue of representativeness from Emersonian presumptions of individual heroism to the constellation of issues involving racial origins, emigration, and American nationalism.

13. Douglass, *The Heroic Slave, The Oxford Frederick Douglass Reader*, ed. William L. Andrews (New York: Oxford University Press, 1996), 134. All further citations are from this edition.

14. The foregoing presentation of the colored convention movement, its relation to the symbolism of the black press, and Douglass's investment in the rhetoric of racial elevation owes much to Levine, *Martin Delany, Frederick Douglass*, 22–32. Douglass's own effort to organize the 1848 colored convention is recalled on pages 86–88.

15. See the intertwined history of the Massachusetts Anti-Slavery Society and freemen associations like the General Massachusetts Colored Association as well as the larger history of interracial tension in Boston's abolition community in Horton and Horton, *Black Bostonians*, 81–94; and Horton and Horton, *In Hope of Liberty*, 224–27. The common political heritage of David Walker and Garrison is argued in Donald M. Jacobs, "David Walker and William Garrison: Racial Cooperation and the Shaping of Boston Abolition," in *Courage and Conscience: Black and White Abolitionists in Boston*, ed. Jacobs (Bloomington: Indiana University Press, 1993), 1–20.

16. Houston Baker, "Critical Memory and the Public Sphere," *Public Culture* 7 (1994): 12–15.

17. Fraser's model of a multilateral, potentially incongruous alliance of disenfranchised interests is re-created in Michael C. Dawson, "A Black Counterpublic? Economic Earthquakes, Racial Agenda(s), and Black Politics," *Public Culture* 7 (1994): 195–224. My insight regarding racial identification and antagonism as a public activity is owed to Michael Awkward, *Negotiating Difference: Race, Gender, and the Politics of Positionality* (Chicago: University of Chicago Press, 1995), 3–20. A critique of the public sphere that recognizes the deconstructive implications of a "war of position" for race-based politics is found in Steven Gregory, "Race, Identity, and Political Activism: The Shifting Contours of the African-American Public Sphere," *Public Culture* 7 (1994): 147–64.

18. Miriam Hansen, foreword to *Public Sphere and Experience*, by Negt and Kluge, xxxvi.

19. I am referring here to a tradition of African Americanist criticism that focused on the influence of Garrison and white abolitionist principles in Douglass's literary and oratorical career. "Where, for example . . . does a protypical black American self reside?," asked Baker, and several critics of the slave narrative genre had the same question. See Houston Baker, *The Journey Back: Issues in Black Literature and Culture* (Chicago: University of Chicago Press, 1980), 43; Peter Walker, *Moral Choices: Memory, Desire, and Imagination in Nineteenth-Century American Abolition* (Baton Rouge: Louisiana State University Press, 1978), 244–45; James Olney, "'I Was Born': Slave Narratives, Their Status as Autobiography and as Literature," *The Slave's Narrative*, ed. Charles T. Davis and Henry Louis Gates Jr. (New York: Oxford University Press, 1985), 150–67; Stephen Butterfield, *Black Autobiography in America* (Amherst: University of Massachusetts Press, 1974), 30–33.

20. Whipper quoted in "Address by William Whipper," *The Black Abolitionist Papers: United States, 1830–1846*, vol. 2 of *The Black Abolitionist Papers*, ed. C. Peter Ripley (Chapel Hill: University of North Carolina Press, 1991), 300. The masculine representations of freemasonry and their availability for the freemen antislavery struggle are explored insightfully in Maurice Wallace, "'Are We Men?': Prince Hall, Martin Delany, and the Masculine Ideal in Black Freemasonry, 1775–1865," *American Literary History* 9 (1997): 396–424.

21. Douglass, *My Bondage and My Freedom*, 237.

22. Douglass's letter to *The Liberator* reprinted in Douglass, *My Bondage and My Freedom*, 226–27.

23. The conflicting role of republican citizenship in the constitution of Douglass's identity is explored in Priscilla Wald, *Constituting Americans: Cultural Anxiety and Narrative Form* (Durham: Duke University Press, 1995), 43–73. The dialogic voice of Douglass's speeches and slave narratives has been the focus of similar critiques in Shelly Fisher-Fishkin and Carla L. Peterson, "'We Hold These Truths to be Self-Evident': The Rhetoric of Frederick Douglass's Journalism," in *Frederick Douglass: New Literary and Historical Essays*, ed. Eric Sunquist (New York: Cambridge University Press, 1990), 189–204; Thad Zolkowski, "Antithesis and the Dialectic of Violence and Literacy in Frederick Douglass's *Narrative* of 1845," in *Critical Essays on Frederick Douglass*, ed. William L. Andrews (Boston: G. K. Hall, 1991), 148–65; and Ann Kibbey and Michele

Stepto, "The Anti-Language of Slavery: Frederick Douglass's 1845 *Narrative*," *Critical Essays on Frederick Douglass*, 166–91.

24. Donald Pease, "National Identities, Post-Modern Artifacts, and Post-National Narratives," in *National Identities and Post-American Narratives*, ed. Pease (Durham: Duke University Press, 1994), 5.

25. Douglass, "Our Paper and Our Prospects," *The North Star*, December 3, 1847, 2.

26. With this observation, I am attempting to mediate a false opposition between oral and written culture that has taken up residence in the scholarship of republican America. Among the strongest statements of a spoken origin of political foundations appears in Christopher Looby, *Voicing America: Language, Literary Form, and the Origins of the United States* (Chicago: University of Chicago Press, 1996), 13–45. See also Sandra M. Gustafson, *Eloquence Is Power: Oratory and Performance in Early America* (Chapel Hill: University of North Carolina Press, 2000).

27. "Frederick Douglass in Boston," *Frederick Douglass's Paper*, August 12, 1853, 2.

28. Douglass, "Colored Newspapers," *The North Star*, December 12, 1847, 2.

29. Garrison, introduction to *Narrative of the Life of Frederick Douglass*, 246, 245.

30. For the importance of racial comparison to the Enlightenment presumption of universal humanity, see Nicholas Hudson, "From 'Nation' to 'Race': The Origin of Racial Classification in Eighteenth-Century Thought," *Eighteenth-Century Studies* 29 (1996): 247–64; Gates, "Writing 'Race' and the Difference it Makes"; and Appiah and Gutman, *Color Conscious*, 47–71.

31. Douglass, "Report of the Committee on Abolition," *Minutes of the Proceedings of the National Negro Conventions*, 32.

32. Douglass, "What Are the Colored People Doing for Themselves?," *The North Star*, July 14, 1848, 2.

33. The contention between Delany and Douglass over the masculine symbolization of the Mason is explored in Levine, *Martin Delany, Frederick Douglass*, 7–11. Delany's own attempt to rescue black male hetereosexuality for an emergent liberal capitalist order is argued in Robert Reid-Pharr, "Violent Ambiguity: Martin Delaney, Bourgeois Sadomasochism, and the Production of a Black National Masculinity," in *Representing Black Men*, ed. Marcellus Blount and George P. Cunningham (New York: Routledge, 1996), 73–94.

34. Stewart quoted in Horton and Horton, "The Affirmation of Man-hood: Black Garrisonism in Antebellum Boston," in *Courage and Conscience*, 134. Stewart's career and her gendered jeremiad discourse is recounted in Carla L. Peterson, *"Doers of the Word": African-American Women Speakers and Writers in the North (1830–1880)* (New Brunswick: Rutgers University Press, 1995), 56–73. Garnet's famous Rochester speech challenging the manhood of his race is recounted in "Henry Highland Garnet at the National Convention of Colored Citizens," in *The Black Abolitionist Papers*, 410.

35. Douglass, "The Slaves' Right to Revolt," in *Speeches, Debates, and Inter-views, 1847–1854*, vol. 2 of Frederick Douglass Papers, Ser. 1 (New Haven: Yale University Press, 1979), 130–31.

36. David Walker, *David Walker's Appeal, in Four Articles*, revised and introduced by Sean Wilentz (New York: Hill and Wang, 1994), 16.

37. A beautifully conducted discussion of this context appears in Hinks, *To Awaken My Afflicted Brethren*, 109–56.

38. Walker, *David Walker's Appeal*, 30.

39. Ibid., 28, 29.

40. Cornish quoted in *The Black Press, 1827–1890: The Quest for National Identity*, ed. Martin E. Dann (New York: Putnam, 1971), 34–36.

41. *The Black Press*, 45.

42. Douglass, "The Folly of Racially Exclusive Organizations," in *Speeches, Debates, and Interviews, 1847–54*, 111.

43. Douglass, "A Few Words to Our Own People," *The North Star*, January 19, 1849.

44. I am taking the contention here from Goodman that anticoloniza-tion constituted a principle aim of black antislavery politics in the antebellum era and reinterpreting it in light of the social structure of the antebellum news-paper marketplace. See Paul Goodman, *Of One Blood: Abolitionism and the Origins of Racial Equality* (Berkeley: University of California Press, 1998).

45. Douglass, "The Claims of the Negro Ethnologically Considered," in *Speeches, Debates, and Interviews, 1847–54*, 501–03.

46. Berlant, *The Anatomy of National Fantasy*, 34.

47. Douglass, "These Questions Cannot Be Answered by the White Race," in *Speeches, Debates, and Interviews, 1855–63*, vol. 3 of The Frederick Douglass Papers, Ser. 1 (New Haven: Yale University Press, 1979), 86.

48. Douglass, "About Ourselves," *The North Star*, December 7, 1849, 2.

49. Martin Delany, "Highly Important Statistics—Our Causes and Destiny—Endowment of a Newspaper," *The North Star,* April 13, 1849, 2.

50. Douglass, *Narrative of the Life of Frederick Douglass, Classic Slave Narratives,* ed. Henry Louis Gates (New York: New American Library, 1987), 325.

51. Douglass, *My Bondage and My Freedom,* 216.

52. Ibid., 248.

53. Garrison, *The Liberator,* January 1, 1831, 3.

54. Garrison, *An Address before the Free People of Color* (Boston, 1831), 9.

55. "Rights of All, September 18, 1829," *The Black Press,* 300.

56. James Forten, "James Forten to William Lloyd Garrison," in *The Black Abolitionist Papers,* 85–86. Forten's contributions to the public culture of Philadelphia are recounted in Nash, *Forging Freedom,* 51–100.

57. William Watkins, "William Watkins to William Lloyd Garrison," in *The Black Abolitionist Papers,* 92.

58. Garrison's debt to Boston's freemen political culture is explored in Horton, *Free People of Color,* 83–88; Horton and Horton, *Black Bostonians,* 32–95; and Jacobs, "David Walker and William Lloyd Garrison."

59. Charles Gardner, "Speech Delivered at the Broadway Tabernacle," *The Black Abolitionist Papers,* 210.

60. This split between Garrison and his black constituency is discussed in Horton and Horton, "The Affirmation of Manhood"; Horton and Horton, *Free People of Color,* 88–92.

61. "Resolution by a Committee of Boston Blacks," *The Black Abolitionist Papers,* 300.

62. One particularly nasty episode concerns Garrison's withdrawal of support from the effort of one Benjamin F. Robert to start a colored newspaper. See "Benjamin F. Roberts to Amos Augustus Phelps," *The Black Abolitionist Papers,* 270.

63. Douglass, "The Liberator," *Frederick Douglass's Paper,* January 14, 1853, 2.

64. "Frederick Douglass vs. Robert Purvis, Wendell Phillips, and C. L. Remond," *Frederick Douglass's Paper,* December 9, 1853, 1.

65. Douglass, "A Review of Anti-slavery Relations," *Frederick Douglass's Paper,* December 9, 1853, 1.

66. The founding of the Massachusetts General Colored Association and Garrison's patronage of Nell are recounted in Horton and Horton, *Black Bostonians,* 57–63; and Hinks, *To Awaken My Afflicted Brethren,* 75–88.

67. Douglass, "Letters from the Editor," *Frederick Douglass's Paper,* August 4, 1853, 1.

68. Garrison's attempt to rein in his black supporters forced him to renounce his earlier position on nonresistance and embrace the militaristic, more "manly" positions provided by Unionism. See Horton and Horton, "The Affirmation of Manhood," 142–50.

69. Douglass, "A Liberal Offer to Subscribers," *Frederick Douglass's Paper,* January 13, 1854, 2.

70. Michael Hutt, "'Making a Man of Him': Masculinity and the Black Body in Mid-Nineteenth-Century American Sculpture," *Oxford Art Journal* 15, no. 1 (1992): 247–64.

71. Ronald Takaki, *Iron Cages: Race and Culture in Nineteenth-Century America* (New York: Knopf, 1979), 3–34.

72. Douglass, "The Lecturer," *Frederick Douglass's Paper,* January 13, 1854, 2.

73. The transformation of oratory from a republican institution of civic pedagogy into a commercial enterprise for the specialized practitioner is described in Scott, "Print and the Public Lecture System," in *Printing and Society in Early America,* ed. William Leonard Joyce et al. (Worcester, Mass.: American Antiquarian Society, 1983), 278–99; Carl Bode, *The American Lyceum: Town Meeting of the Mind* (New York: Oxford University Press, 1956), 28–43; and Clark and Halloran, introduction to *Oratorical Culture in Nineteenth-Century America,* 1–26.

74. My argument here addresses the contention that Douglass regarded speech as inherently manly and powerful, capable of supplying the argument for racial fitness as a foundational category. My contention here is that the public function of the black press was never far from Douglass's regard for oratory or his attempt to present himself as a powerful force in his own right. Cf. James Perrin Warren, *The Culture of Eloquence: Oratory and Reform in Antebellum America* (University Park: Pennsylvania State University Press, 1999), 122–40.

75. Caleb Bingham, *The Columbian Orator* (Boston, 1804), 19. All further citations are from this edition.

76. Matthiessen's assertion that oratory grounded the literary project of America in the preservation of republican virtue has particular relevance here. See F. O. Matthiessen, *The American Renaissance: Art and Expression in the Age of Emerson* (New York: Oxford University Press, 1957), 11–22. More specific in their analysis of pedagogical institutions of republicanism, its legalistic standards,

and the service of "cult of the orator" are Peter Dobkin Hall, *The Organization of American Culture, 1700–1900: Private Institutions, Elites, and the Making of American Nationality* (New York: New York University Press, 1984), 81–94 and 151–77; and Robert Ferguson, *Law and Literature in American Culture* (Cambridge: Harvard University Press, 1984), 11–87.

77. Edward Parker, *The Golden Age of the American Orator* (Boston, 1857), 260, 257.

78. Rogers quoted in "From the Herald of Freedom," *The Liberator,* February 2, 1842, 3.

79. An apt comparison here might be drawn with the compelling argument regarding the displacement of the black male body and the reinstatement of a symbolic discourse based on the value of representation. Cunningham, for instance, regards the absence of black male agency as a condition for the imaginary, while I would stress his point that the importance of the black body is to force a "recursive moment" in the narration of modernity. See George P. Cunningham, "Body Politics: Race, Gender, and the Captive Body," in *Representing Black Men*, 131–54.

80. The link between oratory and textuality through the means of this conformity is explored in Nan Johnson, "The Popularization of Nineteenth-Century Rhetoric: Elocution and the Private Learner," in *Oratorical Culture in the Nineteenth Century*, 139–57.

81. Fisher-Fishkin and Peterson, "'We Hold These Truths to be Self-Evident,'" 189–204.

82. Whipper quoted in "Address by William Whipper," *The Black Abolitionist Papers*, 146.

83. "Declaration of Sentiments," *Minutes of the Proceedings of the National Negro Conventions*, 28.

84. For the significance of the Dred Scott Supreme Court decision to standards of both white male citizenship and African American marginalization, see Smith, *Civic Ideals*, 243–85; Peter D. Schuck and Rogers M. Smith, *Citizenship without Consent: Illegal Aliens in the American Polity* (New Haven: Yale University Press, 1985), 66–89; and Bernard Schwartz, *From Confederation to Nation: The American Constitution, 1835–1877* (Baltimore: The Johns Hopkins University Press, 1973), 107–30.

85. The larger context for the rhetoric of white male paternity in antislavery discourse and its connection to American historiography is explored in Castronovo, *Fathering the Nation*.

86. Douglass, "Slavery, the Slumbering Volcano," in *Speeches, Debates, and Interviews, 1847–54*, 155.

87. The development of an "American School" of ethnology focused on the establishment of racial difference is described in Smith, *Civic Ideals*, 203–06; William Stanton, *The Leopard's Spots: Scientific Attitudes toward Race in America* (Chicago: University of Chicago Press, 1960), 3–12; and George Fredrickson: *The Black Image in the White Mind: The Debate on Afro-American Character and Destiny, 1817–1914* (New York: Harper and Row, 1971), 74–76.

88. Douglass, "The Claims of the Negro, Ethnologically Considered," *Speeches, Debates, and Interviews, 1847–54*, 511–14.

89. According to Levine, Douglass gave this speech during a period, 1853–54, in which he and Martin Delany were conducting a public debate over the question of African American emigration to Africa. For both sides of this debate, see Levine, *Martin Delany, Frederick Douglass*, 90–98.

90. Douglass, "A Nation in the Midst of a Nation," *Speeches, Debates, and Interviews, 1847–54*, 425.

91. Berlant, *The Anatomy of National Fantasy*, 34.

92. Ibid., 5.

93. Garrison, introduction to *Narrative of the Life of Frederick Douglass*, 246.

4. Faneuil Hall

1. Henry Adams, *The Education of Henry Adams*, ed. Ernest Samuels (Boston: Houghton Mifflin, 1973), 3. I am indebted for the Adams reference and for some larger insights regarding the ideological significance of civic memory to James Brewer Stewart's elegant essay, "Boston, Abolition, and the Atlantic World, 1820–1861," in *Courage and Conscience: Black and White Abolitionists in Boston*, ed. Donald Jacobs (Bloomington: Indiana University Press, 1993), 101–25.

2. A revealing account of the Attucks festival, emphasizing its counternationalist politics and its contribution to a vernacular historical consciousness at odds with official memory, appears in Elizabeth Rauh-Bethel, *The Roots of African-American Identity: Memory and History in the Free Antebellum Community* (New York: St. Martin's Press, 1997), 3–16. I again draw my depiction of African American civic culture in Boston and particularly its historical orientation to the ideals of the American Revolution from Horton and Horton,

Black Bostonians, 4–50; and Horton and Horton, *In Hope of Liberty*, 69–76 and 172–200.

3. I am emphasizing this historical dimension for the self-representation of the popular will somewhat at the expense of the spatial, or social, dimension, partly in response to the symbolism of Faneuil Hall itself but partly in response to the arguments concerning African American memory and historical consciousness in relation to civic festivals and monumentality. In addition to Rauh-Bethel, *The Roots of African American Identity*, I have also learned much from Genevieve Fabre, "African-American Commemorative Celebrations in the Nineteenth Century," in *History and Memory in African-American Culture*, ed. Fabre and Robert O'Meally (New York: Oxford University Press, 1994), 72–91; Russ Castronovo, "Radical Configurations of History in the Era of American Slavery," in *Subject and Citizen: Nation, Race, and Gender from Oroonoko to Anita Hill*, ed. Michael Moon and Cathy Davidson (Durham: Duke University Press, 1995), 169–93. The potential for the emergence of a national, synchronic community in the context of the spatial or social configuration of popular demonstrations and celebration is explored in Waldstreicher, *In the Midst of Perpetual Fetes;* and Brooks McNamara, *Day of Jubilee: The Great Age of Public Celebrations in New York, 1788–1909* (New Brunswick: Rutgers University Press, 1997).

4. The convergence of official and critical historiographies of the American republic on Faneuil Hall is explicated brilliantly in Stewart, "Boston, Abolition, and the Atlantic World, 1820–1861."

5. See this connection between corporeality, locality, and historical narratives of citizenship worked out in Berlant, *Anatomy of National Fantasy*, 32–56 and 178–95.

6. William Lloyd Garrison, "To Harrison Gray Otis," *The Liberator*, September 5, 1835, 3.

7. Ibid.

8. Dolores Hayden, *The Power of Place: Urban Landscape as Public History* (Cambridge: MIT Press, 1995), 46.

9. M. Christine Boyer, *The City of Collective Memory: Its Historical Imaginary and Architectural Entertainments* (Cambridge: MIT Press, 1994), 7. A more synchronic connection between the urban landscape, economic development, and cultural formations of Boston is argued in Mona Domosh, *Invented Cities: The Creation of Landscape in Nineteenth-Century New York and Boston* (New Haven: Yale University Press, 1996), 8–34.

10. Anonymous pamphlet quoted in Abram English Brown, *Faneuil Hall and Faneuil Hall Marketplace, or Peter Faneuil and His Gift* (Boston, 1900), 163. My conception of the contradictory gestures of republicanism is drawn from the nuanced description of Boston civic culture at the end of the eighteenth century in Gordon Wood, *The Radicalism of the American Revolution* (New York: Knopf, 1992), 79–90.

11. See Lefebvre, *The Production of Space*, trans. Donald Nicholson-Smith (Oxford: Blackwell, 1991), 220–26.

12. The inquiry into the relation between language and space is conducted throughout Lefebvre's work but particularly in his conception of the production of space in "spatial practice." See *The Production Space*, 16–53.

13. Garrison, "Meeting of Citizens," *The Liberator*, August 9, 1835, 3.

14. Boyer describes the topographical landscape of a city as a civic language of instruction, particularly in those cities that strive to imitate the classical tradition of the polis. See *The City of Collective Memory*, 343–63.

15. Garrison quoted in Stewart, *William Lloyd Garrison and the Challenge of Emancipation*, 55.

16. Stewart, "Boston, Abolition, and the Atlantic World," 120.

17. Jean-François Lyotard, "Judiciousness in Dispute, or Kant after Marx," in *The Aims of Representation*, ed. Krieger, 56.

18. See Lefebrve, *The Production of Space*, 139–40, on the mediation of spatial tropes. An apt comparison here might be to White's conception of metaphor and metonymy in the context of an historical imagination. See Hayden White, *Metahistory*, 31–42.

19. According to White, Nietzsche's concept of critical history does not so much dispense with the recognition of the past as a normative reference but seeks to combine the ways of reading the past, the present, and the future in a generically ironic fashion. I would argue that Garrison's patrilinear discourse was critical to this extent. See White, *Metahistory*, 350–52.

20. The distinction between the imaginary and the symbolic is central to the argument of ideological resistance in Cornelius Castoriadis, "Radical Imagination the Social Instituting Imaginary," *in Rethinking Imagination*, ed. Robinson and Rundell, 87–117.

21. The short history and rationale for this penny press newspaper can be found in Garrison, "Cradle of Liberty," *The Liberator* April 5, 1839, 3; and Garrison and Garrison, *William Lloyd Garrison*, 2: 284.

22. Brown, *Faneuil Hall*, 117.

23. Arendt's concept of the polis as normative for democratic politics is found in *The Human Condition*, 24–38. For a critique that turns the ideological articulation of this civic space against liberal democratic politics, see Jean Luc-Nancy, *The Experience of Freedom*, trans. Bridget McDonald (Stanford: Stanford University Press, 1993), 74.

24. Habermas, *The Structural Transformation of the Public Sphere*, 4.

25. A highly selective bibliography of the literature of critical and cultural theory that has emerged from the critique of the public sphere would include Ajun Appadurai, "Disjuncture and Differerence in the Global Cultural Economy," in *The Phantom Public Sphere*, ed. Bruce Robbins (Minneapolis: University of Minnesota Press, 1993), 269–96; Fredric Jameson, "On Negt and Kluge," in *The Phantom Public Sphere*, 42–74; Jameson, "Cognitive Mapping," in *Marxism and the Interpretation of Culture*, ed. Cary Nelson and Lawrence Grossberg (Urbana: University of Illinois Press, 1987), 347–57; Negt and Kluge, *Public Sphere and Experience*, 1–93; Miriam Hansen, "Unstable Mixtures, Dilated Spheres: Negt and Kluge's *The Public Sphere and Experience*, Twenty Years Later," *Public Culture* 5 (1993): 179–214; and Sudipta Kaviraj, "Filth and the Public Sphere: Concepts and Practices about Space in Calcutta," *Public Culture* 10 (1997): 83–113.

26. Lefebvre, *The Production of Space*, 44.

27. The larger dimensions of this "spatial" critique for post-Marxism is laid out memorably in Ernesto Laclau and Chantal Mouffe, *Hegemony and Socialist Strategy: Towards a Radical Democratic Politics* (London: Verso, 1985). For the particular relevance of this position to the articulation of democratic space, see Ernesto LeClau, "Metaphor and Social Antagonisms," in *Marxism and the Interpretation of Culture*, ed. Nelson and Grossberg, 254. The liberatory vision of "radical democratic hegemony" appears at the conclusion of Mouffe, "Democratic Citizenship and the Political Community," in *Community at Loose Ends*, ed. Miami Theory Collective, 70–82.

28. My argument concerning hegemony and public space can be regarded as supplying a layer of political and critical theory to the social history of urban conflict recorded in Ryan's analysis of public space. See Ryan, *Civic Wars*, 21–57.

29. This reformulation of Marxist class warfare and populist struggle, modulated to accommodate the mediation of "articulatory practices" in the construction of political subjects and spaces, is the central argument of Leclau and Mouffe, *Hegemony and Socialist Strategy*, 129–59.

30. Stewart's abolitionist scholarship is unique for lending the discussion of abolition not only an urban context but a determinate effect on the configuration of urban space and history. See Stewart, "Boston, Abolition, and the Atlantic World"; Stewart, *William Lloyd Garrison: The Challenge of Emancipation*, 43–87.

31. *Annual Report* of *Society* 1838, 40 and 34.

32. Quoted in *Annual Report* of 1838, 33.

33. Austin quoted in *Annual Report* of 1838, 47.

34. My account of Philips's speech relies on reportage relating that the cries of "Take him back" were so loud that his speech could not be heard. See Bode, *The American Lyceum*, 205. A contrary report is found in Stewart's account, which describes a more successful attempt by Philips to appropriate the tradition of the revolutionary forefathers. See Stewart, "Boston, Abolition, and the Atlantic World," 120.

35. Garrison, *An Address Delivered in Marlboro Chapel*, 10.

36. Lefebvre, *The Production of Space*, 115–16.

37. We might regard the scholarship of Nash and Wilentz, for instance, as wedded to the material disposition of urban life for its articulation of "the people" in the context of the American Revolution. A local account of this connection could include Countrymen, while Hartog's similar New York focus situates the instability of the denomination of the people in the discursive, legal conditions for public space. See Gary Nash, *The Urban Crucible: Social Change, Political Consciousness, and the Origins of the American Revolution* (Cambridge: Harvard University Press, 1979); Wilentz, *Chants Democratic*, 61–103; Edward Countryman, *A People in Revolution: The American Revolution and Political Society in New York, 1770–1790*; and Hendrik Hartog, *Public Property and Private Power: The Corporation of the City of New York in American Law, 1730–1870* (Ithaca: Cornell University Press, 1989), 82–100.

38. Hutchinson quoted in William W. Wheildon, *Semi-Centennial Celebration of the Opening of Faneuil Hall and Marketplace* (Boston, 1877).

39. Faneuil quoted in Brown, *Faneuil Hall*, 80.

40. Among the many formulations of the republican political economy that have informed my account are those found in Crowley, *This Sheba, Self*; Pocock, *The Machiavellian Moment*, 401–05; and Wood, *The Radicalism of the American Revolution*, 214–76.

41. An account of the debate over the acceptance of Faneuil's gift appears in Brown, *Faneuil Hall*, 80.

42. This characterization of "liberal" follows from Appleby, *Capitalism and a New Social Order.*

43. Smith's concept of the imaginary "impartial spectator" governing public conduct is given a Foucauldian inflection in John Durham Peters, "Publicity and Pain: Self-Abstraction in Adam Smith's *Theory of Moral Sentiments*," *Public Culture* 17 (1995): 657–75.

44. The distinction between the royally chartered city and the unincorporated town is described in Jon C. Teaford, *The Municipal Revolution in America: Origins of Modern Government, 1650–1825* (Chicago: University of Chicago Press, 1975).

45. My argument here is a variation of the familiar etiology of the public sphere found in Habermas, *The Structural Transformation of the Public Sphere*, 15–30.

46. Quoted in Josiah Quincy, *Municipal History of the Town and City of Boston* (Boston, 1852), 1.

47. For the disparate composition of this public body as well as the modulation of economic interests in urban politics, see Nash, *The Urban Crucible*, 28–32 and 78–82.

48. See Hugh Morrison, *Early American Architecture: From the First Colonial Settlements to the National Period* (New York: Oxford University Press, 1952), 430–33.

49. This lottery system is described in Brown, *Faneuil Hall*, 90.

50. See Warner, *Letters of the Republic*, 40–67. The following argument about the construction of Faneuil Hall draws from his account of the discursive construction of the republican citizenry.

51. For the mediation of the print marketplace in the self-description of this political struggle see Warner, *Letters of the Republic*, 67–72; Edmund S. Morgan and Helen M. Morgan, *The Stamp Act Crisis: Prologue to Revolution* (Chapel Hill: University of North Carolina Press, 1952), 181–87.

52. This practice is recounted in Brown, *Faneuil Hall*, 134; for a transcription of toasts and even a menu, see Wheildon, *Semi-Centennial*.

53. The renovation of Faneuil Hall is recounted in Harold Kirker, *The Architecture of Charles Bulfinch* (Cambridge: Harvard University Press, 1969), 232.

54. An "insider" account of this urban development is found in Quincy, *Municipal History*, 54–132. See also Boston City Council, *Report of the Committee of Both Branches of the City Council on the Extension of Faneuil Hall Market* (Boston, 1826). For analysis of the influence of Faneuil Hall's reconstruction on the regional economy, see Henry Binford, *The First Suburbs: Residential Communities on the Boston Periphery* (Chicago: University of Chicago Press, 1985), 11–34.

55. Quincy, *Municipal History*, 121–22.

56. Quoted in *Annual Report* of 1838, 33.

57. See Hartog, *Public Property and Private Power*; Oscar Handlin and Mary Flug Handlin, *Commonwealth: The History of the Role of Government in the American Economy: Massachusetts, 1774–1861* (Cambridge: Belknap Press of Harvard University Press, 1969), 103–241; Morton J. Horowitz, *The Transformation of American Law, 1760–1860* (New York: Oxford University Press, 1992), 109–39.

58. The calculation of this net loss is taken from figures for the transaction and construction of Faneuil Hall and Quincy Marketplace from Quincy, *Municipal History*, 132; *Report of the Committee*, 22.

59. *Annual Report* of 1838, 42.

60. I am drawing here from the notion of a self-critical public in Claude Lefort, "Human Rights and the Welfare State," in *Democracy and Political Theory*, 21–44.

61. *Annual Report* of 1838, 43.

62. For the testimonials to Quincy and the history of Faneuil Hall that accompanied this celebration, see Wheildon, *Semi-Centennial Celebration*.

63. Resolution quoted in *Annual Report* of 1838, 46.

64. Friedrich Nietzsche, "On the Uses and Disadvantages of History for Life," in *Untimely Meditations*, trans. R. J. Hollingdale (Cambridge: Cambridge University Press, 1983), 72.

65. Garrison, *Annual Report* of 1838, 40.

66. Thomas Russell Sullivan, *Letters against the Immediate Abolition of Slavery* (Boston, 1836), 5.

5. Thoreau's Civic Imagination

1. Henry David Thoreau, "Civil Disobedience," in *"Walden" and "Civil Disobedience,"* ed. Owen Thomas (New York: Norton, 1966), 243. All further citations are from this edition.

2. Thoreau, *Walden*, in *"Walden" and Civil "Disobedience,"* ed. Thomas, 89. All further citations are from this edition.

3. Foucault, *The Order of Things: An Archaeology of the Human Sciences* (New York: Vintage, 1973), 338.

4. Among the most persuasive retellings of the "great transformation" that upholds Thoreau's contention regarding the interpenetration of the state into the private affairs of society is found in Sellers, *The Market Revolution*; and Thomas, *Revivalism and Cultural Change.*

5. My reference here is to Berman's argument regarding the Marxian antimaterialist dialectic in *The Communist Manifesto.* See Marshall Berman, *All That Is Solid Melts into Air: The Experience of Modernity* (New York: Simon and Schuster, 1982), 90–110.

6. Joseph Woods, *The New England Village* (Baltimore: The Johns Hopkins University Press, 1997), 53–95 and 141–46.

7. The citation of Marx is from "On the Jewish Question," in *The Marx-Engels Reader*, ed. Robert C. Tucker (New York: Norton, 1978), 34.

8. This genealogy is articulated in Graham Burchell, "Peculiar Interests: Civil Society and Governing 'The System of Natural Liberty,'" in *The Foucault Effect: Studies in Governmentality*, ed. Burcell et al. (Chicago: University of Chicago Press, 1991), 119–50; Colin Gordon, "Government Rationality: An Introduction," in *The Foucault Effect*, 1–52.

9. See Lefort, "Outline on the Genesis of Ideology in Modern Societies," in *The Political Forms of Modern Society*, 216.

10. An insightful exposition of the relation between social space and modes of production in Marx's political economy appears in M. Gottdiener, *The Social Production of Urban Space* (Austin: University of Texas Press, 1985), 70–73.

11. For Habermas, the distinction between "town" and "court" is constituted for the self-conception of bourgeois society as an autonomous realm. See *The Structural Transformation of the Public Sphere*, 22–32. Pocock's categorization of "country" and "civic" are invoked here and will become more central to my argument. See *The Machiavellian Moment*, 315–419; 519–34.

12. The term "urban-industrial complex" and its signification as a network of social intercourse, social planning priorities, and economic organization are taken from Thomas Bender, *Toward an Urban Vision: Ideas and Institutions in Nineteenth-Century America* (Baltimore: The Johns Hopkins University Press, 1982), 28–51.

13. Walter Benjamin, "On Some Motifs in Baudelaire," in *Illuminations*, 162.

14. See this reading of Baudelaire in Berman, *All That Is Solid*, 147–59.

15. Boyer, *The City of Collective Memory*, 322.

16. These references are drawn widely from *Walden*, 26, 14, 13, 80, 74, 3.

17. I derive the argument that posits a generic connection between aesthetic consciousness and the subjective image of the city from William Sharpe and Leonard Wallock, "From 'Great Town' to 'Nonplace Urban Realm': Reading the Modern City," in *Visions of the Modern City: Essays in History, Art, and Literature* (Baltimore: The Johns Hopkins University Press, 1987), 1–50; and Raymond Williams, *The Country and the City* (New York: Oxford University Press, 1973), 233–47.

18. Michel de Certeau, *The Practice of Everyday Life* (Berkeley: University of California Press, 1984), 94, 98, 100. Jameson's formative argument for his conception of postmodernity appears in "Cognitive Mapping," in *Marxism and the Interpretation of Culture*, ed. Nelson and Grossberg, 347–60; and Jameson, *Postmodernism, or, The Cultural Logic of Late Capitalism* (Durham: Duke University Press, 1991). The conception of "cognitive mapping" originates in a sociological study of urban orientation. See Kevin Lynch, *The Image of the City* (Cambridge: MIT Press, 1960).

19. My argument here is directed against an arguably lapsed critical tradition that sees in *Walden*, to use Miller's words, "the independence of a self-conscious mind." Cavell does much to establish the relevance of political theory and even the prospect of intersubjectivity before concluding that Thoreau's relation to place represents a "solution to the problem of self-consciousness." See Perry Miller, *Consciousness in Concord* (Boston: Houghton Mifflin, 1958), 80; and Stanley Cavell, *The Senses of Walden* (New York: Viking, 1972), 105.

20. See Nash, *The Urban Crucible*, 236–342. The moral and political virtues that American Federalists attached to an urban commercial economy are explicated in Janet A. Reisman, "Money, Credit, and Federalist Political Economy," in *Beyond Confederation: Origins of the Constitution and American National Identity* (Chapel Hill: University of North Carolina Press, 1987), 128–61.

21. See Pocock, *The Machiavellian Moment*, 423–505.

22. I owe this insight regarding Thoreau's statist theories to an explication of those of Lefebvre in Gottdiener, *The Social Production of Urban Space*, 132–47.

23. For this characterization of pastorals, I am relying on Myra Jehlen, *American Incarnation: The Individual, the Nation, and the Continent* (Cambridge: Harvard University Press, 1986), 76–122.

24. The Federalists' project of civic development is celebrated in Beatrice Garden, *Federal Philadelphia, 1785–1825: The Athens of the Western World* (Philadelphia: Philadelphia Museum of Art, 1987). The self-representation of the urban bourgeoisie with republican ornamentation is described as a feature of early national and antebellum civic life in Tamara Plakins Thornton, *Cultivating Gentlemen: The Making of Country Life among the Boston Elite, 1785–1860* (New Haven: Yale University Press, 1989), 14–18. Particularly during the antebellum era, so-called republican institutions operated as a form of civic pedagogy for urban centers increasingly shaped by the influx of the working class and immigration. See Kerber, *Federalists in Dissent*, 67–134; and Robert T. Oliver, *The History of Public Speaking in America* (Boston: Allyn and Bacon, 1965), 430–65.

25. James Spear Loring took special pride in noting that the title of "Athens of America" had been bestowed on Boston by the *Philadelphia Bulletin*. See Loring, *The Hundred Boston Orators . . . Comprising Historical Gleanings, Illustrating the Principles and Progress of Our Republican Institutions* (Boston: John P. Jewett, 1853), 720. New York, on the other hand, did not aggressively develop its civic institutions and consciousness until the rise of the industrial capitalist class and of the City Beautiful movement at the end of the nineteenth century. See Edward K. Spann, *The New Metropolis: New York City, 1840–1857* (New York: Columbia University Press, 1981).

26. The fusion Thoreau seems to have created is represented as an ideological project of colonial and postrevolutionary America in Ralph Lerner, *The Thinking Revolutionary: Principle and Practice in the New Republic* (Ithaca: Cornell University Press, 1987) 195–221; and Drew McCoy, *The Elusive Republic: Political Economy in Jeffersonian America* (Chapel Hill: University of North Carolina Press, 1980).

27. Woods's account of the New England village makes clear that its historical associations were linked closely to an economic discourse of moralized social relations. See *The New England Village*, 112–36. I derive the concept of a contemporary moral discourse of enterprise from Leonard Neufeldt, *The Economist: Henry Thoreau and Enterprise* (New York: Oxford University Press, 1989).

28. This reconceptualization of city and country is owed to Thornton, *Cultivating Gentlemen*, 19–56.

29. See Pocock, *The Machiavellian Moment*, 446–505. Thoreau's relation to this tradition is patiently explicated in Leonard Neufeldt, "Henry David Thoreau's Political Economy," *New England Quarterly* 57 (1984): 359–83.

30. "Cato" quoted in Pocock, *The Machiavellian Moment*, 468.

31. Robert Gross, "The Great Bean Field Hoax: Thoreau and the Agricultural Reformers," *Virginia Quarterly Review* 16 (1985): 483–97.

32. Neufeldt, "Henry David Thoreau's Political Economy," 372.

33. Max Horheimer, "Rise and Decline of the Individual," in *Eclipse of Reason* (New York: Continuum, 1974), 131. The locus classicus of Thoreau's classical education is of course Edith Sybold, *Thoreau: The Quest and the Classics* (New Haven: Yale University Press, 1951).

34. Cf. Michael Gilmore, "Walden and the 'Curse of Trade,'" in *Ideology and Classic American Literature*, ed. Sacvan Bercovitch and Myra Jehlen (Cambridge: Cambridge University Press, 1986), 293–308. Gilmore sees a civic project with direct applicability to Concord derailed in successive drafts and in the second half of *Walden*.

35. See Gilmore, "Walden and the Curse of Trade," 307.

36. Benjamin, "The Work of Art in the Age of Mechanical Reproduction," in *Illuminations*, 223.

37. Fredric Jameson, *The Political Unconscious: Narrative as a Socially Symbolic Act* (Ithaca: Cornell University Press, 1981). I have been influenced as well by the civic structure of neurosis explicated in Rosalind C. Morris, "Surviving Pleasure at the Periphery: Chiang Mai and the Photographs of Political Trauma in Thailand, 1976–1992," *Public Culture* 10 (1998): 341–70. Her theorization of periphery and memory in the self-conception of the marginalized will become more central to this chapter.

38. Morris's brilliant analysis of this temporality in the staging of historical events gives as much emphasis to its utility for the regeneration of power as to fomenting what she calls the "pleasures of survival." See Morris, "Surviving Pleasure at the Periphery," 360–67.

39. The building of the New England village from the institution of "fee-simple" land tenure is recalled in Sam Bass Warner Jr., *The Urban Wilderness: A History of the American City* (New York: Harper and Row, 1972), 8–18.

40. In Woods's account of the New England village ideal as preserved in the works of Hawthorne, Catherine Maria Sedgwick, and Henry Ward Beecher is a unique representation of collective memory in the service of creativity. See Woods, *The New England Village*, 141–44.

41. Homi Bhabha, "Dissemination," *Location of Culture*, 140.

42. Bhabha, "Dissemination," 159.

43. See Benjamin, "Theses on the Philosophy of History," in *Illuminations*, 262.

44. Bhabha, "Dissemination," 147.

45. Benjamin defines the memorable phrase, "empty, homogeneous time," in contrast to the time of materialist historiography, which is defined by the present awareness of writing history. See "Theses on the Philosophy of History," 263. Bhabha's iteration of Benjamin's critique takes aim at not just nationalist historiography but the model of the uniform, internally coherent national community. See "Dissemination," 147–61; and Anderson, *Imagined Communities*, 37–46.

46. Bhabha, "Dissemination," 157.

47. The urban history of Massachusetts rightly focuses on the factory system as it was instituted in places like Lowell and narrates the consequences of its growth on urban, suburban, and rural space. An exemplary account remains Jonathan Prude, *The Coming of the Industrial Order: Town and Factory Life in Rural Massachusetts, 1810–1860* (Cambridge: Cambridge University Press, 1983); see also Thomas Bender, *Toward an Urban Vision*. My argument regarding the suburban renaissance of Concord is taken from Robert Gross, "Transcendentalism and Urbanism: Concord, Boston, and the Wider World," *Journal of American Studies* 18 (1984): 361–81.

48. Henry David Thoreau, in *A Week on the Concord and Merrimack Rivers*, in *A Week, Walden, Maine Woods, Cape Cod*, ed. Robert Sayre (New York: Library of America, 1985), 200.

49. Eric Lampard, "The Nature of Urbanization," in *Visions of the Modern City*, ed. Sharpe and Wallock, 65–66.

50. Henry C. Binford, *The First Suburbs: Residential Communities on the Boston Periphery* (Chicago: University of Chicago Press, 1985), 35. Lewis Mumford also considers the commercial city to have provided the resources for industrialization and thus its own eclipse. See Mumford, *The City in History: Its Origins, Its Transformations, and Its Prospects* (New York: Harcourt, Brace, Jovanovich, 1961), 419.

51. For the development of Boston's commercial infrastructure, see Binford, *The First Suburbs*, 30–34. The preceding and following account of local agricultural economic transformation is culled from Gross, "Transcendentalism," 363–81; Gross, "Culture and Cultivation: Agriculture and Society in

Thoreau's Concord," *Journal of American History* 69 (1982): 42–61; and Thornton, *Cultivating Gentlemen*, 108–30.

52. The development of the financial infrastructure for urban industrialization is described in Peter Dobkin Hall, "Family Structure and Economic Organization: Massachusetts Merchants, 1700–1850," in *Family and Kin in Urban Communities, 1700–1930*, ed. Tamara K. Hareven (New York: New Viewpoints, 1977), 47–55. See also Hall, *The Organization of American Culture*, 79–124.

53. These conversations are given considerable weight in Robert Gross, "'The Most Estimable Place in All of the World': A Debate on Progress in Nineteenth-Century Concord," *Studies in the American Renaissance* 2 (1978): 7–26; and Leo Stoller, *After Walden: Thoreau's Changing Views of Economic Man* (Stanford: Stanford University Press, 1957), 15–25.

54. Betty Hobbes Pruitt, "Self-Sufficiency and the Agricultural Economy of Eighteenth-Century Massachusetts," *William and Mary Quarterly* 41 (1984): 335.

55. Henry David Thoreau, *Journal*, ed. John C. Broderick, 4 vols. (Princeton: Princeton University Press, 1981), 2: 374.

56. Jean-François Lyotard, "A l'insu (Unbeknowst)," in *Community at Loose Ends*, ed. Miami Theory Collective, 42.

57. On the ironic mode of historiography in relation to the aesthetic modulation of modernity, see White, *Metahistory*, 45–68; 375–79.

58. With this formulation I am seeking to build on the aesthetic potential inherent in an orientation toward the present and introduce the register of space in tropes. An evocative statement of this potential that draws on the Baudelarian figure of the dandy is found in Michel Foucault, "What Is Enlightenment?," 157–74. For an exposition of this aesthetic orientation in relation to the "non-cultural" narratives of modernity, see Dilip Parameshwar Gaonkar, "On Alternative Modernities," *Public Culture* 11 (1999): 1–18.

59. Bhabha, "Dissemination," 168, 170.

60. For a historical account of this suburbanization, see Gross, "Transcendentalism," 380.

61. Benjamin, "On Some Motifs in Baudelaire," 160.

6. Douglass's Sublime

1. Frederick Douglass, "What to the Slave Is the Fourth of July," in *The Oxford Frederick Douglass Reader*, ed. William L. Andrews (New York: Oxford University Press, 1996), 109, 114. All further citations are from this edition.

2. As my emphasis in this chapter will be on the rhetorical medium of Douglass's oratory, I am pleased to have learned from an analysis of Douglass's speech that foregrounds the aesthetic structure of his discourse and cites its disturbance to nationalist historiography. See James Jasinski, "Rearticulating History in Epideictic Discourse: Frederick Douglass's 'The Meaning of the Fourth of July to the Negro,'" in *Rhetoric and Political Culture in Nineteenth-Century America*, ed. Thomas W. Benson (Lansing: Michigan State University Press, 1997), 71–89.

3. The mediation of irony in the rhetoric of the black orator is described as a precondition for representing the place of the former slave in John Louis Lucaites, "The Irony of 'Equality' in Black Abolitionist Discourse: The Case of Frederick Douglass's 'What to the Slave Is the Fourth of July,'" in *Rhetoric and Political Culture in Nineteenth-Century America*, 47–69.

4. Bhabha, "Dissemination," 159.

5. These phrases and their argument are taken from Paul Gilroy, *The Black Atlantic: Modernity and Double Consciousness* (Cambridge: Harvard University Press, 1993), 202.

6. Henry Louis Gates Jr., *The Signifying Monkey: A Theory of African-American Literary Criticism* (New York: Oxford University Press, 1988), 49–50. The rhetorical inversion of American discourse is described as a distinctive feature of Douglass's editorial voice in Shelly Fisher-Fishkin and Carla L. Peterson, "'We Hold These Truths to Be Self-Evident'", in *Frederick Douglass: New Literary and Historical Essays*, ed. Sundquist, 189–204.

7. This rendition of Douglass's oratorical and editing career relies on William McFeeley, *Frederick Douglass* (New York: Norton, 1991), 81–160.

8. I am indebted to Baker for this and other evocations of place in this chapter. See Houston Baker, *Blues, Ideology, and Afro-American Literature: A Vernacular Theory* (Chicago: University of Chicago Press, 1994), 68–69.

9. My ambition here is consistent with Gilroy's injunction to reconstruct "the primal history of modernity" from the "slave's point of view. The slave's perspective requires a discrete view not just of the dynamics of power and domination . . . but of such central categories of Enlightenment project as the idea of universality, the fixity of meaning, the coherence of the subject, and, of course, the foundational ethnocentrism in which these have all tended to be anchored." See *The Black Atlantic*, 55.

10. Houston Baker, *Modernism and the Harlem Renaissance* (Chicago: University of Chicago Press, 1987), 101, 95. The significance of the ideal of

rational self-consciousness in the constitution of the violated racial subject is explored in Lindon Barrett, "African-American Slave Narratives: Literacy, the Body, Authority," *American Literary History* 7 (1995): 415–42.

11. Higginson, *American Orators*, 76.

12. Baker, *Blues, Ideology, and Afro-American Literature*, 63 and 192–98.

13. For the importance of Niagara Falls to the inscribing of nationalist history and the ironizing critique of William Wells Brown, see Castronovo, *Fathering the Nation*, 106–76. Castronovo's account focuses on the Niagara Falls as a trope of historical narration, while my focus on the same boundary site is intended to explore its potential as an aesthetic representation of space, or placelessness. The importance of border crossing and Niagara Falls for Brown's literary consciousness is suggested by John Ernest, "The Reconstruction of Whiteness: William Wells Brown's *The Escape: or, A Leap for Freedom*," *PMLA* 113 (1998): 1108–21. An important historical analysis of the number and density of fugitive slave communities in western New York is found in Judith Wellman, "This Side of the Border: Fugitives from Slavery in Three Central New York Communities," *New York History* 79 (1998): 359–93.

14. An insightful restaging of the observance of English emancipation and other counternational public celebrations appears in Rauh-Bethel, *The Roots of African-American Identity*. The alliance between African American and English antislavery movements is recounted in R. J. M. Blackett, *Building an Anti-Slavery Wall: Black Abolitionists in the Atlantic Abolitionist Movement, 1830–1860*, (Baton Rouge: Louisiana State University Press, 1997).

15. The English genealogy of the American sublime is reconstructed through figural and rhetorical art in Elizabeth McKinsey, *Niagara Falls: Icon of the American Sublime* (Cambridge: Cambridge University Press, 1985), 19–53.

16. Frederick Douglass, "Niagara Falls," *The North Star*, June 26, 1848, 3.

17. The place of the aesthetic in the political discourse of modernity is one of the reigning interests of this chapter, and for this formulation I have relied on Luc Ferry, *Political Philosophy 1: Rights, the New Quarrel between the Ancients and the Moderns* (Chicago: University of Chicago Press, 1984), 122–24; and Geoffrey Galt Harpham, "Aesthetics and the Fundamentals of Modernity," in *Aesthetics and Ideology*, ed. George Levin (New Brunswick: Rutgers University Press, 1994), 124–25.

18. Gilroy, *The Black Atlantic*, 38–40 and 215–16. Castronovo plays on a similar note of possibility and disturbance in his concluding, suggestive remarks

on the sublime. See Russ Castronovo, "Compromised Narratives along the Borders," in *Border Theory: The Limits of Cultural Politics*, ed. Scott Michaelson and David E. Johnson (Minneapolis: University of Minnesota Press, 1997), 195–220.

19. J. E. Robinson, "Ode to Niagara Falls," *The North Star*, December 3, 1847, 4.

20. This appraisal occurs as part of the reportage woven into the transciption of one of Douglass's speeches. See Frederick Douglass, "Southern Slavery and Northern Religion," in *Speeches, Debates, and Interviews, 1841–1846*, 27.

21. Gilroy describes "the attempt to differentiate the true, the good, and the beautiful which characterize the junction point of capitalism, industrialization, and political democracy" as a staging of black identity undertaken by both black and white. For this important conception, see Gilroy, *The Black Atlantic*, 8. Gates's account of black literacy and its place in the philosophical narrative of modernity is also influenced by his interest in aestheticism as both basis and critique of Western norms. See Gates, "Writing 'Race' and the Difference it Makes," 1–20.

22. These responses are taken from the compilation of newspaper reportage of Douglass's speeches in John Blassingame, introduction, *Speeches, Debates, and Interviews, 1841–1846*, xxvii, xliv.

23. Philips quoted in Oliver, *The History of Public Speaking in America*, 248.

24. For the origins of the sublime in moral sense theory, see Andrew Ashfield and Peter de Bolla, introduction to *The Sublime: A Reader in British Eighteenth-Century Aesthetic Theory* (Cambridge: Cambridge University Press, 1996), 60. I have been influenced in my conception of this heterogeneity by the work of Honig, who defies the philosophical imperative to find the agency of citizenship within the subject-position of citizen. Her remarks on Kant describing the "fundamental ambivalence that marks subjectivity, the otherness haunting the practices of respect" are suggestive of the political critique she pursues. See Bonnie Honig, *Political Theory and the Displacement of Politics* (Ithaca: Cornell University Press, 1993), 38; and Honig, "Ruth, the Model Émigré: Mourning and the Symbolic Politics of Immigration," in *Cosmopolitics: Thinking and Feeling beyond the Nation*, ed. Bruce Robbins and Pheng Cheah (Minneapolis: University of Minnesota Press, 1998), 192–215.

25. See Longinus, "On the Sublime," in *Critical Theory since Plato*, ed. Hazard Adams (New York: Harcourt, Brace, Jovanovich, 1975), 85–77. Longinus's

derivation of the sublime proceeds from the acknowledgment that the democratic polis is unable to manifest its own idealized image of itself and therefore needs the commanding force of the orator.

26. My model of the transformation of the sublime from rhetorical category of English aesthetics into American monumentalism is taken from McKinsey, *Niagara Falls*, 87–108. An extensive reading of Blair's *Lectures* and its importance in the development of moral epistemology is found in Nan Johnson, *Nineteenth-Century Rhetoric in North America* (Carbondale: Southern Illinois University Press, 1991), 32–44.

27. Rob Wilson, *American Sublime: The Genealogy of a Poetic Genre* (Madison: University of Wisconsin Press, 1991), 4–5.

28. See Myra Jehlen, *American Incarnation: The Individual, the Nation, the Continent* (Cambridge: Harvard University Press, 1986), 6–122.

29. See Smith, *Civic Ideals*, 13–39. Smith attempts to go beyond an immanent critique of American liberal democracy or the exposure of contradiction to demonstrate the racially exclusive requirements of the laws of citizenship. Matthiessen's throwaway line concerning the aesthetic foundations of American civic discourse continues to grow larger in my thinking in this chapter. See *The American Renaissance*, 19–20.

30. David Lloyd, "Race under Representation," *Oxford Literary Review* 13 (1991): 65.

31. Immanuel Kant, *Critique of Judgment*, trans. James Creed Meredith (Oxford: Clarendon Press, 1991), 153. All further citations are from this edition.

32. Terry Eagleton, *The Ideology of the Aesthetic* (Oxford: Blackwell, 1990), 96.

33. Ibid., 405.

34. Ferry's theorization of the aesthetic will become increasingly important to my critique of Douglass. These remarks concerning the problem of sociality are found in Luc Ferry, *Homo Aestheticus: The Invention of Taste in the Democratic Age* (Chicago: University of Chicago Press, 1993), 25, 20.

35. Jean-Luc Nancy, "The Sublime Offering," in *Of the Sublime: Presence in Question* (Albany: SUNY Press, 1993), 28.

36. Slavoj Žižek, *Tarrying with the Negative: Kant, Hegel, and the Critique of Ideology* (Durham: Duke University Press, 1993), 1–2.

37. See Žižek, *The Sublime Object of Ideology* (London: Verso, 1989), 21.

38. For historical accounts of the emergence of white manhood as civic norm in Jacksonian America, see Smith, *Civic Ideals*, 165–242; Alexander Saxton,

The Rise and Fall of the White Republic (London: Verso, 1990); and Dana Nelson, *National Manhood: Capitalist Citizenship and the Imagined Fraternity of White Men* (Durham, N.C.: Duke University Press, 1998), 29–60.

39. See Žižek, *The Sublime Object*, 104, where this structural condition is put in racial terms.

40. This discrepancy appears as a historical development within American constitutional theory in Gordon Wood, *The Creation of the American Republic, 1776–1787* (New York: Norton, 1969), 471–564.

41. In retrospect, the world of coffeehouses, salons, and epistolary exchanges that Habermas described so memorably as the historical basis for the liberal public sphere can be said to belong also to a world of aesthetics and manners. Eagleton's own account of the public sphere lays bare this aesthetic dimension in its attention to the faculty of criticism, while Shields's historical analysis of eighteenth-century American sociality reveals the irreducibility of manners and aesthetic convention. See Habermas, *The Structural Transformation of the Public Sphere*; Terry Eagleton, *The Function of Criticism: From the Spectator to Post-Structuralism* (London: Verso, 1984), 12–22; and David S. Shields, *Civil Tongues and Polite Letters in British America* (Chapel Hill: University of North Carolina Press, 1997).

42. On this point regarding the inflection of manners in the social discourse of republican egalitarianism, see Gordon Wood, *The Radicalism of the American Revolution* (New York: Knopf, 1992), 193–218.

43. Lloyd, "Kant's Examples," in *Unruly Examples: On the Rhetoric of Exemplarity*, ed. Alexander Gelley (Stanford: Stanford University Press, 1995), 258.

44. I take this critical distinction of the aesthetically mediated public sphere from Ferry's revealing critique of Schiller and from Lyotard's analysis of Kantian taste. See Ferry, *Political Philosophy 1*, 96–124; and Jean-François Lyotard, *Lessons on the Analytic of the Sublime* (Stanford: Stanford University Press, 1994), 2–15 and 191–202. See also the revealing commentary on the mediation of pleasure in the formation of society in Paul Guyer, "Pleasure and Society in Kant's Theory of Taste," in *Essays on Kant's Aesthetics*, ed. Ted Cohen and Guyer (Chicago: University of Chicago Press, 1982), 21–54.

45. See Richard Brodhead, *Cultures of Letters: Scenes of Reading and Writing in Nineteenth-Century America* (Chicago: University of Chicago Press, 1993). In his theorization and exposition of literacy in its social setting, Brodhead emphasizes its normative, pedagogical function.

46. Here is a point at which I depart both from the print-mediated and

orally mediated conception of the public sphere, or the attempt to bring them into alignment in a way destructive to them both. Looby faults Warner's conception of impersonal recognition for dismissing the importance of oral performance in public, but could any performance be completely vernacular, or dismissive of the formal, i.e., printed rules for expression? See Warner, *Letters of the Republic*; and Looby, *Voicing America*, 3–6.

47. Bingham, *The Columbian Orator*, 19.

48. Quoted in Philip Foner, ed., *The Life and Writings of Frederick Douglass: Early Years, 1817–1849*, vol. 1 of *The Life and Writings of Frederick Douglass* (New York: International Publishers, 1950), 47.

49. Quoted in Blassingame, introduction, *Speeches, Debates, and Interviews, 1841–46*, xxxvii.

50. See William Charvat, *The Origins of American Critical Thought, 1810–1835* (New York: Russell and Russell, 1971), 21–45. The political potential for uniform inclusion within the public sphere is suggested in Eagleton, *The Function of Criticism*, 14. Taylor, on the other hand, seeks to uncover the "false homogeneity" within the operation of mutual recognition. See Charles Taylor, *Multiculturalism and the "Politics of Recognition"* (Princeton: Princeton University Press, 1992), 44–51.

51. Quoted in Blassingame, introduction, *Speeches, Debates, and Interviews, 1841–46*, xxix.

52. Ibid., xlvii.

53. Quoted in Foner, *Life and Writings of Frederick Douglass*, 25.

54. See this term explicated in Gates, *Signifying Monkey*, 75–76.

55. Douglass's facility with mimicry and his mocking treatment of the oratory of American statesmen is recounted in Blassingame, introduction, *Speeches, Debates, and Interviews, 1841–46*, xxxi.

56. Higginson, *American Orators*, 88.

57. Quoted in Oliver, *History of Public Speaking*, 248.

58. Ephriam Peabody, "Narration of Fugitive Slaves," *Christian Examiner* 12 (1849): 61, 63 n., and 74.

59. Quoted in Blassingame, introduction, *Speeches, Debates, Interviews, 1841–46*, xxx.

60. This aesthetic condition, simultaneously legalist and limiting, on intersubjectivity is a central feature of arguments in Ferry, *Political Rights 1*, 97–99; and Lyotard, *Lessons*, 218–23.

61. Charvat, *Origins of American Critical Thought*, 55.

62. Hugh Blair, *Lectures on Rhetoric and Belle Lettres* (Philadelphia, 1854), 27. All further citations are from this edition.

63. Johnson's major argument, which I adopt, is that the rhetorical discipline becomes altered from its civic function to its moral epistemological function, which seeks similitude in the structures of the mind rather than of society. See Johnson, *Nineteenth-Century Rhetoric*, 22–32.

64. Jacques Derrida, *Truth in Painting* (Chicago: University of Chicago Press, 1987), 42 and 45.

65. See Ferry, *Political Philosophy 1*, 112–24.

66. I take this familiar formulation of Kant's philosophical deduction of beauty from Žižek, *Tarrying with the Negative*, 46–47.

67. This lapsarian account of the public sphere as mediated by the exercise of taste is suggested by Rundell's rather brilliant rethinking of the dual role of imagination in the premise of happiness and in the failure to conceive unanimity. See John Rundell, "Creativity and Judgment: Kant on Reason and the Imagination," in *Rethinking Imagination*, ed. Robinson and Rundell, 96–110.

68. Mary Poovey, "Aesthetics and Political Economy in the Eighteenth Century: The Place of Gender in the Social Constitution of Knowledge," in *Aesthetics and Ideology*, ed. George Levin (New Brunswick: Rutgers University Press, 1994), 90.

69. Bassett quoted in Blassingame, introduction, *Speeches, Debates, and Interviews, 1841–46*, xxxix.

70. Bhabha, "The Other Question," in *Location of Culture*, 70.

71. Žižek quoted in Bhabha, "The Postcolonial and the Postmodern: The Question of Agency," in *Location of Culture*, 184–85.

72. Bhabha, "Of Mimicry and Man: The Ambivalence of Colonial Discourse," in *Location of Culture*, 86. A similar formulation of the uncanniness of the black orator can be found in Catronovo's Bhabha-inflected discussion of Douglass. See Castronovo, *Fathering the Nation*, 195–210 and 219–26.

73. The distinction from the synchronic and the subsequent analysis of the diachronic is taken from Bhabha, "Interrogating Identity: Frantz Fanon and the Postcolonial Prerogative," in *Location of Culture*, 50.

74. See Lloyd, "Race Under Representation," 68–74.

75. See Lloyd, "Kant's Examples," 261–63.

76. Lloyd, "Kant's Examples," 262.

77. "Frederick Douglass in Philadelphia," *The Liberator,* August 31, 1844, 3.

78. Weigman, *American Anatomies,* 90.

79. "From the Herald of Freedom," *The Liberator,* February 27, 1842, 3.

80. Quoted in Blassingame, introduction, *Speeches, Debates, and Interviews, 1841–46,* xlvii.

81. Peter Fenves, introduction to *Raising the Tone of Philosophy: Late Essays by Immanuel Kant, Transformative Critique by Jacques Derrida,* ed. Fenves (Baltimore: The Johns Hopkins University Press, 1993), 8.

82. Žižek, *The Sublime Object,* 128 and 43.

83. Derrida, *Truth in Painting,* 127. The racial composition of the sublime concentrated on the "pre-modern" aspects of Western rational peoples. For Blair's veneration of the "artless" Ossian, see Hugh Blair, "From a Critical Disseration on the Poems of Ossian," in *The Sublime,* ed. Ashfield and de Bolla, 207–12.

84. Frederick Douglass, "A Nation in the Midst of a Nation," *Speeches, Debates, and Interviews, 1847–54,* 425–26.

85. Douglass, *The Heroic Slave,* 132.

86. Peabody, "Narration of Fugitive Slaves," 75.

87. Žižek, *Tarrying with the Negative,* 47.

88. Derrida, *Truth in Painting,* 131. The philosophical deduction of the sublime describes invariably the implicit determination of the faculty of reason in the "free play" of the imagination. See Paul Crowther, *The Kantian Sublime: From Morality to Art* (Oxford: Clarendon Press, 1989), 45–103; and Gilles Deleuze, *Kant's Critical Faculties: The Doctrine of the Faculties* (Minneapolis: University of Minnesota Press, 1984), 46–58.

89. See Davis, *The Problem of Slavery,* 557–64.

90. Especially useful in this modulation toward the gendered dynamics of the sublime have been Jenny Franchot, "The Punishment of Esther: Frederick Douglass and the Construction of the Feminine," in *Frederick Douglass: New Literary and Historical Essays,* ed. Sundquist, 141–65; and Maurice Wallace, "Constructing the Black Masculine: Frederick Douglass, Booker T. Washington, and the Sublimits of African-American Autobiography," in *Subjects and Citizens,* ed. Moon and Davidson, 245–70.

91. See Lyotard, *Lessons on the Analytic of the Sublime,* 179–81.

92. Barrett, "African-American Slave Narratives," 431.

93. Douglass, *My Bondage and My Freedom*, 59.

94. See this critique of the sublime in Paul de Man, "Phenomenology and Materiality in Kant," in *Aesthetic Ideology*, ed. Andre Warminski (Minneapolis: University of Minnesota Press, 1996), 70–90.

95. Lyotard, *Lessons on the Analytic of the Sublime*, 108–09.

96. See de Man, "Phenomenology and Materiality," 77.

97. Lyotard, *Lessons on the Analytic of the Sublime*, 109.

98. Ibid., 22.

99. Žižek makes this point in reference to the fragility of the "Big Other" in the Lacanian "quilting of the subject." See Žižek, *The Sublime Object of Ideology*, 146–49. A similar point regarding the destruction of a totalized society by the agency of the law is found in Roberto Mangabeira, *Law in Modern Society: Toward a Criticism of Social Theory* (New York: Free Press, 1976), 61–62.

100. Douglass quoted in Benjamin Quarles, *Frederick Douglass* (New York: Atheneum, 1970), 126.

101. My comment here is meant to suggest a common derivation of the aesthetic image of the beautiful tragic mulatto and the political narrative of liberation. The potential for this inquiry is opened by the new scholarship and primary sources appearing in Robert S. Levine, ed., *Clotel, or The President's Daughter*, by William Wells Brown (New York: Bedford Books of St. Martin's Press, 2000). For a more aesthetic genealogy of the tragic mulatto, see Werner Sollors, *Neither Black nor White Yet Both: Thematic Explorations of Interracial Literature* (New York: Oxford University Press, 1997). For more gender-inflected critiques of the same, see Anne DuCille, *The Coupling Convention: Sex, Text, and Tradition in Black Women's Fiction* (New York: Oxford University Press, 1993); Hazel V. Carby, *Reconstructing Womanhood: The Emergence of the Afro-American Woman Novelist* (New York: Oxford University Press, 1989).

102. Douglass's opposition to the construction of an African nationality and colonization are recounted in Levine, *Martin Delany, Frederick Douglass*, 58–98 and 208–23.

103. Douglass, "Farewell to the Nation," *Speeches, Debates, and Interviews, 1847–54*, 27–28.

104. Lyotard, *Lessons on the Analytic of the Sublime*, 223.

105. Douglass, "Agitation, Agitation," in *Speeches, Debates, Interviews, 1847–54*, 396.

106. In *Critique of Judgment* Kant makes clear the pointlessness of judgment concerning the faculties of reason and understanding and contends that it contributes nothing to our objective knowledge of the world. We judge for the sheer pleasure of feeling our faculties accord. See *Critique of Judgment*, 29–42. For the amplification of this point in the deduction of freedom and necessity, I am endebted to Deleuze, *Kant's Critical Faculties*, 46–58.

107. Douglass, "Southern Slavery and Northern Religion," in *Speeches, Debates, and Interviews, 1841–1846*, 24.

Conclusion

1. William Lloyd Garrison, "The Dangers of the Nation," in *Selections*, 47 and 58.

2. With this depiction of Garrison's historiography, I am extending significantly the presentation of him as an agitator in Henry Mayer, *All on Fire: William Lloyd Garrison and the Abolition of Slavery* (New York: St. Martin's Press, 1998).

3. Immanuel Kant, "Idea for a Universal History with a Cosmopolitan Perspective," in *Kant: Political Writings*, ed. Reiss, 44–45. All further citations are from this edition. Several recent commentaries on this text have stressed the relation of his humanitarian aims and ethical dimension to the spatial figure of nationalism. See Thomas McCarthy, "On Recovering Cosmopolitan Unity and National Diversity," *Public Culture* 11 (1999): 175–208; Allen W. Wood, "Kant's Project for Perpetual Peace," in *Cosmopolitics*, ed. Cheah and Robbins, 59–76; and Pheng Cheah, "Given Culture: Rethinking Cosmopolitan Freedom in Transnationalism," in *Cosmopolitics*, 290–328.

4. See Kant, "Idea for a Universal History," 51. The frailty and imbalance of the imagination in this endeavor has been described as a historical condition of the exercise of reason. See John Rundell, "Creativity and Judgment: Kant on Reason and the Imagination," in *Rethinking Imagination*, ed. Robinson and Rundell, 1994, 9–113.

5. My reading of the novel's relation to epic history is taken from Georg Lukacs, *The Theory of the Novel: A Historical-Philosophical Essay on the Forms of the Great Epic Literature* (Cambridge: MIT Press, 1971). My reference to overlapping periodization in the novel is taken from Raymond Williams, *Marxism and Literature* (New York: Oxford University Press, 1977), 132–33.

6. Paul Ricoeur, "Imagination in Discourse and Action," in *Rethinking Imagination*, 134.

7. Kant, "The Contest of the Faculties," in *Kant: Political Writings*, 189.

8. Foucault's rereading of Kant stresses this very act of self-orientation in the aesthetic constitution of modernity. See Michel Foucault, "What Is Enlightenment?," in *Interpretive Social Science*, ed. Rabinow and Sullivan, 163.

9. Garrison, "Forbearance of the Abolitionists," *The Liberator,* September 29, 1835, 2.

10. *Annual Report* of 1845, 2: 62.

11. With this insight, I am drawing on Williams's concept of the "structure of feeling" as a mode of historical orientation. See *Marxism and Literature*, 134–47.

12. For the "anthropological perspective" unique to the sublime, see Rundell, "Creativity and Judgment," 114.

13. Lyotard, "Judiciousness in Dispute, or Kant after Marx," in *The Aims of Representation*, ed. Krieger, 33.

Index

"abolitionize," xii, xv, xx, xxvi, 260. *See also* abolition movement: publicity campaign of

abolition movement: as democratic revolution, xv, xvi–xvii, xxxvii, 2, 3, 50, 76, 79, 80, 130, 168, 201; historical representation of, xv–xvi, xxviii–xxxv, xxxviii–xli, 6, 7, 11–12, 26–28, 39–41, 45, 49, 62–63, 66–67, 70, 76–78, 84, 107, 127, 219, 250, 252, 254–55, 257–60; historiography of, xvi–xvii, xix, xxii–xxiv, xxvii–xxviii, xxx–xxxix, 1, 4–5, 7, 21, 26, 40–41, 49, 58, 128, 130–35, 251–54, 257–60; marginal status of, xii, xiv, xxi–xxii, xxiv, xxvi, xxx, xxxiii, xxxv–xxxvii, 8, 12, 27–28, 38, 40, 135, 142, 162–65, 167–68, 178, 201–2, 208–9, 252 (*see also* marginality); petitions of, 7, 9, 22–23, 25, 27–28, 30; print culture of, xvii–xviii, xix, xxi, xxvi, xxvii, 2, 45, 48, 53, 63, 89, 95, 98, 106, 113, 162; public identity of, xv–xvii, xxi, xxvi–xxviii, xxxvi, 5–9, 11–13, 35, 39, 40–41, 49–50, 56, 58, 62–63, 66, 67, 70, 74, 75–76, 84, 86, 103, 105, 132, 134–35, 142, 144–45, 162, 168, 212, 219, 222, 250; publicity campaign of, xi–xvii, xix–xxi, xxiii, xxiv–xxviii, xxix, xxxvi, xxxix, xl, 1–2, 5–6, 11–13, 22, 27–28, 39, 45, 58, 106, 167, 170, 198, 252–53, 260; vs. public opinion, xi, xv, xvii, xxii, 2, 9, 11, 26, 39–40, 144, 145, 158, 163, 212, 260; reading public of, xii, xv, xx–xxi, xxvi, 1, 23, 81, 105, 107, 109, 260; right of free speech of, xxvii, 6–8, 11–14, 27, 32, 34–35, 37–41, 43, 51, 53, 55, 61, 65, 67, 73, 132, 135, 141–43, 145, 151, 160–61, 163–66, 170, 260; vs. state, xii, 1–2, 8–9, 11–12, 20–23, 27, 34–35, 37–38, 43; women's

Robert Fanuzzi is associate professor of English at St. John's University in New York. He contributed to the anthology *The Black Press: New Historical and Literary Essays* and is editing an anthology of American and transatlantic antislavery literature.